SOUTHSIDE
VIRGINIA FAMILIES
Volume II

by

John Bennett Boddie

CLEARFIELD COMPANY
REPRINTS & REMAINDERS

Reprinted for Clearfield Company, Inc. by
Genealogical Publishing Co. Inc.
Baltimore, MD 1991

Originally Published
Redwood City, California
1956

Reprinted with permission

Library of Congress Catalog Card No. 66-28239

To my esteemed cousins
J. Byron Hilliard
and
Claiborne Thweatt Smith, Jr.
whose aid and assistance
is greatly appreciated

PLEASE NOTE

The families of BRANCH, pages 52-65, DICKENS, pages 101-115, HILLIARD, pages 172-270, and HILLIARD-HUNT, pages 271-275, as contained in the original edition of 1955, have been omitted from this edition as they have been reprinted with corrections in Volume IX of the HISTORICAL SOUTHERN FAMILIES series.

TABLE OF CONTENTS

EXPLANATION OF ABBREVIATIONS

A. C.	Alumni Cantabrigiensis, by Venn.
A. O.	Alumni Oxoniensis.
A. P. R.	Albemarle Parish Register.
B. J.	Journals of the House of Burgesses.
Bell.	Old Free State.
Boddie	Designations used by others to denote "17th Century Isle of Wight" or "Colonial Surry".
Brown	Brown's Abstracts of Somerset England Wills in 6 volumes.
Burgess	Revolutionary Soldiers of Virginia, by Burgess.
Chapman or C	Mrs. Blanche Adams Chapman's Abstracts of Elizabeth City County, or Isle of Wight.
C. P.	Cavaliers and Pioneers (Abstracts of Virginia Land Grants) by Mrs. Nell M. Nugent.
do.	Ditto; meaning the same reference as previously shown.
D. A. B.	Dictionary of American Biography.
D. B.	Deed Book.
dsp.	Died single person.
dvp.	Died before parent.
D. N. B.	Dictionary of National Biography.
E.	Essex.
Foster	Alumni Oxoniensis, by Foster.
Fleet	Abstracts of Virginia County Records, by Beverly Fleet.
G. E. C.	The Complete Peerage, by G. E. Cokayne.
G. B.	Grant Book.
Harl.	Harleian Society Publications.
Hasted	Hasted's History of Kent County, England.
Hathaway	North Carolina Historical and Genealogical Register.
Hayden	Virginia Genealogies, by Hayden.
Heitman	Historic Register of Officers, American Revolution, F. B. Heitman.
Hotten	Original Lists of Immigrants to America, by Hotten.
I. P. M.	Inquests Post Mortem.
J. H. B.	Journals of the House of Burgesses.
K. G.	King George County, Virginia.
L. B.	Land Book at Virginia State Library.

M. C. B.	Magna Carta Baron.
M. C. G. C.	Minutes of Court and General Council.
M.	do.
N. N.	Northern Neck Land Grants.
N. E. G. R.	New England Genealogical and Historical Register.
Nash	Nash's History of Worcestershire, England.
O.	Orders.
O. B.	Order Book.
P. B.	Patent Book.
P. C. C.	Prerogative Court of Canterbury Wills, England.
P. G.	Prince George County.
P. R.	Patent Rolls of England.
P. W.	Prince William County.
R.	Register of Parish.
Reg.	do.
R. B.	Record Book.
S.	Stafford County.
17 C.	Seventeenth Century Isle of Wight County.
S. P.	St. Paul's Parish or Parish Register of Stafford County.
sp.	Single Person.
S. P. R.	St. Paul's Parish Register, Stafford County.
S. P.	Calendar of State Papers of England.
S. P. Col.	Calendar of State Papers, Colonial.
Sweeney	Abstract of Rappahannock Wills, by Sweeney.
T.	Tyler's Magazine.
Tyler's	do.
V. B.	Vestry Book.
Vic. His.	Victorian Histories of the Counties of England.
V.	Virginia Historical Society Magazine.
V. M.	do.
W.	William and Mary College Quarterly, Series (1) and (2).
W. M.	do.
W. B.	Will Book.

Abbreviations are not uniform because some chapters were written before Dr. Swem's Index was published using T. W. and V. to designate the above magazines. Also, other persons contributing used other forms of abbreviations which were not changed.

A CORRECTION OF MISTAKES APPEARING IN VIRGINIA HISTORICAL GENEALOGIES

In V.H.G. on page 106 is a chart called "The Scottish Succession". It shows that Helen McDonald, daughter of Alan McDonald, Earl of Galloway, married Roger de Quincy. Helen McDonald was the daughter of a first wife of Alan McDonald whose name is not known. Helen McDonald in her own right was Constable of Scotland.

Alan McDonald married secondly in 1209 Margaret, eldest daughter of "David, Earl of Huntingdon, brother of King William the Lion of Scotland.

It was an error to show that Helen was a daughter of Margaret, the second wife of Alan, Earl of Galloway.

There is an error in the chart on page 227. Instead of showing that "Johan Harris" married Thomas Ligon, Jr., the chart should read as follows:

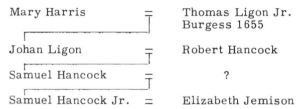

Mary Harris ＝ Thomas Ligon Jr.
Burgess 1655

Johan Ligon ＝ Robert Hancock

Samuel Hancock ＝ ?

Samuel Hancock Jr. ＝ Elizabeth Jemison

This was a printer's error as it was correctly shown on page 342 of V.H.G. that Mary Harris, instead of Johan Harris, married Thomas Ligon Jr.

In a chart on page 233 two generations were dropped out of the chart. The chart should correctly read as follows.

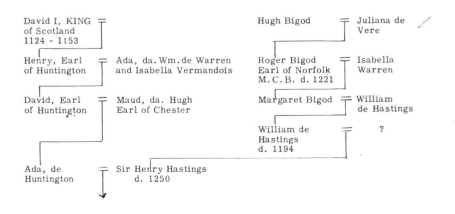

David I, KING of Scotland 1124 - 1153 ＝

Henry, Earl of Huntington ＝ Ada, da. Wm. de Warren and Isabella Vermandois

David, Earl of Huntington ＝ Maud, da. Hugh Earl of Chester

Ada, de Huntington ＝ Sir Henry Hastings d. 1250

Hugh Bigod ＝ Juliana de Vere

Roger Bigod Earl of Norfolk M.C.B. d. 1221 ＝ Isabella Warren

Margaret Bigod ＝ William de Hastings

William de Hastings d. 1194 ＝ ?

x

The Aston chart on page 277 should be corrected in accordance with the chart below. It appears that Katherine Wingfield who married Michael de la Pole, 1st Earl of Suffolk (1330-1389) was not descended from the Hastings family.

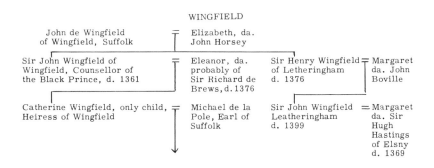

WINGFIELD

John de Wingfield of Wingfield, Suffolk = Elizabeth, da. John Horsey

Sir John Wingfield of Wingfield, Counsellor of the Black Prince, d. 1361 = Eleanor, da. probably of Sir Richard de Brews, d. 1376

Sir Henry Wingfield of Letheringham d. 1376 = Margaret da. John Boville

Catherine Wingfield, only child, Heiress of Wingfield = Michael de la Pole, Earl of Suffolk

Sir John Wingfield Leatheringham d. 1399 = Margaret da. Sir Hugh Hastings of Elsny d. 1369

This correction is made by Mr. G. Andrews Moriarty, a fellow member of the American Society of Genealogists. See his articles in the N. E. H. G. Reg. Jan. 1942 and for October 1949, p. 287, on the early origins of the Hastings and Wingfield families.

The Aston chart on page 276 should also be corrected. Agatha who married Edward The Atheling, was not a daughter of Henry II, Emperor of Germany, as shown by Hume in his "History of England". The Emperor died without issue. Agatha was a daughter of the Emperor's sister, Gisela, who in 1008 married St. Stephen, the first Christian King of Hungary. (See N. C. H. G. Reg. Jan. 1952, p. 52).

Page 132 V. H. G. should read that "Mumford De Jarnetts married Frances Hannah Pickett, daughter of Martha Terry Pickett and Major James Pickett. Major Pickett was a soldier in the Revolution from Wilmington District (N. C. Roster, p. 410). He was a son of James and Hannah Rennolds Pickett; a grandson of John and Mary Pickett and a great grandson of Henry and Sarah Pickett. The basis of this is said to be a lawsuit of Pickett Vs. Daniel but party sending information did not give any reference. The Bible records of the family of Frances and Mumford De Jarnette are printed in the "De Jarnette Family" by Earl and May Frost, pp 159-160.

Page 33. The name Lavinia Brooks should be spelled "LAVINA".

Page 35 should read that Henry Creswell Fleming Jr. and Marjorie Nixon Bell were married "Nov. 22, 1942". Their daughter, Marjorie Fleming was born Nov. 2, 1943, at Columbus, Ga. Their son, Henry Creswell Fleming III was born in Laurens, S. C.

Nov. 2, 1944. Captain Henry Creswell Fleming Jr. is now a banker in Colorado Springs, Colorado.

Page 32. Elizabeth Butler married Zachariah Smith Brooks. They had an only son, Col. Whitfield Brooks who married Mary Carrol. They were the parents of Preston Smith Brooks of S. C. Inasmuch as P. S. Brooks did not have any uncle by the name of "Brooks" he did not therefore have any first cousins. (Error 4th line of page 62).

Page 32. Two of the children of Nancy Butler and Elisha Brooks were omitted. Their children were: (1) J. Wesley; (2) Matilda R. m. Robinson; (3) Edna m. George Caldwell; (4) Lavina m. first Richard Watson and second Dr. John P. Barrett; (5) Mary, m. first Charles Chappell and second Richard Watts; (6) Stanmore Butler; (7) William Butler.

Errors appearing in the Eaton and Haynes families have been corrected in the Eaton chapter in "S. V. F." Vol. I.

ARRINGTON OF NASH COUNTY

By Claiborne Thweatt Smith, Jr.
and J. Byron Hilliard

The Arrington family of Nash County, N. C. descends from one William Arrington who appears in the records of Isle of Wight County, Virginia, about 1700. It is not known where he came from. A William Arrington was security for the appearance of William Rose in Henrico County in 1692 (Minute Book, 1692). The will of John Arrington, dated 4-20-1712, is on file in Westmoreland Co., Va. The will of Thomas Arrington, dated 10-16-1715, recorded in the same county, mentions among others, a brother Wandsford Arrington. A Samuel Arrington is mentioned in a patent in Goochland Co. Va. in 1731. (P.B. 14-265). The relationship between these Arringtons and William Arrington of Isle of Wight is not known. The name Arrington is of English extraction. Arrington is a parish ten miles south west from the city of Cambridge and in the Diocese of Ely. The parish took its name from the more ancient word, Ermington. The name of the place is said to have been taken as a surname by some local landowners there in the 13th Century. The parish church of St. Nicholas in Arrington dates from the Norman Conquest. (Oxford Dict. English Place Names, London, 1936)

William Arrington of Isle of Wight, first known ancestor, married Elizabeth Pedin of Isle of Wight. On June 9, 1703 William Arrington and his wife Elizabeth discharged William Boddie of a deed of gift William Boddie gave to James Pedden, his father-in-law 20 years ago (17th C.-p. 650). James Pedden was in Isle of Wight by 1667, at which time he witnessed a power of atty. (Ibid: 550). The will of James Pedden of the Lower Parish, mentioning his wife Jane, and dated Oct. 16, 1693, was recorded 8-9-1694 (G.B. 347). William Arrington was a witness. Jane was formerly the widow of the Rev. Matthew Huggens. (Admns. 31)

The will of William Arrington, dated 5-9-1725 was recorded in Isle of Wight G.B., p. 169. He mentioned his wife Elizabeth, sons Arthur, William, John, and Benjamin and daughters Mary Sykes, Elizabeth Crumpler and Sarah Riggan.

The will of a John Arrington, probably the son of William above, dated 4-26-1761 is recorded in Southampton Co. Va., and lists son Benjamin, wife Anne, daughter Anne Holt, and grandsons Jesse and John Arrington. His son John Arrington, Jr. will dated 4-5-1761, had predeceased him a few weeks. He mentioned wife Anne, son Jesse, daughters Patience and Elizabeth and named his wife and honored father as executors.

William Arrington, son of William Arrington, seems to have moved to Northampton Co. N. C. where his will was probated in

1

1752. He devised his estate to his two sons Briggs and William
Arrington. Also mentioned in the will were James Ross, son of
Sarah Ross, and Elizabeth Riggan, daughter of Daniel Riggan.
Col. John Dawson and friend Nathaniel Williams were appointed
executors.·
2. Arthur Arrington, son of William Arrington. He was granted
90 acres in Isle of Wight on n. side of Nottoway River bordering
on Wm. Crumpler, Wm. Arrington and James Chapple for im-
porting 2 persons in the colony 6-16-1727. (P.B. 12-134). He
witnessed a deed from John Exum to Robert Johnson on 10-11-1748
in Isle of Wight. According to family tradition, the surname of his
wife Mary was West. Arthur Arrington and his sons moved to the
western part of Edgecombe Co. N.C. about 1760. After 1777 this
section was Nash Co. The will of Arthur Arrington was dated Nash
Co. 4-1-1779 but was not recorded until Aug. 1801. Issue, according to his will, and family records.

I.   Arthur Arrington Jun. - of whom later
II.   Benjamin Arrington - untraced
III.   Joseph Arrington m. Martha Crafford - of whom later
IV.   Mary Arrington m. Benjamin Whitehead, Nash will dated
       1794
V.   Elizabeth Arrington m. John Drury
VI.   James Arrington m. Miss Portis, untraced
VII.   Ann Arrington m. Mathew Drake, Nash will dated 1810.

Arthur Arrington (3). On 2-9-1769 Arthur Arrington Jr. of Edgecombe Co. N.C. sold 180 acres in Southampton Co. Va. (D.B.
4-159). He settled a few miles east of Hilliardston on the north
side of Swift Creek where his homeplace is still standing. He became prominent in the new county of Nash. In 1777 when Nash
County, N.C. was created by the General Assembly, Arthur Arrington was appointed one of the commissioners to survey the line
dividing it from Edgecombe. Arrington was one of the first justices of Nash and was appointed first sheriff of the county by Gov.
Richard Craswell. According to the Nash Court Minutes in 1778,
the justices ordered that "the house of Arthur Arrington be appointed for a gaol for the county of Nash until there is one built."
In 1781, he was Quarter Master Commissioner of Nash County
under Joshua Potts, Special Quarter Master Comm. Halifax
District. (S.A.R. Lineage Book-N.C.-p.9). Arthur Arrington
married in Virginia 4-14-1758 Mary Sandefur, the daughter of
William Sandefur.

SANDEFUR EXCURSUS: This name also appears as Sandiford
and Sandifor. Mary Sandefur, wife of Arthur Arrington (3) was
the daughter of William Sandefur of Southampton Co. Va. and his
wife Mary, the daughter of Samuel Tompkins whose will was probated in Southampton in 1763, W.B. 2-19. Samuel Tompkins was
born in York Co. Va. 6-19-1696. Through the parish records of
Charles River and York Hampton Parishes, the Tompkins family
can be traced back to one Humphrey Tompkins who was in York
Co. by 1635. (W16-96). He is probably the same Humphrey Tompkins who was "allowed a bill of adventure due him from a five
shilling lottery 1-12-1619. (Records of the Va. Co. Vol. I - p.295).
According to the old family Bible of Wm. Sandefur, he was born

10-14-1707 and his wife Mary 2-12-1719. Their children were: Martha, b. 9-18-1738; Mary, b. 9-29-1741; William, b. 10-14-1743; Patsy, b. 1-9-1745; Ann, b. 4-1-1753, and Tompkins, b. Sept. 1755. The entries for Hill and Samuel Sandefur were illegible. The will of Wm. Sandefur was recorded in Southampton Co. Va. in 1755 and mentioned only his wife, sons Hill, Samuel and William and posthumous child. This child was given the mothers name of Tompkins. The daughters are not mentioned in the will but are listed in the will of their grand-father Samuel Tompkins in 1763. Mary Tompkins, widow of Wm. Sandefur, m. (2) Benjamin Hasty and had Benj., b. 1758 and Mary, b. 1762 m. Joseph Vick. The Sandefurs moved to western Edgecombe (later Nash) with their Arrington kindred. According to the Edgecombe Court Minutes in 1772, Wm. Sandifur was appointed administrator of Hill Sandifur decd. The will of Tompkins Sandifur was recorded in Nash County in 1783, mentioning his children and brother-in-law Arthur Arrington.

The will of Arthur Arrington (3) dated 5-23-1795, was probated in Nash Co. Nov. 1795. The executors were sons Joseph, John, and William Arrington. The witnesses were William Lewis and James Sandifur. The will of his widow Mary was probated in Nash Co. in 1805. Mentioned were her five youngest children; Henry, Richard and Arthur Arrington and daughters Mary Hunter and Nancy Sandifur. Arthur Arrington (3) and Mary Sandifur had issue. The dates are from the family Bible.

I. Martha Arrington, b. 4-3-1759, m. James Battle of Nash Co. They had issue Mary Battle and Elizabeth who m. Littleberry Hines. (S.V.F.-274)
II. Elizabeth Arrington, b. 8-29-1760, m. Henry Vick - 6 children
III. Joseph Arrington, b. 3-27-1762, m. Mourning Ricks - of whom later
IV. John Arrington, b. 1-16-1764, m. Eliza Nicholson - of whom later
V. William Arrington, b. 3-2-1766 - of whom later
VI. Peter Arrington, b. 6-4-1768 - of whom later
VII. Lucy Arrington, b. 8-3-1770. She is said to have m. Archibald Griffin and moved South.
VIII. Mary Arrington, b. 2-27-1773, m.(1) Archibald Hunter of Nash. (2) Mr. Blick. No issue by either marriage.
IX. Ann Arrington, b. 9-23-1777 - According to family tradition, she m. Alexander Hines but this appears unlikely. (S.V.F.-p. 274). She is mentioned as Nancy Sandifur in her mother's will in 1805.
X. Henry Arrington, b. 4-4-1779, will dated 12-23-1837, probated Nash Co. May, 1838. The name of his wife Rebecca is said to have been Southal.
   Children:
   1. Robert Arrington - no record
   2. Elizabeth Arrington m. (1) John Ward (2) Crafford Arrington, Nash M.B. dated 6-9-1845. Issue only by first marriage.
   3. Holman Arrington - will probated Nash Co. Nov. 1847

      4. John Simmons Arrington (1802-1849) m. 1826 Sallie
        Drake. Issue.
      5. Henry Arrington Jr. - no record
      6. Martha Arrington m. Thomas Alston - M.B. II-II-1823,
        Nash Co.

XI.   Richard Arrington, son of Arthur (3), b. 11-30-1781. He m.
(1) Maria Johnson, d. 7-31-1826. He m. (2) Temperance
Green Boddie, b. 3-24-1787, the daughter of William Boddie
(1749-1817) and Martha Jones of Halifax. She m. (1) 1812
Arthur Whitehead and (2) 5-29-1827 Richard Arrington.
The will of Richard Arrington, dated 11-17-1838, was prob.
Nash Co. Feb. 1839. The will of his widow Temperance was
prob. Feb. 1864.
Issue of first marriage.
1. Mary Arrington m. W.A. Cooper and had issue.
2. Martha Arrington m. Mathew Bolivar Drake and had issue.
3. Susan Arrington m. J.N. Conan
Issue of Richard Arrington by second marriage.
4. Temperance Arrington - no record
5. Eliza Arrington m. George W. Powell
6. Richard William Arrington m. 11-2-1858 Ruina Avent
   and had issue.

XII.   Arthur Arrington, son of Arthur Arrington (3), b. 10-25-
1784, d. Halifax Co. 7-3-1825. He m. 10-25-1806 Elizabeth Wright Alston, b. 12-20-1786 daughter of Col. Willis
Alston of Halifax, whose will, prob. Nov. 1819, W.B.
3-646, mentions son-in-law Arthur Arrington. The will of
Arthur Arrington, dated 2-20-1824, was probated Halifax
Co. 1825, W.B.4.
     Children:
1. Elizabeth Wright Arrington, b. 3-27-1809, m. James
    R. Battle
2. Mary Sandiford Arrington, b. 1-25-1812
3. Willis Alston Arrington, b. 3-9-1814
4. Arthur Arrington, b. 3-16-1816
5. Jack Patrick Arrington, b. 9-7-1818 - To Alabama
6. James J. Harrison Arrington, b. 10-5-1821
7. Marial Louisa Arrington, b. 3-25-1824

Joseph Arrington (4), 1762-1836; son of Arthur Arrington (3). At
one time he was sheriff of Nash County. He m. Mourning Ricks,
b. 3-10-1766, the daughter of James Ricks of Edgecombe and his
wife Mary Crudup. (17th C-243). His will, dated 3-8-1836, pro-
bated May 1836, lists only his three daughters Mary Person,
Temperance Mason, and Rhoda, the wife of Carter Arrington.
Issue of Joseph Arrington and Mourning Ricks.
I.   Ricks Arrington m. Miss Bunn. Only record of issue, Capt.
       William T. Arrington. See S.V.F. p.274 for descendants.
II.   Anthony Arrington - no record
III.   Temperance Arrington m. Nathaniel Mason. Untraced
IV.   Mourning Arrington m. Dr. Wood Tucker
V.   Mary Arrington m. Presly Person
VI.   Rhoda Arrington m. her cousin Carter Arrington, son of
       Joseph (3). See later for descendants.

VII. Dr. Joseph Arrington, d. 7-24-1827, m. 12-31-1822 Elizabeth Barker Tunstall, widow of John Hilliard. (S. V. F.-261).
She died 4-1-1827. See First Tunstalls in Va. by Morris,
p. 85, for descendants.

VIII. Thomas Arrington (1793-1828) m.1-21-1812 his cousin Martha Arrington, daughter of Joseph (3). Their descendants
moved to Twiggs Co. Ga.
Children:
1. Harriet Arrington m. Stephen Miller
2. Robert Ricks Arrington, d. 1849, m. Nancy Fulton
3. Eliza Arrington m. Henry Land
4. Mourning Arrington, m. Tillman Denson
5. Henry Crafford Arrington m. Jane Chappel
6. Thomas Nicholson Arrington m. Lucinda Melton

John Arrington (4), b. 1764, son of Arthur Arrington (3). He resided near the village of Hilliardston and represented Nash County
in the legislature for several terms. He m. 1804 Elizabeth Ann
Nicholson, b. 8-17-1777, the widow of Allen Mann and daughter of
Thomas and Ann Nicholson. Thomas Nicholson was a soldier in
the Revolution and the son of Lemuel Nicholson of Halifax Co.
N. C. John Arrington seems to have married a second time as the
marriage bond of John Arrington Sen. and Sarah Gardener was
recorded in Nash 4-14-1823. Sarah Arrington made her will
10-11-1826 mentioning only son Holman Gardener. John Arrington was a witness. The will of John Arrington dated 6-10-1830,
was probated Nash Co. Nov. 1844.
Issue by Elizabeth Nicholson.

I. Samuel Lewis Arrington - of whom later
II. Archibald Hunter Arrington - of whom later
III. Elizabeth Ann Nicholson Arrington (1808-1851). She m.
1824 Henry G. Williams. (See Tunstall Book, p. 113 and
Alston Book, p. 453 for issue)

Samuel Lewis Arrington (5), son of John Arrington, above. b.
Nash Co. 3-9-1806, d. 12-15-1879 Montgomery Co. Ala. m.
12-19-1826 his cousin Eliza Ann Nicholson, of whom later,
daughter of Mary Arrington and James Nicholson.

Children:
I. Mary Ann Eliza Arrington, b. 11-26-1827 - d.s.p.
II. Thomas Mann Arrington, b. 8-29-1829; of whom later
III. Laura Elvira Arrington, b. 4-13-1831 - d.s.p.
IV. James Nicholson Arrington, b. 1835-d.8-12-1894.Capt.C.S.A.
V. John Richard Arrington, b. 12-24-1836, d.4-27-1882
VI. Samuel Lewis Arrington, b. 1-2-1839, d. 12-14-1862; C.S.A.
buried in Montgomery
VII. Archibald H. Arrington, b.6-27-1843, d. 7-15-1862, C.S.A.
VIII. Mary Laura Arrington, b. 1-27-1845 - d.s.p.
IX. Henry Linn Arrington, b. 1-27-1845 - d.s.p.
X. Eliza Ann Arrington, b. 5-23-1841, m. 2-10-1860 Abner
F.Ellsbury, Lt. C.S.A., the son of Michael Ellsbury and
Eliza Ponder, at the Arrington Plantation which is now the
Country Club.

Children of Eliza Ann (Arrington) and Abner F. Ellsbury:
1. Samuel Arrington Ellsbury, b.1860, d.1879, m.1886 Amelia Palmer Ready, b.1864, d.1948.
    Children:
    (1) Samuel Arrington Ellsbury, b.Feb.14,1888; m.1921 Lillian La Marr, in Dallas, Texas. Issue:
        a. Samuel Arrington Ellsbury, b.Dec.1923; m.Martha Ann McDavid Feb.1950. Issue:
            (a) Samuel Arrington Ellsbury,b.May, 1954.
    (2) Edward Ready Ellsbury, b.Dec.19,1892. Lives in Los Angeles, Calif.
    (3) Palmer Ready Ellsbury, b.Dec.19,1892; m.Aug.28, 1918, Herbert Jones of Liverpool, Eng. Now lives in Houston, Texas. Issue:
        a. Margaret Ready Jones, b.Sept.13,1919; m. S. Donald Cook. Issue:
            (a) Donald David Cook, b.June 3, 1942.
            (b) Herbert Neal Cook, b.Oct.13, 1944.
            (c) Wayne Howard Cook, b.Dec.3, 1947.
        b. William Herbert Jones, b.June 14, 1921.
        c. Arthur Evan Jones, b.Apr.4, 1923; m.1953 Helen Ann Darnielle in Houston, Texas. Issue:
            (a) Lisa Darnielle Jones, b.Feb.1954.
2. Michael Ellsbury, b.Nov.2,1862; d.s.p. Aug.30,1891.
3. Edward Foster Ellsbury, d.Feb.28,1928, in Houston; m.Cora Underwood in Geneva,Ala.,Apr.12,1910.
    Children:
    (1) Michael Ellsbury, b.Jan.31,1911; lives in Dallas, Texas, has a son.
    (2) Louise Ellsbury, b.Aug.13,1912; d.May 5,1954; m. Apr.23,1949 Henry Feldman. No issue.
    (3) Laura Ellsbury, b.1914; d.1916.
    (4) Benjamin Richard Ellsbury, b.Dec.10,1916; m.1951, Mildred _____. One child.
4. Lida Ellsbury, b.ca.1870; d.Jan.1912; m.Hervey Brown of Montgomery.
    Children:
    (1) Hervey Abner Brown, b.ca.1894; m.Pauline Vineintelli, Issue:
        a. Pauline Lida Brown.
    (2) Elizabeth Brown, b.ca.1895; m.ca.1914, W.A.Arnold, Manager of St.Luke's Hospital, Jacksonville, Fla. Issue:
        a. Bill Arnold
        b. Betty Arnold
5. Mary Laura Ellsbury,b.Dec.10,1872; d.Oct.30,1907; m.Apr.21,1895, Edgar Robert Malone, b.Dec.1867; d.May 30,1951.
    Children
    (1) George Yewell Malone,b.Jan.21,1896; m.Sept.19, 1920, Johnnie Logan Ress. Issue:
        a. Annie Laurie Malone, b.Aug.5,1922; m.Sept.10, 1947, William Belling. Issue:

          (a) Virginia Ress Belling, b. Jan. 31, 1949.
          (b) Elizabeth Malone Belling, b. Jan. 31, 1949.
          (c) Catherine Belling, b. Jan. 3, 1952.
       b. Mary Elizabeth Malone, b. Dec. 19, 1925; m.
          Sept. 6, 1948 Wallace E. Calhoun. Issue:
          (a) Drucilla Patton Calhoun, b. July 16, 1950.
          (b) Wallace Everett Calhoun, III, b. Sept. 17, 1952.
          (c) Laurie Calhoun, b. Feb. 18, 1954.
          (d) Ann Ross Calhoun, b. July 29, 1955.
     (2) Lida Ellsbury Malone, b. Dec. 10, 1903.
   6. Benjamin Richard Ellsbury, b. 1875; d. 1909 in Montgomery, Ala.

XI.   Ellen Nicholson Arrington, b. 4-29-1850, m. Archibald Pitt Tyson (1844-1922) of Montgomery, Ala. Issue:
   1. Anne Arrington Tyson - (1876-1945)
   2. Sarah Nicholson Tyson, b. 4-24-1878, m. 12-5-1900 O. C. Maner and had issue Pitt Tyson Maner who m. Dorothy Vernon McAlpine
   3. Archibald Pitt Tyson Jr. b. 3-25-1880, m. 11-23-1938 Mrs. Willie Creagh Wilson Chapman, b. 11-3-1910, and had Ellen Tyson, b. 9-27-1939.
   4. May Tyson, b. 2-28-1882, m. Robert Harris, born in N. C. 2-24-1879 of Montgomery, Ala., and had issue: Archibald Tyson Harris, d. while a student at Washington and Lee. d. s. p.; Robert Lea Harris, b. 7-24-1919; Major Anti-Air Craft; Aide to Gen. Benj. Lockwood; $42\frac{1}{2}$ mo. South Pacific and Ellen Arrington Harris, b. 11-2-1915 m. 8-8-1942 Oscar Dahlene, Jr., and had: Anne Tyson Dahlene, b. 3-30-1944; Ellen Harris Dahlene, b. Sept. 1946.

XII.   Martha Nicholson Arrington, daughter of Samuel Lewis Arrington, b. 3-6-1852, d. Jan. 1, 1933. Was a babe in arms when her parents moved to Alabama from Nash Co. N. C.; m. Laban Warren Tyson, Montgomery, Ala. Issue:
   1. Archibald Lowndes Tyson, b. 9-27-1874, d. 4-27-1932, m. 7-17-1907 to Allene Nabors of Tuscaloosa, Ala. Issue Robert Nabors Tyson, b. 9-11-1911. General in Army in World War II. Still in Service; m. Lillian Nalli, b. in Phillipines. They had: Lucy Tyson; Robert Nabors Tyson, Jr.; William Tyson.
   2. Laban Warren Tyson Jr., b. 4-9-1880, m. 7-17-1907 at Florence, Ala. Mildred Keller, sister of Helen Keller. Issue: Katharine Keller Tyson, b. 10-27-1910; Pattie Arrington Tyson, b. 9-24-1915, m. 11-10-1938 William Tipton Johnson, Jr., and had: Wm. T. Johnson, III, b. 4-20-1941; Warren Tyson Johnson, b. 4-28-1945; Mildred Keller Tyson, m. 3-26-1942 William Gray Bickley, of Tuscaloosa, Alabama, who was a Major in U. S. Regular Army in World War II; at Anzio Beach; 2 years in Korea. Issue; Wm. Grey Bickley, Jr., b. Oct. 16, 1944.

   Thomas Mann Arrington, (6) son of Samuel Lewis Arrington, was born July 29, 1829; d. Nov. 30, 1895; married Dec. 18, 1861, Mary Robins, b. 8-15-1840; d. 10-29-1940, daughter of George

Goldthwaite, Adjutant General, State of Alabama, 1861-1885; Judge of Supreme Court of Ala., and U.S. Senator; b. 1810, d. 1879 at Tuscaloosa, Ala., and his wife Olivia Price (Wallach) who was born in Boston, Mass., 1810 and died in Montgomery, Ala., 1878.

Thomas Mann Arrington graduated from the University of North Carolina before he moved to Montgomery, Ala. In 1861 he volunteered in the Metropolitan Guards of Montgomery, 3rd. Ala. Infantry. While he was absent he was elected to the Legislature, which relieved him of military service. He declined this privilege,, and helped to raise a company of which he was made Captain. Later he was elected Lieutenant Colonel of his regiment serving throughout the war. After the war he was elected Judge of City Court of Montgomery, with concurrent, dignity and jurisdiction with the Circuit Court and with Chancery Court. He held this office from reconstruction days until his death. They had issue:

I.   George Goldthwaite Arrington, b.7-27-1863, d.s.p.
II.   Samuel Lewis Arrington, b.5-26-1866, d. 6-11-1923
III.   Olivia Goldthwaite Arrington, b. 8-10-1868, d. 5-27-1946
IV.   Thomas Mann Arrington, b. 7-4-1870, d. 8-25, 1934
V.   Richard Henry Arrington, b. Nov. 30, 1872; d. Aug. 12, 1929; m. Feb. 17, 1903, Pauline Seabrook White of Cheraw, S.C. He was a lawyer, and State Senator from 25th. District 1900-1903, and 1915. He lived in Elba, Ala; moved to Enterprise, Ala. and in 1916 to Montgomery, where he formed a Law partnership with his brother, Archibald Hunter Arrington. They were Division Council for Atlantic Coast Line R.R. He was elected to the Legislature from Montgomery in 1923. In 1904 he enlisted in 1st. Infantry, Ala. National Guard, and was Captain of Company I. Issue:
       1. Richard Henry Arrington, Jr., b. Aug. 17, 1919; m. Sept. 9, 1925, Mary Burnett Black of Brownsville, Texas. He an Army Air Force Captain in Intelligence in World War II, and enlisted before Pearl Harbor. Issue:
          (1) Mary Arrington, b. Nov. 21, 1946.
          (2) Lucy Arrington, b. March 24, 1948.
          (3) Pauline Arrington, b. June 29, 1949.
          (4) Richard Henry Arrington, III, b. June 16, 1952.
          (5) Laura Arrington, b. Dec. 15, 1953.
VI.   Archibald Hunter Arrington, b. 9-13-1874, d. 8-8-1946 m. 4-2-1914 Ethel Pelzer of Summerville, S.C. He was Judge of City Court of Montgomery.
       Issue:
       1. William Pelzer Arrington, b. 1-7-1916
VII.   John Arrington, b. 6-10-1876, d. 1946, m. Jesse McKee Lund of Marietta, Ohio. They had issue:
       1. Frances Mary Arrington m. Barnett Savery
VIII. Robert Goldthwaite Arrington, b.6-2-1878, d.8-11-1945 m. 4-26-1906 Olive Pierce. He was educated at Sewanee; and was Assistant Solicitor for Montgomery Co. for 30 years; retired 1943. Issue:
       1. Miriam G. Arrington m. 1944 Victor Block of Austria. Issue: Elizabeth A. Block, b. Montreal, Can. 1946; Victoria A. Block, b. Ithaca, N.Y. 1953

2. Robert Pierce Arrington, b. 5-5-1920, m, Marion S.
Graves of Tuscaloosa, Lieut. Navy Air Force, World
War II. Issue: Jean Pierce Arrington, 1946, Robert
Goldthwait Arrington, b. 4-15-1952; Stuart Graves Ar-
rington, b. 8-14-1954.

IX. Eliza Nicholson Arrington, b. 9-9-1880, Montgomery, Ala.
and died 7-18-1951 Atlanta, Ga. m. 2-28-1905 Joseph
Lloyd Lyon, b. 6-20-1877 at Chicago, died Pittsburg, Pa.
12-29-1945. They had issue:
1. John Flavelle Lyon, b. 11-11-1908 m. 1952 Mrs. Bess
Dowe. He was a Lieut. Commander in Navy in World War
II.
2. Elisa Lyon, b. San Juan, Peurto Rico, 1-10-1906, educated Randolph Macon and University of Ala., m. 7-7-1928
Howard Clinton Traywick, b. Clayton, Alabama 9-4-1903.
Issue: Olivia Arrington Traywick, b. 5-2-1929, grad.
University of Ga.; m. 5-30-1952 Richard Warren Cheat-
ham of Atlanta, Ga. and has two children; Olivia, b. 5-9-
1953, and Richard b. 5-27-1955

X. Mary Arrington, b. 11-27-1882, d. 10-16-1924 m. Archibald C. Goldthwaite, (1877-1927) Issue:
1. Archibald Campbell Goldthwaite, b. 12-16-1914
2. Mary Robbins Goldthwaite, b. 9-7-1917 m. Dr. James
Jeffrey of Edinburg, Scotland. Issue: Ethel Susan Jeffrey,
b. 1940; Stewart; Hebe Elizabeth; and Eleanor all b. in
Edinburg, Scotland.
3. Alfred Witherspoon Goldthwaite, b. 8-12-1921, with Patton's Army World War II. Judge Advocate U.S.A. after
the war.

Archibald Hunter Arrington (5), son of John Arrington (4) and his
wife Eliza Nicholson. b. Hilliardston, Nash Co. N.C. 11-13-1809,
studied at Louisburg College; member of the 27th and 28th Congresses, a member of the Secession Convention in N.C. 1861, a
member of the Confederate Congress and Chairman of the Co.
Court of Nash 1866-1867. He died 7-20-1872 and was buried on his
plantation near Hilliardston. He m. (1) his cousin Mary Jones
Arrington, b. 9-22-1820, d. 11-27-1851, daughter of Peter Arrington (4) of whom later, on 5-24-1839. He m. (2) Catherine E.
Wimberly of Edgecombe Co. on 3-14-1855. She was b. 3-1-1834
and died 5-3-1871.
Issue of First marriage.
I. Mary E. Nicholson Arrington b. 1833, m. Judge William
Lewis Thorp of Rocky Mount, N.C. Issue:
1. Archibald Arrington Thorp, b. 5-26-1875, died unmarried
2. Virginia Thorp, b. 1-26-1879, died 1903, m. 7-10-1901
Richard Henry Gregory of Rocky Mount. No issue.
II. John Peter Arrington, b. 5-11-1851 - of whom later
Issue of Second Marriage.
III. James Mann Arrington, b. 2-22-1856, killed by a falling tree
1-22-1872.
IV. Thomas Mann Arrington, Rocky Mount, N.C., d. Dec. 1917,
m. Florence J. Avera.

       They had issue:
1. Thomas Mann Arrington Jr., Wake Forest, N.C., m.
Hallie Powers
2. Samuel Lewis Arrington, b.5-3-1899, U.N.C. 1921,
Rocky Mount, N.C.
V.   Archibald Hunter Arrington, b.7-30-1858, U.N.C. 1876,
died unmarried on 12-19-1892.
VI.   Samuel Lewis Arrington, b. 3-11-1860, prominent in Civic
affairs in Rocky Mount, died unmarried 2-13-1918.
VII.   Robert W. Arrington, b.7-14-1862, d.6-24-1928, m.Eula
Knight. Issue:
1. Louise Wimberly Arrington m. Arthur Dowding
VIII. George Wimberly Arrington, b.8-18-1864, d.6-29-1885;
U.N.C. 1884
IX.   Joseph Calhoun Arrington, b.1-5-1867, d. 9-15-1897
X.   Margaret Powell Arrington, d. 1-1-1865
XI.   Henry Wise Arrington, b.2-21-1858, died in childhood

John Peter Arrington (6), son of Archibald H. Arrington, b. 1851,
d. Aug. 1904, m. 2-26-1873 Laura Maud PHILIPS of Edgecombe
County. Issue:
I.   Mary Jones Arrington, b. 1-7-1874, d.6-28-1950 unmarried.
For many years she was the County Historian for Nash
County and collected much of the information on the Arrington family used in this chapter.
II.   Kate Wimberly Arrington, b.8-30-1875, unmarried
III.   Florence Elizabeth Arrington, b.10-14-1876, d.4-16-1946,
m. 5-17-1901 William Burt PHILIPS. They had issue:
1. John Arrington Philips
2. William Burt Philips
3. Maude Arrington Philips
IV.   Harriet Burt Arrington, b.6-28-1878, m.8-28-1912 Richard
Henry Gregory of Rocky Mount. They had issue.
1. Jane Gregory, b. 5-8-1916, M.D. Duke University, m.
8-17-1945 James Chalmers Marrow and had issue; James C.
Marrow, Jr. b.7-11-1947; Henry Gregory Marrow, b.5-18-
1949; and Harriet Burt Marrow, b.11-11-1952
V.   Archibald Hunter Arrington, b.6-1-1880, m.1905 Maude
Latta. Issue:
I. Archibald Hunter Arrington, Jr.
VI.   James Jones Arrington, b.3-9-1882, died unmarried
VII.   Maude Philips Arrington, b.8-22-1883, m. Hugh Horne
Battle of Rocky Mt. on 5-8-1916. She died 10-2-1940. They
had issue:
1. Maude Arrington Battle, b.5-31-1918, m.9-10-1949 Lawrence Porter Johnson, Jr. They had issue: Lawrence P.
Johnson, Jr., b.10-2-1950 and Philip Battle Johnson,
b. 10-1-1953.
2. Hugh Horne Battle Jr., b. 4-2-1921, Davidson College,
m.6-5-1948 Evelyn Cooper Jeffreys, daughter of Wm.
and Eva Cooper Jeffreys.

Gen. William Arrington (4), son of Arthur Arrington (3), b.1766.
He was a prominent citizen of Nash Co., a general in the State

Militia and a State Senator in 1796. He married (1) about 1789
Anne Jackson, a native of England. At her death, he m. Dec.1804
Mary Ann Williams (1768-1816) daughter of Maj. John Williams
of Halifax Co. and widow of Capt. William Battle of Nash Co.(See
Boddie and Allied Families). The obituary of Gen.Wm.Arrington
appeared in "The Raleigh Register" for 10-2-1812. "Communi-
cated: Died, at his seat in Nash Co., the morning of the 24th of
Sept., Gen. Wm.Arrington after an illness of ten days which he
bore with great fortitude. This death is lamented by all who had
the pleasure of his acquaintance. As a neighbor, a citizen or member of society, Nash County has sustained an injury, such a one,
it is feared, providence will never replace." Gen. Arrington's
will was probated in Nash in 1812. The will of his widow Mary was
probated Nov. Term 1816.
Issue of 1st Marriage.
I.   Mary Jackson Arrington, b.8-29-1790, m. (1) James M.
     Nicholson who died leaving only a daughter Elizabeth Arring-
     ton who m. her cousin Samuel L. Arrington above. Mary
     J. Arrington m. (2) her cousin Gen. Joseph Arrington, son
     of Joseph (3).
II. John D. Arrington, b. 5-4-1792, m.1812 Joanna Drake,
     daughter of John Hodge and Frances Williams Drake. They
     had 7 children
III. William Arrington m. Ann Brinkley, daughter of James
     Brinkley and had issue, William Arrington, m. Maria Al-
     ston and had issue Maria Arrington m. William Kitchin of
     Halifax Co., N.C., the parents of, among others, Hon.
     Claude Kitchin, Speaker of the House during the Wilson Ad-
     ministration and William Kitchin, Gov. of N.C.
IV. Martha Arrington, b.11-7-1795, d.1870, m. Lawrence
     Battle. (See Battle Book for descendants).
Issue of Gen.William Arrington by second marriage.
V.   Anne Arrington (1805-1825) m. 1822 Peyton Randolph Tun-
     stall (See Tunstall Book, p. 52). They had issue:
     1. Virginia Caroline Tunstall, b. 1-17-1823 Nash Co.N.C.
        d. 1914 Huntsville, Ala., m.Clement Claiborne Clay, Jr.,
        U.S. Senator 1853-1861 and m. (2) Judge David Clopton.
        She was the author of the book A Belle of the Fifties and
        at the time of her death was president of the United
        Daughters of the Confederacy.
VI. Nicholas Williams Arrington - of whom later.

Nicholas Williams Arrington (5), son of Gen. William Arrington,
b.12-25-1807, d. 2-14-1865, m. 4-18-1827 Temperance Arring-
ton Drake, daughter of Francis and Elizabeth Drake. He was a
wealthy planter and resided at his plantation in Nash Co. known
as the "Cedars". There is a chapter on him in Bishop Cheshire's
book "Non Nulla". His will, dated 3-16-1863, was probated in
Nash Co. Aug. 1805 W.B.I. p.595. Issue according to his will.
I.   Elizabeth Francis Arrington - of whom later
II. John G. Arrington - untraced
III. Josephine Arrington m. a Mr. Howerton
IV. Nicholas W. Arrington Jr. - unmarried
V.   Temperance Ann Arrington m. Mr. Harris

VI.   Mary Williams Arrington - untraced
VII.   Celestia C. Arrington m. Mr. Smith

Elizabeth Francis Arrington (6), daughter of Nicholas W. Arring-
ton, b. 3-16-1828 d. 1-7-1867 "Woodlawn", Nash Co. N.C. m.
7-5-1845 William Thomas Wright of Halifax Co., the son of Arche-
leus Wright and Nancy Avent. They had issue:
I.   Dr. William Arch. Wright, b. 5-26-1846, Jefferson Med.
       College. d. s. p.
II.   Laura Virginia Wright m. 1866 James Avent
III.   Silas Henry Wright, of whom later
IV.   Nicholas Williams Wright, b. 1851, d. 1908 in Lee Co. Ar-
       kansas, m. in N.C. Martha Sherrod and had issue four
       children.
V.   Junius Paul Wright, b. 1853, d. 1935 Birmingham, Ala. m.
       Lulu Russell of Athens Ala., and had issue.
VI.   Frances Drake Wright - d. s. p.
VII.   Lena Thomas Wright m. Mr. Bradley
VIII. Samuel Pitts Wright (1864-1934)

Silas Henry Wright (7), son of Elizabeth Arrington Wright, b. 1849
Nash Co., N.C., educated at home by tutors and attended Louisburg College where he was a fine Latin and Greek Scholar. He
went West after the Civil War and was first President of Wright
Bros. Tobacco Co., St. Charles, Mo., and later President of
the Deerfield Lumber Co., Little Rock, Ark. He m. 11-7-1877
in Athens, Ala. Emma May Cox (1857-1890) the daughter of Elizabeth Tyus and Dr. Thomas Cox, a graduate of Jefferson Medical
College. Silas Wright died 12-4-1938 and is buried in Oak Lawn
Cemetery, Little Rock. Issue:
I.   Byrd Arrington Wright, attended Central College, Lexington,
       Ky. m. (1) Augustine Feeny 4-14-1903. She m. (2) 8-24-1922
       J.C. Anderson.
       Issue by first marriage.
       1. Martha Feeny m. 1928 Eugene Lohman. Issue, Judith and
          Gail Lohman.
       2. Jack Feeny, b. 2-21-1909 m. Helen Johnson
       3. Joseph Feeny, b. 10-13-1914 - died young
II.   Arch Tyus Wright, d. 1943, of New Orleans, La. m. Aileen
       Brooks and had issue:
       1. Jack Wright
III.   Annie Laurie Wright, grad. Hosmer Hall, St. Louis, Mo.,
       m. 6-26-1909 to William Edward Smith of Woodstock, Ill.,
       the son of W.E. Smith of Bedford, England and his wife Ade-
       laide Church. Mr. Smith was a graduate of the University
       of Wisconsin in 1902, was interested in Canadian Mining and
       died Sudbury, Ontario, 5-25-1939. They had issue:
       1. Adelaide Smith, grad. Sweet Briar College, m. 1939 Dr.
          Willis Joret Nelson of New Orleans and has issue; Ade-
          laide and Jennifer Nelson.
       2. Lawrence Wright Smith, b. 1-17-1920, in the Air Force,
          World War II, was graduated from Univ. Arizona 1948,
          m. Elsa Lilystrand 6-1-1943 and had issue; Constance
          and Deborah Wright.

3. Constance Caroline Smith, b.10-13-1914 - died young
IV. Emma May Wright, m.1908 St. Louis, Ernest Abner Green, son of Judge James Franklin Green. They had issue:
   1. Marjorie Harriet Green, m. June, 1937 Joel A. Rogers
   2. Ernest Alan Green, grad.Washington University, St. Louis
   3. John Leslie Green - Amherst College, Lt. in Navy, World War II, m. Miriam Symmes Nash of Winchester, Mass.

Peter Arrington, (4), son of Sheriff Arthur Arrington, b.1768, d. 7-3-1837. He m. (1) Ann Jones, the widow of one Armstrong and daughter of Lewellyn Jones of Franklin Co., N.C. He m. (2) Barbara Height of Franklin Co. His will was dated 6-8-1837 and probated Nash Co. Nov. 1840. The will of his widow Barbara, which mentions her brother Francis Height and her two daughters, was dated Nash Co., 1-13-1848 and probated the same year.
Issue of Peter Arrington (4) by first marriage:
I.   Dr. John Arrington - of whom later
II.   Peter Arrington Jr. - of whom later
III. Lewellyn Arrington m. Miss Bunn and had six children
IV.   Elizabeth Arrington m. George Cooper and had issue.
V.   Nancy Ann Arrington m. James Drake. Record of issue from the will of Peter Arrington: Mary Drake, Harriet Adelaine Drake, Elizabeth Drake, Richard Arrington Drake, and Mourning Sessums. Harriet Drake died unmarried leaving a will probated in Nash in 1846 mentioning sister Eliz Harris, sister Mary Rawls and children of sister Mourning Screws.
VI.   Arthur Arrington m.(1) his cousin Leah Arrington, daughter of Joseph Arrington (3). He m.(2) Dec.1830 Elizabeth Irwin of Edgecombe.
      Issue of First marriage:
      1. Mary Arrington m.4-11-1833 Thomas Wiggins and had issue among others, Rozella Wiggins m. George A.Smith of Scotland Neck, son of William R. Smith and Susan Evans. (V.H.G. p.355) They had issue.
      2. Leah Caroline Arrington, b.1820, m.Thomas B. Irwin. (See S.V.F.-280)
      3. Martha Arrington m.Robert Hart and had issue 7 children of whom Leah Hart m. (1) John H. Hyman of Scotland Neck, and (2) William H. Shields. Issue, among others, Pauline Arrington Shields m. Charles H. Herring, Scotland Neck, N.C. 6-6-1905.
      4. Dr.Thomas C. Arrington m. Anna Langford and had issue.
Issue of Peter Arrington (4) and his second wife Barbara Height.
VII. Barbara Sandiford Arrington m. Wm. K. A. Williams of War-Co. but had no issue. (See Alston Book, p.434)
VIII. Mary Jones Arrington. the first wife of her cousin Archibald Hunter Arrington (5), see above.

Dr. John Arrington (5), son of Peter Arrington, b.1-5-1800, d. Petersburg, Va. 4-23-1878, m.9-20-1825 Martha Smith Westray, b.11-10-1805, d.1-30-1848, the daughter of Samuel Westray of "Westrayville", Nash Co. N.C. and his wife Sally Bradford Turner, the widow of David Short of Northampton Co. N.C. (See will of Sarah Westray, dated 1838, Nash W.B. 1-434). Dr. Arrington

was a physician and practiced medicine at Hilliardston, Nash Co.
He m. (2) Mrs. Mary Ann Kearney Boyd of Warrenton (1800-1878)
but had no issue by her.
Issue of Dr. John Arrington and his first wife.

I.   Sally Ann Arrington, b.12-22-1827 m. Dr. John T. Watson
    of Petersburg, Va. Issue, 8 children, of whom Alice Watson m. her cousin Peter Arrington, son of Peter Arrington
    (5).
II.   Samuel Peter Arrington - of whom later.
III. Richard Turner Arrington, b.1-3-1833, removed to Petersburg, Va. where he became a wealthy merchant. He m.
    Elizabeth Plummer, daughter of Kemp Plummer of Warrenton, N.C. (S.V.F. p.357). Issue:

    1. Sallie F. Arrington, b.10-2-1854, d.s.p.
    2. Martha S. Arrington m. William Wright of Petersburg and
       had issue; Bettie M. Gaston Battle and Mattie m. Jacob
       Battle, Jr. (Battle Book).
    3. William P. Arrington, b.7-11-1857
    4. John Arrington, b.4-12-1859 - d.s.p.
    5. Henry Lynn Arrington, b.7-24-1860 - d.s.p.
    6. Col.Richard T.Arrington, b.4-1-1862, d.5-6-1915 m.
       Judith Beane and had issue two children.
    7. Kemp Plummer Arrington, b.7-28-1865
    8. Austin Peete Arrington, b.1-26-1867
    9. Samuel Watson Arrington, b.2-5-1868 - M.D. died unmarried
   10. Herbert Arrington, b.8-2-1869, d.4-12-1899 m. Miss
       Boisseau and had issue, Helen Elizabeth and Ann Lee
       Arrington.
   11. A.Warren Arrington, b.8-29-1870 - d.s.p.
   12. Ivy Lewis Arrington, b. 1-10-1872 m. Miss Thornton.

Samuel Peter Arrington (6), son of Dr. John Arrington (5). He settled in Warrenton, n.C. m. (1) Susan Eaton, S.V.F. p. 183, who died without issue and m. (2) Hannah Bolton White, b. 11-17-1839, d. Sept. 1938, the daughter of John White of Warrenton. Samuel P. Arrington was b. 1-1-1839 and d. 4-6-1893.
They had issue:

I.   Pattie Arrington, b.11-23-1861, d.s.p.
II.   Rosa Gilmour Arrington m.Tarleton Heath of Petersburg,
    Va. Issue:
    1. Jesse Heath
    2. Samuel A. Heath
    3. Tarleton Heath m. Mary Carter Riddle 4-20-1926
    4. Rosa Heath m. William Lunsford Long, son of Lemuel
       McKinnie Long and Bettie Mason of "Longview", Northampton Co. N.C. They live in Warrenton, N.C. and had
       issue: Rosa Heath Long m. James Payne Beckwith of
       Raleigh; Ruth Mason Long m. Peter Pescud Williams
       of Raleigh, and Dr. William Lunsford Long of Raleigh,
       m. Rebecca Williams, daughter of Walker Williams and
       sister to Peter P. Williams above.
III. Sallie Watson Arrington, b.7-28-1867 m. Walter G. Rogers

IV.   Mary White Arrington, b.11-4-1868 - d.s.p.
V.   Peter Arrington, b.12-26-1869, d. 1917, prominent tobac-
      conist, m. Katherine Pendleton of Warrenton, N.C. but had
      no issue. She died 1955. For many years she was president
      of the N.C. Art Association and was active in other Civic
      affairs.
VI.   Jessie Key Arrington, b.5-10-1871, d.1899 m. (1) Malvern
      Hill Palmer by whom she had issue; and (2) Andrew W.Falk-
      ner.
VII. Richard Bolton Arrington, b.6-17-1873, m.6-17-1903 Ethel
      Lewis and had issue, four children.
VIII. John White Arrington - of whom later
IX.   Lily Arrington, b.4-7-1876, m. Howard Alston - no issue.
X.   William Jones Arrington, b.1-29-1875
XI.   Charles Spruill Arrington, b.11-21-1877 - died young

John White Arrington (7), son of Samuel Peter Arrington (6). b.
2-28-1866 Warrenton, N.C., d. 11-14-1938 Greenville, S.C.,
m. 4-9 1889 Manchester, Va. Mary Carter Sublett, b. 7-31-1863,
d.10-15-1953, daughter of Lucy Nelson Page and James Madison
Sublett. They had issue:
I.   John White Arrington, Jr., b. 3-1-1890, m.9-9-1913 Hen-
      derson, N.C. Cornelia Graham Crittenden, b.10-16-1891,
      daughter of Effie Graham and Stephen Stanley Crittenden. Mr.
      Arrington resides in Greenville, S.C.
      Issue:
      1. Effie Graham Arrington, b.1-16-1915, m. W.Jack Wel-
         born
      2. Mary Carter Arrington, b.3-18-1916,m.James Bryan
         Little
      3. John White Arrington, III, b.8-21-1925, m.Jane Taylor
II.   Mary Carter Arrington, b.1-22-1892 - d.s.p.
III. Richard Westray Arrington, b.7-11-1893, m.Adelaide Bar-
      row
IV.   Octavia Page Arrington, b.9-18-1895, m.Don Cameron
V.   Nelson Battle Arrington, b. 2-25-1897, m.Polly Harrell.

Peter Arrington (5), son of Peter Arrington (4) and his wife Ann
Jones. He m. Sarah Ann Burt, the daughter of William Burt. The
will of Peter Arrington, dated 9-24-1851, prob. Nov.1852 Nash
Co. mentioned his 6 children and appointed his nephew Dr.Thomas
C.Arrington executor.
Peter Arrington and Sarah Ann Burt had issue.
I.   Susan Arrington m.10-18-1853 John B.Odum. 3 daughters.
II.   Peter Arrington Jr. m. his cousin Alice Watson. She d.
      3-23-1904. They had issue:
      I. Watson Young Arrington of Petersburg, Va.
III. William Burt Arrington married but had no issue.
IV.   Kearney Williams Arrington m.Sallie Marsh - issue 5 chil-
      dren
V.   Lucy Jones Arrington m. Lemuel Boyce and had issue:
      1. Sallie Arrington Boyce m. John W. Steele
      2. Dr. William Boyce
VI.   Harriet E. Arrington m. William E. Spruill of Martin Co.

16

N. C. Issue:
1. Peter Arrington Spruill, Littleton, N. C. m. Harriet Burt Parker. See PHILLIPS
2. Elizabeth Ballard Spruill, m. James B. Boyce - 6 children
3. William Emry Spruill m. Annie Ward. 3 children
4. Harriet Arrington Spruill - unmarried
5. Susan Sims Spruill m. Elijah Boddie Perry. Issue
6. Lucy Arrington Spruill m. Eugene Gay and had issue.
7. Alice Henry Spruill m. John Carter Mitchell. No issue.
8. John Arthur Spruill - unmarried
9. Frank Shepherd Spruill, atty for the Atlantic Coast Line, Rocky Mount, N.C., m. Alice Winston, sister of Judge Robert Winston of Bertie Co., N.C. 3 children

Joseph Arrington (3), son of Arthur Arrington (2) and brother of Sheriff Arthur Arrington (3), came to Nash County, then a part of Edgecombe, with his brothers and settled on the north side of Swift Creek. He married in Virginia, Martha Crafford, the daughter of Elizabeth Kearney and Carter Crafford (V.H.G.-297). Elizabeth Kearney, b. 6-11-1724, was the grand-daughter of Col. Thomas Godwin, Speaker of the Va. House of Burgesses and his wife Martha, the daughter of Hon. Joseph Bridger of Isle of Wight. (17th Cent. 469-70). Leah Crafford, sister of Martha Crafford Arrington married Isaac Hilliard who settled not far from the Arringtons on the south side of Swift Creek. Joseph Arrington represented Nash County in the Legislature 1781-82. His will, dated 11-12-1818 was probated Nash Co. Feb.1819. His widow survived him.
They had issue:
I. Carter Arrington - of whom later
II. Crafford Arrington m. Elizabeth Spruill and had issue 8 children, of whom Sallie m. Larkin Battle. (See "The Battle Book")
III. James Henry Arrington m. Mary Blount Spruill and had issue 9 children.
IV. Elizabeth C. Arrington, b.4-30-1784, d.10-10-1832, m. 4-19-1804 John Nicholson of Halifax Co. N.C. They had issue, 5 children.
V. Leah Arrington m. her cousin Arthur (5), son of Peter Arrington (4), see above.
VI. Martha Arrington m. Thomas Arrington (5), son of Joseph (4). See above for descendants.
VII. Ann Arrington m. Alexander Culpepper and moved to Starkville, Miss. She is said to have attained the age of 105 years.
VIII. Gen. Joseph Arrington m. his cousin Mary Jackson Arrington, widow of James Nicholson and daughter of Gen. William Arrington (4). They had issue 14 children and removed to Livingston, Ala.

Carter Arrington(4) son of Joseph Arrington (3). He married his cousin Rhoda Arrington, daughter of Joseph Arrington (4) and his wife Mourning Ricks. Carter Arrington settled in Halifax County near Culpeppers Bridge. His will dated 8-22-1834, and probated

Halifax Co. W.B. 4-173 mentions his wife and 3 sons and appointed his son Benjamln and Isaac Hilliard (his first cousin) executors. The will of his widow Rhoda Arrington, dated 11-24-1851, probated Nov. 1853, Halifax W.B. 4, 355, mentions son James and Benjamin and children of deceased son Joseph Arrington. They had issue:
I.   James Carter Arrington m. (1) the widow of his brother Joseph, but had no issue. He m. (2) Sallie Jones and had issue.
      1. Carter Arrington - untraced.
II.   Joseph John Arrington - of whom later
III. Benjamin Whitehead Arrington - of whom later.

Joseph John Arrington (5), son of Carter Arrington (4) resided in Halifax Co. N.C. He married Sarah Rebecca Moore, daughter of Alfred Williams Moore (1793-1865) of Halifax Co. and his wife Martha Williams. Alfred W. Moore was the son of James Moore who served in the Revolutionary Navy and a relative of Judge Bartholomew F. Moore, Atty. General of N.C.
Joseph Arrington and his wife had issue.
I.   Florence Arrington m. Dr. Frank Drake of Nash Co. Untraced.
II.   Joseph Carter Arrington m. (1) Ella Jones and (2) Betty Fields.
      Issue of Ist Marriage.
      1. Blanche Arrington m. Ed Huffines and had issue: Earnest Huffines
      Issue of 2nd Marriage.
      1. Joseph Carter Arrington, Jr. married and left issue, 9 children.
      2. Frederick Arrington - died unmarried while in service
III. Benjamin Franklin Arrington - of whom later.

Benjamin Franklin Arrington (6), son of Joseph John Arrington (4). b.9-29-1839 at Glenview, Halifax Co. - d. 3-12-1907 at Rocky Mount, N.C. m. 1-13-1875 at Ringwood, Halifax Co., Cora C. Tyree, b. 9-7-1853, d. 11-4-1916, daughter of John P. Tyree and Eliza Faris. (See S.V.F. for Tyree Ancestry). Mr. Arrington was a member of the Episcopal Church.
They had issue:
I.   John Hiram Arrington, b.7-2-1876, d.5-1-1901 unmarried
II.   Benjamin F. Arrington Jr., b.4-22-1878, d.12-15-1903 unmarried
III. Edwin Tyree Arrington, b. 3-13-1880, d. 5-5-1952 unmarried
IV.   Faris Moore Arrington, b.7-10-1882, m. Ame Oplinger - No issue.
V.   Cora Corinne Arrington, b.8-18-1884, m. Thomas Edgar Jenkins 11-7-1908 at Rocky Mount, N.C. He was b. 3-15-1874 and d. 3-5-1944, the son of Samuel Freeman Jenkins and his wife Saral L. Price of Edgecombe Co. N.C. Issue:
      1. Benjamin Freeman Jenkins, b.8-16-1909, m. Virginia Cade
      2. Cora Tyree Jenkins, b.4-26-1915

3. Martha Price Jenkins, b.12-13-1917
4. Thomas E. Jenkins, Jr., b.8-6-1912 m. 1-15-1946 Dora Hardy, and had issue; Thomas E. Jenkins III, b.2-2-1947

VI. Annie Rebecca Arrington, b.7-14-1886, m.6-2-1909 Roderick Goldston Murchison, b.1-6-1885, son of Robert Alexander Murchison and Mary Kate Goldston. Mr. Murchison is an official of the A.C.L. Railway and a member of the Episcopal Church. They had issue:
  1. Ellen Alice Murchison, b.6-26-1914
  2. Roderick G. Murchison, Jr., b.10-3-1918 m. 8-20-1949 at Ann Arbor, Mich. Helen Johanna Heikkinen, b. 9-19-1918, daughter of Lauri Isaki Heikkinen and his wife Lyyti Saari. They had issue: R. G. Murchison III, b. 7-4-1950; Donald H. Murchison, b. 10-2-1951, and Ross Arrington Murchison, b. 11-28-1953

VII. Ellen Alice Arrington, b.7-23-1888 - unmarried
VIII. Sarah Emily Arrington, b.12-18-1895 - died in infancy
IX. Pattie Simpson Arrington, b.10-23-1890, m.10-6-1926 Frank Parker Philips, son of Joseph Battle PHILIPS. They live at "Oak Forest", Battleboro, N.C.
Issue:
  1. Frank P. Philips, Jr., b.9-2-1927, m.9-9-1950 at Battleboro, Naomi Fisher. They have issue: Frank P. Philips III, b. 2-20-1953
  2. Neil Arrington Philips, b. 12-2-1930 m. Dr. William Blair Bryan of Battleboro.

X. Robert Lee Arrington, b.12-28-1892, m.6-14-1924 Dorothy Lee Harris, b.5-17-1899, the daughter of Andrew Jackson Harris and Lee Mitchell of Henderson, N.C. Mr. Arrington is a tobacconist and lives in Rocky Mount, N.C. They had issue:
  1. Dorothy Lee Arrington, b.4-15-1929, attended Salem College, m.2-19-1951 in the Church of the Good Shepherd, Rocky Mount, N.C., Richard Evans Richards, b.1-18-1928 Lancaster, S.C., the son of Hon. James Prioleau Richards M.C. and his wife Katherine Wylie. They have issue: Robin A. Richards, b. 2-15-1953 and Katherine W. Richards, b. 3-19-1955.
  2. Robin Tyree Arrington, b.8-16-1930, m.1-18-1953 Brian Pierce Power-Waters, b. 12-19-1922, London, England, son of Pierce Power-Waters and his wife Alma Shelley. Issue: Robin Shelley Power-Waters, b.5-17-1954

Benjamin Whitehead Arrington (5), son of Carter Arrington, b. 1818, d.1879, lived in Halifax Co. N.C. He married Martha Fluellyn Moore, daughter of Alfred W. Moore and sister to the wife of his brother Joseph.
They had issue.
I. Cornelia Arrington - no record
II. Pattie Crawford Arrington - of whom later
III. Benjamin Ricks Arrington, b.4-19-1844, d.4-7-1917 m. Annie Fitts and left issue.
IV. Mary Temple Arrington - of whom later

V.   Ella P. Arrington, b. 1850, d. unmarried 1919.
VI.   Bartholomew Arrington m. Mamie Pope and left issue.
VII. Alfred Williams Arrington - of whom later
VIII. Frank Arrington - of whom later.

Pattie Crawford Arrington (6), daughter of Benjamin Arrington (5), b. 6-15-1840 Halifax Co., d. Rocky Mount, N.C. 9-3-1928, m. Frederick Sterling Pierce who died in Halifax Co. N.C. in 1878. They had issue.
I.   Carrie Arrington Pierce, b. 3-21-1866, m. Joseph Farmer
II.   Annie Moore Pierce, b. 6-1-1867, d. 6-12-1950, m. John Daffin Odum, b. 1-14-1865, d. 5-15-1909 at Rocky Mount, N.C. They had issue.
    1. John D. Odum, Jr., b. 4-13-1894, m. Mary Alice Davenport. No issue.
    2. Annie Mae Odum, b. 9-3-1896, m. John Byrd Keller. No issue.
    3. Willie Pierce Odum, b. 7-16-1898, m. William C. Cooper, b. 8-31-1903, the son of Rastus and Lou (Duncan) Cooper. They had issue; William C. Jr., 6-5-1934; and Doris Ann Cooper, b. 11-11-1930.
III. Mattie Fluellyn Pierce, b. 7-1-1871, m. Edgar Zenus Parker, Rocky Mount, N.C. Issue:
    1. Louise Parker, Phi Beta Kappa from Duke University, 1928, Latin teacher Rocky Mount High School.
    2. Pierce Arrington Parker

Mary Temple Arrington (6), daughter of Benjamin Arrington (5). b. 1848, d. Rocky Mount, N.C., m. Harlow D. Avera of Rocky Mount, b. 1854, d. 1890. They had issue:
I.   Florence Avera m. Mr. Joyner but had no issue.
II.   Ella Avera m. D. L. Christian of Rocky Mount. They had issue:
    1. Mansfield Christian
    2. Dr. J. D. Christian of St. Louis, Mo.
III. Thomas Arrington Avera, b. 2-20-1890, d. 5-2-1952, Rocky Mount, N.C., m. 2-12-1920 Fannie Hill Herring, daughter of James Roswell Herring and his wife Julia Henrietta Hill of Noonan, Ga. They had issue:
    1. Thomas A. Avera Jr., b. 2-21-1921 had
    2. Frances Hill Avera, b. 6-3-1926, m. 11-18-1949 William G. Gaither, Jr., of Elizabeth City, N.C. Mrs. Gaither attended St. Marys School and the University of N.C. Issue: Helen Robinson Gaither, b. 12-25-1953
IV. William Whitehead Avera, b. 1877, d. 1940, m. (1) Minnie Haynes (1890-1919) of Mt. Airy, N.C. and (2) Mary Woodward, the daughter of Frederick William Woodward and his wife Mary Bowles of New Kent Co., Va. Issue of first marriage:
    1. William H. Avera Jr., b. 10-7-1919 Issue of second marriage:
    2. Mary Woodward Avera, b. 10-17-1934

Alfred Williams Arrington (6), son of Benjamin Arrington (5), b. 1-15-1842, Halifax Co. N.C., d. 4-4-1918. He removed to Rocky Mount where he was prominent in the early development of that

city. He m. (1) Florence Lindsey (2) Mary Ballard Bunn (See
S.V.F. p.271) and (3) Betty Hammond, the daughter of Col. Gray
W. Hammond of Rocky Mount.
Issue of first marriage.
I.   John L. Arrington - died unmarried
Issue of 2nd marriage.
II.   Lucy Bunn Arrington - of whom later
III.   Bennet Bunn Arrington, Rocky Mount, N.C. m. Mary Allen.
        Issue:
        1. Margaret Ballard Arrington
        2. Martha Bunn Arrington
        3. Frances Allen Arrington
Issue of 3rd Marriage.
IV.   Charles Hammond Arrington

Lucy Bunn Arrington, b.1-25-1879, d.12-26-1950, m.11-9-1898
Edward Garland Johnston of Rocky Mount, b.11-7-1872. They had
issue.
I.   Edward G. Johnston, Jr., b.6-2-1900, m.Julia Walling
        Moore, b.9-17-1902, Kinston, N.C., the daughter of Edward
        Orr Moore and Elizabeth Parrott. Mr. and Mrs. Johnston
        were married 6-28-1922. Mr. Johnston is Sales Supt. Rocky
        Mount Tobacco Board of Trade. Issue:
        I. Julia Moore Johnston, b.5-28-1925, m.1-28-1952 Henry
           Mowry Cook. Issue: Henry M. Cook, Jr., b.6-17-1953
           and Stephen Reid Cook, b.5-19-1955
II.   Alfred Arrington Johnston, b.12-1-1901, m.11-5-1927 Lil-
        lian Thompson. They had issue:
        I. Lillian A. Johnston, b.9-30-1940
III.   James Marion Johnston, b.9-23-1908, m. 4-10-1937 in Wash-
        ington, N.C. Lucy Tayloe Bowers, daughter of Ben F. Bow-
        ers and his wife Lucy Alston Tayloe. They had issue:
        1. James M. Johnston, Jr., b.1-23-1942
        2. Franklin Bowers Johnston, b.3-6-1945
IV.   Nell Burt Johnston, b.5-23-1912, Rocky Mount, N.C. m.
        11-14-1941 Earl Thomas Baysden, b.5-31-1909, son of
        Eugene J. Baysden and his wife Ida Simpson. They had issue:
        1. Earl Thomas Baysden, Jr., b.1-11-1943
        2. Edward Johnston Baysden, b.11-22-1947

ARRINGTON OF SUNCOMBE COUNTY, N.C.

William Arrington, the first known ancestor of this Arrington family, first appears in the public records in 1818 when on Dec. 5th of that year, he was granted 100 acres in Buncombe County on Casebolt's Branch of French Broad River on James Arrington's line. (P.B. 11-261). He was undoubtedly the son of an earlier James Arrington who appears in the Census of 1790 as residing in Burke County, N.C. the county from which Buncombe was formed in 1791. In the Census of 1830 James Arrington is listed as being between 70 and 80 years old. Thus he could have been the father of William Arrington who was born about 1795. The will of a James Arrington, dated 5-13-1831, was probated in Buncombe County, N.C. July 1831. He mentions his wife Milly and his children, but doesn't list them by name.

It is not known where this James Arrington came from. Arthur Arrington (2) of the Nash County family, who settled in North Carolina about 1760, mentioned a son James Arrington in his will, dated 1779. On 8-21-1771, Arthur Arrington deeded 185 acres to James Arrington in Edgecombe Co., bordering on Griffin and Douglas. (Deed B. "D"-376). This land fell in the new county of Nash in 1777. On 7-30-1785 James Arrington sold this tract to Joseph Arrington. Arthur Arrington's corner is mentioned in the deed. (Nash Book 3). He evidently moved away from Nash at this time as there is no mention of him in the Nash and Edgecombe records except for the two deeds shown above. He was born by 1750 as he was deeded land in 1771. Hence, he could have been the same James Arrington who was 70-80 years old in Western N.C. In 1830 (See Above). However, further research is needed to establish this connection. There was also a James Arrington living in Anson Co. N.C. at the time of the 1790 Census. According to traditions preserved in the Arrington family of Nash County, James Arrington, son of Arthur Arrington (2) married a Miss Portis and had issue; four sons - James, Henry, Lewis, and Littleton Arrington. The Portis family settled in the extreme upper portion of Nash County at an early date. The well known Portis Gold Mine was later discovered on their property.

William Arrington (I), first known ancestor, born in Buncombe County, N.C. about 1795. In 1850, he was living in Yancey County and later moved to Madison County, N.C. near Marshall where he died. He married Judith Gillespie (1804-1882), the daughter of Silas Gillespie and his wife Mary Emaline Neal.
They had issue:
I.   Elizabeth Arrington, b. circa 1816, m. Henry Grooms
II.   James Arrington, b.1817, m. Lucinda Ramsey
III.   Lewis Arrington, b.1818, m. Mary Rice
IV.   Joseph Arrington, b.1825, m. Delanie McHone

V.   Mary Arrington, b.1826, m. Gabriel Cody
VI.   Talitha Arrington, b.1828, m. John Tilson
VII.   Silas Arrington - of whom later
VIII. Edith Arrington, b.6-27-1831, m. Sidney S. McLean
IX.   Richard Arrington, b.1834
X.   William Arrington, b.1835
XI.   Robert Wilson Arrington,(b.1838, m. Sarah Gentry
XII.   Minerva Arrington, b.1840, m. Stewart F. Higgins

Silas Arrington (2), son of William Arrington, b.2-10-1830,N.C.,
died 3-5-1901 Read Hill, Cocke County, Tenn. He was a Free
Will Baptist Minister. He married 6-25-1853 Madison Co. N.C.
Mary Caroline Henderson, b.4-6-1834, Laurens Co. S.C. died
3-30-1936 Fountain City, Tenn. They had issue:
I.   Elizabeth Jane Arrington, b.1-28-1855, m.Manson Winfield
       Cook
II.   LeRoy Madison Arrington, b.6-8-1857 - of whom later
III.   Lucinda Arrington, b.5-13-1859, m. Robert Cleveland
       Harper.

LeRoy Madison Arrington (3), son of Silas Arrington, b. 6-8-
1857 Madison Co. N.C. died 8-13-1946 Twin Falls, Idaho, m.
May, 1879 Priscilla Jane Brisendine, b.8-27-1857 at Chucky
Knobs, Cocke Co., Tenn., d.10-19-1949, Twin Falls. In 1891
they became converted to the Church of Jesus Christ of Latter-
day Saints and in 1901 moved to Idaho. They had issue:
I.   Bruce Sidney Arrington, b.7-19-1880, m. Bessie Mae
       Emerson
II.   LeeAnner Arrington, b.4-3-1883, m.William Orvile Fisher
III.   Grover Nicholas Arrington, b.9-5-1885, m. Katheryn
       Hasenbalg
IV.   Jacob Franklin Arrington, b.10-19-1887, m. Annie Mar-
       garet Shields
V.   Noah Wesley Arrington - of whom later
VI.   Callie Belle Arrington, b.11-26-1891, Cocke Co. Tenn.
       m. 5-8-1930 Salt Lake City George David Ward, b.10-18-
       1883, Cassia, Idaho.
       They had issue:
       1. LeRuth Ward - b.1-19-1932 - m. Elmer D. S. Tyau
       2. Elaine Ward, b.5-6-1934, m. Craig Kimball Mayfield
VII.   Robert Glenn Arrington, b.6-6-1893, m. Annie L. Tuttle
VIII. Joseph Earl Arrington, b.6-21-1895, m. Genevieve
       Thornton
IX.   Pearl Arrington, b.4-19-1898 Cocke Co. Tenn. m.6-26-1929
       Salt Lake City, Lee Ray Sparks, b.3-8-1904, Leavenworth,
       Kansas. They reside in Oakland, California, and had issue:
       1. Naomi Mae Sparks, b.8-8-1931, m. John Duke Allen
       2. Lloyd Arrington Sparks, b.7-29-1933
X.   Silas Arrington, b.1900 - died in infancy

Noah Wesley Arrington (4), son of LeRoy Arrington. b.11-30-1889,
Cocke Co. Tenn. m.6-1-1913 Lawton, Oklahoma, Edith Grace Corn,
b.Ireland, Indiana 11-26-1894.
They had issue:
I.   LeRoy Wesley Arrington, b.1-15-1914, m. Mary F. Nix

II.   Thelma Eileen Arrington, b. 2-14-1916, died in infancy
III.   Leonard James Arrington, b. 7-2-1917, m. Grace Fort
IV.   Marie Arrington, b. 5-5-1919, m. 9-23-1938 Ezra Earl
       Davidson, b. 5-6-1917 Oakley, Idaho. They had issue:
       1. Milton Earl Davidson, b. 9-16-1938
       2. Deanna Marie Davidson, b. 6-6-1940, d. 6-10-1952
       3. Charles Ezra Davidson, b. 7-1-1944
       4. Jerry Dean Davidson, b. 1-10-1948
V.   Kenneth Richard Arrington, b. 11-10-1923, m. Doris Baldwin
VI.   Asa Wayne Arrington, b. 5-10-1925
VII.   Doris Elaine Arrington, b. 9-23-1927
VIII. Donald Charles Arrington, b. 7-25-1929 m. Cleone Baird
IX.   Ralph Marvin Arrington, b. 12-11-1930
X.   Ross Lamont Arrington, b. 2-7-1934

THE ANSELM BAILEY FAMILY OF SURRY

Anselm Bailey I was a footman in the Surry Militia in 1687. The date of his death is not known but his widow married Thomas Tarver sometime before Dec. 13, 1711, when her second husband, Thomas Tarver, made his will (Bk. 6, p. 125). Anselm Bailey's children are mentioned in the will of his son, Robert Bailey, dated Oct. 4, 1712 and probated Mar. 18, 1714, as follows: "To my Mother, Elizabeth Tarver, a horse and at her death to sister, Sarah Boyce. To sister, Sarah Tarver, dishes. To Samuel Tarver, a gun; to Benj. Bailey, my brother Anselm's son, to sister, Jane Lother bed and furn. Cozen William Warren a jacket. Bros. Anselm and Walter Bailey, exrs. Wits: John Tooke, Thos. Waller (Bk. 6, p 34).

Anselm Bailey II lived in Surry where he made his will in 1754 as follows: "To Granddau. Hannah Hargrave plantation whereon I dwell, 300 A on my branch adj. Joseph Hargrave, David Holloway, Joseph Pettway; To grandsons, Elijah and Joseph Bailey, 190 A. at upper end of above mentioned adj. Edward Harris, Nathaniel Sebrell; to grandson Samuel Bailey 190 A; portion of estate to be divided equally among my 3 children, Benjamin, Anselm & Martha; to dau. Martha Hargrave 1 negro. Exec.: Samuel & Elijah Bailey. Dated 7/7/1754. Recorded 10/16/1759. Tryal Bailey, Anselm Bailey Jr., Benj. Bailey Jr. (W.B. 1754-68, part 1, p. 208).

Children:

I. Anselm III, m. a daughter of Lemuel HARGRAVE who calls him "son-in-law" in his will probated Sept. 15, 1742 (Bk. 9, p 415). Anselm's will was dated April 1770 and probated Jan. 21, 1772. He bequeathed his wife, Mary, a plantation of 175 acres for life; to son Anselm 220 acres where he now lives; to son in law, Samuel Pretlow the balance of his account with me; son John Bailey land and plantation bought of Joseph Holleman, also part of a tract I bought of Anselm Bailey at run of Tarapan Swamp; dau. Ann Hunnicutt 2 negroes; son, Michael, 240 acres where he now lives bought of Michael Holloway; son Lemuel land and plantation where I now dwell 125 acres divided from lands I have given sons Anselm & John. Samuel and Anselm Bailey to be execs. This 6th day of the 4th month called April (Quaker designation) Wits: Arthur, William and Joseph Holloman (W.B. 1769, p 176).

II. Benjamin's will was dated April 18, 1784, pro. Feb. 10, 1785. His legatees were: sons, Tirah, Absalom, Joseph, Edmund, and Abidon (Executor); daus., MIRIAM HARGRAVE; Mourning Russell, Rhoda Sadler, Sarah Brook; sons Joshue; Josiah Davis, Elijah Bailey and wife, Sarah. (Southampton Wills)

III. Martha, m. Joseph Hargrave.

24

BARHAM OF SURRY

Captain Charles Barham of Surry descends from the ancient family of Barham in Kent, whose pedigree begins with Warine de Barham, who in 1210 held lands in Berham, near Canterbury, by Knight service as one of the military tenants of the Archbishop of Canterbury. (See article by R.G. Fitzgerald-Uniache, B.A. F.R.S.A. Sussex Arch. Soc. LVI (1914) p.110) This family has also resided in Surry County Virginia continuously for more than 300 years. It's present representative is Mr. S.B. Barham, now Clerk of the County Court.

Captain Barham first appears in the Surry records in 1654 as a witness to a bond of Andrew Robinson to Dorothy Kew. (D.W. 1645-1715 p 43) He was a vestryman of Lawne's Creek Parish first appearing on the list May 24, 1661. On Feb. 2, 1663, Charles Barham, gent., of Lawne's Creek Parish bought 300 acres on Hog Island, formerly owned by John Medmore, willed to him by heirs in England. Captain Barham paid 63 guineas sterling with bills of exchange drawn on his brother RICHARD BARHAM of London. Wits.; Wm. Cockerham, Andrew Robinson, David Williams. (Id.-228). In 1666, Capt. Wm. Cockerham and Mr. Charles Barham were granted 850 acres on the Blackwater for the transportation of 17 persons, among whom were John and Mary Cockerham. (C.P. 562) In 1668 Captain Barham was appointed a Justice of the County Court and in 1672 he and Robert Caufield presented the estate of Capt. Corkerham to the Court.

Captain George Watkins in his will made in 1673 refers to "Cousin Charles Barham, son of my loving Uncle, Capt. Charles Barham; and makes a bequest of 1000 lbs. of tobacco to Captain Barham, whom he made co-executor with his wife Elizabeth Watkins. The exact relationship between the families has not been definitely determined. (48V.278-279) Captain Barham's wife was Elizabeth.......last name unknown. His two daughters, Elizabeth and Priscilla Barham are given bequests in the will of Wm. Ridley of Isle of Wight, dated May 1, 1671 and probated Oct.16, 1671. (W.D.& W.no.2-p.98.) Capt. Barham was appointed Sheriff in 1673, and in 1677, after Bacon's Rebellion, was confirmed as a Justice by Governor Berkeley. He probably served on the County Court until his death.

In 1680 Captain Barham deeded Joseph Rogers, for 8000 lbs. tobacco 830 acres heretofore patented by him and Capt. Wm. Cockerham in 1666. John Barnes, a prominent Quaker, in his will dated Mar. 2, 1690, stated: "What is due me from my kinsman, Robert Barham, son of Capt. Charles Barham, late of Merchant's Hundred, decd., be paid to my wife Jane." Capt. Barham evidently moved to Merchant's Hundred shortly before his death. His will probably perished in the destruction of the James City records.

25

Children, mentioned in wills of relatives:

I.   Elizabeth, m. Thomas[2]Binns (?) (See Binns, V.H.G.)

II.   Priscilla, m. Robert Hart. (See Hart)

III. Charles[2] inherited land in James City as proven by a petition of his son Charles[3] in 1734, of which Dr.B.C.Holtzclaw secured a copy from the Public Records Office in London. This shows that there were four children as given herein, but that "Perilee" as given in Dr.Holtzclaw's article in the last line of page 279,48 Virginia Magazine should be "Priscilla".

IV. Robert, m. Elizabeth Clark. (See later)

2. Robert Barham appears first as a tithable in 1695, indicating his date of birth as 1679. This is confirmed by a petition dated January 4, 1697-8, to have his estate "being near full age". He married, about 1700, Elizabeth, daughter of John and Mary Clark of Lawnes Creek Parish. She is mentioned in the will of her father in 1717, in which he bequeaths legacies to five of his Barham grandchildren. John Clarke's wife, Mary, was a daughter of Robert Flake of Isle of Wight.

Robert Barham apparently lived most of his life in Surry but moved to Southampton County in his old age. His will dated January 18, 1748, was probated in Southampton, April 14, 1760 (W.B. I. p. 332)

Children:

I.   John, m. Elizabeth, daughter of Elizabeth (NEWSOM) and Thomas EDWARDS. (See later)

II.   Robert, b. prior to 1711, and died in Surry in 1770. His will, dated March 27, 1770 and probated July 17, 1770, mentions only his son William and granddaughter Elizabeth Barham. The granddaughter, Elizabeth, was probably a daughter of Thomas Barham, d.1764, and his wife Lucy Holt, daughter of Benjamin Holt of Surry Co., whose will in 1770 mentions his daughters Lucy Barham and Ann Bell, and sons Joseph, Michael, and Philip Holt.

III. Thomas Barham, b. in Surry after 1711, m. Sarah NEWSOM. He lived for some time in Isle of Wight Co., though born in Surry. He later moved to Sussex Co., where he died in 1784. His will, dated August 17, 1782, and probated September 16, 1784, mentions only his wife Sarah and his daughter Lucy. There were other children, however. Mary Moss, in her will in Sussex in 1775, mentions her daughter Elizabeth Barham and her son-in-law, Thomas Barham, Jr. Another daughter, Patty, is mentioned in the Albemarle Parish Register; while Charles Barham and Benjamin Barham, whose children's births are recorded in the same Register, were probably also sons of Thomas and Sarah Barham. The following dates are taken from the Albemarle Parish Register.

Children:

1. Thomas Barham, m. prior to 1775 Elizabeth Moss; had at least one daughter Mary (Polly), born October 29,1775, christened February 11, 1776.

2. Charles Barham (probably), m. Mary (Harwood?); and

had issue: (1) Elizabeth, b. January 23, 1763, christened
March 27, 1763; (2) Rebecca, b. April 17, 1764, christened May 20, 1764; (3) Amy, b. February 19, 1766,
christened March 23, 1766; (4) Charlotte, b. June 14,
1768; christened September 4, 1768; (5) Mary Harwood,
b. January 19, 1771, christened March 17, 1771; (6)
Daniel, b. December 2, 1773, christened March 13,
1774.

3. Benjamin Barham (probably), m. Sarah, and had issue
at least one son, John Barham, b. February 13, 1771,
christened June 9, 1771.

4. Martha Barham (Patty), b. January 4, 1763, christened
March 27, 1763.

5. Lucy Barham, b. May 2, 1768, christened June 12, 1768.

IV. Benjamin, b. in Surry after 1711, d. in Southampton Co.,
Va. in 1797; m. (perhaps) Mary Judkins, dr. of John Judkins of Surry Co. (see Judkins Family). His will, dated
March 30, 1776 and probated in Southampton June 10, 1779,
mentions his wife Mary, sons William, John and Benjamin,
daughters Lucy, Fanny and Elizabeth Barham.

IV. Benjamin, b. in Surry after 1711, d. in Southampton Co.,
Va. in 1797; m. (perhaps) Mary Judkins, dr. of John Judkins of Surry Co. (see Judkins Family). His will, dated
March 30, 1776 and probated in Southampton June 10, 1779,
mentions his wife Mary, sons William, John and Benjamin,
daughters Lucy, Fanny and Elizabeth Barham.

V.   Charles, b. in Surry Co. prior to 1711. He first appears
in the Surry records May 19, 1727 (D. & W. 1715-30, p. 750),
which indicated about 1706 as the probable date of his birth.
In 1733 he petitioned the House of Burgesses to enable him
to sell certain entailed lands and settle others more conven-
ient (Journal of the House of Burgesses, 1727-40, pp. 138,
139, etc.). In 1738 he was deeded land by Thomas Holt Jr.
in Isle of Wight Co. (Isle of Wight D.B. 5, p. 249) and lived
in Isle of Wight for a number of years, receiving also numerous land-grants in that county, most of which fell into Southampton on the organization of that county. He died in Southampton Co. in 1791 at an advanced age. His will, dated
September 17, 1783 and probated June 9, 1791 (W.B. 4, p.
432), leaves his property to his son Robert Barham and
granddaughter Milly Barham; daughter Lucy Deloach; Dewry
Parker husband of his daughter Elizabeth; grandsons Joel
and Barham Newsom and daughter Mary Harris; son James;
and makes his grandson Joel Barham his executor. Charles
Barham married the first time, probably, Sarah Judkins,
daughter of John Judkins of Surry (Dr. Holtzclaw V.M. 48,
p. 359). His second wife was Ann Arrington, widow, of
Southampton.
Children:

1. James, b. about 1730, m. (probably) Mary Thorpe, granddaughter of Timothy Thorpe of Southampton Co. (the
latter's will in 1751 in Southampton mentions his granddaughter Mary Barham); Lieutenant of Militia in 1755 in

Southampton Co.; d. 1792, his will, dated February 26, 1791 and probated in Southampton June 9, 1792, mentioning his son Joel Barham, drs. Martha Harris, Sarah Fisher and Rebecca Holliman, son James, daughters Mary Barham and Susannah Meacom, Sons Judkins Barham, Samuel Barham, Timothy Thorp Barham and John Barham, granddaughter Phoebe Barham dr. of Judkins, and sons-in-law Edward Fisher and William Holliman.

2. Robert, m. Hannah_____; d. in Southampton 1797; will dated March 20, 1792, probated May 15, 1797, mentions his wife Hannah, daughters, Peggy, Charlotte and Sally Barham, Mary Cooper, Milly Hutchings, Patsy Gilliam, and Betsy Gilliam; son Howell Barham.
3. Mary, b. about 1735, m. David NEWSOM.
> 4. Elizabeth, m. Drewry Parker.
5. Lucy, m._____De Loach.

John[3] Barham, son of Elizabeth (Clark) and Robert[2] Barham, married Elizabeth, daughter of Elizabeth (Newsom) and Thomas Edwards. John's will was dated Sept. 29, 1770, proven July 1771. He named the following children:
I.   Jesse, m. Faith Judkins.
II.   John, m._____Judkins (?)
III. Joseph, m. Sally Lane. (See later).
IV.   Mary, m. Benjamin Judkins before 1770.
V.   Ann, m. Thomas Lane, Jr.
VI.   Elizabeth, m. James Adams.
VII. Martha.

Joseph[4] Barham, who was born about 1745 in Surry County, Virginia, died there in 1823. In 1765/6 he married Sally Lane, daughter of Mary and Thomas Lane, who was born about 1748 in Surry and died there in 1826. (See Lane)
Children:
I.   Joseph, b. 1768; m. Ann Cocke Hunnicutt. (See later)
II.   James, b. about 1770 d. s. p.
III. Thomas, b. about 1772.
IV.   Charles, b. about 1774; d. s. p.
V.   Mary Ann, b. about 1776, m. Batts Lane.
VI.   Nancy, b. about 1778.
VII. Elizabeth, b. about 1780, m. in 1808, Robert B. Hunnicutt, Jr.

Joseph[5] Barham, Jr., son of Sally (Lane) and Joseph[4] Barham, was born in Surry County, Virginia, in 1768, and died there in 1834. In 1824 he married Anne Cocke, daughter of Elizabeth (Binns) and Robert B. Hunnicutt, Sr., who was born in Surry in 1801 and died there in 1873. (See Binns, V. H. G.)
Children:
I.   Joseph A. S. Barham, b. Mar. 22, 1828; m. Pamela J. Howell.
II.   Allen Cocke Barham, b. Nov. 1, 1829; m. Virginia Crittenden.
III. Caroline Virginia Barham, b. Dec. 7, 1830, died at the age of 12.
IV.   Claudius A. W. Barham, b. Apr. 27, 1832; m. Alexine G. Ballard. (See later)

Claudius[6] A. W. Barham, son of Ann Cocke (Hunnicutt) and

Joseph[5] Barham, was born April 27, 1832, in Surry County, Virginia and died in Asheville, N.C. August 19, 1911. At Goldsboro, N.C. Oct.18, 1859 he married Alexine Goldsborough, daughter of Martha Partial (Wells) and Jethro Ballard, who was born Dec. 17, 1839 in Suffolk, Nansemond County, Virginia, and died May 13, 1884 in Durham, N.C.

Mr. Barham served in the Confederate Army, and later engaged in the Tobacco Business.

Children:

I. Claude Virginia Barham, b.Apr.27,1862; m.E.E. Bishop
II. Virginius Ballard Barham, b.Mar.4,1865; d.s.p.
III. Charles A.W. Barham, b.Apr.16,1867; m.Mary H.Wilkinson. (See later).
IV. Undine Urquahart Barham, b.Nov.4,1869; m.John E.Hardin.
V. Fredericka Barham, b.July 20, 1872; d.s.p.
VI. Lenore Barham, b.Oct.18,1875; m.(1) Ernest L. Holland; (2) J.B. Harrison.
VII. Jethro Ballard Barham, b.Nov.30, 1878; d.s.p.
VIII. Landon Earle Barham, b.Dec.15, 1881; d.s.p.

Charles[7] A.W. Barham, son of Alexine Goldsborough (Ballard) and Claudius[6] A.W. Barham, was born April 16, 1867 at Goldsboro, N.C., died at Sarasota, Florida, January 4, 1952, although his home was in Nashville, Tenn. On February 20, 1889, at West Point, Virginia, he married Mary Hannah, the daughter of Jane (Dyke) and Edwin Wilkinson, who was born April 2, 1865 in Philadelphia, Penn; and died April 13, 1928.

Mr. Barham was Vice-President of the Nashville, Chattanooga & St. Louis R.R.; a 33 degree Mason; Grand Master of the Masonic Lodge of Tenn. President of the Nashville Chamber of Commerce, and Chairman of the Southern Freight Association.

Children:

I. Peyton Earle Barham, b.Nov.11, 1889; m. (1) Lenore Bell; (2) Gladys Belleville.
II. Jane Alexine Barham, b.Oct.17, 1891; m.Albert H.Peoples.
III. Helen Louise Barham, b. Apr.20,1894; d.s.p.
IV. Martha Elizabeth Barham, b.Oct.31, 1895; m. E. Gray Smith; divorced.
V. Charles[8] A.W. Barham, Jr., b.Oct.18,1903; m.Emma Louise Wheeler. (See later).

Charles[8] Barham, Jr., the son of Mary Hannah (Wilkinson) and Charles Barham, was born Oct.18, 1903, at Nashville, Tenn., and married Oct. 10, 1928, at Mt. Pleasant, Maury Co., Tennessee, Emma Louise, daughter of Marie Louise (Stitzel) and Franklin Sheldon Wheeler, who was born March 9, 1903, at Louisville, Kentucky.

Mr. Barham received his B.A. degree from Vanderbilt University, 1924 and now lives at Farmington, Charlottesville, Virginia. He is a partner in Radio Station WCHV; Vice-President and Treasurer of Thomas Jefferson Memoria Fd.; President of Commerce; and Chairman of the Albermarle Planning Committee.

Children:

I. Frank Wheeler Barham, b.April 11, 1930.
II. Charles Barham, III, b.Oct.6, 1931.

BARKER OF SURRY

John Barker, Master of the good ship, "Abraham", set sail from London "bound for Virginia about November 20, 1635 (Hotten 138) with 51 passengers. It is not known whetern or not he was any relation to William Barker, Master of the "America" who sailed from Gravesend June 23, 1635 with 88 persons. William Barker, Mariner, is known to have patented land in Charles City county 1635 (VHG-146).

A John Barker patented 300 acres in James City county, Nov. 29, 1649, "lying upon the very head of the main branch of Lower Chippokees Creek bounded upon the land of Master Dunston and William Carter for the transportation of 6 persons" (C.P.187). He may not have been John Barker, Master of the Abraham.

On Jan. 9, 1653, Theodrick Bland, of John Bland and Co., merchants, for 10000 pounds of good tobacco conveyed unto John Barker, Planter, a plantation bounding upon the main river of Upper Chippokes Creek (Surry, 1645-72, p. 38) Wits: Richard Stevens, John Holmwood.

John Barker Sr. on Sept. 2, 1673, with his wife, Anne Barker, conveyed unto John Barker, Planter, a plantation bounding upon the main river of Upper Chippokes Creek (Surry Co. Wills, Deeds, Orders Vol. 1671-84, p. 32) "To all people whom this deed, sale or writing of Bargain & Saill shall come, wee, Joh: Barker, Senr. of the parish of Southwick in the County of Surry in Virga and Anne, my wife, the late wife and Executrix of the last will and testament of Geo. Marshall, late of Martins Brandon in Charles City County, decd. send greetings. Whereas, the sd Geo. Marshall was in his lifetime possessed ----of a certain Plantation--scituate att Martins Brandon, Containing 75 acres--which the said Geo. Marshall purchased of the wido. & orpht of one Joh: HASKER---the sd. Geo: Marshall by his last will and testament in writing p'ved in Charles Citty County Courte, 9 March 1672, did give and bequeath to the sd. Anne, his wife---and I the sd John Barker have since married with the sd Anne---wee the sd Joh: Barker Senior and Anne, my wife, for a very valuable consideration to us by Joh: Barker, the Younger, of the p'sh & county aforesd, have given----unto the said Joh: Barker, the Younger----the aforesd Plantion--scituate att Martins Brandon----"

Wits: Wm. Sherwood   Signed   John Barker
       Robt. Lee   Ann Barker

Mrs. Ann Barker was the "mother in law" (stepmother) of John Barker, the Younger, as proven by the following deed, dated March 3, 1673/74, in which John Barker, Junior, conveyed the previously mentioned 75 acres back to his father and stepmother:

"Whereas Mrs. Anne Barker, Mother in law to me, John Barker, Junr. did convey unto me a p'cell of land scituate in Maritins Brandon being 75 acres by a deed bearing date 2^d 7br 1673---
(No witnesses)   (Signed) Jno Barker Junr".

"Whereas my son John Barker Junior, did convey unto me, John Barker, Senior, both then of Surry County----75 acres lying in Martins Brandon in Charles Citty County---   John Barker (No wits)   (Id. 1671-84, pp. 43, 68)

On Aug. 10, 1678, John Barker, Senr. of Martins Brandon in Charles Citty County, planter, with the approbation and consent of Ann, his wife, for 16000# of good merchantable Toba conveyed unto Benjamin Harrison---of that part of Devident of land in Surry County above the head of Upper Chippokes Creek whereon I formerly lived---patent granted unto me 18 Dec. 1662 being in quantity 1800 acres.

Wits: Elias Osborne   John Barker
    his   Ann Barker
 Jethro B Barker
   mark

    his
 Samuel z Newell   (Id-185)
   mark

Letitia Barker, probably mother of John Barker Jr. witnessed the following deed in 1671:------that I Vincent Inge doe constitute ---my loving friend, Isaac Watson To be my ---lawful attorney to sue---from any person in James City County or Surry County in Virga

Wits: Letitia Barker   Vincent Inge
   Hen: Knight

John Barker, the Elder, had two sons other than John Barker, his son and heir, as proven by the following Court order: (Charles City County Orders 1687-1695, p. 328, Date 5 January 1690)

"Judgement is granted Joel Barker agst John Good of Martins Brandon for 8000 pounds of Tobo & casq which appears from ye sd Good to the sd Barker by ye will and testament of John Barker father to the said Joel. He the said (Good) having intermarried with the Admtrx of the said decedent & it is ordered ye upon receipt of the said Tobacco both ye sd Joel and Jethro Barker signe a sufficient discharge therefor & allsoe allow in discount from this judgement what tobo: already received from ye Goods on this account----".

John Barker Jr. of Surry Co., Va. on Oct. 5, 1657 patented 600 acres on Upper Chippokes Creek (C.P. 415). The dates of his birth and marriage are unknown. He married Grace, probable daughter of Thomas Busby and probable granddaughter of Francis (Capt.) Grey and his wife, Grace, about 1680. Since John Barker Jr. executed a deed in 1673, he was born by or before 1652. It appears that Thomas Busby and John Barker were among the "Rebels" who took possession of "Bacon's Castle" (Arthur Allen's home) during the Rebellion, for "Bacon's Lieutenant, Thomas Busby, at whose house no guard was found during the critical days of Mid-September, along with a number of Bacon's men (among whom was JOHN BARKER) agreed to pay Arthur Allen damages, Nov. 15, 1677" (Co. Surry 138-9).

John Barker Jr. died in Surry County, after the 9th Oct. 1713 and before 19th May 1714. His will was recorded in Surry County

Deeds No. 5, 1709-1715. Abstract follows:
> Daughter, Elizabeth Andrews, 5 shillings (m. (1) Christopher Foster; (2) Thomas Anderson.
> Daughter, Sarah Lanier, 10 shillings, (m. Robert ? Lanier)
> Daughter, Hannah Lashley, 20 shillings, (m. Walter Lashley)
> Grandson, Robert Foster, 40 acres
> Son, John Barker, 400 acres (See later)
> Son, John Barker, 222 acres
> Son, Josiah Barker, 400 acres (See later)
> Son, Josiah Barker, 222 acres
> wife, Grace Barker, 300 acres
> Daughter, Grace Barker, the 300 acres plantation after her mother's death.
> "My son Josiah Barker to take into his possession the Estates of Christopher, Grace and Robert Foster and not to be appraised and to pay them as they shall come of age"---I do constitue and appoint my loving wife Grace Barker my Executrix & my son Josiah Barker Ex^r. with her of this my last Will and Testament
> Wits.: Thomas Cotten, John Johnson, Elizabeth Figures
> Dated Oct.9, 1713, probated May 19, 1714.

Elizabeth, probable eldest child of John and Grace----? Barker, m. (1) Christopher Foster: (2) Thomas Andrews. Christopher Foster was the son of Mary (Jordan), sister of Lt.Col.George Jordan of Surry County. Mary Jordan m. (1) Arthur Bailey, (2) -------Foster, first name unknown. However, we know from the will (1678, Surry Co.) of Lt. Col. Jordan that among seven nephews one was Christopher Foster (See Jordan).

Christopher Foster, nephew of Lt. Col. Jordan, was born 1649 (Surry Co. depositions), place unknown. He died after March 27, 1711 (will) and before July 18, 1711: m. between 1689 and 1696, Elizabeth, daughter of John and Grace-----Barker. John Foster was named in his will as the eldest son and was probably the eldest child. On the 20th Feb. 1711/12, John Foster appeared in Court (Surry Co. Orders, 1691-1713, p.388) and "made choice of Edward Bailey for his guardian". Thus we know that his parents were married by 1696.

The will of Christopher Foster was recorded in Surry County Deeds, etc. No.5, 1709-1715. Abstract:
> my eldest son John Foster----
> my youngest son Christopher Foster----
> Rest of the estate divided between wife and four children, John Foster, Christopher Foster, Faith Foster and Elizabeth Foster.
> "and I do also nominate and appoint my loving wife Elizabeth Foster and her father, Mr. Jn⁰ Barker Execut^x and Execut^r Joyntly----
> "Whereas the upper part of this will hath been Long made and it hath pleased God to bless me with three children more since to say Grace Robert and Fortune"----
> Dated 27 March 1710/11; Proved July 18th, 1711
> Teste   Christopher Foster   Sealed
> Edward Bayley   by C mark - with red wax
> Tho: Ho: Andrews

Christopher Foster of Isle of Wight and Southampton, son of Christopher and Elizabeth (Barker) Foster, was born about 1700; died Southampton Co., Va., before March 12, 1767; married before 1728 Alice, daughter of Elias Fort III. (His older brother, John Foster, married Mary, sister of Alice, see will of Elias Fort III, Surry Co., 1739). (See Fort in Vol.I)

The will of the above Christopher Foster is of record in Southampton Co. Will Book 2, p.191: date Nov.17, 1766; Rec. Mar. 12, 1767. Abstract:

Son, John Foster---
Grandson Richard, son of Elias Foster---
Son, Moses Foster---
dau. Amy Foster ---
wife, Alice Foster---
son, Newit Foster---
"I likewise resign the guardianship of the orphans of Jno Westbrook, decd, to them my excrs."---
Exs. sons Newit and Moses Foster.
Wit: Arthur Foster, John Fort, John Westbrook.

Alice (Fort) Foster survived her husband six years. Her will was recorded in Southampton Co. Will Book 3, p.24; Dated Aug. 7, 1770, Rec. Feb.11, 1773. Abstract:

Son Moses; daughter Amey Foster; grandson Elias Westbrook.
Ex. son Moses Foster.
Wit. Arthur Foster, Joshua Fort.

John Westbrook, son of John Westbrook and "beloved wife" (Will Book 3, p 357, I. of W) married (1) daughter of Christopher and Alice (Fort) Foster, as proved by the court records of Southampton County. There was born to them sons, John, William, Moses, James, and Elias. After the death of his first wife, ---- (Foster) Westbrook, he married Honour Ramsey by whom there were sons , Burwell and Gray. John Westbrook's will is of record in Southampton Will Book One, p 391; Dated Apr.7,1761; rec.Aug. 13,1761. Wit.John Person, Joshua Cland, Richard Taylor Jr. John Westbrook predeceased his father-in-law, Christopher Foster who became guardian of John Westbrook's children by his first wife, the daughter of Christopher Foster, vis., John, William, Moses, James, and Elias. All of the children, including Gray and Burwell by the second wife, removed to No. Carolina. (For descendants see Westbrook). (Compiled from records furnished by Mr. William Blair Jones of Pell City, Alabama)

John[3] Barker, son of Grace and John[2] Barker, Jr., was bequeathed by his father "400 acres where he now lives joining the plantation I live on", and "my plantation on the Nottaway River, 222 acres on Indian Cabin branch after his mother's decease." On June 16, 1721, John Barker and Mary, his wife, of Southwark Parish sold Thomas Peters 223 acres on Cabbin Branch adjoining William Hunt. Wits.: Benj. Chap. Donaldson, John Mitchel, Gerald Green (BK 8-p.367) This land, consisting of 446 acres, had been patented by his father, July 12, 1718," on the north side of the Nottaway River adjoining Wm. Hunt". (P B 10, -390)

John Barker made his will may 21, 1725; probated April 21, 1742. He gave his son, JOHN BARKER land between Reedy Branch and Cattail Swamp; to son CHRISTOPHER. "land that parts my father's and me to one Cattail Branch;" daughter Mary mentioned; other estate to be divided between wife Mary and five other children not mentioned by name. wife MARY extrix; Wits.: John Collier, Nicholas Cocke; Joshua Nicholson. Presented in court by MARY MORRIS late MARY BARKER, extrix. (W.B. 1738-54 p. 407)

Josiah[3] Barker, brother of the above John Barker, married Faith Washington, daughter of Richard Washington. On Feb.14, 1720/21 he sold to Richard Parker, Jr., 223 acres in Cabbin Creek; wits.: James Washington, Thomas Bailey, Samuel Briggs. (1715-20-p.306) On Aug.16, 1729, he bought 115 acres on Blackwater Swamp, from John Allen. (Id.967) He and wife Faith on Jan. 17, 1737, sold David Jones two tracts on Main Blackwater Swamp: one 115 purchased from John Allen, and 195 patented by him Sept. 28, 1732. (1730-38-p.800) Josiah made his will Feb.23, 1760, proven March 17, 1761. He gave son, JOHN BARKER 150 acres, where he dwells; son ARTHUR 100 acres; son RIVERS BARKER, plantation where he formerly dwelt for life, then to his son William; son SAMUEL, "plantation where I dwell and land adjoining John Barker to Trudy Branch, he to pay his sister FAITH BARKER Ł 20 and Sarah, Fathy and Mary Ellis, 20 shillings each..... Mentioned Grace Barker; wife Faithy, chattles, ect., Exrs.; sons John and Samuel; wits.: Philip Reekes, Benj. Emrey, Faith Emery (W.B. 1754-68 p.250).

Grace[3] Barker, sister of the above John Barker and Josiah Barker made her will Feb. 19, 1741, proven May 15, 1750. Her legatees were: brother Josiah; cousin Richard Barker; "my plantation with 300 acres, 100 acres to go to his brother John Barker when of age; to cousin Josiah Barker; cousin Mary Bishop; Mary Bishop's son James; cousins William, Joshua and Joell Barker; gifts to Faith and Elizabeth Barker. Richard Barker, exr.; Wits.: Robert Lanier, Josiah (C) Barker, Josiah Barker. (W.B. 1738-54 p.673.) Grace Barker died Nov. 3, 1749.

Joell[2] Barker, son of John[1] Barker, Sr., together with his brothers John and Jethro of Southwark Parish, sold him 200 acres in that parish for 1000 lbs. of tobacco. This was part of a patent of 261 acres granted Jethro Oct.20, 1689, adjoining Joell's plantation. The deed was dated April 20, 1693; wits.; Benj. Harrison, Silas Smith. (B.K.4-298). On May 6, 1707, Joell sold this land to William Killingsworth for 2000 lbs. of tobacco; wits.: Wm. Edmunds, Francis Clements. (BK.1694-1702, p.370). In 1694, Joel Barker was listed with two tithables, consisting of himself and Howell Edmunds, who was evidently between the ages of 16 and 21. The estate records of Joel have not been found, so date of his death is uncertain. From other wills and deeds it appears that his children were: JOHN BARKER, whose will was dated April 11, 1736 and proven Sept. 1740. He bequeaths his plantation to sister MARY BARKER, after her death it was to go to his brother, JOSHUA BARKER. Mary Barker, executrix; wits.: Josiah (J) Barker, Faith Barker. Will was presented in court by MARY BISHOP, executrix named. Inventory presented by James Bishop, husband of Mary. (1738-54-p.211.)

On Feb. 8, 1750, WILLIAM BARKER of Southwark Parish, HENRY (Z) BARKER, of Martin's Brandon, Prince George, and Joshua Barker of Southwark Parish Surry sold 130 acres on Reedy Branch and Cattail Branch to James Bishop and wife Mary, BROTHER-IN-LAW and SISTER of the Grantors; wits.: Joseph Carter, Caleb ELLIS, Robert Ray. (D.B. 6,1749-53 p.147.)

JOELL and RICHARD BARKER mentioned in the will of Grace Barker may have been two other sons of Joell[2] Barker, Sr. The children of some of the above sons of Joell[2] Barker appear in the Albermarle Parish Register.

Jethro[2] Barker was the son of John[1] Barker, Sr., and brother of John[2] and Joell[2]. (ante) Jethro's first appearance in the county records was on Sept.10,1678, when he witnessed a deed, as Jethro (B) Barker, from his father to Benj. Harrison for 1800 acres patented Dec.18,1662, (D.B.2, 1671-84, p.186). John Barker, Sr., and Ann his wife were of Martin Brandon's Parish, Charles City County, (later Prince George) and that land was on Chippoakes Creek where they formerly lived. On the back of a patent for 240 acres, granted to John Barker, Sept.9, 1682, was an assignment by John Barker and Grace his wife, for a consideration, of all right and title, dated July 4, 1685; wits.: Benj. Harrison, Richard Taylor. (D.B. 3, p.31.) This patent was located on the north side of Otterdam Swamp, adjoining Benj. Harrison and Mr. Jordan. (P.B. 7-189).

Jethro Barker patented 261 acres Oct.20, 1689 on the south side of Otterdam Swamp at Edward Gunnell's line; 165 acres April 1, 1717 on south west side of main Blackwater Swamp and 120 acres Sept. 5, 1723 on the south side of the same place. (P.B. 8 p.7;10 p.314;11, 267.)

On July 6, 1685, Jethro sold to John Harris 120 acres of a patent located above Jethro's dwelling place. This was evidently one half of the patent he received from his brother John. Jethro Barker and Mary his wife, Sept. 1, 1690, sold 60 acres on the south side of Otterdam Swamp to William Killingsworth, wits.: Adam Heath, Richard Skogeny (?). (D.B.4-158). William Harvey of Southwark Parish, Surry, Jan.15, 1694, sold him 235 acres of a Patent of 335 acres granted Thomas Cotton April 16, 1683 and sold by him Nov.3, 1685, to said Harvey, on Otterdam Swamp, adjoining Jethro Barker's own land. Wits.: Benj. and Nathaniel Harrison. (BK.1694-1709-p.51)(P.B. 7-280) (Wm. Harvey made his will in 1704.)

Jethro[2] Barker held 240 acres in Surry in 1704 Quit Rents. On Sept. 9, 1744, he deeded to Jethro Barker, Jr., 270 acres on Otterdam Swamp at Harris Branch. (D.B.4,1741-46-p.246.) He also deeded to his son, John Barker, both of Albermarle Parish, Oct.19, 1747, a patent to said Jethro April 1, 1717. (D.B.5, p.141)

Jethro Barker made his will Jan.25, 1744; proven Mar.15,1747/48 as follows: to son JOHN BARKER plantation where he lives and all land ajdoining, also £ 3; son JETHRO BARKER, £3; son HENRY BARKER, £ 3; daughters JANE FIELD and MARY ANDROSS (Andrew) each £ 3; to hree grandaughters, children of son GEORGE, Agnes, Mary and Elizabeth, 150 acres on north side of Otterdam Swamp where GEORGE BARKER lived; to grandaughter Sarah, daughter of son JEHU BARKER. £ 5; to JEHU BARKER and his heirs "plantation where I now live." Jehu Barker, exr. Wits.: Nicholas Partridge, Hugh Ivie, Nicholas Partridge, Jr. (W.B. 1738-54, p. 567)

Children:

I.   John[3] made his will in Sussex, July 8, 1762, and mentions following children: (W.B. "B"-16)

     1. Drury, given 265 acres where his father lived, on Feb. 14, 1775 deeded 150 acres heired by the death of his brother Joseph Barker, formerly the property of their father, John Barker, granted to him July 4, 1759. (Sussex D.B. "E"-324). He made his will July 8, 1762, proved April 18, 1782. He died without issue as he gave his sister Mary Barker plantation he lived on; and bequests of money to nephews and nieces: John Henry Barker, Charles Barker, Nehemiah Barker, Susanna and Elizabeth Barker; sisters Elizabeth and Mary Barker to divide balance of estate. Wits.: Faddo Garrad, Daniel Ivey, Nath. Barker.

     2. Mary, with will dated Feb. 7, 1779, proven Nov. 18, 1779, predeceased her brother Drury for she gave him all her estate and Drury seems not to have changed his predated will. (W.B. "C"-347.)

     3. Elizabeth, living in 1777.

     4. Joseph, d. 1771, inventory filed. (No children).

II.   Jethro, Jr. His will was dated Dec. 3, 1754, proven Dec. 12, 1754, as follows: to daughter-in-law, Alice Barker, chattles; to son JOHN. 170 acres north side Otterdam Swamp where Jethro resides; daughter, SARAH BARKER, £18 when 18 years old; son JETHRO £5 and estate he now has; daughter ELIZABETH SHOFFEL. her estate; and son John remainder "of my estate" he to be executor. Wits.: Samuel Cocke, John Barker, (W.B. 1754-68, p. 26).

III. Jane, M. John Field.

IV. Mary, m. _____ Andross or Andrews.

V.   George, m. Agnes _____. Inventory of his estate was recorded May 16, 1744. (W.B. 1738-54-p. 472.) He appears to have had three daughters: Agnes, Mary and Elizabeth.

VI. Jehu, m. Mary _____. His will was dated Jan. 13, 1779, proven Feb. 21, 1782, as follows: to daughter SARAH JOLLY and her child Rachel Jolly, negroes; to daughter-in-law, Lucy Barker, (wife of son Jehu who died 1773)--(W. BK. "C"-85) "use of plantation I live on"; grandson, Richard Barker 200 acres on Reedy Branch; grandson Nicholas Barker, "plantation I now live on" at 20 years of age; granddaughters, Mary, Sarah and Elizabeth Barker; Exrs.: Isham Inman, Lucy Barker, daughter-in-law; Nicholas Barker, grandson. Wits.: Jesse Wallis, Mary Jarrad, Richard Wallis. (W.B. "C"-430) (The grandchildren mentioned in will were children of Jehu Barker, Jr.)

VII. Henry[3] Barker, m. Catherine _____. After Henry died, Catherine married Timothy Rives. (Henry was probably the third son of Jethro[2] Barker but is placed here for convenience because his is the line carried down). (See later).

Henry[3] Barker, son of Jethro[2] , married Catherine, family

name unknown. After Henry's death she married Timothy Rives
Feb. 12, 1763. She died April 4, 1772. Henry died March 21,
1759 (A.P.R.)

Henry Barker patented 175 acres, Sept. 28, 1732, on south
side of main Blackwater Swamp and on July 5, 1751, he patented
800 acres on south side of Blackwater Swamp. (P.B. 14-503; 29-
464) On June 19, 1738, John[3] Barker deeded Henry[3] Barker, for
love and affection that he bears for his brother Henry Barker, 100
acres on south side of Blackwater Swamp where he now lives,
same granted to John Barker, April 1, 1717. (D.B. 1730-38, Vol.
2, part 2, p.863) Wits. Nicholas Partridge, Robert Jones Jr.,
John Tatum. Henry on Jan. 4, 1755 made three deeds to his sons.
He gave to son Benjamin 225 acres on south side of Blackwater
Swamp; son James 200 acres in the same place; and son Nathaniel
200 acres. (D.B. "A"-46-47-49) These gifts and 175 acres given
in his will to his son Henry accounts for his 800 acre patent obtained in 1751. His will was dated Dec. 4, 1758, and proven April
20, 1759. His legatees, to whom he gave negroes except HENRY
who received 175 acres, were: wife to have use of plantation during
her life or widowhood; sons BENJAMIN, CHARLES, JAMES,
NATHANIEL; daus. ANN and MARY. Sons Henry & James, exrs.
Wits: John Irby, William Briggs, Henry Briggs. (W.B. "A"-125)

Children of Henry and Catherine Barker:
I. Mary Barker, b.Sept.12,1739; Robert & Mary Long, Mary
Figures, Sponsors.
II. Ann Barker, b.Feb.11, 1733. No sponsors given.
III. Benjamin Barker, m.Mary. They sold to James Barker for
£ 45, 225 acres on Sept. 18, 1766, part of patent to father
Henry Barker July 5, 1751.
Children, from A.P.R.
1. Katherine, b.Jan.26,1745; John Irby, Kath & Jane Bar-
ker, Sponsors.
2. William, b.Oct.22, 1747; Wm.Cook, Wm.Brown, Frances
Chambliss, Sponsors.
3. Nathan, b.Jan.13,1749; Chas.Barker, John Baird, Eliz.
Cook, Sponsors.

A Benjamin Barker Jr., died Jan.30, 1772, death reported by
John Adkins. Adkins also reported the death of Katherine Hobbs,
the wife of Frederick Hobbs on Jan.30,1772. Katherine Hobbs was
probably the above Katherine Barker born Jan.26,1745. She and
Frederick Hobbs had the following children A.P.R.:
1. William Hobbs, b.Feb.24, 1764, Benj.and Mary Barker,
Jos.Denton, Sponsors.
2. Lucy Hobbs, b.Jan.22, 1766, Wm.Tomlinson, Rebecca
Ivy, Hannah Hancock, Sponsors.
3. Bolling Hobbs, b.July 8, 1767, Nathan Cotton, Daniel Ivy,
Agnes Dunn, Sponsors.
4. Edmund Hobbs, b.Aug. 25, 1771, Don McInnish, David
Lessenberry, Frances Barker, Sponsors.
The above Benjamin Barker Jr. probably had the following
children attributed to Benjamin & Mary Barker:
1. Nathaniel, b.Mar.21,1766, Don McInnish, Thos.John-
son, Eliz. Wilkinson, Sponsors.

2. Amiss, b. Apr. 20, 1771, John Underhill, Nathan Barker, Frances Barker, Sponsors.

IV.   Henry Barker, m. Elizabeth   . On Sept. 18, 1788, he and wife Elizabeth made a deed of gift to their daughter Elizabeth of 110 acres on south side of Blackwater, part of a patent granted John Barker of 165 acres April 1, 1717. They gave to son Charles Barker 155 acres on south side of Blackwater in Sussex whereon said Henry Barker now lives.

Children of Henry and Eliz. Barker A. P. R.:
1. Susanna, b. April 30, 1762. No Sponsors given.
2. Elizabeth, b. Oct. 5, 1764, no Sponsors given.
3. John Henry, b. Dec. 26, 1766, no Sponsors given.
4. Charles, b. Feb. 15, 1769; m. Johanna.
5. Jeremiah, b. Dec. 27, 1771. John and Lucy Gilbert, Richard Cook, Sponsors.
6. Katherine, b. Mar. 17, 1774, Fred Andrews, Lucy Johnson, Joan Hight, Sponsors.

V.   Charles[4] Barker Sr. , m. Ann. (See later)

VI.   James Barker. On Aug. 19, 1763, James Barker made the following deed to his sister Mary Barker "Whereas will of father Henry Barker dated July 4, 1758, gives certain negroes to his wife during her life or <u>widowhood</u>, the first child to go to Mary Barker, after end of widowhood, negro Patt to go to James. James now gives title to Patt to his sister Mary (B-317).

The "widowhood" was ended by his mother, Catherine, marrying Timothy Rives, Feb. 12, 1763.

Benjamin Barker, and wife Mary, on Oct. 18, 1766, deeded to James Barker, 225 acres for Ł 25, part of patent to father dated July 1, 1751. (C-207).

An inventory of James Barker's estate was filed in Sussex in 1772 (Id. -4).

The children of James Barker Jr. and wife, Johannah, are shown in the Albemarle Parish Register as given below. He may have been younger than another contemporary James Barker.

Children of James & Johanna:
1. Jesse, b. Mar. 13, 1758. No sponsors.
2. James, b. June 11, 1760. No sponsors.
3. Elizabeth, b. July 17, 1762. No sponsors.
4. Ann, b. July 18, 1771. Robt. Winfield, Mildred Wynne, Martha Rainy, Sponsors.
5. Nathaniel, b. May 11, 1769. Wm. Harrington, Joel Davis, Sarah Sheffield, Sponsors.

VII.   Nathaniel Barker, m. Sarah _____ . Their children were A. P. R.:
1. Lucy, b. Dec. 12, 1755. Jas. Barker, Ann Barker, Anne Stacy, Sponsors.
2. Rebecca, b. Feb. 23, 1757, Henry Barker Jr. , Mary Cook, Mary Barker, Sponsors.

Nathaniel Barker died June 27, 1785. His will wherein he gave his lands to his wife during life, then to be equally divided between his two daughters, Lucy, wife of Charles Davis, and Rebecca, wife of John Judkins, was recorded by his wife, Sally, July 21, 1785. (Bk. F-424)

Charles[4] Barker, Sr., was born about 1741 in Surry County, Virginia, where his father and mother, Henry and Catharine Barker lived. Henry died in Surry County in 1759.

In 1761, Charles, Sr., and Ann Barker his wife, received a patent for 100 acres of land in Surry County. About 1766 he moved to Nottoway Parish (later to become Nottoway County, Amelia County, Virginia) and there bought 263 acres on Nov. 24, 1766. Four years later in 1770, he sold his Surry County land and in his deed described himself and wife as residents of Amelia.

Charles[4] Barker, Sr., may have served as a private in the 11th. Virginia Regiment, Col. A. Buford, commanding. A Charles Barker received his discharge from the Army at Hillsborough, Oct. 25, 1780. However, there were three slave holding Charles Barkers, heads of families in the Virginia Census of 1782-1784; one in Amelia, one in Cumberland, and one in Hanover.

The Revolutionary record of Charles Barker was as follows:

BOUNTY WARRENT

CHARLES BARKER, 1784, Req. C6554.

The bearer Charles Barker having served as a soldier in the Continental Army the term of three years in the full time for which he enlisted, he is therefore discharged from the said service. Given under my hand at Hillsborough, North Carolina, October 25, 1780.

Signed: A. Buford, Col.,
11th. (?) Vig'a Reg't.

The original of the above discharge loged in the Auditor's Office, Apr. (?) 10, 1783.

B. Mark.

***

Sir, Please to send by the bearer a Certificate for the land that I am entitled to for the within service in the Continental Army. Witness my hand this 3rd. day of May, 1783.

Charles Barker.

Teste
Levin Powell
To the (?) Clk. of the (?) Council.

I do certify, that Charles Barker is entitled to the proportion of land allowed a Private of the Continental line, for three years service.

Council Chamber Tho. Meriwether.
Ap'l 20th, 1784.

Benj. Harrison.

In 1781 and 1783, Charles, Sr., furnished rations to the Continental Armies and was allowed claims in Amelia County therefor. (Amelia, Court Booklet 1, -pp.21,61)

The personal property records of Amelia for 1782 showed him as having 9 slaves, including "George". This is interesting, because in the will of Henry Barker, Charles father, Henry bequeathed a slave named "George" to his son, Charles. Charles, Sr., continued on the personal property lists of Nottoway County until 1793.

Charles Barker, Jr., from 1793 to 1799 appears on the personal property lists in Nottoway County.

Charles, Jr., bought 770 acres in Halifax County in 1797 and 540 acres in 1800. The 1797 deed describes the grantee as "Charles Barker of Nottoway County, Virginia."

Charles Barker, Jr., married Barbara Walton August 18, 1791, in Mecklenburg County. If we assume that he was 21 when he married, then Charles, Jr., was born in 1771, after his father had moved to Amelia County.

Charles Meriwether of Albemarle County bought lands in Halifax County in 1801. He married Mary Daniel, formally Mary Walton, in Halifax County in 1808. Charles Barker, Jr., sold both tracts of his Halifax County land. In 1809 Charles Meriwether sold his land. They both moved to Kentucky in 1809.

The will of Charles Barker, Sr., is dated Halifax County, Jan. 8, 1801. He refers to a granddaughter, Jane Anderson, who at that time was a minor living with her uncle, Charles, Jr. Charles was his only known son.

Sometime prior to August 1791, in the Halifax County Virginia Court "Charles Barker, Jr., an infant by Charles Barker, Sr., his father as Plaintiff, brought suit for a debt due December 1790, against James Pauls, defendant. In March 1793, the case was continued and at this time Charles Barker, Jr., appeared in his own right and not as an infant.

Charles Barker, Jr., married first Barbara Ann Walton, the daughter of Barbara (Hester) and Edward Sims Walton, in Mecklenburg County, Virginia, in 1791. Barbara was born in Mecklenburg County, in 1772 and died at "Fairfields", Montgomery County, Tennessee in 1821. His second wife, whom he married in 1824, was born at Hopkinsville, Christian County, Kentucky.

When Charles Barker and his friend and brother-in-law, Dr. Charles Meriwether reached Kentucky in 1809 they settled on a strata of rich loam so far south in Kentucky that later, when the Federal Government did survey the line between Kentucky and Tennessee much of their land fell in Montgomery County, Tenn; also the Barker's home "Fairfield". This survey is noted in the Day Book of "Woodstock" farm rather as an interruption to the farm work than as an historical event; in several instances through the first years the inconvenience of the rock piled markers in the big rolling fields is noted.

Children by first wife:

I. John Walton Barker, b.1793; m. (1) Mary Minor Meriwether (see later); m. (2) Ellen (Morris) Carr.
II. Richard Henry Lee Barker, b.1795; d.s.p.
III. Alexander Meriwether Barker, b.1798; m. Lucy Ann Meriwether.

IV. Edward Simpson Barker, b. 1800; m. Marion Anderson.
V.   Caroline Hunt(d)ley Barker, b. 1804; m. "Chas." Nich. Minor Meriwether.
VI. Mary (Polly) Walton Barker, b. 1806; m. "Prof." James Hunter Ross.
VII. Ann Minor Barker, b. 1810; d. s. p.
VIII. Lydia Laurie Barker, b. 1812; m. Dr. John Thornton Gilmer.
IX. Charles Meriwether Barker, b. 1814; m. Maria Anderson, sister of Marion, supra.
X.   Richard Henry Barker, b. 1816; m. Caroline Matilda Sharp.

John Walton Barker, who was born in Nottoway County, Virginia, in 1793, and died at his home, "Cloverlands", Montgomery County, Tennessee, in 1867, married first, in the Brockman home in Louisa County, Virginia, Mary Minor Meriwether, the daughter of Ann Minor and Thomas Meriwether, who was born at "Sunninghill" Louisa Co., Va; in 1798, and died at "Cloverlands" in 1831.; his second wife was Mrs. Ellen Carr, the daughter of Nancy (Watson) and William Morris, who was born in 1814 and died at "Cloverlands" in 1888; they were married in 1840.

Mr. Barker graduated from the University of North Carolina in 1808. He was one of the founders of the Northern Bank in Clarksville, Tenn. He was a planter, and exported his tobacco to England; sending it by "flat-boat" to New Orleans, down the Cumberland and Mississippi Rivers.

Children of first wife:
I.   Thomas Meriwether Barker, b. 1815; d. s. p.
II. Chiles Terrell Barker, b. 1816; m. Mary Louisa Hutchison. (See later)
III. Barbara Ann Barker, b. 1819; m. Robert French Ferguson.
IV. Ann (Nanny) Minor Barker, b. 1820; m. Judge Alex. M. Clayton son.

Children of second wife:
V.   Mary (Molly) Walton Barker, b. 1841; m. Edward Walton Barker.
VI. Louisa McTyer (Tex) Barker, b. 1844; m. (1) Maj. Thos. F. Henry; m. (2) Dr. C. W. Bailey.
VII. Harriet (Hattie) Morris Barker, b. 1846; m. Joseph Watkins Scales.
VIII. Hortense Barker, b. 1846, d. s. p. (Twins)
IX. Ellen Morris Barker, b. 1851, m. Capt. Patrick Henry.

Charles Terrell Barker, who was born in 1816 at "Cloverlands" Montgomery County, Tenn., and died at "Glenburnie" Christian County, Ky., in 1898; married as his first wife, in 1841 at Green Spring, Louisa Co., Va., Mary Louisa, the daughter of Louisa Minor and Elija Hutchison, who was born at Green Spring in 1823 and died in Hopkinsville, Ky., in 1909.

Mr. Barker was the most extensive land owner in Christian Co., Ky. He had $100,000.00 on deposit in the Bank of England at the time of his death in 1898. He had contributed a like amount in gold to the cause of the Confederacy. He founded "Glenburnie".

Children:
I.   Thomas Meriwether Barker, b. 1842, m. Mary Love Morris.

II.   John Walton Barker, b.1843; m.Fannie Elliott.
III.   Chiles Terrel Barker, b.1845; d.s.p.
IV.   Mary (Lulie) Louisa Barker, b.1847; m. W.M. Cloud
V.   Sallie Watson Barker, b.1849; m. Ben H. Logan
VI.   Nancy (Nannie) Minor Barker, b.1852; m.Wm.H.Jesup
VII.   Barbara Ann Barker, b.1854; m.Logan Williamson.
VIII. Charles Edward Barker, b.1857; m.Mary Friend Lester
          (See later)
IX.   Peter Meriwether Barker, b.1859; m.Annie L. Johnston
X.   Elizabeth (Ledlie) Barker, b.1862; m.William S.Moore
XI.   Susie Morris Barker,b.Aug.5,1865; m.Joseph L. Hall
XII.   Frances Pendleton Barker, b.Aug.5,1865 (Twins); m.Morris
          K.Clark

Charles Edward Barker, who was born May 1, 1857 at "Glen-burnie", Christian Co., Ky., and died October 26, 1931 at Clarkes-ville, Tenn., married at Petersburg, Va., on Nov.26, 1884, Mary Friend Lester, the daughter of Virginia (Jordan) and Robert Fountain Lester, who was born in Charlotte County, Va., Nov.26,1850 and died Dec.2,1923 at Clarksville, Tenn.

Mr. Barker received an A.B. degree from Southwestern Presbyterian University in Clarksville, Tenn., about 1881; was one of the organizers of the Lester Memorial Church. He was a farmer, and founded "Wheatlands".

Children:
I.   Virginia Fountain Barker, b.Oct. 13, 1886, m.Dr. Maurice
          L. Hughes.
II.   Frank Pendleton Barker, b.Aug.5,1889, m.Mildred Buchanan. (See later)
III.   Mary Lester Barker, b.April 27, 1891.

Frank Pendleton Barker, who was born Aug.5, 1889, in Pembroke, Ly., was married in Winnetka, Illinois, June 1, 1918, to Mildred Claiborne Buchanan, daughter of Nathalie Claiborne and John W. Buchanan, who was born in Louisville, Ky., June 20,1891.

Mr.Barker holds an A.B. from the University of North Carolina 1912, and an L.L.B. from the Law School of Columbia University, 1915. He was a Captain in the U.S.Army, World War I; President of Kansas City Lawyer's Assn. 1938, and is a lawyer and a member of the firm of Barker, Winger, Bagby and Smith. Mr. and Mrs. Barker reside at 613 West 59th St., Kansas City, Missouri.

Children:
I.   Frank Pendleton Barker, Jr., b.Aug.20,1919; m.Maujer
          Moseley. He served in World War II as a Judge Advocate
          General in the Navy.
II.   Nathalie Claiborne Barker, b.July 26,1921; m.James H.
          Baldwin.
III.   Mildred Buchanan Barker, b.Dec.5, 1922; m.Joseph E.
          Johnson.

BRANCH of ISLE of WIGHT and NORTH CAROLINA

The first one of this family in Isle of Wight was George Branch who with James Sampson witnessed a power of attorney in April 1664 (17C-504). On June 9, 1666, George Hardy deeded Francis England 100 acres where George Branch formerly lived called "Shadow Rock". (Id, 545). John Oliver, July 2nd, 1650, patented 300 acres on the Blackwater near Lower Chippokes Creek. On Jan. 5, 1666, John Collins, who had married Eleanor, dau. of John Oliver, with her consent sold George Branch ½ of the above patent. John Wakefield who married the youngest dau. of John Oliver, sold him the other 150 acres (Id. 541). George Branch evidently lived on the above land for on Jan. 9, 1679, Thomas Carter sold 56 acres to John Parsons on the main Blackwater "at George Branch's" Id. 586).

George Branch married about 1652 Ann England, daughter of Captain Francis England. Captain Francis England was born in England in 1609 and came to Virginia when he was very young for "ffrancis England of the age of twenty years or there abouts", testified in a case concerning one Thomas Hall, 25 March 1629 at a court held in Jas. City" (M.C.G.C. p. 194). On June 20, 1642, Francis England received a patent of 746 acres of land in Isle of Wight County. (17 Cent. p. 669) On Sept. 26, 1668 Gov. William Berkeley granted the commission of captain to Francis England. However, it appears that the duties of this commission were not made clear to him for this record is found: "Wm. Berkeley, having granted a commission to Capt. Francis England for the command of a company of Foot, declares he is not to meddle or have anything to do with the other companies belonging to the parish, etc... 26 Sept. 1668. (Id. p. 553). Captain Francis England was a strong supporter of Gov. Berkeley in Bacon's Rebellion, and was one of those who signed the reply to the Grievances of His Majesty's "Poor but Loyal Subjects" in 1677. (Id. p. 161) During Bacon's Rebellion Colonel William Groves, one of Bacon's colonels, who had been taken prisoner, on Dec. 25, 1676 ran from his guard. Thirty or forty men under Capt. Consent were sent after him; they found him and three rebel companions at Capt. Francis England's house which they had captured. There Capt. Consent shot the colonel dead and brought away his horse" and the three rebels and Capt. Francis England back to his ship the "Young Prince"(Id. p. 669)

Captain Francis England was twice married. His first wife was Sarah____, whom he married shortly after her coming to Virginia. In 1642 he received a patent for her transportation. (Id. p. 669) She died prior to 1664 and Capt. England married Joyce, daughter of the wife of Robert Flake, one of the largest landowners in Isle of Wight. Capt. England in his will dated May 13, 1677, probated June 9, 1677, gave to his dau. Ann Branch, wife of George

Branch, 4000 lbs. tbco. and to daughter's sons, George, Francis and John Branch, 12 pence each English money (Bk. 1-144). Joyce England, widow of Francis, married George Cripps and in her will gave a legacy to George Branch's three children, Francis, Anne and John Branch (Id. 202). George Branch Jr. not mentioned in above will appraised the estate of Nicholas Davis April 9, 1680.

George Branch Sr. died intestate. An appraisal of his estate was taken in presence of GEORGE BRANCH, JAMES LUPO, FRANCIS BRANCH, JOHN BRANCH, ANN BRANCH, May 18, 1688 Id. 285). These were his children, his daughter, Sarah, having married James Lupo.

George Branch Jr., with his father, George Branch Sr., signed the Loyalist petition to the Commissioners of England in 1677 (17C 160-161).

Inasmuch as his father died intestate, George, as his eldest son, inherited all of his land. In a series of deeds he sold land to his brothers, all except John who evidently had been given his land which he sold in 1709. On Mar. 6, 1688, George Branch and Susanna, his wife, "of Southwark Parish, son and heir of George Branch and Ann, his wife, only dau. of Francis England of Blackwater in I. of W. whereas Francis England, his grandfather, in his will 13 May 1677, gave 1300 acres to Joyce, his wife, who afterward married George Cripps and gave the land to said Cripps, George Branch as lawful heirs to his grandfather now sells to George Moore". (17C-599). On Aug. 4, 1688, he sold to Francis Branch of Upper Parish of Isle of Wight, for 3000 lbs. tbco., that plantation where he lives of 50 acres. On the same day for the same sum he sold land to James Lupo, land where he now lives. On Oct. 31, 1688, he sold to Ann Branch of the U. P. for 6500 lbs. tbco. 50 acres where John Branch now lives". (Id).

Children of Ann (England) and George[1] Branch:

I.   George[2] Branch, Jr., married Susanna, daughter of Capt. William Corker, Burgess from James City, 1655-56. (Col. Surry, p. 93)(S. V. F., p. 169) George Branch was a titheable in Surry in 1688, but does not appear in subsequent tax lists. After selling the above mentioned land in 1688-89 he evidently moved to Chowan County in N. C. (See later)

II.   Sarah Branch married before 1679, James Lupo, son of Phillip Lupo, Jr., and grandson of Phillip Lupo, Goldsmith of London. James Lupo died in 1713 leaving children: 1. Phillip; 2. Sarah, m. Mr. Lilbourne and died in 1728; 3. Ann, m. John Bidgood, Jr., who died in 1726; 4. Mary; 5. John.

III. Francis Branch, m. Elizabeth daughter of William Norwood. (See later)

IV.   Ann Branch, m. Robert Hodges, Jr., and moved to Chowan County, N. C. (See later)

V.   John Branch, m. Catharine   He patented 100 acres in Isle of Wight Sept. 5, 1720; also on Feb. 18, 1722/3 he patented 200 acres on the south side of main Blackwater and on both sides of Cabbin Branch. (P. B. 11-167) This land afterwards fell in Southampton County. On Feb. 13, 1735 he and his wife sold the patent of 100 acres to Thomas Kitchen of Nansemond (D. B. 5-11) John Branch died before June 10, 1756, for on that date WILLIAM BRANCH, planter and wife Ruth sold to Richard Kello 50 acres on the South side of Main Cabbin Branch, being part of 200 acres formerly granted to John Branch, father of William, on Feb.18, 1722, and by the LAST WILL of the said John Branch given and devised unto the said William (D.B.2, p.106). William Branch died intestate 1768 leaving wife Ruth.

Francis[2] Branch, son of George[1] Branch and his wife Ann England, was born about 1660. In 1690 he purchased land in Surry County from William Baldwin and his wife Elizabeth (Deeds, Wills, Etc. No. 4, p.135). He evidently sold this land before 1704 as he is not shown in the Quit Rent List for that year.

On August 4, 1688, George Branch, brother of Francis, and his wife Susannah deeded to Francis Branch of Upper Parish of Isle of Wight for 3000 Lbs. Tobacco "that plantation where he lives" (17C., p.598). On Oct.24, 1713 Francis Branch purchased from Benjamin Chapman of Surry County for 5,000 Lbs. of Tobacco 380 acres bound according to a patent from Spottswood dated May 2, 1713. This land was located on the south side of Nottoway River in what was then Isle of Wight County but later Southampton. The witnesses were Francis Sowerby, George Norwood and Richard Norwood (Deed Bk. 2, p. 263).

Francis Branch married before 1703 Elizabeth Norwood, daughter of William Norwood of Surry Co., Va., and his wife Lydia. William Norwood was born in England prior to 1623 and was the son of Richard and Elizabeth (Stuard) Norwood of Leckhampton, Gloucestershire, England. His descent from King Edward III appears in Virginia Historical Genealogies.

Francis Branch made his will in Isle of Wight April 27, 1717, pro. 22 Aug. 1720. He gave land to wife, to son, FRANCIS, land; to son, GEORGE and BENJAMIN, land at 16, wife to have use of plantation for bringing up 4 youngest children until Benj. is 16; to daus. ELIZ, MARY, SARAH and LYDIA, cows, to daus. JANE, HANNAH and MARTHA, furn. To Cousin Catherine Branch's dau. Ann. 3 sons and 7 daus. Wits. Eliz. Doid, Eliz. Benson, John Joyner.

Elizabeth Branch, wife of Francis, made her will in Southampton Oct. 28, 1749, pro. Dec. 12, 1750.

Children of Francis Branch and his wife Elizabeth Norwood:

I.   Francis Branch, mentioned in the will of his father but not in that of his mother. He probably died without issue or was a son by a former marriage.
II. Benjamin Branch moved to Northampton Co., N.C. before Dec. 7, 1753 when he sold his lands in Southampton Co., Va. to his brother, George Branch (D.B.2, p.10).
III. George Branch. (See later)
IV. Liddia Branch.
V.   Ann Branch, m. John Tyas. (See Tyas)
VI. Elizabeth Branch, m._____ Cord.
VII. Mary Branch, m._____ Brewster.
VIII. Jone Branch, m._____ Williams.
IX. Martha Branch, m._____ Williamson.
X.   Sarah Branch, m._____ Williams.
XI. Hannah Branch, m. Joseph Williamson.

George Branch, son of Elizabeth and Francis Branch, made his will in Southampton Sept. 14, 1770, pro. Nov. 8, 1770. His legatees were: sons BAILEY, HOWELL, HENRY, BENJ; wife MARTHA; daughter LUCY; granddaughter Mary, dau. of son ED-MUND BRANCH; Son Newsom. Exrs. sons Bailey and Newsom. Wits: R. Kello, Moses Phillips (Id. -347). Martha Branch, wife of George, died before April 9, 1772, when her will was recorded.

Children of George Branch and wife Martha;

I.   Edmund Branch
II.   Bailey Branch who died in Southampton County in 1809-1819 (W. B. 6, p. 707). The name of his wife is not known.
      Children:
      1. Pamela Branch married in 1792 Amos Washington.
      2. Goodman Branch married in 1796 Sally Nebeth.
      3. Joseph Branch moved to Sussex Co., Va.
      4. Sally Branch.
III.   Howell Branch (see later).
IV.   Benjamin Branch married Nancy _____ before 1801 and sold the land which had been devised to him by his father (D. B. 9, p. 563).
V.   Henry Branch married Mary____and died in 1808 (W. B. 6, p. 563).
      Children:
      1. Francis Branch
      2. Benjamin Branch
      3. Polly Branch
      4. Burwell Branch
      5. Elizabeth Branch.
      6. Edwin N. Branch
      7. Sally Branch
VI.   Lucy Branch
VII. Newsom Branch married Mary_____and died in 1802-1803 (W. B. 5, p. 427).
      Children:
      1. George Branch
      2. Orson Branch
      3. Valentine Branch
      4. Lewis Newsome Branch
      5. Sally Branch
      6. Hannah Branch married in 1795 James Johnson
      7. Diana Branch married in 1790 James Davis

Howell Branch, son of George and Martha Branch, was born in Southampton Co., Va., about 1738. He first purchased land in in 1759 (D. B. 2, p. 331). He married about 1765 Elizabeth, family name unknown, who was living in 1810 (D. B. 12, p. 344). Howell Branch made his will Oct. 12, 1781 and the same was probated on Nov. 8, 1781 (W. B. 3, p. 346).

Children of Howell and Elizabeth Branch:

I.   Drewry Branch married in 1791 Lucretia Summerill.
II.   Peter Branch died before 1810 without issue.
III.   Martha Branch married John Warren.
IV.   Jesse Branch (see later)

Jesse Branch, son of Howell and Elizabeth Branch, was under 16 when his father made his will. He married (1) Olivia Holden in

1803 and (2) Elizabeth Britt in 1809 (Southampton Register of Marriages, p. 155). Between 1810 and 1820 he moved to Halifax County, N.C. His plantation was located about four miles northwest of Halifax town. He made his will on June 22, 1842 and the same was probated in the Nov. Court for that year. According to the census records of 1820 and 1830 Jesse Branch had several children who were not mentioned in his will. (W.B. 4, p. 214).

Children of Jesse Branch (mentioned in his will):
I. Patrick H. Branch (see later).
II. Willie Branch married Sarah Bass.
By second marriage:
III. Mary Branch.
IV. Martha Ann Branch

Patrick H. Branch, son of Jesse Branch and his wife Olivia Holden, was born in Southampton Co., Va., about 1805 and died March 14, 1855 in Halifax County, N.C. About 1839 or 1840 he married Jemima Powell (b. 1808; d. Feb. 6, 188?), daughter of Daniel Powell and his wife Holly Merritt, daughter of Ephraim Merritt who died in Halifax County in 1788-89 (Family Records & Hal. Co. W.B. 3, p. 160). Daniel Powell was the son of Zachariah Powell and his wife Mary Jones.

Children of Patrick H. Branch and his wife Jemima Powell:
I. James Branch b. 1834.
II. Mattie Branch b. 1837.
III. Susan Ann Branch b. 1839 married as his second wife Balaam Dickens. Children under father. (See Dickens herein).
IV. Thaddeus Branch b. 1841, m. Mary Jane Dickens.
V. Mary L. Branch, b. 1843.
VI. Margaret Branch, b. 1847.
VII. Caroline B. Branch, b. 1850.
VIII. Martha S. Branch, b. 1852.

George[2] Branch (George[1]) evidently moved from Surry to Chowan County, North Carolina in 1694 for in that year he proved his rights for the importation of George Branch, Mary Branch, WILLIAM BRANCH, Elizabeth Branch, Phyllis Branch and George Branch. He assigned his rights that day to Nicholas Crisp.

It seems that the above mentioned persons were his children, and that his wife Susanna was deceased.

William Branch and his brother Francis Branch appear later in the above locality adjoining Nicholas Crisp. Francis Branch does not appear in the above list of names. However he may have been over 21 years of age in 1694 and imported himself, or arrived after that date.

At present time no further evidence concerning George Branch, the elder and his son George, has been ascertained.

On Jan. 6, 1707/8, Francis Branch bought 137 acres from Jeremiah Exum and Anne his wife, at the mouth of Mattacomack Creek, bounded on the southeast by the land of NICHOLAS CRISP and on the northwest by the land of Nathaniel Chevin. (Hathaway 1-94) His brother William Branch had previously bought, on July 4, 1704, 50 acres at the head of Mattacomack Creek from John Dennis and his wife Mary. (Id. 91)

William Branch appears in Albermarle County, N.C. in the
years 1695 to 1699 inclusive. On July 17,1716, July 16, 1717 and
July 21, 1717, the Court for Chowan Precinct met at William
Branch's house. (Id.149-151-153). On April 23, 1717, he patented
292 acres on the Mattacomack at Bonner Creek (Id.16). He sold
this land to Col. Edward Moseley Oct.31,1717. Wits: Thomas and
Elizabeth Swann. (Id 1618) He married Margaret Wheatley, who,
after his death, married Wm. Arkill.

William Branch of Chowan County made his will Nov.24,1720,
proven Jan.1721. He bequeathed to his wife MARGARET land in
Edenton on Queen Anne Creek; son WILLIAM plantation near Edenton; son ISSACHAR plantation on S.W. side of Mattacomack Creek;
son SOLOMON; dau. ELIZABETH. Extrxs. wife Margaret Branch
and BROTHER FRANCIS BRANCH. Wits: Jno New, Anne Branch,
Thomas Branch (Grimes-44).

The above abstract from Grimes Wills omitted legatees, Henry
Bonner, William Bonner, and Paul Palmer, and also an unnamed
infant child (N.C.Reg.p.32).

Margaret Branch, widow of William Branch, married secondly,
William Arkill, for in 1725, William Arkill and his wife Margaret,
made a deed of gift of lot B, in the town of Edenton, "...to Issa-
char Branch, son of William Branch and his wife Margaret, now
my wife.....in case of death to his sister Martha (Margaret ?)
Branch."(Id.123) On Feb.18,1724/25 William Arkill and wife
Margaret made a gift of lots in Edenton to Elizabeth Robertson
and Martha (Margaret ?) Branch. The deed was witnessed by
Francis Branch. Evidently Elizabeth Branch had married Mr.
Humphrey Robertson. They had two children, Elizabeth and Francis.

On June 18, 1737, William Arkill deeded to William Branch,Jr.,
175 acres at the head of Queen's Creek, "where the said Branch
now dwells...." (Id.115) On July 28,1732, William Branch,Jr.,
married Elizabeth, daughter of John Howcutt and wife, Mary
STANDIN, sister of Samuel[2] Standin and daughter of Edward[1]
Standin (will 1721) and Mary Wiatt.

This appears to account for all of the children of William
Branch except Solomon, who probably died young.

Issachar Branch, son of Margaret and William Branch, in
1735 sold to Edmond Gale, 146 acres on Queens Creek, being $\frac{1}{2}$ of
tract belonging to William Branch, deceased, on Bonner's Cove.
(Id.108). He married in 1737 Sarah Steward, daughter of William
Steward, Jr., 1697. Issachar, Sr. died in 1802 leaving a will.
His children were: JOB; ISSACHAR, JR.; and ARKILL BRANCH.

Job Branch, son of Sarah Steward and Issachar Branch, Sr.,
was born in 1760 in Perquimans County, N.C. and died there on
May 5, 1802, his will recorded in Edenton, N.C., 1805. On April
10, 1781 he married Rachel Bratten, daughter of Nathaniel[2] Bratten, b.1722; who married Mar.24,1744, Sarah Minge (daughter of
James Minge, Jr., and Mary Horth, d. Jan.23,1723) and granddaughter of John[1] Bratten.

Job Branch enlisted, Nov.29,1776 in Martin's Company, 2nd.
N.C. Battalion, commanded by Col. John Patton and fought at
the Battle of White Plains in Washington's Army, Sept.9, 1778.
In 1783, as a Corporal in the Continental Line he received 350

acres of land for 46 months service. (N.C. Roster, pp.59,263,605)

His children were: SARAH BRANCH who married in 1805, Jesse Standin (see later); JOSEPH BRANCH; JOB POWELL BRANCH; daughters: Penelope, Elizabeth and Mary.

Issachar Branch, Jr., made his will in 1801, probated Feb. 15, 1802 as follows: wife Rebecca (Bratten sister of Rachel) Branch to have use and occupation of house and land during her natural life. Sons: (1) Issachar Branch 3rd. to have tool chests and all moulding, planes likewise two sets of tools and oyl stones; (2) John Branch to live and abide with son Issachar 3rd., after the manner of an apprentice until he arrives at the age of 21 years; (3) William Branch to be bound out by Executors of said will at their discretion until he is 21 yrs.... Negroes to be sold and proceeds to pay all debts.... Beloved wife Rebecca and son Issachar, Geo. Bain, Sr., Geo. Bain, Jr., Executors. At Rebecca's demise all land and property to be equally divided among his three sons.

Francis[3] Branch, brother of William[3] in addition to the land bought of Jeremiah Exum in 1707/8 previously mentioned, on July 14, 1712 bought 166 acres lying at Barrowhole from Richard Lewis. Francis Branch and Ann his wife later sold this 166 acres to William Woodley of Nansemond. On July 15, 1712, Francis and Ann his wife sold 136 acres bought of Jeremiah Exum.(Id. 98) On Aug. 6,1719 Francis Branch patented 230 acres N.W. side Mattacomack Creek and 124 acres at head of same creek.

Francis Branch of Chowan Co., made his will Nov.14,1739 proven Dec.4,1739. His legatees were: Phillip Magnier 100 acres on Rockyback Neck; Phillip Magnier, Jr., Samuel Magnier; son WILLIAM BRANCH; Son ISSACHAR; daughter SARAH DONOVAN. Extrs: James Donovan, wife ANNE. Overseers: friends Wm. Arkill, and Wm.Luten. Wits.: Const. Luten; Wm.Luten, Wm. Lewis (Grimes-44; N.C.Reg.-29)

Sarah Donovan, daughter of Francis Branch, afterwards married William Lewis; for on Oct.19,1745, William Lewis and Sarah his wife, daughter of Francis Branch, sold to John Hodgson 124 acres at the head of Mattacomack Creek.

Sarah Branch, daughter of Job Branch and Mary Bratten, was born in 1785 and married in 1805, Jesse Standin, who was born in Perquimans County in 1789, the son of William[3] Standin, (twin of Edward), who was born July 25, 1743; died May 1815; and Elizabeth Perry. whom he married Feb.4, 1764.

Jesse Standin's grandfather was Samuel[2] Standin (brother of Mary Standin Howcott, ante) and son of Edward[1] Standin who died in 1721 and his wife Mary Wiatt. Samuel[2] Standin married Sarah, the daughter of Major Thomas Luton, whose will was probated Feb.16,1729. Samuel died in 1752.

Jesse Standin's mother was Elizabeth, daughter of Jesse[2] Perry of Little River, N.C. who died in 1751 and his wife, Sarah, the daughter of Thomas[1] Walton, Sr., and his wife Sarah Hunter. Elizabeth Perry Standin's grandfather was Philip[1] Perry,Jr., died July 5, 1751, who married Elizabeth Hunter, daughter of Isaac Hunter. (Grimes-177)

William Branch Standin, son of Sarah (Branch) and Jesse
Standin, was born in Perquimans County, N.C., in 1818; died
suddenly Feb. 1, 1853 and was buried on his farm. On March 1,
1840 in her home he married Mary Frances Haskett, who was
born in 1822 and died Nov. 1890; the daughter of William[4] Haskett
(B.1775) and his wife, Frances, daughter of Thomas[3] Parson
(b.1728; d.Feb.13,1747) and his wife Sarah, who was the daughter
of Elizabeth and William[2] Bogue, and grandaughter of Ellener and
William[1] Bogue.

One of Mary Frances Haskett's grandfathers was Samuel[2]
Parson, Jr., (b.Dec.24,1696; d.1745) who married in 1720,
Sarah, daughter of Elizabeth and John Arnold. Her great grand-
father was Samuel[1] Parson, Sr., who married May 4, 1694,
Elizabeth, daughter of Capt. Ralph Fletcher.

Her other grandfather was Thomas[3] Haskett, (b.1750) who
married in Oct. 1773, Mary_____. He was the son of William[2]
Haskett (b.1703; d.1772) who married another Mary   . His
grandfather was Anthony[1] Haskett, (b.1675; d.Oct.1735) who
married, in 1697, Diana_____.

Children of Mary Frances (Haskett) and William Branch
Standin:
I.   Martha Elizabeth Standin, b.Sept. 24, 1845; m.James Henry
       Bratten. (See later)
II.   Sarah Frances Standin, b.May 1, 1849; m. Augustus Warren
       Spruill. They had a son, A. W. Spruill.
III.   William Thomas Standin, b. Oct.23,1851.
       Two sons, John Henry Standin and Jesse Jerome Standin
       died in infancy.

Martha Elizabeth Standin, daughter of Mary Frances (Haskett)
and William Branch Standin, was born in Perquimans County Sept.
24, 1845; d. Dec. 20, 1923, in Baltimore, Md; on Dec.21,1865
at Edenton, N.C. married James Henry Bratten, who was born
March 20, 1845, at Edenton, and died Sept. 21, 1902, at Baltimore,
Md. He was the son of Deborah, daughter of Lesley Smith and
John Lesley Bratten, Sr., who enlisted Feb.28,1862, as 1st.
Lieutenant of Co.A. 1st.N.C. Regiment, C.S.A. He was wounded
at Chancellorsville, Va., May 3rd. 1863, and was a cripple all
his life. He died June 30, 1893 at the Confederate Soldier's Home
in Pikesville, Md., and was buried with all military honors in
Louden Park, Baltimore, Md.

James Henry Bratten enlisted May 10, 1861 at Edenton, in the
same regiment of First North Carolina, Company A, in which his
father had a commission. James Henry Bratten was wounded at
the last battle of Gettysburg, Pa.

After the War, James Henry Bratten married and later moved
to Baltimore, Md., from whence in 1876 he joined the United
States Navy for four years. He was on the U.S.S. "Dispatch" in
the engineers department and stationed at Constantinople during
the Truke-Russian War, as a tender to the U.S.Minister. He told
his wife that he gave four years of his life to the South, and four
years in the Navy to the North, and he was sure that God would
not hold anything against him.

51

Children of Martha (Standin) and James Henry Bratten:
Gertrude Bratten, James Thomas Bratten and Martha Frances
Bratten, their first three children, died in childhood.
IV.   Lily May Bratten, b.Aug.27,1875; m.Mar.4,1896, Allen C.
       B. Dorsey. (See later)
V.   Florence Milan Bratten, b. June 10, 1881; m.Sept.1903,
       Louis B. Crowley.
VI.   Mary Edith Bratten, b.Oct.11,1885, m. Charles C. Keyes.
VII.   Henry Clifton Bratten, b.Dec.26,1888; d.March 18,1906.
       (See later)

Henry Clifton Bratten, who was in the U.S. Navy, died of
spinal meningitis in the Hospital at Portsmouth, Va., in his
eighteenth year, and is buried in the Naval Cemetary.

Lily May Bratten, the daughter of Martha (Standin) and James
Henry Bratten, was born August 27, 1875, in Baltimore, Md.
There, on March 4, 1896, she married Allen Clifton Boothe Dor-
sey, who was born Feb.14, 1867, at Washington, D.C., and died
Oct.12,1951, at Baltimore. He was the son of Amanda Warfield
(Stevens) and John Warfield Dorsey; and was a Veteran of the
Spanish War.
    Mrs. Allen C.B. Dorsey is a member of the Carter Braxton
Chapter, D.A.R.; the Maryland Historical Society; James R.
Wheeler Chapter, U.D.C; and Auxiliary of Goldsborough Post,
Spanish War Veterans. She now resides at 411 Edsdale Road,
Apt. F, Uplands Apts., Baltimore 29, Maryland.
       Children:
I.   Audrey Florene Dorsey, b.Feb.26,1897; m.April 9,1916,
       William Spaulding Albert. Issue: Audrey Dorsey Albert,
       b.Apr.21,1917.
II.   Vera Elaine Dorsey, b.Sept.6,1898; m.(1) June 25,1919,
       George Hassen, who enlisted in Co.A, 115 Infantry, 29th
       Division A.E.F., May 28, 1917. He served until June 5,
       1919; and was in the Meuse Argonne Offensive, Oct.8-29,
       1918, was awarded the "Silver Victory Button", Aug.15,
       1919; Purple Heart, Nov.13, 1933. He died Jan.2,1951.
       Issue: George Albert Hassen, Jr., who was born Sept.21,
       1924, and was a member of the 4th Marine Division, World
       War II. Mrs. Hassen married, secondly, Dec.15,1951,
       Irving Lloyd Brohawn.
III.   Leone Edith Dorsey, b.April 18,1900; m.(1) 1918, Melvin
       Rogers. Issue: Allen Dorsey Rogers, b.Aug.16,1920.
       m. (2) June 2, 1931, Victor K. Butler, d. April 25, 1944.

Branch
of Halifax County, North Carolina

The material on the Branch Family of Halifax County, North Carolina, included on pages 52-65 of the first edition, has been reprinted with corrections in Volume IX of HISTORICAL SOUTHERN FAMILIES.

⅄ CHAPPELL OF SURRY

The later generations of this family are treated fully in the Chappell Genealogy by Phil E. Chappell (Kansas City, 1900). However, there are several mistakes in this genealogy regarding the earlier generations. In particular, the first two Thomas Chappells, father and son, are telescoped into one in that genealogy, so that one generation is left out.

The first of the family was Thomas Chappell of Charles City Co., Va. who is probably identical with a Thomas Chappell, b. 1612, who came to Virginia on the ship "America" in 1635. This Thomas Chappell died in Charles City Co., in 1658, leaving his lands to his eldest son, two breeding cattle to each of his other children, and the rest of his estate to his wife, no names of wife or children being mentioned (Charles City Order Bk., 1655-65, p. 159). The widow Chappell married (2) Walter Vernham (Id. p. 158).

Thomas Chappell, second, first appears in the records April 30, 1661, when he acknowledged receipt of a legacy to his daughter from Lt. John Bannister (Id., p. 271, p. 588). Thomas Chappell's wife may have been a daughter of John Banister. The latter died in 1661. (Id., p. 302), and his wife, Joan Banister m. (2) James Wallace. Thomas Chappell was granted 80 acres of land in Charles City Co. Oct. 20, 1665 (Nugent, "Cavaliers and Pioneers", p. 535).

Thomas Chappell, third, first appears April 21, 1690,- when he was granted 904 acres of land in Charles City (later Prince George) Co. (Grant Bk. 8, p. 77). Other large grants were made to him later, some of the land being in Surry and Isle of Wight Co.'s. Thomas Chappell was still living June 3, 1702, when he deeded some of the land in Surry to his brother-in-law, James Jones Jr., who conveyed it to his son, Robert Jones (Surry D. & W. 1715-30, p. 295) He was dead by June 22, 1704, when his widow, Elizabeth, entered into a marriage contract with Thomas Taylor. Elizabeth Chappell was the daughter of James Jones of Prince George Co. (See Jones Family). She and her second husband, Thomas Taylor, were still living in Surry Co. on Oct. 19, 1736 (Surry D. & W. 1730-38, p. 628). They had at least four children:

I.   John Taylor (cf. above deed).
II.   Thomas Taylor (Ibid).
III.   Elizabeth Taylor m. John Chambliss (Prince George D. & W. 1713-28, p. 1108).
IV.   Katherine Taylor m. Edward Holloway (Id. p. 1109)

Thomas Chappell, third, and Elizabeth Jones, his wife, had four sons. (It is stated in the Chappell Genealogy that he had a daughter who m. John Williams, but this is a mistake. John Williams was the husband of his sister-in-law, Mary Jones, who m. (2) Richard Darden). They were:

I.   Robert Chappell. (See later)
II.   Thomas Chappell. (See later)

III.   James Chappell, born 1694. (See later)
IV.   Samuel Chappell, b. 1696.(See later)
    Robert Chappell (Thomas, Thomas, Thomas) died in Prince
George Co. in 1724, his will being dated Feb.3,1723 and probated
Feb.12, 1724/5. He m. Sarah_____, who survived him and m. (2)
William Crawley, Sr., moving to Amelia Co., where she d. 17ɜ1.
They had 6 children, all under age in 1723, namely Robert, Sarah,
Mary, John, Ann, and James Chappell.
    Thomas Chappell (Thomas, Thomas, Thomas) married in 1710
Hannah Hunnicutt, a Quaker, and himself became a Quaker. He
died in Prince George Co. before 1726. Issue (from Quaker re-
cords):
I.   Margaret Chappell m. Jan. 12, 1736 Aaron Hill.
II.   Thomas Chappell m. May 10, 1731 Margaret dr. of Robert
        Hunnicutt.
III.   Rebecca Chappell m. July 3, 1731 Peter Binford.
IV.   Samuel Chappell m. 1741 Ann Simons.
V.   Martha Chappell m. June 2, 1751 James Binford.
VI.   Benjamin Chappell m. June 7, 1754 Anges Binford.

    Samuel Chappell (Thomas, Thomas, Thomas) receipted his
uncle, James Jones Jr. for property inherited from his father,
Thomas Chappell, on May 14, 1717, thus indicating his birth as
1696 (Prince George D. & W. 1713-28, p.168). He married prior
to 1724 Elizabeth, daughter of John Scott of Prince George Co.
(See Vol.I, p.101) Samuel Chappell lived in Surry Co., where his
will, dated 1748, was probated Nov.21, 1749. It mentions the
following children: Samuel, Elizabeth, Sarah, Bethia, Mary,
Emelia, Thomas, James, John, Benjamin, Robert, Drury, and
Nancy Chappell. Descendants of several of these are given in the
Chappell genealogy.
    James Chappell (Thomas, Thomas, Thomas) was born in
Prince George Co. in 1694, as he acknowledged receipt of his
property from the estate of his father, Thomas Chappell from
James Jones May 10, 1715 (Prince George D.&W., 1713-28, p.
52). He married about 1720 or 1721 Elizabeth Briggs, daughter
of Henry and Elizabeth (Lucas) Briggs of Surry Co. She died Sept.
26, 1744 in Surry Co. (Albemarle Psh.Reg.). James Chappell was
a vestryman of Albemarle Parish from 1743 till his death, was a
Justice of Surry Co.(latter Sussex) from 1738, and was Sheriff of
Sussex Co. in 1754 (Wm.and Mary Quarterly, New Series Vol.II,
p.52; Sussex O.B. 1754-6,p.1; Exec.Journal of Council of Va.Vol.
4,p.417).He died in Sussex Co.Feb.12,1769(Albemarle Pshe.Reg.).
James Chappell's will,dated Oct.31,1768,was probated Mar.16,
1769 in Sussex Co.It mentions his sons,James and Thomas,daugh-
ters,Elizabeth Mason,Mary Gee,Sarah Mason,Rebecca Northington,
grandsons Thomas and Howell Tatum,daughter Amy Smith,son John,
daughter Lucretia Carter,son Howell,and grandchildren James and
Henry Chappell, sons of James, Howell Chappell, son of John, and
Mary Chappell, daughter of Thomas.
        Children:
I.   James Chappell Jr., born about 1720-25, died 1778 in Sus-
        sex Co., m. (1) Elizabeth Briggs, daughter of William and
        Mary Cook Briggs (See Briggs family). She died June 11, 1762,
        and James Chappell m. (2) Judith_____, who d. Mar.1,

1769. Children of first marriage:
1. Elizabeth Chappell, b.July 6, 1745, m.Philip Reeckes (Sussex D.B.1768-72, p.198)
2. James Chappell, b.Mar.5,1746/7, m. Sally Hines. (See later)
⤳ 3. Henry Chappell, b. Mar.5, 1751, m. Elizabeth, dau. of Christopher and Elizabeth Mason Rives.
4. John Chappell, b.Mar. 8, 1755.
5. Amy Chappell, b.May 19, 1758.
6. Rebecca Chappell, b. May 21, 1760.
7. William Chappell, b. June 10, 1762.
   By his second marriage, James Chappell had:
8. Mary Chappell (probably) mentioned in her father's will but not shown in the parish register, married Sterling Neblett.(See later)
9. Benjamin Chappell, b.Aug.20,1765.
10. Martha Chappell, b.Dec.7, 1766.
11. Kinchen Chappell, b.1769.

II. Thomas Chappell married Mary Briggs, daughter of William and Mary (Cook) Briggs of Sussex Co. He moved to Charlotte Co. (See later)

III. Elizabeth Chappell married Major John Mason of Sussex Co. They had at least three children, John, William and Ann Mason (Sussex D.B.1768-72, pp.392,434)

IV. Mary Chappell married Charles Gee, son of Capt. James and Boyce (Scott) Gee.

V.   Sarah Chappell m. Christopher Mason. She died 1796 in Brunswick Co. and her will shows the following children (W.B.6, p.57):
1. Sterling Mason b. 1747 (Albemarle Psh.Reg.), d. before 1796.
2. John Mason.
3. Joseph Mason, d. before 1796.
4. Thomas Mason.
5. Elizabeth Mason m._____Speed.
6. Sarah Mason m.Randolph Newsom
7. Christopher Mason.
8. Martha Mason, m._____Johnson.
9. Henry Mason.

VI. Rebecca Chappell m. Nathan Northington
VII. Amy Chappell m. James Smith.
VIII. John Chappell m. Mary, dau. of Thomas Hines, and died in Sussex Co., Va. in 1803. Children:
1. Howell Chappell, b. April 22, 1759.
2. Martha Chappell, b. July 17, 1761.
3. John Chappell, b. Sept. 30, 1763.
4. William Chappell, b. Aug. 1, 1765.
5. Elizabeth Chappell, b. July 27, 1767.
6. Mary Chappell, b. Sept. 21, 1769.
7. Thomas Chappell, b. Jan.17, 1772.
8. Henry Chappell, b. Aug. 19, 1774.
9. Peggy Chappell.

IX.   Ann Chappell, b.Dec. 22, 1739; she perhaps married a Tatum, and was mother of Thomas and Howell Tatum, grandsons mentioned in James Chappell Sr.'s will.

X.   Lucretia Chappell, b.Feb.10, 1741/2 (A.P.R.), m._____ Carter.

XI.   Howell Chappell, b. Aug.26, 1744 (A.P.R.) m. Rebecca, daughter of William and Mary (Cook) Briggs, and died in Sussex Co. in 1806. Children:

1. Howell Chappell.
2. Briggs Chappell.
3. Henry Chappell, b.Sept.16, 1764.
4. James Chappell, b. Feb.12, 1767.
5. William Chappell, b. Aug. 30, 1769.
6. Frances Chappell, b. July 27, 1774.
7. Susannah Chappell, b. Oct. 24, 1771.
8. Rebecca Chappell.
9. Elizabeth Chappell.

Mary Chappell, daughter of James Chappell, Jr., and Elizabeth Briggs, married Sterling Neblett. In 1776, James Chappell of Sussex County, for love and affection makes over one negroe girl to Sterling Neblett and Mary his wife of Sussex County, son in law and daughter of the said Chappell, (BK E p.361).

"Haymarket" on the Nottoway River was the home of Nathaniel Neblett, a veteran of the war of 1812. He was the son of Sterling Neblett and Mary Chappell of "Woodlawn in Lunenburg County". He married Elizabeth Davis, nee Fisher, the widow of Ashley Davis, and had: ELIZA, REBECCA, and ANNE. Eliza married Charles Smith, Treasurer of Lunenburg County, Ann married Dr. W.H. Perry, also of Lunenburg County, and Rebecca died unmarried. (Turner, "Old Homes and Families of Nottoway." p. 65).

Eliza D. Neblett, b. Oct. 21, 1811, d. March 5, 1845 in Lunenburg County, m. May 13, 1830. Charles Smith, b. Sept. 10, 1795 in Addison County, Vermont, d. June 30, 1857, at Rubermont, Lunenburg County, Va. Mr. Smith was an A.B. of Middlebury College, Vermont, 1815, and Commonwealth's Attorney for Lunenburg County, Va. Their daughter was Rosamond Smith. Turner says: (p.124) "Roseland" was the home of Col. William Purnell Dickinson, born 7 Sept. 1810, died 6 Oct. 1874. He married (1) Miss Barkesdale, (2) Miss Venable, (issue 2 daughters); (3) Miss Rosamond Smith, born 20 June, 1833, died 3 Sept. 1896, and had Mary Purnell Dickinson.

Mary Purnell Dickinson, born Aug. 7, 1807, at "Roseland", died Nov. 19, 1933, at Newport News, married Feb.7, 1883 at "Roseland", Charles Lewis Putzel, born April 18, 1848, at Martinsville, Henry County, died Oct. 25, 1907, at Richmond, Va.

Their daughter, Mary Putzel, born Sept. 23, 1887, at Martinsville, married January 19, 1911, at Newport News, Schuyler Otis Bland, born May 4, 1872 in Gloucester Co., Va., died Feb. 16, 1950 in Washington. He was the son of Schuyler Bland and his wife Olivia James Anderson of Gloucester. Mr. Bland was graduated from the College of William and Mary and the Law School of the University of Va. He belonged to the Kappa Alpha fraternity and was also a Phi Beta Kappa. He was a lawyer and was a representative in Congress for the first district of Virginia for 32 years.

James Chappell, son of Elizabeth (Briggs) and James Chappell, born March 5, 1747, died 1818, married April 20, 1769, Sallie Hines, died 1824. He was a private in the 2nd. Virginia Regiment, commanded by Colonel Alexander Spottswood and later by Colonel Febiger. He enlisted February 15, 1776, discharged February 21, 1778. He served later in Captain Everade Meade's and Captain William Taylor's companies.

His will was probated in Sussex November 5, 1818. His children were:

I.   James IV, b. 1770, m. (1) Polly Sturdevant, (2) Martha B. Gregory.
II.   Elizabeth, b. 1771, m. Lewis Parham.
III.   Littleberry, b. May 21, 1772, m. Clairmond Dobie. (See Later).
IV.   Edmund, b. 1774, dsp.
V.   Rebecca Parham, b. Apr. 23, 1775, m. Stephen Lucas.
VI.   Mary, b. 1779, m. William Dobie.
VII.   Sally, b. 1780, m. Harwell Caraway?

7. Littleberry Chappell, b. November 21, 1772, died April 5, 1827. He married February 4, 1802, Clairmond Dobie, born 1778, died September 26, 1826. He resided in Sussex all of his life. His children were: Littleton, b. September 28, 1804 (see later No. 8); Nathaniel; Albert; Joseph; Robert (see later No. 9); Edmond; Jane; Sarah.

8. Littleton James Chappell, born September 28, 1804, married November 3, 1828, Betsy Graves, and had

John Lewis Chappell, born October 10, 1835, died January 10, 1907; married December 19, 1854, Lucy Ann West, born June 23, 1832, died November 14, 1907, and had

Littleton James Chappell, born April 5, 1858, died August 23, 1835; married December 23, 1885, Rebecca Valetine Ellis, born February 14, 1869, died July 28, 1940. Mr. Chappell is buried in Neville Church yard in Sussex.

Their son, John Wallace Chappell, was born at Homeville, Sussex, March 4, 1890, and resides at 525 East Speedway, Tucson, Arizona.

9. Robert A. Chappell, born June 24, 1818, died 1863 at Waverly, Sussex, married Jan. 5, 1843, Elizabeth R. Cotton, born April 1824, died 1895 at Waverly. A daughter, Sally Bet Chappell, born August 17, 1850, died November 5, 188?, married Nov. 27, 1874, Purnell Fleetwood, born Aug. 17, 1847 in Sussex Co., Delaware, died Apr. 17, 1828 at Waverly, Va. Mr. Fleetwood was president of the Waverly and Claremont Banks in Sussex and Surry.
    Children:
I.   Harvey Fleetwood, m. Lottie Arnold.(See later).
II.   Purnell Fleetwood, Jr., M. Madeline Davis.
III.   Blanche Fleetwood, m. Jack Baird.
IV.   Mary Elizabeth Fleetwood, m. (1) Nicholas Burt, (2) Joseph Leslie Bradshaw. (See later).

V.   Sally Bet Fleetwood, m. Walter Daniel.
VI. Holt Fleetwood.

   Mr. Harvey Fleetwood, born 1880 in Waverly, Sussex, died
Mar. 1, 1939, son of Sally (Chappell) and Purnell Fleetwood,
married Oct. 18, 1905, Lottie Arnold, born 1885, daughter of
Judge Richard Watson Arnold, succeeded his father as president
of the Waverly and Claremont Banks in 1928 and served as presi-
dent until his death.
      Children:
I.   Arnold Prince Fleetwood, b. Mar. 18, 1909, m. Miss Butler.
II. Harvey Fleetwood, Jr., b. Feb. 2, 1916, m. Maria Fraile.

   Mary Elizabeth Fleetwood, born June 6, 1884, died Aug. 19,
1925; married, (1) Nicholas Burt, (2) on Jan. 8, 1915, Joseph
Leslie Bradshaw, born Aug. 17, 1874, died Mar. 15, 1918. Mr.
Bradshaw was educated at the University of Richmond, and Mrs.
Bradshaw was educated at Randolph-Macon Womans College.
      Children of 1st. Marriage:
I.   Elizabeth Fleetwood Burt, b. Dec. 28, 1911, m. Frank
     P. Pulley, Sr.
      Children of 2nd. Marriage:
II. Leslie Chappell Bradshaw, b. Feb. 13, 1916 at Waverly,
     Va. m. Dec. 21, 1940 George Benjamin Fleetwood Traylor,
     b. Dec. 21, 1915. Mr. Traylor was educated at Lee's
     Junior College, Lexington, Ky., and Atlanta Dental College,
     Atlanta, Ga. He served in the Navy as a Lieutenant in the
     Dental Corps in World War II. Mrs. Traylor was educated
     at State Teachers College, Farmville, Va., and now resides
     at 7100 Hampton Blvd., Norfolk, Va. They have one child,
     Sarah Fleetwood Traylor, b. Dec. 22, 1943.
III. Maude Osborn Bradshaw.

   Thomas Chappell, son of Elizabeth (Briggs) and James Chap-
pell, married Mary daughter of William BRIGGS. His parents
deeded him land which afterwards fell in Southampton. Deeds in
that county show that he removed to Charlotte and Lunenburg
counties. His will was probated in Lunenburg October 14, 1790.
(W. B. 1788-90, p. 370)
      Children:
I.   James, m. Elizabeth, daughter of William Briggs.
II. Thomas IV, m. Elizabeth, dau. Mary and William Malone.
     (See later)
III. William.
IV. John
V.   Mary, m. Clay.
VI. Annie, m. (1) Daniel Malone, (2)   Robertson. Grand-
     children, William, Thomas, Mary, and Rebecca Malone,
     were mentioned in will of Thomas Chappell IV.

   Thomas Chappell IV married August 20, 1772, in Sussex,
Elizabeth Tucker Malone. Her father, William Malone, consented
to her marriage because she was under age. On April 1, 1771,
his father deeded him land in Sussex which he sold when he moved
with him to Lunenburg. In the deed it is stated that land was patented by the elder Thomas Chappell June 25, 1747.

Thomas Chappell sold his property in Charlotte and moved back to Sussex after the death of his father, where his will was probated in May 1, 1823 (Bl, p. 351).

Children:
I. Robert, dsp.
II. Mary, m. December 9, 1797, Thomas Chappell Malone.
III. Martha, m. February 13, 1800, James Anderson.
IV. Phoebe, m. April 20, 1801, John Rainey.
V. Lucretia Tucker, m. November 8, 1801, George RANDOLPH.
VI. Ann, m. April 15, 1809, Samuel Owen.
VII. Sarah, m. December 7, 1809, Balaam Green (Sussex marriage Bonds).

CLOUD of PENNSYLVANIA, VIRGINIA, and SOUTH CAROLINA

William[1] Cloud, ancestor of this family, came from Calne, Wiltshire, England, and settled in Chester Co., Penn., where William Penn granted him 500 acres of land on Sept. 8, 1681. He made his will the 20th day of the 7th month 1700 which method of dating is usually a Quaker designation, and same was probated at Chester Aug. 25, 1702, as follows: "I, WILLIAM CLOUD of Concord Sem, in county of Chester, being aged and well stricken in years, do give unto my son WILLIAM CLOUD 100 acres of my purch.land; to my son JEREMIAH CLOUD 200 acres of my purchased land, to sons, JOSEPH, JOHN and ROBERT CLOUD one English shilling if demanded; to my grand daughter, HANNAH CLOUD, daughter of JEREMIAH CLOUD, all the rest of my estate, both real and personal, she to be Executrix. Son JEREMIAH to be Overseer". Wits: Robert Pyle, Ann Pyle, Sadie Pyle (Register of Wills, Phila). Children: William, d. 1720, m. Grace; Jeremiah[2], m. Elizabeth Bailey (See later); Joseph, m. Mary Moore; John, m. Ann Beesom; Robert, dsp? Susanna, m. Lukens.

Jeremiah[2] Cloud, who inherited 200 acres from his father William, had a much larger estate upon his death 17 years later. Jeremiah made his Will Feb. 20, 1715/16 same probated Dec. 1, 1717, as follows: "I, JEREMIAH CLOUD of Rexland Manor in County of New Castle upon the Delaware in Penn., cordwainer, being "sick and weak" give unto my beloved wife, ELIZABETH, and son, WILLIAM CLOUD, whom I constitute executors of my Will, my manor plantation where I now dwell with cattle etc. Immediately after wife's death it is to become property of WILLIAM; to sons, JEREMIAH and MORDECAI 500 acres in Township of Marlborough, Chester Co.; to son, DANIEL, tract of land known as "Mount Pleasant", formerly land of Nathaniel Lampley near Chichester containing 200 acres; to son JOHN one shilling; to daus. SARAH, HANNAH, ELIZABETH at 21 certain pounds of ancient money". Wits: Geo. Robinson, Rob. GILLINGHAM (Dover Deleware Book C, Vol 1, p. 118).

William[3] Cloud, son of Elizabeth (Bailey) and Jeremiah [2], is said to have also married an Elizabeth Bailey. He was of age in 1716 at the time his father made his Will as he was the executor. He made his Will at Brandywine Hundred, County of New Castle, Del., May 12, 1747, "in perfect health and memory", to son HENRY CLOUD, 400 acres in Frederick County, Va., where he hath made his choice at the lower end of my land"; to son, JEREMIAH CLOUD 400 acres in the same Colony where he hath made his choice adjoining to my son before mentioned; to son, DANIEL CLOUD, the reversion of the said tract except the bottom part to be equally divided between my three sons heretofore mentioned; to my wife, ELIZABETH, thirty pounds and all profits of my plantation until son WILLIAM comes of age; also to William tract of

73

land bought from John Little John, adjoing land to son JOSEPH; to dau. MARGARET CLOUD Ł 50; to daus. ELIZABETH and MABLE 5 sh. each. Wife extrix. Wits; Joseph Pyle, William Ford, Benjamin Ford. (Reg. New Castle, Del.)

The first three sons above named were evidently living in Frederick Co., Va., where they "had made their choice" at time the above Will was made.

Daniel Cloud served in the Revolution as a private from Virginia, enlisting June 8, 1776 and serving until 1778. Mordecai Cloud's will was probated in Frederick Co. 1789.

William[4] Cloud, son of William of Brandywine Hundred, first appeared in S.C. by official records on the third day of January 1765 when he took a land grant on Fishing Creek in Chester Co., S.C., then old Craven County. He took two successive land grants for "increase in family". Sometime before 1775 William Cloud deeded this land on Fishing Creek in Chester County to his daughter, Mrs. Alice Boyleston. This land is still owned by the Boyleston family. The other grant of William Cloud on Fishing Creek in Chester County was deeded to their son, James Cloud. William Cloud then removed to Virginia until after the Revolution when he came back to S.C. and records show that he was buying lands in this county on the first of January 1787.

The family record is that William Cloud married in Virginia to Alice Hardin before coming to S.C. originally. There are deeds in Fairfield and in Charleston showing Alice Cloud, the wife of William Cloud, as signing dower rights.

William Cloud made his Will March 14, 1810, probated Aug. 30, 1811, as follows: To wife and son, JOSEPH, certain negroes, cattle and furniture, remainder to be sold and divided equally between my daughters, SIN FORD, ALICE BOYLESTONE and grandson, VINCENT BELL; to grandson, WILLIAM CLOUD, son of DANIEL, all my lands lying on south side of Thorntree Creek at death of my wife; to daughter, ANN GUPHILL 5 schillings; JOSEPH CLOUD, my son and VINCENT BELL, my grandson, to be exrs. Wits: Leod Godbolt, Ananias Godbolt, Samuel Loughdote (Winnsboro Bk. 5-539). His children were: Joseph[5], b. Mar. 23, 1770, m. Martha Nettles (See later); James, m. Jane McKennie; Ann, m. _____ Ford; Alice m. _____ Boyleston; David; dau. m. Bell, and had Vincent Bell who was to take his deceased mother's portion.

Joseph[5] Cloud, (William[4]) born Mar. 23, 1770, in Fairfield County, S.C. died Oct. 5, 1851 in Fairfield, m. Dec. 25, 1801, Martha Nettles, born Oct. 15, 1785 in Fairfield, died May 2, 1852. Mr. Cloud was a planter and raised a large family. His Will was that of a wealthy man as he disposed of a large quantity of personal property including negroes and cattle. It was dated Feb. 20, 1851 and probated Oct. 13, 1851. He bequeathed his wife, MARTHA, one half of plantation where I now live including houses, 25 head of cattle, etc. Other legatees, sons, AUSTIN N., JAMES H., WILLIAM A., ANDERSON J., DOUGLAS B., FRANKLIN D., Daughters were ALICE BARBER, ANNE BAILEY, ELIZA H. HOOD, JANE MCKEY. Other legatees, WM. BARBER, CHARLES BAILEY, JAMES HOOD. Executors, sons Austin, John and Franklin Cloud. Wits. I.F. Cloud, L.H. Boul-

ware, I.C. Boulware. (Bk.19-319). Children:
I.   Alice, m. William Barber.
II. Jane[6], b. Dec. 31, 1804, m. William Land McKey (See later).
III. Eliza, m. James Hood.
IV. Anne, m. Charles Bailey and had: James Bailey; Walter Bailey m. Helen Cloud; Douglas Bailey m. Hattie Steele, Lavinia Bailey, m. Dr. Anderson Bowen, first wife; Eliza Bailey, m. first Richburg, second E. T. Lomas of England; Eunice H. Bailey, m. Dr. J.G.B. Bulloch; Alice Bailey m. Dr. J.E. Jarnigan; Joseph Bailey; Arrabella Bailey.
     The following data obtained from tombstones at old Smyrna Church - located between Ridgeway and Camden, S.C.:
     No marker found for Anne Cloud-daughter of Joseph and Martha Nettles Cloud, found only marker for husband-Charles Bailey-Died March 25, 1857- aged 58 years.
     Children of Anne Cloud and Charles Bailey buried at Old Smyrna:
     1. James A. Bailey, born Nov.16, 1841, died May 25,1862.
     2. Alice Bailey- Beloved wife of Dr. J.E. Jarnigan- Born May 16, 1852- married May 4, 1875- Died Nov.25,1896.
     3. Arrabella Josephine- daughter of C. and A.C. Bailey-Born March 28, 1855, Died Sept. 19, 1857.
V.   Anderson, m. Martha Barber.
VI. Douglas B. m. Cornelia Webb.
VII. Franklin[6] D., b. Nov. 4, 1824, m. Sarah Hogan. (See later)
VIII. John Benjamin, b. Oct.26, 1810, m. Margaret Montgomery.
     Data from tombstones Old Smyrna Church:
     John Benjamin Cloud- Born Oct.26, 1810- Died Oct. 7,1895.
     Margaret D. Cloud- daughter of David and Mary Montgomery and wife of J.B. (John Benjamin) Cloud- Born Nov.16, 1818- Died Feb.19, 1885.
     Children:
     1. T. E. (Ellison) Cloud- born Dec.21, 1838- died April 15, 1882.
     2. David Gamewell Cloud- born April 16, 1841, died July 4, 1871.
     3. Mrs. C. L. Rouseborough, wife of T. L. Rouseborough, born Jan.31, 1844, died Feb. 20, 1877. (Louisa Cloud)
     4. Mary Alexina Cloud, born May 25, 1848, died Dec.19, 1863.
     5. Helen C., wife of W. A. Bailey, born July 27, 1845, died June 6, 1910. W. A. Bailey, born May 19, 1843, died May 9, 1909.
IX. James, m. Sarah Bell.
X.   Austin, m. Mary (Polly) Ruff.

Jane[6] Cloud, daughter of Martha (Nettles) and Joseph[5] Cloud, was born Dec.31, 1804, died Jan. 26, 1853; married Feb. 17, 1825, William Land McKey, born Nov.3, 1800, died Nov. 9, 1856. Children from McKey family records now in possession (July 8, 1954) of Miss Lillian Jordan McKey, 513 W. Hill St., Valdosta, Ga.

I.   Martha Elizabeth McKey, b. Nov. 20, 1825, died April
      25, 1857, married Sept.3, 1845 Aaron Woodward and
      had children: John Woodward, James Woodward and Annie
      Woodward.

II.   Jonathan Leval McKey, b.Oct.23,1827, m.June 24,1857
      Emma R. Lawson and had three children.

III. Dr. James Taylor McKey, b. July 24, 1833, m. Jan.19,
      1869 Mattie Lorena Brassington and had one child who died
      in infancy.

IV.   Alice Jane McKey, b.April 21, 1829, d.Sept.16,1866,m.
      Jan.8, 1849 Henry B. Holliday.

V.   William Harrison McKey, b.Oct.17,1837, d.Feb.19,1890,
      m. Oct.25,1876 Martha Ann Watson, b.Nov.29,1861,
      d.March 19, 1930. Their children were:

1.   Earle Sinclair McKey, b.Jan.6,1878,d. March 18, 1930,
      m. Dec.4, 1907 Susan Catherine Converse, dau. of
      Mary Ann Keller and Thomas Briggs Converse and had
      children:

      (1) Earle Sinclair McKey Jr., b. Sept. 1908, m. (1)
           Alys Katherine Keiley on Nov. 6, 1940 and had
           one child: Earle Sinclair McKey III, b. Oct. 18,
           1942. m. (2) Oct. 22, 1948 Martha Augusta Wise-
           man.

      (2) William Converse McKey m. Martha Jane Gates
           Nov.12, 1938 and have a son born Aug.19,1951,
           William Clay McKey.

      (3) Robert Wilburn McKey married Lucille Adams,
           Nov. 6, 1942 and have:
           a. Robert Wilburn McKey,-Jr., b. Nov.9, 1944.
           b. Lucille, b. Jan. 19, 1947.
           c. Sally Catherine, b. Jan. 18, 1953.

      (4) Susan Converse McKey, m. Lyndle Eugene Thomas,
           Dec. 16, 1943 and have
           a. Lyndle Eugene Thomas Jr., b. Dec.31, 1946.
           b. William Converse Thomas, b. Oct. 10, 1950.

2.   Lillian Jordan McKey, b. Aug. 24, 1883 - unmarried.

3.   Wilburn Hampton McKey, b. May 12, 1887, d. June 10,
      1954- unmarried.

4.   Alva Bulloch McKey, b.Aug.30,1889 - unmarried.

Franklin[6] Darrington Cloud, b.Nov.24, 1824, Fairfield Co.,
S.C., d. Sept. 29, 1885, Fairfield Co., S.C., m.June 2, 1846,
Fairfield Co., S.C. Sarah Hogan, b. Jan. 4, 1825, Fairfield
Co., S.C., d. June 16, 1888, Fairfield Co., S.C. Their children
are:

I.   Danman Cloud, killed in the Confederate Army.
II.   Mary Eliza Cloud.
III. William Cloud m. Josephine Fullwood.
IV.   Joseph Cloud married and moved to Texas.
V.   Martha, m. Hon. William J. Johnson, Banker and Member
      of S.C. Assembly.
VI.   Cynthia, m. Richard Hogan.
VII. Milton, died young.
VIII. Ernest Eugene, b. July 16, 1864, d. May 30, 1925, m.

Sept. 21, 1894 Jessie Walker Hough, b. June 8, 1870, d. Dec. 31, 1952. Their children were:

1. Mary Evelyn, b. Oct. 5, 1895.
2. Esther Eugenia, b. July 11, 1900.
3. Sarah, b. May 29, 1904.
4. Jessie, b. March 10, 1910, m. James Patterson McAliley.
5. Ernestine, b. March 10, 1910, m. William Raynolds Paden (Twin)

IX.　Alice Ann[7] m. Samuel Duke (See later)

Alice Ann[7] Cloud, b. Oct. 11, 1861, Fairfield Co., S.C., d. April 25, 1951, Columbia, Richland Co., S.C., m. Dec.20, 1880, Fairfield Co., S. C., Samuel Charleton Duke, b. Sept. 29, 1854, Fairfield Co., S.C., d. June 22, 1895, Fairfield Co., S.C., Children:

I.　Ruth Estelle[8] Duke, b. Feb.4, 1884, m.March 31, 1917, John L. Dove, b. Aug. 18, 1883, d. July 25, 1949, son of Nancy Weir Dove and Richard Dove. Children:
1. Ruth Dove, b. May 15, 1918, m. Norman Des Jardins.
2. Dorothy Dove, b. Feb. 15, 1922, m. (1st) Raymond L. McKenzie and had
a. John Raymond McKenzie, b. May 21, 1942.
Dorothy Dove, after divorce, m. (2) Richard Wilson and had
b. Richard Peter Wilson, b. Jan. 20, 1949.
c. Shelley Dove Wilson, b. Jan. 7, 1950.
d. Sherry DuBois Wilson, b. Jan. 7, 1953.

II.　Ernest Charlton Duke, b. 1881, d. 1899 - unmarried.
III.　Sarah[8] Duke, m. Benjamin Frampton Griner- had one son- Benjamin Charlton Griner who m. Mary Moulder.
IV.　Lila Christine[8] Duke, b. Oct. 11, 1894, d. May 10, 1939, m. April 24, 1924 Charles Watson Holland, b. June 24, 1896. Children:
1. Carolyn Cloud[9] Holland, b. July 30, 1926, educated at Winthrop College, Rock Hill, S.C. m. Aug.7, 1944, Burrell Marion Ellison, Jr., b. Nov.15, 1920.
Ch Children:
(1) Burell Marion[10] Ellison III, b. Feb. 28, 1946.
(2) Laura Carolyn[10] Ellison, b. Aug. 8, 1948.
(3) Elizabeth Jones[10] Ellison, b. May 2, 1953.
(See V.H.G. page 165 for Mr. Burrell M. Ellison, Jr.)
2. Charles Duke Holland, b. April 25, 1929, married.-- has two adopted children--is now serving with the Army in Germany.

COLLIER of SURRY

John Collier who appears in Surry in 1668 is the first of this family from whom descent is clearly traced. He may have been a son of Thomas Collier (Coluer) who, on Oct. 31, 1643, acknowledged a debt to John Flowers of 4000 lbs. tbco. to be paid each year beginning Oct. 31, 1643 (B 1, p. 112, Recorded 1657).

In 1659 George Stephens and Susanna, his wife, sold 300 acres to Edward Collier on Chippokes Creek called "Cabin Point". (B 1, p. 143) Edward Collier of Charles City in 1668 sold this 300 acres called "Cabin Point" to Richard Rogers. Witnesses: John Banks and John Rawlings. (B 1, p. 321)

John Collier was a nephew of this Edward Collier, for at the same time the above deed was executed Edward Collier gave a power of attorney to his "loving cousin" (nephew), John Collier. (Do)

John Collier married Mary, possibly a daughter or relative of Thomas and Ann Sowerby, which is proven by the following records. John Collier died in 1676 for an inventory of his estate was filed May 27, 1676. (D. B. 1671-84, p. 151) On Sept. 24, 1677, a marriage contract between John Rawlings and Mary Collier was made. "John Rawlings and Mary Collier now being disposed to marry it is agreed upon that John Rawlings has no right nor title to estate of Mary Collier, signed before marriage Sept. 24, 1677". Wits.: Thomas and Ann Sowerby. (D. B. 1671-84, p. 172). On Nov. 15, 1677, another inventory of John Collier's estate was presented by John King. Mary Rawlings. the relict, appeared in court and certified to the correctness of the inventory. (B 2, p. 15).

On May 7, 1678, Thomas Sowerby recorded the following gift, "Thomas Sowerby about 4 years since gave John Collier, son of John Collier, deceased, one yearling and prays that gift be recorded for good of the child". (D. B. 1671-84, p. 171). In 1679 an inventory of John Collier's estate in hands of John Rawlings was filed and the names of the orphans of the deceased were shown as Thomas, John, Joseph and Mary Collier. (Do. p. 211).

Thomas Sowerby died about 1694 and his widow, Ann, married James Jordan. She made a will as Anna Jordan Oct. 2, 1697 and gave a servant boy to John Rawling's son.

Children of John and Mary Collier:
I.   Thomas. In 1683 a court decree gave permission to Thomas Collier to live permanently with Thomas Sowerby provided Thomas gave bond to teach John Collier "the rudiments of Christian religion and bring him up according to his quality". Thomas Collier was a horseman in the Surry Militia in 1687; was a Justice of the County Court in 1714 and High Sheriff in 1720. His will was recorded in Surry Mar. 20, 1725 as follows:
(D. B. 1715-30, Part 3, p. 795). Will of Thomas Collier of Surry: "to grandson, Thomas, plantation whereon I now

78

dwell and all land thereunto belonging on south side of Mill
Swamp and also my water mill and 2 acres adjoing; to
grandson, John Collier, all my land on north side of Mill
Swamp except 2 acres already given to grandson Thomas;
to my daughter-in-law, Jane Lowther for life or widowhood
one third of the plantation whereon she now dwells, then to
grandson, John. To grandson, Thomas, plantation in Isle of
Wight where Thomas Browning now liveth, 220 acres; to
grandson, John Collier, 220 acres whereon William Wood
now liveth in Isle of Wight adjoining Alchamoufork Swamp.
To grandson, Thomas, all stock of cattle on plantation
where Thomas Browning does live to be delivered to him
when he attains the age of 18; to grandson, John, stock of
cattle on plantation where William Wood does live when he
attains the age of 18. Four negroes to daughter, Sarah Marriott, wife of William Marriott; to grandson, Thomas, when
he attains age of 18 years, 3 negroes in consideration of
his part of his father's estate the same being in my hands
received of his mother; same to grandson, John, when he
attains age of 18; to granddaughter, Mary Marriott, 1 bed,
1 rug, 1 blanket and new sheets when she is 18 or married;
to grandsons, Thomas and John. Executor, son-in-law
William Marriott and grandson, Thomas". Witnesses: Nicholas Maggett, Robert Watkins, Henry Barnes.
     Children:
1. John, died in 1716. His wife, Jane, was appointed admnx.
   of his estate July 18, 1716. She married John Lother who
   was appointed admns. with her in 1718. (B 7, p.22). She
   was Jane Thomas, dau. of William THOMAS.
   Jane (Collier) Lother made her will as follows:
   "To grand dau. Rebecca Andrews, one half dozen leather
   chairs, etc. To grand-daughter, Pricilla Andrews,
   three chests and four cattle to be equally divided among
   her four granddaughters. To dau. Martha Andrews, a
   side saddle. Sons Thomas and John Collier to be exrs.
   To dau. Martha Andrews rest of estate. Dated Jan. 28,
   1740-1; prob. May 20, 1741. Wits.: Nicholas Maget,
   Peter Warren, Benj. King (B 9, p.332)
        Children of Jane (Thomas) and John Collier:
   (1) Thomas, not 18, 1727.
   (2) John, not 18, 1727.
2. Sarah, m. William Marriott.

II.   John. The following interesting court order was entered in
      April, 1683 concerning him:
         "John Collier, son of John Collier, decd., having for-
      merly lived with John Rawlings who entered into bond to
      teach said Collier rudiments of the Christian religion
      and bring him up according to his quality but said Col-
      lier now living with Thomas Sowerby and said Rawlings
      in court consenting that he should continue there provided,
      etc.". (O.B. 1671-90, p.413).
      He was in the list of foot soldiers in 1687 and an inventory
      of his estate was filed in 1693. William Goodman who moved

to North Carolina was guardian of his orphans. (D 5, p.49).
III. Mary
IV. Joseph, m.Jane, dau. of William and Susan Halso of Surry
which is proven by a deed made in 1718 by William Halso
as follows: (Deeds 1715-30, p.115)
"William Halso of Surry to William Cocke for 25 lbs.
plantation of 165 acres called Swan's Bay purchased of
George Nicholson, decd. Dec.2, 1695 adjoining Robert
Nicholson and William Cocke, reserving 40 acres which
my son-in-law, Joseph Collier, holds and the land I gave
my son, William Halso, decd., being 50 acres and 4
acres to Mr. John Simmons May 21, 1718. Witnesses:
Harry Floyd, Nicholas Cock and Thomas Cocke".
Joseph's children were:
1. John, d. 1732 (See later)
2. Joseph Collier
3. William Collier
4. Thomas Collier
5. Mary Collier
6. Jeane Collier
7. Elizabeth Collier
8. Sarah Collier

John Collier, son of Joseph, married Sarah, dau. of Samuel
BRIGGS. His will was probated in 1732 as follows: (Deeds and
Wills 1730-38, Vol. I, Part II, p.246.)
Will of John Collier of Surry: to daughter Mary 1 guinea and
to Moses Johnson 1 guinea and all he owes me; to son, John,
plantation whereon he lives and what he owes me; to son, William,
1 guinea; son Thomas, land; dau. Gr____; son Benjamin; son
Charles; son Henry; remainder of money and pewter to be divided
between Benjamin, Henry and Charles; son Henry to son William
until he comes of age of 21; give son Charles to Moses Johnson
until he comes of age of 21; appoints Moses Johnson and sons
John and Thomas, executors. Dated 7/3/1732. Witnesses: Wm.
Hus, Solomon Hawkins, Charles Lucas.
His children were: Mary, m. Moses JOHNSON; William;
Thomas; Grace; Benjamin; Charles; and Henry Collier.

Moses Johnson chose William Lucas as guardian, April 18,
1711. He was born about 1697; was sub-sheriff of Surry in 1716;
Inspector of Warehouses for Merchant-Brandon and Cabin Point,
1731, and patented 1737 acres in Brunswick in 1732. His wife
was Mary, daughter of John Collier. His inventory was recorded
in Sussex, Feb. 18, 1762.
Children:
I. Lewis Johnson, m. (1) Elizabeth Moore, daughter of Thomas Moore the Elder, and his wife, Mary; Elizabeth died
Feb.4,1767. Lewis married (2) Dec.3, 1768, Mary Heron;
Mary died April 17, 1771. Lewis married (3) Lucy Ezell,
Sept. 16, 1772. Lewis' will is recorded in Sussex Mar.16,
1786.
Children of first marriage:
1. Mary Johnson, b.Feb.11,1753, m.Silvanus Bell and had:

(1) John Bell, b.Dec.24, 1772;
(2) Elizabeth Bell, b. July 11, 1772; (?)
(3) James Bell, b. Feb.11, 1774.
2. Jemima Johnson, b.July 13, 1772; m.William Stuart
(See STUART).
3. Peggy Johnson, b. Nov.15, 1757.
4. Rebeckah Johnson, m._____ Thomas.
5. Benjamin Johnson, b. Aug.19, 1750 or 1760 (Not clear)
6. Elizabeth Johnson, b.May 31, 1766.
Children of second marriage:
7. Edmund Johnson, b.Dec. 12, 1769.
8. Robert Johnson, b.Dec. 6, 1770.
Children of third marriage:
9. John Johnson, b.Aor. 21, 1773.
10. Swan Johnson.

II.　Moses Johnson Jr. owned plantations in Sussex and Brunswick. He petitioned to build a water grist mill in 1746; he was Overseer of the Highways in 1749; commissioned as Ensign of Brunswick Militia in 1749; and as Lieutenant in 1756; was Gentleman Justice, 1758. He made his will in Sussex in 1763. His wife, Mary, died Nov.18, 1772.

Children:
1. William Johnson, d. before 1776; wife Elizabeth_____.
He had children:
(1) William Johnson
(2) James Johnson, m. Elizabeth; d. 1785; had: Frederick,—
Benjamin and 3 other sons.
(3) Rebecca Johnson, b. Sept. 7, 1747.
(4) Charlotte Johnson, b. Aug. 11, 1748.
(5) Elizabeth Johnson, b. Aug.30, 1750.
(6) Nathaniel Johnson, b. Aug.25, 1762.
2. Moses Johnson, m. Agnes Battle, Jan.20, 1767; m. (2) Sally Girl, Feb. 1, 1786. He gave aid in American Revolution together with son Moses (Tyler's Quarterly, Vol. 6, p.109); d. 1789. Children:
(1) David Johnson.
(2) Moses Johnson.
(3) Nathan Johnson.
(4) Sarah Johnson, m.James Moore, April 3, 1774.
3. Richard Johnson, inherited land in Brunswick; wife Lucy; they had son, William, b. Dec. 4, 1762.
4. Elizabeth Johnson.
5. Ann Johnson, m. Burwell Gilliam and had following children:
(1) Patty Gilliam, b. Nov. 25, 1746.
(2) Franky Gilliam, b. Oct. 22, 1747.
(3) William Gilliam, b. Oct. 11, 1749.
(4) Anne Gilliam, b. Mar. 3, 1752.
(5) Rebecca Gilliam, b. Jan.3, 1755.
(6) Moses Gilliam, b. Nov. 17, 1756.
(7) Miles Gilliam, b. Feb. 21, 1759.
(8) Wyatt Gilliam, b. Apr. 6, 1762.
6. Martha Johnson, m. Anselm Gilliam and had the following

children:
- (1) Richard Gilliam, b. Oct. 24, 1757.
- (2) Robert Gilliam, b. June 20, 1761.
- (3) Stephen Gilliam, b. July 21, 1759.
- (4) Carter Gilliam, b. Oct. 6, 1763.
- (5) Martha Gilliam, b. Mar. 4, 1766.
7. Lucy Johnson.
8. Sarah Johnson.

COKER, COFFER, COFER, COCER, COPHER of SURRY

The name "Coker" was spelled in various ways by the county clerks as they spelled by sound in the early days. Often in a single document names were spelled differently. Sometimes the same name was spelled in four of five different ways. It does not seem that the name "Coker" was derived from "Corker" but "Coffer", "Cofer" and "Copher" were derived from "Coker" as shown later.

A John Coker, aged 20, appears in the muster of William Gayne and Robert Newman in Elizabeth City taken in February 1623/24 (Hotten-253). On November 21, 1624, John Coker made a deposition "touching the difference betwwen Capt. Ralph Hamor and Justinian Cooper and his wife". He said he was servant only to Ensign James Harrison, deceased, and not to John Cofter or David Barry and knew nothing about any agreement between the three. He also said that James Harrison had no part or parcel of what was bought off of Mr. Robert Bennett, decd. by John Cofter or David Barry. (M.C.G.C.-35). Justinian Cooper who married Ann, wife of Ensign James Harrison, patented 1050 acres in Isle of Wight, Sept. 13, 1636, at head of Lawnes Creek. Among his headrights was John Coker who evidently had made a voyage to England and returned (C.P.47)

A John Coker, aged 21, embarked on the "Plaine Joan" for Virginia, Capt. Richard Barham, May 15, 1635 (Hotten 79).

An early immigrant to Virginia was William Coffer of Surry who first appears in that county in 1640. John Spiltimber on Nov. 16, 1648, patented 100 acres of land in James City county, now Surry, "lying about $1\frac{1}{2}$ miles above Smith's Fort Creek, bounded Westerly upon the land of JOHN CORKER, Southerly upon a swamp that parts it from the land of Thomas Warren, 50 acres formerly granted to WILLIAM COFFER, Feb.10, 1640 and purchased of him, and 50 acres for the transportation of Dorothy Bishop" (C.P. 185).

A Mr. William Cocker, probably a resident of Nansemond, married the relict of Capt. John Whitby and was much involved in defending suits for debts against the Captain. These suits were brought between April 20 and March 29, 1672, when an order was entered to have the Sheriff of Nansemond bring his attorney, James Hyre, before the next General Court (M.C. 215, 217, 218, 234, 304). Captain John Whitby may have been a ship captain. He patented 1450 acres in Northumberland May 15, 1661.

William Coffer's place in Surry appears to be next to John Corker's land and these very similar names appearing together are confusing. It was first assumed that the two families were the same but the Corker family died out in the male line. However, the above entry of 1640 may have referred to William Corker, son of John Corker, who died without male heirs (See Corker, S.V.F. p.170).

There was a Coker family long seated at Mapowder in Dorset. Their arms were "Argent on a bend gules 3 Leopard faces" and their pedigree connects with many distinguished families (Baker's Northampton, Vol. II-266; Hutchins Dorset III-723; Collinsons Somersett II-343). A Robert Coker of Mapowder, born 1563, died 1624, had three sons with names very similar to hose of the Cokers of Surry, namely: William, b. 1598, Robert, b. 1605; Thomas, b. 1610. The wills of this family are numerous and should be searched. This is suggested because several wrong connections have been submitted.

A John[1] Cocer was a headright of William Boddie who patented 3350 acres of land in Isle of Wight at the head of Cypress and Western branches July 12, 1665, for the transportation of 67 persons. Among the list of persons whose headrights he probably bought was "John Cocer" (C. P. 476).

This John[1] Cocer, name now spelled "Coker", was probably the John Coker who was a witness to the will of Henry Combs Oct. 11, 1677, in Isle of Wight (Bk 2, p. 156). John[1] Coker was also a witness to the marriage of Hugh Bressie and Sarah Campion, Quakers, May 14, 1680. (Chapman's Mar. p. 103)

On April 20, 1684, John Coker received a grant of 400 acres on Cypress Swamp in the Lower Parish of Surry for the transportation of 8 persons (P. B. 5-371). One year after his first grant, April 20, 1685 John Coker received a grant of 1450 acres. This patent included the former 400 acres and the land was described as being on "Cypress Swamp of ye main Blackwater in the Lower Parish of Surry" (Id. 464).

John[1] Coker appears in the list of tithables in Surry in 1683, 1688, by himself, but in the tithables of 1694 he had two tithables, the other one being William "Cocker", his only son, showing that William was then over 16 years of age. The name is "Cocker" in 1694, "Coker" in 1698 and "Cocker" in 1702 (Colonial Surry) "Coker" may have been given the English accent of "Cocker" or "Coccer"" in those days.

John Turner in his will dated 1705 in Isle of Wight gave sons James and John the plantation where JOHN COFFER did live and sons Joseph and Simon land on Boddie's Branch (C-1-63). This seems to identify John Coker as the person of that name who was a headright of William Boddie in 1665. The above way of spelling "Coker" was another variation for Turner was referring to John Coker of this text. (See later).

John Coker and Margaret Coker, his wife, of Lawnes Creek Parish, Surry, on Mar. 3, 1687/8 sold to Richard Bennett, the younger, of the Upper Parish of Isle of Wight, 450 acres granted to him April 20, 1685 on Blackwater and in the Parish of Lawne's Creek (D. B. 3-31). On July 5, 1690, John and Margaret Coker sold to SION HILL for 1600 lbs. of tobacco 160 acres on Blackwater adjacent to Richard Bennett (Id. 143).

Sion Hill had married Mrs. Elizabeth Spiltember, widow of John Spiltember, who died in 1677. It will be recalled that John Spiltember patented 100 acres in 1648, 1½ miles above the head of Smith's Fort Creek adjacent to the land of John Corker and Thomas Warren. John Corker had witnessed the will of Thomas

Warren dated Mar. 16, 1669 (V.H.G.-246). From this it has been surmised that John Coker had deeded land near Spiltimber and the Corkers which he had inherited from Capt. John Corker. However, it is plainly shown here that this land had not been inherited but had been patented by John Coker on the Blackwater. Also Sion Hill resided on the Blackwater and not on Spiltimber lands for the will of Col. William Browne, dated 4 December 1704, and proved at a Court at Southwark for Surry County, Va., on 3 July 1705, contained the following clause:

"The land whereon Sion Hill lives and has built a mill contained in my patent of a tract of land on the South side of Blackwater, my will is that my herinafter named Executor do make a conveyance of said land to said Sion Hill beginning at the nearest place of the said land to down to the lower end, the said Hill having already made satisfaction for the same".

On April 11, 1693, John and Margaret Coker of Lawne's Creek sold to Elizabeth Caufield 100 acres bought of Hon. John Lear, Esq. (Id. 286) On Feb. 15, 1692 they sold land to Anthony Evans adjacent to Sion Hill. Rec. Mar. 16, 1714 (W.B. 5-227). They sold to Sam Vasser, 70 acres Sept. 3, 1716 (W.B. 1715-30, p. 111)

Richard Bennett's daughter, Jane, married John[1] Coker's grandson, John[3] Coker. Richard Bennett in his will dated 1720 gave legacies to his daughter, Jane Coffer and to his grandchildren, Robert, John, Richard and Magdalen Coffer (See Bennett)

John Coker held 900 acres in the rent rolls of Surry in 1704. He was relieved of paying taxes July 18, 1701, when he probably reached the age of 60. This would make his date of birth in the year 1641. It would appear that he was 24 years of age when he came to Virginia (D.B. 1691-1714, p. 371).

Both John Coker and his wife lived to be aged. John's will is dated 1711 and recorded 1720. Margaret's will was dated Sept. 21, 1721 and recorded Dec. 20, 1721. Sons, grandsons and great grandsons are mentioned in their wills.

John Coker's will dated May 22, 1711 was as follows: to son WILLIAM COKER for life 100 acres of land at my upper old plantation and after his decease to his son JOHN Coker forever, to my wife, Margarette all rest of my lands and remainder of my estate whatever it may be, she to be sole executor. Wits: John Atkinson, John Phillips, Pricilla Coker. The same persons witnessed Margaret's will (W.B. 1713-30-281).

Margaret's will was as follows: to grandson, JOHN Coker 50 acres of land lying in Surry where he now lives, beginning at James Bennett's line to Saml. Vasser's line. To JOHN Coker Jr. that is the son of my grandson, JOHN Coker, 230 acres lying in Surry on W. side of Cypress Swamp, E. of Saml. Vasser and WILLIAM Coker's land. If said JOHN Coker Jr. die without issue land to his brother, THOMAS Coker. Appoint JOHN Coker, the father of said child and Anthony Evans to keep land in their possession until JOHN Coker Jr. is 18. Grandson JOHN Coker to have one bible, etc. at my son WILLIAM Coker's. All rest of my estate at WILLIAM Coker's I give to my son WILLIAM Coker. Rest of estate in general to grandson JOHN Coker to be executor (Do-384).

It appears from her will that Margaret was living with her son, William Coker.

William[2] Coker was the only known son of John[1] and Margaret Coker. He was living at the date of his mother's will 1721 but probably died soon afterwards. He married Margaret, dau. of Caleb Cartwright of Nansemond (Surry O.B. 1691, p. 30). Caleb is said to be a son of John Cartwright of Nansemond (Surry O.B. 1691, p. 30), and a grandson of John Cartwright who witnessed John Rolfe's will in Jamestown March 10, 1621/22 and was "among the living" there in the Census of February 16, 1623/24 (Col. Surry 63) (Hotten 174)

They had an only son, John[3] Coker who married Jane, daughter of Richard Bennett Jr. of Isle of Wight.

From the wills of John and Margaret Coker, also that of Richard Bennett, it appears that John and Jane Coker had the following children:

I.   John[4], m. Pricilla, dau. of James Geddings (See later).
II.   Thomas[4], m. Oliff (Olive), dau. of Thomas Ward (See later).
III.   Robert;
IV.   Richard;
V.   Magdalen.

John[4] Coker Jr. is said to have married Pricilla Geddings. She witnessed John Coker's will in 1720. John Jr. is mentioned in the will of his great grandmother, Margaret Coker as follows: "To John Coker, Jr., that is to say the son of my grandson, John Coker, 230 acres of land lying in Surry on w. side of Cypress Swamp, E. of Samuel Vassar and Wm. Coker's land on the West. If said John Coker shall die without issue then I give the said land to his brother, Thomas." John Coker Jr. seems to have been his father's eldest son. He lived on the above land in Surry. This land fell in St. Andrew's Parish, Brunswick, when a great area of Surry was cut off to form that county about 1720. He made his will Dec. 16, 1758, probated May 22, 1759 and named the following children: (Information about children from old letters).

I.   John[5], said to be the John Coker with sons William, Samuel and Jesse in Christian County, Ky.
II.   Joseph[5], m. Mary Aldridge of Roanoke, Va. (See later)
III.   Priscilla, m. her cousin, Thomas Coker and had Lt. Thomas Coker of Mars Bluff in the Revolutionary War.
IV.   William of Old Cherans, S.C., is said to have had sons, Francis, Nathan, Benjamin and others.
V.   James, said to be of Greenville Co., Va. (cut off from Brunswick). His will was dated Nov. 30, 1792, pro. 1793 (D.A.R. Mag. 1933, p. 295); children: Thomas, Sally, Dolly, Lucy, Betsy, Mafsey. This Thomas may be the one who died in Bibb Co., Ala. with will 1818.
VI.   Robert of Laurens, S.C., is said to have married an "Abercrombie" and had children Harper, Phillip, Robert and others.
VII.   Honour, m. Drury S. Smith.
VIII. Mary, m. _____ Floyd.

-   Joseph Coker, son of John , married Mary Aldridge of Roanoke, Va. He lived in Laurens Co., S.C. where he made his will

March 20, 1792 (Rec. Bk. A-71) and named the following children:
I.   William, not named in will because previously given his
      part, m. Honoria Garlington (See later)
II.   Drury, m. Betsy Gray, made his will in S. C.
III. Thomas, died 1835 in Harlan Co., Ky. Rev. War Pension
      S. 30957;
IV.   Collins.
V.   John, youngest son
VI.   Jeannette, m. Col Armstrong.

William Coker, son of above Joseph , m. 1780 in Orangeburg
District, Elizabeth Honoria Garlington, born 1760, daughter of
Christopher Garlington (1729-1805) of Charleston, S. C. William
made his will in Laurens, S. C. in 1830 (Bk. F p. 312, box 15).
Known children, probably had more;
I.   Ann Amanda (Nancy), b. Mar. 24, 1784, m. Isaac Dial in
      1801 (See later)
II.   Garlington (1790-1856) m. 1816, Martha Babb, b. 1799, had
      15 children: Abner, Henry, Drury, Harvey, Hastings, Nancy,
      Kellett, Polly, John, Martha, William, Benjamin, Robert,
      James, Joseph, m. Martha, dau. of Mary (Avery) and Cotten
      Attaway, d. Athens, Texas, 1906.
III. James Geddings, had Drury, Nancy, James, Aldridge and
      William.

Nancy Amanda Coker, b. Mar. 24, 1784, d. Aug. 7, 1826; m.
1801 as his first wife, Isaac Dial, b. Feb. 19, 1772, d. May 18,
1835, m. Laurens, S. C., son of Col. Hastings Dial and his wife,
Rebecca, dau. of Attorney General James Abercrombie. Mr. Dial
made his will Mar. 14, 1835 in Laurens County (will not copied,
names and number of children not known).

Captain Garlington Coker Dial, son of Isaac Dial, b. Mar. 20,
1810, d. 1861 near Hearne, Texas, m. 1845 Pamelia Scrogan, b.
1818, d. 1878, dau. of John Scrogan (1770-1841) and wife, Mary
Long (1775-1839) of Caddo Parish, La; son of Capt. John Scrogan
and wife, Ann Wagoner. Children:
I.   Mary I. H. Dial, m. Major J. B. Scruggs (See later)
II.   Emma M. Dial, m. Wm. Hearne
III. Martha Dial, m. Dr. John Carrington
IV.   Robert Dial, m. Mary B. Carnshaw

Mary Isabella Hasting Dial, daughter of Captain Garlington Coker Dial, born 1846, d. 1910, m. Major James Briscoe Scruggs,
born Jan. 5, 1868 in Robertson County, Texas, died Oct. 2, 1939,
in Dallas, Texas, married Nov. 18, 1890 Marion Stuart Price, born
July 18, 1869 in Jessamine County, Ky. Mrs. Scruggs was educated
at Mary Nash College. Mr. Scruggs was educated at the University
of the South, Sewanee, Tenn., and was the owner and founder of
Gross R. Scruggs Insurance Co., and Agency, Dallas, Texas. He
also was interested in ranching in Stephens County, Texas on which
was located large coal and oil deposit. He was a Trustee of the First
Presbyterian Church at Dallas and an active member thereof until
his death. Children:
I.   Margaret Ann, b. Feb. 18, 1892, m. Raymond Percy Carruth
      (See Lane)

II.   Stuart Briscoe, b. Dec. 14, 1894, m. Bess Thornton.

Thomas[4] Coffer, son of Jane (Bennett) and John Coffer lived in Isle of Wight. His will was dated Nov. 3, 1783, recorded Feb. 4, 1784 (W. B. I, 1779-85, p. 213). His wife Oliffe was a daughter of Thomas Ward who died in 1728. Oliffe Coffer on Mar. 22, 1784 deeded her son, Jacob, land she had inherited from her father Thomas Ward, decd. (D. B. 15-399). This Thomas Ward was a son of Thomas Ward of Surry who made his will in Surry Feb. 20, 1678; pro. July 4, 1675; Legatees: wife Eliza; son Thomas Ward $\frac{1}{2}$ my land; son John Ward land, the rest between my wife and all my children. Exrs. Friends Jas. Reddick and Jos. Richeson; Wits: John Person, James Stringfellow (Surry Bk. II, p. 2). In 1697, John Ward and wife Elliner sold to Thomas Ward, both of Lawnes Creek, 100 acres formerly granted Wm. Cook and left to me by will of my father. Wits: Henry Gray, Jas. Briggs, James Bynam, Joseph Ford (Surry 1694-1709 -217). In 1707, Thomas Ward bought 100 acres of land on 1st swamp of Blackwater in Isle of Wight from Robert and Elinor Monger (I of W B 2-184). Thomas sold his home plantation in Surry in 1710 and moved to Isle of Wight where he had acquired more land. His wife Joanna was a daughter of Francis Reyner of Isle of Wight who made his will Sept. 29, 1716 and mentions his daughter Joanna, wife of Thomas Ward (G. B. #2, p. 9). Thomas Ward in his will dated April 15, 1727 mentions his dau. Olive

Thomas and Olive Copher raised a large family all evidently reaching maturity as he mentions several grandchildren in his will. Children:
I.   Thomas, m. Eliz. Moody. (See later)
II.   James, m. (1) Mary Simmons, (2) Mourning Pitman. (See later)
III.   Jacob, m. Milly Braswell, Dec. 26, 1793.
IV.   Olive, m. _____ Griffin.
V.   Charity, m. Jesse Holleman.
VI.   Mary, m. John Stephenson.
VII.   Ann, m. _____ Pitman.
VIII.   Sarah, m. Hunter.
IX.   Jane, m. Dewell.

Thomas[5] Cofer, eldest son of Oliff and Thomas Cofer, married Elizabeth Moody. On Feb. 11, 1775, Thomas Cofer and Elizabeth his wife deeded land near Atkinson Bridge to the people of the Baptist Society "one acre more or less for a place to meet at for the worship of Almighty God." (D. B. 13-308). In the possession of Mrs. Russell Syer Barrett of Smithfield, Virginia, who kindly furnished this information about the Cophers, is a list of Thomas Copher's children "Transcribed from Gill's Divinity" formerly owned by the Rev. Josepher Cofer, 5th child of Thomas and Elizabeth Cofer as follows:
I.   Diana Cofer, born Aug. 16, 1768.
II.   Moody Cofer, born May 20, 1770.
III.   Samuel Cofer, born Oct. 3, 177-.
IV.   Mathew Cofer, born Jan. 24, 177-.
V.   Joseph Cofer, born Sept. 8, 1775
VI.   Cherry Cofer, born Apl. 7, 177-

VII.   Elizabeth Cofer, born Sept. 20, 177-
VIII. Nancy Cofer, born June 11, 1783
IX.   Thomas Cofer, born Feb. 28, 1785
X.   Isaac Cofer, born April 30, 1789
XI.   Patsy Cofer, born Nov. 12, 1791
    All eleven children and wife Elizabeth were mentioned in Thomas[6] Cofer's will, dated Nov. 29, 1802 and probated April 24, 1806 (Surry W. B. 1-712).

    Joseph[6] Cofer, son of Thomas[5] and Elizabeth, his wife, a Baptist Minister, married Sept. 15, 1799 (1) Jerusha Lancaster; (2) Sept. 7, 1824, Patsy Delk. He died Jan. 4, 1839.
        Children of 1st wife:
I.   Rebecca Cofer, born Sept. 27, 1800
II.   Charity Cofer, born Aug. 27, 1802
III.   Susanna Cofer, born July 26, 1804
IV.   Isaac Cofer, born Oct. 26, 1806
V.   James H. L., born Nov. 28, 1808
VI.   Mathew M., born Nov. 2, 1810
VII.   William L., born Nov. 27, 1812
VIII. Martha C., born Aug. 24, 1814
IX.   Josiah Cofer, born Sept. 24, 1816
X.   Elizabeth M., born July 10, 1818
        Children of Joseph Cofer by second wife:
XI.   Mary V. Cofer, born Oct. 3, 1825
XII.   Thomas W. Cofer, born Mar. 22, 1827
XIII. Junius D. Cofer, born June 18, 1830

    James Henry Lancaster Cofer, 5th child of the Rev. Joseph Cofer, married Keturah Jones of Isle of Wight, dau. of Abraham Jones, Jan. 26, 1832. He died Dec. 2 or 3, 1863. Keturah Jones Cofer was born June 29, 1810 and died Sept. 12, 1888. Children from "Gills Divinity":
I,   Andrew Jackson Cofer, born June 27, 1833
II.   Ann P. Cofer, born July 27, 1835
III.   Joseph Abraham, born Mar. 9, 1837
IV.   James Owens, born Mar. 14, 1839
V.   Octavius Adolphus, born Nov. 25, 1840
VI.   Nathan Pliny, born Nov. 15, 1842
VII.   Carson Pinkney, born May 11, 1884
VIII. Alonzo Malcom, born July 20, 1847
IX.   Thos. Jefferson, born July 1, 1849
X.   Alberta Keturah, born July 1, 1849

    Carson Pinkney[8] Cofer, 7th above child, m. Dec. 22, 1868, Margaret Sarah Parker, dau. of Wm. H. Parker and Sarah (Everett) Parker.

    James[5] Copher, second son of Oliff and Thomas Copher, married in 1761 Mary, daughter of James Simmons of I. of W. who died before Sept. 5, 1751. A guardians account recorded on that date for his children shows that Mary Simmons, his daughter, was born March 13, 1740 (Guar. Acct. Bk. 4). She died before Aug. 1785, as James married, secondly, Mourning Pitman on Aug. 2, 1785. James died before June 6, 1796, as his will was probated on that date. Children: (All marriges from I. of W.

marriage bonds): 1. Olif, m. _____ Gray; 2. Joanna, m. John
Cooks, of Southampton, Dec. 20, 1783; 3. Cloe, m. Edward Gay,
Oct. 26, 1786; 4. Mary m. Jesse Edwards, April 17, 1794;
5. James, m. Susanna Brock, Aug. 21, 1801; 6. Ann m. John
Edwards, Mar. 5, 1798; 8. Sally; 9. Winifred m. Daniel Whiteley
Mar. 24, 1811. Children of second wife: 10. Rhoda; 11. Jermima;
12. Nathan (O. B. 1797, p. 82)

James[6] Cofer, Jr., son of Mary (Simmons) and James Cofer
Sr., married Aug. 26, 1801, Susanna Brock, dau. of William
Brock, of I. of W. Mr. Brock's will was probated Sept. 7, 1807
(W. B. 12). James Jr. died seven years after his marriage leaving
three orphan daughters. His wife married, secondly, William
Hicks, Nov. 16, 1809. Children of James Jr.:
I.   Margaret Cofer, m. May 17, 1818, Robert Montgomery.
II.   Winifred Cofer, m. Dec. 24, 1822, Watson White.
III.   Polly S. Cofer, m. Jan. 22, 1822, Wm. C. Edwards. (See
        later)

Polly[7] S. Cofer at the age of 15 married William Chapman Edwards, aged 18. He was the only child of William Chapman Edwards Sr., and his wife, Holland Edwards. William Jr. was born
in 1804 and died in 1863. He was appointed Deputy County Clerk
in 1829 and made a Justice of the County Court March 15, 1832.
The plantation where he lived was on James River near Margaret's
Beach. As a widower 54 years of age, he married secondly, Ro-
setta Nock, aged 24, single, from Accomac County, Dec. 2, 1858.
His will was probated Sept. 7, 1863. Children:
I.   Christopher Edwards, killed in an accident.
II.   James, m. Peninnah Stringfield, 1853.
III.   Marth C. m. _____ Arthur.
IV.   Sarah Jane, m. John Mitchell.
V.   Mary Ann, m. Robert Barrett (See later) 1855.
VI.   Evilina m. Barzilla Joyner, May 4, 1858. They lived in
        Richmond, Va. Children: Walter Joyner, Lillie m. Mr.
        Lytle, no children: Evelyn m. Mr. Schakleford.

Mary Ann[8] Edwards, daughter of Polly Cofer and William C.
Edwards, born 1832, married Robert Foster Barrett, April 26,
1855 and died in Smithfield, Va., June 21, 1897. He was born 1820
in Portsmouth, Va., moved to Smithfield in 1855 and lived there
until his death in 1891. Children:
I.   Robert Smith Barrett, b. 1856, d. 1870.
II.   Ida Belle Barrett, b. Aug. 25, 1857, d. Nov. 25, 1928, m.
        John Rouse of Smithfield; Children:
        1. Park Shepard[9] Rouse, b. Oct. 9, 1891; m. Sept. 15, 1914,
           Pauline Dashield, b. Feb. 17, 1891. Children:
           (1) Park Shepherd Rouse Jr., b. July 20, 1915, com-
               missioned Ensign in Navy Aug. 26, 1942, entered
               Harvard Oct. 1, 1942, where he graduated in Naval
               Communications 1943-44, served on U. S. S. James
               O'Hara.
           (2) Randolph Dashiel Rouse, b. Dec. 30, 1916, commis-
               sioned Ensign in Navy May 19, 1942, reported for
               duty in Washington with Bureau of Ships.

(3) John Dashiell Rouse, b. Apl. 3, 1919; May 19, 1942 inducted in Army at Camp Lee, Va., as a private 8th Armored Division, commissioned 2nd. Lieut. in 1943, served in Newfoundland and elsewhere until end of World War II. He was recalled to active duty December 1950 from Army Reserve. He was killed in action Sept. 2, 1951, while leading his mortar company in against the Chinese Communists in Korea. He was posthumously awarded the Silver Star for gallantry in action. He was a graduate of Washington and Lee University and belonged to Pi Kappa Alpha fraternity. He married Anne Colonna of Hampton and left one son, John D. Rouse, Jr.

(4) William Rouse, b. 1925, entered the Navy Dec. 10, 1943, and was assigned to the Hospital Ship "Refuge" and served throughout World War II.

III. Albert Sydney[8] Barrett, b. 1861, m. Julia Deane Cofer, and had Andrew J. and Mollie Cofer on June 11, 1884 and Robert Cofer Barrett, b. Feb. 2, 1885, d. Dec. 5, 1922 and two other children who died in infancy.

IV. William Edward Barrett, b. 1863.

V. Frederick Mitchell[9] Barrett was born Nov. 17, 1869 and died Feb. 10, 1918, at Newport News, Va. He resided in Smithfield for a short time and went to Newport News to live May 1894. Children:

1. Charles Syer Barrett, b. Aug. 25, 1898,

2. William Sydney Barrett, b. Feb. 1, 1896, Lieut Colonel in U.S. Army, m. Bertha G. Loeffer, Aug. 31, 1917, divorced June 19, 1928; m. (2) Nellie Minon of Texas. They have adopted two children, Barbara Ann in 1937 and Wm. Sydney in 1939.

3. Russell Syer Barrett, b. Aug. 5, 1897, m. Ethel Alexander Fowler, April 15, 1927 and have one child, Russell Syer Barrett, b. Dec. 27, 1928. Mr. Barrett was recalled to the Navy on Dec. 1942 with rank of Lieut Commander and was promoted to Commander April 1943.

4. Frank Syer Barrett, b. April 10, 1899, married Anita O. Kloss of Switzerland June 10, 1922. Children:
   (1) Elaine May Barrett, b. Aug. 20, 1923, Newport News, Va.
   (2) Barbara Anne Barrett, b. Aug. 30, 1925, Clearwater, Fla.

5. Frederick Mitchell Barrett Jr., b. April 10, 1899, m. Ann Lee Cowling, April 24, 1926, was called to Navy Dec. 1942 with rank of Lieut. Commander. Children:
   (1) Frederick Mitchell Barrett III, b. Oct. 15, 1931, appointed apprentice in Va. Pilots Association Oct. 1951.
   (2) Anne Littleton Barrett, b. Oct. 26, 1932, m. Richard Madison Driver, Sept. 2, 1951.

6. Robert Syer Barrett, b. Jan. 13, 1908, m. Myrtle May Curry of Huntington, W. Va., April 26, 1940. He entered active service in Army April 1940 as 1st. Lieut. Aviation Medical Corps; Nov. 1, 1941, promoted to Captain. Flight

Surgeon Sept. 27, 1941. August 1942, promoted to Major
Medical Staff in 13th Bombardment Group. Children:
(1) Grace Syer Barrett, b. Jan. 22, 1941, Washington D.C.
(2) Robert Syer Barrett II, b. Jan. 22, 1943, New York, N.Y.

COFER OF BEDFORD COUNTY, VIRGINIA

Thomas Cofer, the first of the name from whom this family is traced, lived in Culpepper County. It is probable that he was a descendant of the Isle of Wight Cofers. His wife was named "Mary" family name unknown. He may have been the Thomas Cofer who was a vestryman of the Pohick Church.

Thomas Cofer made his will in Culpepper County, April 24, 1782, same probated Dec. 17, 1791. He bequeathed to wife MARY all realty and personalty for life. "Son JAMES having had an equal part with the rest I hope he will be content therewith. ...to son JOSIAS five pounds; son JESSE, ten pounds; after legacies are paid, sons JACOB, JOEL, GEORGE and REUBEN to have what is left equally divided; to son REUBEN, 90 acres I bought off of John Stockdill adjoining Joel Cofer; to son JAMES, 90 acres I had of James Rucker, and 10 acres of Mr. Twain; to daughter ELIZABETH 20 pounds; daughter ANNE GIBSON five pounds; to daughter PHEBE a negro. George Anderson and Joel Cofer, extrs. Wits.; Joseph and Nathan Underwood, Charles Cock. (W. B. "D"-38)

Josias Cofer, son of Thomas, moved to Bedford County, Va., and married Mary Catherine, daughter of John Christopher Lauchart. He made his will April 14, 1814, probated Aug. 22, 1814, as follows: ...to wife MARY land I live on and certain negroes for life. After her death, son OBDIAH to have land for his life under the care of Cathy Lauchart, and after his death for her trouble she was to have land for her life; then the land to be divided between GEORGE, JEMIMA and THOMAS. Son JACOB to have tract where he lives at $3.50 per acre; son JESSE tract where he lives at $10.00 per acre; son GEORGE tract where he lives and tract bought of William Harris at $5.00 per acre; daughter JEMIMA 200 acres at Elk Creek at $7.00; son THOMAS tract of 200 acres next to Jemima at $7.00 per acre. Sons ABRAHAM and ELISHA and daughter SUSANNA to have equal part of personal estate to that of the other children on basis of land valuation. Sons Joseph and George Extrs. Wits. Jakey Leftwich, Dudley Jones, Joseph Slaughter. (W. B. 4-135.)

Children:

I.   Jacob, m. (1) Dec. 22, 1807, Virginia (Jimmy) Bateman; (2) March 27, 1827 Nancy Bateman.
II.   Abraham, m. Nov. 6, 1818 Barshaba Sharp
III.   Elijah
IV.   Obediah
V.   Jesse, died before 1843; m. Nov. 9, 1807 Sarah Crenshaw, dau. of David and Elizabeth Crenshaw.
VI.   Thomas, m. April 9, 1815 Lucretia E. Luck, dau. of Nathaniel Luck.
VII.   Joseph, m. March 1, 1796, Hope Sutton, dau. of Nathaniel Luck
VIII. George, m. (1) Frances Dawson Oct. 16, 1806; (2) Mary A. Cobb March 25, 1824. (See later)

IX.   Susannah, m. Aug.23, 1806, James Bunch
X.   Jamima Salmons Cofer, m. Mar. 9, 1815 Pleasant Dawson.

George Cofer, born Sept. 1, 1784; died Jan.8, 1831, Bedford Co., Va., married (1st) Oct. 16, 1806, Frances Dawson, born Oct. 13, 1786, Amherst Co., Va.; died June 27, 1823; daughter of Robert Dudley Dawson and Mary Lightfoot Slaughter. George Cofer married (2nd) March 25, 1824 Mary A. Cobb and had: Amanda FitzAlan who married Lafayette Lee and Mary E. who married John W. Andrews.
Children by first wife:
I.   Josias Eaton Cofer, b. Dec.26, 1807, m. Mary Reid
II.   Roderick Cofer, b. Nov.14, 1809, died April 3, 1910'
III.   James Madison Cofer, b. July 1, 1811, m. Mary Etta Duncan. (See later)
IV.   Catherine Lauchart Cofer, b. Mar.24, 1813, m.John Winston Schenck
V.   Pleasant Dudley Cofer, b. April 27, 1814, m. (1st) Anna Eliza Dawson, (2nd) Caroline R. Garrett
VI.   Minerva Cofer, b. June 15, 1816, m. William Barnett
VII.   Robert Cofer, b. Oct. 27, 1817, died 1822
VIII. Sarah Ann Cofer, b. Nov.9, 1819, m. Samuel Barnett

James Madison Cofer, born July 1, 1811, Bedford Co., Va.; died 1897 or 6?, Bedford Co., Va., married Feb.23, 1837, Mary Etta Duncan, born Feb. 23, 1819, Buckingham Co., Va.; died April 10, 1879; daughter of George Duncan and Elizabeth Walton. Rev. James Madison Cofer was ordained as a minister of the Protestant Methodist Church in May 1835 in Lynchburg by the Right Rev. W. M. Meade D.D. and ordained to the full work in Richmond in 1836 by the beloved Bishop Richard Channing Moore and held charges in Buckingham, Abingdon and Bedford Co. He also had at times charge of classical schools and a female academy at Abingdon and at Bedford (Liberty).
Children:
I.   George Bedell Cofer, b. Dec.17, 1837, m.Mary E. Ligon (See later)
II.   Martha Anne Cofer, b. Feb.29, 1840, d.Sept.22, 1855
III.   Mary Eliza Cofer, b. Feb. 7, 1842, d.April 22, 1842
IV.   Elizabeth Clay Cofer, b. Aug. 4, 1843, d. same day
V.   Sally Nelson Cofer, born April 12, 1853, d. June 16, 1853

George Bedell Cofer, born Dec. 17, 1837, Bedford Co., Va.; died Feb. 26, 1899, Chula, Amelia Co., Va.; married Aug.8, 1860, Amelia Co., Va., Mary Elizabeth Ligon, born Feb. 1, 1844, Washington Co., Va.; died Feb. 4, 1884, Chester, Chesterfield Co., Va., daughter of William Ligon and Martha Davis. One of the oldest telegraph operators in Va., he was appointed agent and operator at Chula, Va., for the Richmond and Danville R.R. on Mar. 1, 1862 and was connected with the R. & D.R.R. continuously up to his death.
Children:
I.   James Madison Cofer, b. May 13, 1861, m. Fannie Poindexter Spears (See later)
II.   Georgiana Dixon Cofer, b. Mar.18, 1864, m. Claiborne

Gooch Whitworth
III. Frank Henry Cofer, b. Nov. 28, 1866, m. Minerva Fields
IV. Charles Wm. Talcott Cofer, b. Jan. 27, 1869, m. Carrie
Sturdivant.
V. Grace Davis Cofer, b. May 22, 1871, m. James Curtis
Carter.
VI. Martha Blanche Cofer, b. Aug. 28, 1873, m. Henry Irwin
Carter.
VII. Mary Cofer (twin), b. Mar. 14, 1876, m. William Andrew
Light
VIII. Sarah Cofer (twin), b. Mar. 14, 1876, did not marry
IV. Ernest Cofer, b. Sept. 16, 1878, m. Corinna

James Madison Cofer, b. May 13, 1861, Chula, Amelia Co.,
Va.; died Sept. 24, 1924, Chester, Chesterfield Co., Va.; mar-
ried June 17, 1885, Hallsborough, Chesterfield Co., Va., Fannie
Poindexter Spears, born Feb. 1, 1857, Hallsborough, Chesterfield
Co., Va.; died Jan. 1, 1944, Richmond, Henrico Co., Va.,
daughter of William Edward Spears and Rebecca Porterfield Hund-
ley. James Madison Cofer was a railroad employe and telegraph
operator of the Seaboard R.R.
Children:
I. William Edward Spears Cofer, b. April 7, 1886, m. Edna
N. Gill
II. George Bedell Cofer, b. July 17, 1888, m. Ethel Hogwood
III. Julian Poindexter Cofer, b. Nov. 27, 1890, d. Jan. 23, 1891
IV. Mary William Cofer, b. Jan. 24, 1893, m. Jacob Krone
Halder II
V. Philip Hancock Cofer, b. May 11, 1895, m. Emma C. Ad-
kins (See later)
VI. Elizabeth Cofer, b. April 12, 1897, m. Wm. King

Philip Hancock Cofer, 2108 Kirkwood Ave., Charlotte 3, N.C.;
born May 11, 1895, Hallsborough, Chesterfield Co., Va.; married
Dec. 5, 1923, Elkton, Maryland, Emma Clifford Adkins, born
Feb. 17, 1903, Vienna, Dooly Co., Georgia, daughter of Tilden
Alvan Adkins and Florrie Salter Morgan. She was a U.S. Army
Nurse, Walter Reid Hospital. Philip H. Cofer was in the Lafayette
Esquadrille World War I. He has been associated with Ford cars
and tractors since World War I and is the Ford Tractor Dealer
in Rock Hill, S.C.
Children:
I. Philip Hancock Cofer, Jr., b. Feb. 20, 1926, m. Georgia
Ellen Wilson and have children: (1) Georgia Elizabeth Cofer,
b. Jan. 11, 1950, (2) Philis Clifford Cofer, born Jan. 14,
1953.
II. (Twin) Clifford Morgan Cofer, born Feb. 20, 1926, not mar-
ried.
Philip and Clifford Cofer were in the U.S. Air Force in
World War II.

DARDEN-DURDEN OF NANSEMOND

The ancient home of this family in England seems to have been at Dearden, a small town located near Edenfield in Lancaster. There was a family of this name long seated at Rockdale Manor who trace their descent from Elias de Duerden, of the time of Henry VI. However, the Durdens seem to have been located near Dearden as early as the 13th. century. (Cl. State Papers.) The Darden arms were:

"Gules, six crosses, croslet or on a chief or, a martlet gules" (Burke).

The ancestor of this family in the Southern states was Stephen Durden, who, on March 14, 1649, patented 150 acres in Upper Norfolk (Nansemond) "on the Eastward side of the Northwest Branch of Nansemond River at Indian Creek adjacent to George Chewing (Chewning) and Francis Maldin. Formerly granted unto Thomas Brice Oct. 19, 1643; 100 acres of which was granted to him by patent Nov. 11, 1640, and 50 acres for transportation of one person whose name was not given. Assigned to George Chewing (Chewning) who assigned same to said Durden" (C.P. 189)

It was Thomas Brice who patented the 100 acres in 1640 and not Stephen Durden as formerly stated. (C.P. 148)

On March 1, 1668, Stephen Durden patented 250 acres in Nansemond adjoining his own land and that of Robert Hooks, Israel Johnson, Thomas Powell and Thomas Gale. (Bk. 5-p. 208)

The records of Nansemond are destroyed, but Stephen left a will in that county dated 1679. This is shown by a grant to Jacob Darden of 435 acres in Isle of Wight in 1682 "land on the Western Branch of Nansemond River being one half of a patent granted to Robert Hooke and Bream and conveyed to Stephen Durden, late of Nansemond County. The same given to Jacob by order of the General Court 1681. (G.B. 7, p. 137) (17 C.-p. 693)

On April 30, 1694, John Darden was granted 300 acres of land in Nansemond, late in the possession of Stephen Durden, deceased, and found to escheat to their Sacred Majesties, land now granted to John Durden. (G.B. 8-p. 374.) (See also Bk. 9-p. 82)

Robert Hooke, on Aug. 6, 1692, of the Lower Parish of Isle of Wight sold to Jacob Darden, 200 acres part of 400 granted into Robert Hooke, deceased, Oct. 30, 1662. Administrator's Sale to Jacob Darden. (D.B. 1-48)

It appears from these grants that Stephen[1] Durden had two sons: Jacob of. Isle of Wight and John of Nansemond. John may be the John Darden who married Elizabeth, daughter of Edward Powers, Sr. (C.M-14)

Jacob[2] Darden, planter, of Isle of Wight on April 24, 1684, for 1000 lbs. tobacco sold 100 acres to William Murphy adjacent to Robert Hooke, Wits.: Robert Hooke, Thomas Oglethorpe. (17 C. 596). Jacob patented 330 acres in 1697. (G.B. 9-81). He, with consent of wife Anne sold $\frac{1}{2}$ of the above patent to Henry Pope, September 17, 1698. (17 C-635). Jacob Darden made his will April 14, 1719, probated Feb.29, 1718/20. He devised a to son STEPHEN all land in Wainoke Neck; to sons JOHN and BENJAMIN all land where my son Jacob lives at Currawaugh to be equally divided; sons JACOB and LAWRENCE all land I live on after their mother's death......son SAMUEL.. ; My son JACOB to have mill allowing his mother 20 bu. corn meal yearly. Have given to sons JOSEPH and HENRY no land, they to have 1000 lbs.tobacco when 21; to Thomas Giles child, my daughter's child, 1 sh; Wife Anne and son Jacob, extrs. Wits.: Wm. and Sarah Murphy, Charles Roberts (W & D.1-654.)

Jacob[3] Darden (Jacob[2] Stephen[1]) married Anne, a daughter of George Williamson, who in his will dated July 23, 1723, probated Oct.29, 1723, mentions his grandson Jacob Darden, evidently son of the above Jacob (17C-p.427). George Williamson's wife was Hester, the daughter of Colonel Joseph Bridger. (id.)

Joseph[4] Darden, Jr., on Aug.13, 1747 rendered an account of his father's Jacob's estate. Among the items received was one of "Cash my father received as a legacy to me from my grandfather George Williamson" (W.B.5, p.77; C.-2-130). Jacob[3] Darden married, secondly, a sister of Samuel Lawrence of Nansemond as he mentions his "brother-in-law Samuel Lawrence" in his will. Also Jeremiah Lawrence in his will probated Dec.2, 1756, gave a legacy to "Charles, the son of Jacob Darden". (W.B.6,p.246; C-2-180) on June 16, 1714, Jacob patented 54 acres on the east side of the Blackwater also Chowan River in Nansemond.

Jacob made his will Mar.25, 1739, probated Apr.27, 1741, as follows: "to son JACOB the manor plantation where I live provided he will acknowledge to son CHARLES the plantation where he dwells; if not CHARLES to have the manor plantation and the mill; to son CHARLES all land in Nansemond and £10 out of estate for schooling. Samuel Lawrence to take care of Charles until 19. Brother-in-law Samuel Lawrence and son Jacob, exrs. Wits.: George Lawrence, John Marshall. (   ) Estate appraisal returned July 5, 1750. Elizabeth Darden, administratrix.

Jacob[4] Darden, on Sep.7, 1749, sold to loving brother Charles Darden to fulfill father's will, one half of two patents of land granted Jacob Darden, the elder, by estimation 237 acres and bequeathed by said Darden to his son, Samuel, and sold by him to his brother JOSEPH of North Carolina, and made over to Jacob Darden,Jr., by Michael Reynolds and Elizabeth his wife. (D.B. 8-268). This was evidently the 247 acres of land patented by Jacob Darden, June 20, 1733, on s. side of Blackwater at land of Thomas Bracey and Stephen Darden. (P.B. 15, p.73) Jacob[4] Darden and wife Elizabeth signed the above deed. She was probably a daughter of John Murphy (and wife Sarah) who made a his will Dec.6, 1769, and mentioned his daughter Elizabeth Darden.

John Darden[3] (Jacob[2], Stephen[1]) son of Jacob[2] Darden who made his will April 14, 1719, and gave John land at Currawaugh, deeded this land March 6, 1775, to his loving son HARDY DARDEN, 200 acres north side of Currawaugh Swamp and Reedy Branch. (John moving) March 6, 1755. (D.B.9, p.335). It seems that

John[3] Darden was deeding his land to his sons instead of making a will for he made three other deeds to his sons and son-in-law.

On March 4, 1755, John[3] Darden of Isle of Wight, gentleman, and MARY his wife deeded to Joseph English, 150 acres of land. Id. 334). On March 6, 1775, he deeded to loving son, BENJAMIN DARDEN 320 acres on Chowan River. (Id. 334). On Feb. 23, 1763, John Darden for love and affection deeded JOHN DARDEN, JR., land on the north side of Flat Branch ruggning to Cogpit; to a marked tree on Col Bridger's land; to Jacob Spivey's; to Joseph English; John Powell and Abraham Johnson, 200 acres. Wits.: John Eley, Jr., Henry Hedgepeth, Hardy Darden. (D.B. 11-169).

Hardy[4] Darden (John[3] Jacob[2] Stephen[1]) made his will Oct. 2, 1773, probated Dec. 3, 1792, as follows; to son, HARDY DARDEN land where I now live; to son JOHN DARDEN 100 acres called "Bennett's", to daughter ALICE HOLLAND, negro called Hannah and what she already has; to son JONAS, Negro; to wife land and plantation where I now live...at her death to son DEMPSEY; to son Elisha....; Wits.; Jesse Watkins, Priscilla Watkins, Jethro Powell. (W.B. 10-239) (See S.V.F. Vol. 1. pp. 93-3). Hardy Darden was the great[2] grandfather of Mr. James G.W. MacClamroch of Greensboro, N.C., who was instrumental in obtaining this data about the Dardens. For his descent from Hardy Darden, see Vol. I pp. 92-93.

John[4] Darden, brother of Hardy Darden, was seemingly the John Darden who was a Captain in the Isle of Wight Militia in 1777. (17C. 187). In 1778 John Darden was appointed an Ensign in the company whereof John Darden was Captain. (Id. 188). In 1781 this John Darden was appointed a Second Lieutenant in the place of William Eley. (Id. 192)

John[4] Darden made his will May 11, 1788, probated Feb. 5, 1789. He gave a legacy to wife CHARITY; son, JOHN, plantation bought of Elisha Darden; son, HENRY GOODMAN DARDEN; son ELISHA: son MILLS; son, WILLIAM; daughter SALLIE; Henry Goodman and William Goodman to have charge of estate given sons HENRY GOODMAN and ELISHA DARDEN. Exrs.: Benj., ELEY. William Goodman, Henry Goodman; Wits. _____ ,

Joseph[3] Darden (Jacob[2], Stephen[1]) was given 3000 lbs. tobacco in the will of his father, Jacob[2], probated in Isle of Wight 1719. In the deed made by Jacob[4] Darden (Jacob[3], Jacob[4]) on Sept. 7, 1749, to his brother Charles in order to fulfill his father's will, it was stated that the 237 acres was bequeathed by the said Darden[2] to his son SAMUEL DARDEN, same to his brother JOSEPH DARDEN of NORTH CAROLINA, etc., (ante)

Joseph[3] Darden was residing in North Carolina and Samuel, his brother, was previously mentioned as being in Nansemond.

A Mrs. Anne Leigh made her will in Beaufort Precinct, N.C. Aug. 9, 1732, probated March Court 1732/33. She bequeathed to son SAMUEL DARDEN a plantation with three negroes; mentions son, JOSEPH DARDEN; daughters Anne Adams and Jane Watkins; grandsons JACOB DARDEN and James Adams; granddaughters Sarah Adams, and Mary Watkins. The executor was SAMUEL DARDEN, evidently her son. (Grimes 213)

It is evident that she was Anne, the widow of Jacob[2] Darden of Isle of Wight who died in 1719. She seems to have moved to

North Carolina with her sons Joseph and Samuel and had married secondly, a Mr. Leigh. The will of Joseph Darden, son of Anne Darden Leigh, of Bertie Precinct was dated Feb.18, 1733/4, probated at the August Court of 1735, - five months after Mrs. Leigh's will was probated. He bequeathed son WEST 119 acres of land; son JOSEPH 110 acres; son HENRY 320 acres; legacies to daughter AMERICA DARDEN and REBECCA DARDEN wife and executrix, Also. Executor, Arthur Williams, Wits.: Elizabeth Jones, Mary Powers, John Edgerton. (Grimes -91)

A Stephen Darden, Sr., was living in Nansemond on June 24, 1734, for on that day Benjamin Faircloth of Bertie Precinct, N.C., sold to STEPHEN DARDEN, SR., of Upper Parish of NANSEMOND, 200 acres on the s. side of the Blackwater granted to Faircloth's father Nov.13, 1713, and he to son land and water mill; and he to STEPHEN DARDEN. Wits.: Jacob Darden, John Darden. (BK.4-327)

John Durden, said to be the son of John Durden of Isle of Wight is said to have served in the Revolution in North Carolina. A John Durden was a private in the Continental Line and received 640 acres for serving 84 months (Roster 265). A John Durden served in the Militia from the New Bern District (Id.377). A Jacob Durden also served in the Militia from the New Bern District. (Id.378)

John Durden may also have been the John Darden, Jr., who was deeded land by his father, John, Sr., in Isle of Wight in 1755 (ante). John, Sr., may have deeded land preparatory to moving or in lieu of a will. Anyway, John Darden moved to Wilkes County, Georgia, where he was the owner of 400 acres of land in 1789. John was born about 1734 and died in 1800. According to Bible records his wife was Sarah, born 1736, died 1786, whom he married in 1753.

Children of Sarah and John Darden:
I. Jacob, born 1755, a soldier of the Revolution in N.C. and a refugee soldier in Georgia, (Georgia Roster); married Mary Anne Hilliard, daughter of Elias Hilliard of Granville County, N.C. (VHG 260). Jacob received a grant of 1000 acres from the State of Georgia, 1805. Their children were: Zeipher, m. Joshua Rountree; Jacob, dsp; Henry Hilliard Darden and others.
II. Sarah, m. Leonard Delk of Isle of Wight.
III. William, b. 1775; d. 1805; m. Mary Delk (1784-1855) of Emanuel Co., Ga.

Children:
1. Dennis Durden, m. Phoebe Dillard. (See later)
2. Ellis Durden, m. Mary Bawrick.
3. William Durden, m. Elizabeth Bawrick.
4. Mahaley Durden, m. James Dillard.
5. Simon Durden, m. Eliza Bawrick, the third sister
6. Lucinda Durden, b. Nov.10, 1818; d. Jan.27, 1891; m. Jan.17, 1829, Manning Rountree, b.Jan.27, 1818; d.Dec.28, 1893, buried at Canoochee Church, Emanuel Co., Ga.
7. Ebenezer Durden, m. (1) Roxie Rountree (2) Mrs. Lydia

(Bryant) Boatright.
8. Malinda Durden, b. 1814.
9. Jordan Sutton Durden, b. 1804.

Dennis Durden, the son of Mary (Delk) and William Durden, was born May 10, 1802, died May 25, 1876; and married 1824 Phoebe Dillard who was born Feb. 26, 1807, and died Apr. 26, 1874.
    Children:
I.   Rowan Durden, b. Jan. 8, 1828; d. Aug. 11, 1900; m. Dec. 1, 1852, Lydia Burnett.
II.   Albert Neal Durden, b. Mar. 2, 1828, d. Mar. 28, 1904; m. Jan. 23, 1851, Eliza Lewis Brinson. (See later)
III.   Allie T. Durden, m. Millicent Moore.
IV.   Mary A. Durden, b. Jan. 30, 1833; d. July 17, 1881; m. Jesse Adam Brinson, on May 11, 1851.
V.   Berrian W. Durden, b. June 7, 1838; d. June 17, 1922; m. Jane E. Rountree, March 3, 1859.
VI.   Jane Durden, b. Dec. 16, 1836, d. Aug. 15, 1918; m. Lee Turner.
VII.   Fair Durden, m. Kate Stephens.
VIII.   Elizabeth Durden, b. Mar. 14, 1831, d. Nov. 2, 1908; m. Jan. 11, 1849, Noah Brinson.
IX.   Nancy Durden, b. 1835, d. May 25, 1913; m. 1856 William Stephens.
X.   Dennis, Lieutenant, 48th Georgia Regiment, killed at Weldon RR. in War between the States. Interred at Petersburg, Virginia.

Albert Neal Durden, the son of Phoebe (Dillard) and Dennis Durden, was born on Mar. 2, 1828, and died March 28, 1904. On Jan. 23, 1851, he married Eliza Lewis Brinson, who was born April 8, 1833, and died Oct. 6, 1911.
    Children:
I.   William Matthew Durden, m. Emma Kennedy. (See later)
II.   Dennis Brinson Durden, m. Clara Coleman.
III.   Frank Rowan Durden, m. Carrie Harris.
IV.   Sara Phoebe Durden, m. James Madison Roberts.
V.   Fanny Durden, m. Matthew S. Farmer.

William Matthew Durden, the son of Eliza Lewis (Brinson) and Albert Neal Durden, was born on Aug. 26, 1853, and died May 15, 1918. On May 2, 1883, he married Emma Kennedy, who was born July 10, 1863, and died Dec. 7, 1915.
    Children:
I.   Pearl Durden m. Robert Carter Roberson.
II.   Ruby Durden m. Thomas Harkness Buttrill.
III.   Jewell Durden
IV.   Emmie Durden, m. Samuel F. Smith, Jr.
V.   Carl Durden, Lieutenant 20th Machine Battalion, 7th Division, World War I.

The above data was kindly furnished by Mrs. Thomas H. Buttrill in 1928.

Dickens of Halifax, North Carolina

The material on the Dickens Family of Halifax, included on
pages 101-115 of the first edition,
has been reprinted with corrections in Volume IX of
HISTORICAL SOUTHERN FAMILIES.

GREEN OF HALIFAX
by
Oliver Harold Carper and William Marion Mann

Members of this family of Green were long seated in the county of Stafford in Virginia, but due to the destruction of the records of that county proof of the various connections of the family before 1720 can not be obtained. This family therefore traces back to Daniel Green who was born probably in Stafford County about 1720. On Oct. 16, 1750 he married Sarah Foxworth of that County. (Overwharten Parish Register) Before Oct. 1776 Daniel Green moved to Halifax County for on that date William Branch and his wife Elizabeth sold to Daniel Green for Ł. 10 money of Virginia a tract of land adjacent to lands of Edward Robinson, Wm. Jones and others. (D. B. 9, p. 364) On Nov. 13, Daniel Green gave his son George Green all this tract which lay on the north side of the road, and three days later he gave the land which was on the south side of the road to his son Philip Green. (D. B. 17, pp. 798, 802) On Nov. 13, 1794, Daniel Green gave to his son George Green all the property "I now possess since the late division with my children" indicating that there were other children than George and Phillip. Sarah (Foxworth) Green was dead at this time. Daniel Green was dead before 1800 as he was not on the tax list of that year.

Children:
I.   Lizzie Green, b. April 1, 1754.
II.   Mary Green, b. Aug. 25, 1756.
III. George Green, b. 1758. (See later)
IV.   Philip Green, b. ca. 1760. On Aug. 24, 1795 he sold to his brother George Green his land and seemingly left the country. (D. B. 17, p. 850).

George Green was born in Stafford County, Va., in 1758 and died in Halifax County, N. C. in 1848. During the Revolution, he volunteered and served under Capt. Frank Jones in Halifax County. In the spring "of the year before the fight at Guilford" he was placed under the command of Capt. Poynter at Halifax Town guarding prisoners. Later he was in the Battle of Guilford Court House and the Battle of Camden.

On March 26, 1842, George Green gave a lot to the M. E. Church out of his regard for the said Church, "it being the lot on which Ebeneezer Church now stands" (D. B. 31, p. 220) Although the deed would seem to indicate that the church was of recent origin, it was one of the oldest Methodist Churches in the County, being established before 1787 when Methodism was very young.

At the time of his death George Green's wife was Mary_____ . It is thought that she was his second wife but this has not been proven.

116

Children:
I.   Rebecca Green, b.ca.1783; d.1813; m.(1) Samuel Dickens,
      son of William and Mary (Kinchen) Dickens: (see DICKENS)
      m. (2) July 24, 1809 in Warren Co., N.C. Abner Mills.
      Children:
      1. Nancy Dickens Mills, b.1805; d.1861; m.Malachi Dickens,
         son of Bennett and Hannah (Lovell) Dickens. Children under
         father. (See DICKENS)
      2. Malicia (Leecy) Mills, b.1810; m.April 27, 1827, Luns-
         ford James Dickens, b.1805; d.1883; son of James and
         Martha Dickens; child under father. (See DICKENS).
      3. Louise Eliza Mills, b.1812, d.1880; m.Oct.9,1830, Rich-
         ard Britt.
            Children:
            (1) Mary Britt, b.1832; m. Aug.5, 1853, Iley N. Dickens.
                Children under father. (See DICKENS)
            (2) William Britt, b.1838; k. in War, CSA; m.Jan.1859
                Elizabeth Eure. Issue 3 children.
            (3) Matthew Britt, b.1843; d. in service CSA; m.ca.1863
                Rebecca E., daughter of Enoch D. Dickens. (See
                DICKENS)
                   Children:
                   a. Eliza (Lizzie) Britt, b.1864; m.Albert T. Dickens,
                   son of Jacob D. and Melissa J. (LEWIS) Dickens.
                   (see below)
            (4) Sarah Elizabeth Britt, b.Feb.14, 1846; d. 1886; m.
                Alexander A. Hux. Children under father. (See DICKENS)
            (5) Margaret West Britt, b.Feb.1849; d.May 14, 1890;
                m.Jan.1,1868 Wm. H. Hux. Children under father.
                (See DICKENS)
II.   Nancy Green, m. James Neville.
III. Jesse Green, b.ca.1786; m. Sally_____who after his death
      m. Jacob Dickens as his second wife in 1826.
IV.   George Green Jr., b.1789; m.Jan.22, 1822, Temperance
      Hart.
         Children:
         1. Caroline Green, b.1829.
         2. Jesse Green, b.1832.
         3. John Green, b.1837
         4. Martha Green.
V.   Sarah Green.
VI.   Elizabeth Green, m.John Phillips.
VII. Frances Green, m. David Morris
VIII. Lucretia Green, M. March 18, 1824, Egbert Lewis. (See later)
         Children:
         1. Henry Lewis, b.1827.
         2. Melissa J. Lewis, b.1835; m.June 2, 1853, Jacob D.
            Dickens, son of Emsley Dickens. Children under father.
            (See DICKENS)
         3. Robert Lewis, b.1838.
         4. Jesse Lewis, b.1842.
         5. James Lewis, b.1844.

Lucretia (Green) Lewis died and Egbert Lewis then married Margaret Dickens, daughter of Malachi Dickens, and had three children.

IX.   May Green m. Francis Asbury Smith. Untraced.

X.   Elisha P. Green, m. Martha _____ .

      Children:

1. Ambrose G. Green, b. 1842.
2. Elizabeth Green, b. 1845
3. Louise P. Green, b. 1854
4. Elisha P. Green, Jr.
5. Lafayette Green.

EDMUNDS of SURRY and BRUNSWICK

Captain Howell Edmunds who died in Surry in 1729 appears to be the first of the name in Surry from whom the family can be clearly traced.

It is said that he was a son of Howell Edmunds of Charles City County (Barksdale, p. 505). This Howell Edmunds was brought over by William Farrar who received a patent June 11, 1637, for 2000 acres in Henrico for the transportation of 40 persons. Among the 40 persons was a Howell Edmunds.

The first person of the name in Surry was Samuel Edmunds, who, on May 9, 1636, patented 350 acres, "E. upon land of Jeremiah Clements, N. upon mouth of Upper Chippokes Cr., W. upon land of William Rookins. This patent was renewed in 1637 for 350 additional acres. On Sept. 7, 1638, Samuel Edmunds, together with Thomas Plomer, patented 400 acres adjacent to his other holdings.

A William Edmunds died in Surry March 9, 1739. His death was reported by Mary Edmunds. He made his will in Surry February 19, 1730, and same was probated July 16, 1740. He names: sons, William, David, John, Gray; daughters, Mary, Sarah, Susannah, Elizabeth, Faith, Christian, and Phyllis; wife Mary. He may have been a son or grandson of Samuel Edmonds as he mentions lands next to the Clements (Bk. 9, p. 197).

Captain Howell Edmunds, from whom this family is clearly traced, married Elizabeth, daughter of Thomas BLUNT of Shingleton and his wife, Priscilla BROWNE. Thomas Blunt deeded land to his daughter, Elizabeth and her husband, Howell Edmunds in 1701.

The Council of Virginia sent the following message in 1728 to Howell Edmunds, Sheriff of Surry Co.: "It is ordered by the Council that Surry Court House be built on land of Mr. Howell Edmunds near the great road that leads from the bridge through his plantation as near as may be to his Spring". (33 V 20)

Captain Edmunds made his will in Surry December 24, 1728; same probated August 20, 1729, (B 7, p. 962). He gave eldest son, Thomas Edmunds, "plantation where I now live and land I lately had as a patent on Wild Catt, entry on Nottoway adjacent Benjamin Clements and Thomas Butts; to son, Howell, a tract of land on Blunt's Swamp in Isle of Wight and 300 acres on Great Creek; son Nicholas 500 acres on Great Creek in Brunswick, daughters, Sarah Jones, Elizabeth Edmunds, and Ann Edmunds, negroes. Son Thomas, exr.

Children:

I.   Thomas m. Ann SIMMONS. daughter of John Simmons, Burgess of Isle of Wight, 1736-49. Thomas was a Captain of Surry Militia and Burgess for Surry 1736-38, but died intestate before the end of his term. His wife, Ann, was ap-

pointed admn. of his estate May 12, 1737. (B.8, p.697).
She married Edmund RUFFIN, for on October 19, 1743 she
and her second husband were appointed to administer upon
his estate on that date (B 9, p.453).

II.   Howell, will probated in Southampton 1770.
III. Nicholas, m. Elizabeth FLOOD. (See later)
IV.   Sarah, m. James Jones.
V.   Elizabeth.
VI.   Ann.

Nicholas Edmunds was born about 1710 in Surry and died 1789
in Brunswick. He married first Elizabeth, granddaughter of Walter FLOOD, secondly, June 2, 1755, Mrs. Mary Nicholson (No
children). He removed to Brunswick about 1739 and was a Justice
of the County Court in 1740. In 1746 he qualified as a Captain of
a company of foot and again in 1748. He was a major of foot in
1743, and High Sheriff of Brunswick County in 1759. He qualified
as Colonel "in Chief" of Brunswick Militia in April 1772. He was
for many years a vestryman of St. Andrew's Parish.
Children of first wife;

I.   Colonel Thomas (1748-1825), m. Sarah Eldridge (1754-1836),
      daughter of Elizabeth (Jones) and Thomas ELDRIDGE. He
      was commissioned a Captain, 15th Va., November 25, 1776;
      wounded at Brandywine September 11, 1777; regiment de-
      signated 11th Va., September 14, 1778; transferred to 3rd.
      Va., February 12, 1781; transferred to 1st. Va., January
      1, 1783, Brevet Major September 20, 1783. Served to Close
      of War, died 1791. (Heitman) (D.A.R. Mag. Vol.49, p.240
      gives the above as the record of Thomas Edmunds who mar-
      ried Sarah Eldridge and died in 1825. D.A.R. Mag. Vol.117,
      p.218, gives this as the record of Thomas Edmunds who
      married Martha Short in 1784 and died in Sussex in 1791.)
          There was another Thomas Edmunds, a Lt. and Capt.
      of Va. State Regiment, 1777 to February 1781. (Heitman).
      Others of the family who served as officers in the Revolution
      were: Elias Edmunds, Major and Lt. Co. Va. State Regt.
      1777 to Feb.1781; Nicholas Edmunds, Capt. 3rd. N.C. 1777.
II.   John Flood, d.1797, m. Lucy Gray of Southampton. He was
      Sheriff of Brunswick in 1797.
III. Colonel Sterling, d.1801. Sheriff of Brunswick and Colonel
      of Militia during Revolutionary War.
IV.   Sarah, m. _____ RUFFIN.
V.   Elizabeth, (1751-1806), m. Samuel Garland. (See later)

Elizabeth Edmunds, born August 19, 1751, died May 13, 1806,
at "Pleasant Hill" Lunenburg County, Va., married May 13, 1771,
Captain Samuel Garland, born August 25, 1746, in Lunenburg, died
August 1, 1797. He served in the General Assembly 1775-76, and
is said to have been a Captain in the Revolutionary War.
Children:

I.   Mary Garland, b.April 1, 1772, m.Copeland Davis. (See
      later).
II.   Eliz. Garland, b. June 17, 1774, m.David Dunn.
III. Edward Garland, b.Jan.31, 1776.

IV.   Sallie Garland, b. Feb. 1, 1778, m. Robert Chappell.
V.   Lucy Garland, b. Nov. 12, 1784, m. Samuel Bagley.

Mary Garland, born April 1, 1772, died June 20, 1821, married Copeland Davis, November 21, 1791. He was a planter and resided in Lunenburg.
    Children:
I.   Nicholas Edmunds Davis, b. Oct. 16, 1792, m. Eliz. Lewis Lamkin. (See later)
II.   Maria Davis, m. John Flood Lewis.
III.   Elizabeth Davis, m. Gray Dunn.
IV.   Jane Davis.

Nicholas Edmunds Davis, born Oct. 16, 1792, died 1872, married (1) April 3, 1819, Amanda Melvina Lewis, born Jan. 13, 1805, died March 28, 1822, daughter of Benjamin Lewis and Elizabeth Edmunds (cousins); married (2) on May 30, 1826, Elizabeth Lewis Lamkin, born Dec. 23, 1807, died Jan. 11, 1867, at "Oakland", Lunenburg County, and served as a soldier in the War of 1812.
    Children:
I.   Mary J. Davis, b. April 20, 1830, m. Edmund Webb Wilkins. (See later)
II.   Ashley Lewis Davis, b. April 10, 1831, died April 7, 1903, married Sallie (Cabell) Epes, Jan. 20, 1864, at "Bridgewater" near Danville, by Rev. Thomas Ward White.
III.   Nicholas Edmunds Davis, b. Aug. 28, 1840, killed at the Battle of Gettysburg, July 1863.

Mary J. Davis, born April 20, 1830, at "Oakland", died June 30, 1900, at "Belmont", Northampton County, N. C., married November 10, 1855, Dr. Edmund Webb Wilkins, born May 31, 1830, at "Belmont" and died there January 28, 1899.
Dr. Wilkins was educated at the Universities of North Carolina and Virginia and received his M. D. Degree at the University of Pennsylvania.
    Children:
I.   Ashley Wilkins, b. Feb. 8, 1855, d. May 7, 1938 in an automobile accident.
II.   Nicholas Davis Wilkins, b. Feb. 16, 1857, d. Apr. 10, 1912, unmarried.
III.   Elizabeth Garland Wilkins, b. July 28, 1859, d. Jan. 10, 1938, unmarried.
IV.   Edmonia Cabell Wilkins, b. Apr. 9, 1865, kindly furnished this information about the Edmunds family. She lives in the Star Route near Roanokd Rapids, N. C.
V.   Mary Wilkins, b. March 24, 1867, m. C. D. Miller

FOLIOT of YORK COUNTY

The Reverend Edward Foliot, shown in the Berkeley-Norwood chart, was a son of Sir John Foliot and his wife, Elizabeth Aylmer, daughter of Rt. Rev. John Aylmer, Bishop of London. He matriculated at Hart Hall, Oxford, April 13, 1632, aged 22; B.C.L. Nov. 24, 1632, Rector of Alderton, Northants, 1634, until sequestered by the Parliamentary Committee. (A.O.) He came to Virginia and was minister of Westover Parish 1661 and also Hampton Parish in York County. His will was probated in York in 1690. (See Berkeley Chart V.H.G. p.344)

Children:

I. Elizabeth Foliot, m.(1) Josias Moody of York; will of Josias Moody was probated 1677; m.(2) Capt. Charles Hansford of York.

II. Mary Foliot, m. Dr. Henry Power of York whose will was probated Sept. 26, 1692. (W.M.7, p.129)

Children:

1. Elizabeth Power, m. Col. Cole Digges of Bellfield, b. 1692, d. 1744, member of Council. Children: (1) Col. Edward Digges of Belafield, (2) William Digges, (3) Dudley Digges, (4) Mary Digges, (5) Susannah, m. Benj. HARRISON of Wakefield, Surry.

2. Major Henry Power of James City, d. Dec. 1739.

3. John Power, married Mary Lockey, dau. of Edward Lockey Jr. She married John Mybill, 1668, and then John Power. He made his will in York 1720.

Elizabeth Foliot, dau. of Rev. Edward Foliot, married Capt. Charles Hansford of York. He was a son of John Hansford of Chickasee who patented land in York County.

In 1647, John Hansford was appointed administrator of the estate of Thomas Weston, a Puritan merchant of Maryland who died in Bristol, Eng. (T.10, p.210). John Hansford made his will May 9, 1654 and same was probated Aug. 29, 1661. His children were Charles, William, Thomas, John and Elizabeth Hansford.

He gave his sons, Charles and Thomas Hansford, 500 acres of land at head of Felgate's Creek which he had bought of Mr. Weston'.

Thomas Hansford was hung by Sir William Berkeley for his part in Bacon's Rebellion. Elizabeth, his sister, married (1) Christian Wilson in 1661; m.(2) Randall HOLT of Surry.

Capt. Charles Hansford's will was probated in York in 1702. He mentioned wife, Elizabeth, and children: 1. John; 2. Charles; 3. William; 4. Elizabeth; 5. Mary; 6. Lydia, m. HENRY DUKE (See later), dau. m. Samuel Hill of York (Will 1712). Hansford Hill, who made his will in York 1789 was probably grandson of Samuel.

Lydia Hansford, daughter of Capt. Charles Hansford, married Henry Duke. Henry Duke was a Justice in James City in 1860, Burgess 1692, 1699 and Member of the Council 1703-13. He pattented 1000 acres on the Chickahominy in 1690. He may have been a son of John Duke who in 1673 patented 438 acres on the Chickahominy abutting on Tyassum Swamp. This John Duke married Jane, daughter of Major John Scasbrook of York County and a deed recorded in York 1697 shows he had a son John. Jane Duke, his widow, married Capt. Thomas Mountfort (W. M. 2, p. 275; 14, p. 126; 24, p. 200; Tyler 7, p. 214).

An inventory of the estate of Henry Duke was filed in Prince George 1719.

Henry Duke had a daughter, Elizabeth, who married (1) James MASON of Surry who died in 1701; (2) Ethelred Taylor. (See later) (See Duke-Symes Family, p. 25).

Ethelred Taylor of Surry married about 1702 Elizabeth Duke, daughter of Henry Duke, and widow of James Mason. On March 2, 1702, Ethelred and Elizabeth Taylor presented an inventory of the estate of James Mason, decd., and on May 4, 1705, Taylor filed a supplementary inventory. He bought 332 acres in Lawne's Creek Parish from Nathaniel Harrison, et. al., in 1714. His will was dated May 31, 1716 and probated June 26, 1716. He gave his brothers, Samuel and John, and his sister, Rebecca, 20 shillings each to buy rings. (These persons have not been located in adjacent counties.) To John Clements two cows. Loving wife, Elizabeth executrix.

Children:

I.   Samuel Taylor of Surry. He deeded to Thomas Drew 166 acres in Lawne's Creek, Feb. 15, 1734, and is mentioned in his brother William's will March 8, 1735.

II.   Henry Taylor, m. Charlotte _____, moved to Charles City County.

III. Ethelred Taylor II, m. Patience Kinchen. He moved to Isle of Wight, now Southampton County, and was a member of the House of Burgesses from Southampton from 1752-55. On Sept. 11, 1755, he qualified as Colonel of Militia for Southampton County. His will was probated in Southampton Nov. 13, 1755. He left a large number of children. (See V. M. 23, p. 104).

IV.   William Taylor

DESCENDANTS OF ETHELDRED TAYLOR of SURRY
by
William Marion Mann, Jr.

Etheldred Taylor of Surry County, Virginia, appears to have
been the emigrant ancestor of this family of Taylor in America
as the brothers and sisters mentioned in his will (see WILL) can
not be located in Surry or Isle of Wight counties. They probably
resided in England. Etheldred Taylor appears in the records of
Surry in 1702. He was appointed Sheriff of that county in 1710, his
bond bearing date of July 4th. He married Elizabeth, the widow
of James Mason of Surry. On March 2, 1702, Etheldred and Elizabeth Taylor presented an inventory of the estate of James Mason,
deceased, and on Mary 4, 1705, Taylor filed a supplementary
inventory. Before her marriage Elizabeth Taylor was Elizabeth
Duke, daughter of Henry Duke and his wife, Lydia, the daughter
of Charles Hansford. (See HOLT)
    On Feb. 15, 1714, Etheldred Taylor bought from Nathaniel
Harrison, Esq., William Robinson of Williamsburg, and Nathaniel
Ridley of Isle of Wight County, gentlemen, 332 acres in Lawnes
Creek Parish in Surry County. When he died in 1716 he devised
this land to his sons.
        Children of Etheldred Taylor and his wife Elizabeth Mason
        nee Duke:
I.   Samuel Taylor (see later).
II.   Henry Taylor lived first in Surry and afterwards in Charles
        City County, Va. On Feb.10, 1734, he sold his land to Wil-
        liam Ball. He died in 1749.
            Children:
        1. Charles Taylor, no issue.
        2. Charlotte Taylor, m. Rev. Samuel Smith McCorkey.
III.   Etheldred Taylor, moved from Surry County to the part of
        Isle of Wight which later became Southampton County. He
        died there in 1755 (W.B.1, p.182). He married Patience
        Kinchen, daughter of William Kinchen and his wife Elizabeth
        Ruffin, daughter of Robert Ruffin of Surry and his wife,
        Elizabeth Watkins nee Prime, daughter of Edmund Prime.
        He was a member of the House 1752-55 and Colonel of Mili-
        tia 1755.
            Children:
        1. William Taylor died in Southampton County in 1772. The
            name of his wife is unknown.
                Children:
            (1) Nancy Taylor m. _____Browne.
            (2) William Taylor was devised the plantation on which
                John Morgan "is overseer" which "I purchased of
                Henry Adams."

(3) Mary Mason Taylor.
(4) Martha Taylor.
(5) Robert Taylor.
2. Henry Taylor was devised the plantation on which James Railey lives.
3. Etheldred Taylor, d. 1777, no issue.
4. Kinchen Taylor m. Ridley Browne, daughter of Dr. Jesse Browne of St. Luke Parish.
5. John Taylor.
6. Richard Taylor.
7. James Taylor was devised land on "Meherrin".
8. Elizabeth Taylor m. Miles Cary.
9. Mary Taylor m. _____ Peterson.
IV. William Taylor died without issue in 1736.

Samuel Taylor, son of Etheldred Taylor and his wife Elizabeth(Duke)Mason, sold the land which was devised him by his father to Thomas Drew on Feb. 15, 1734. On March 8, 1735 he was named in the will of his brother, William Taylor. Samuel Taylor moved to Bertie County, N.C. and on Feb. 11, 1734 as Samuel Taylor of Surry County, Va. he bought from Joseph Wall 100 acres on the south side of Meherrin River adjacent Thomas Howell, Senr. (Bertie County, N.C. D.B. D, p. 25). On Feb. 1, 1738, he bought 175 acres from Joseph Wall Sr. adjacent Cypress Swamp, William Deloach, Arthur Cook, and his own land (Ibid. D.B.E. p. 248). In 1746 he made his will but the date it was probated is not recorded (Grimes: Abstract of North Carolina Wills, p. 373). His wife was named Cecelia, last name unknown.
Children of Samuel and Cecelia Taylor:
I. Robert Taylor was devised "my plantation".
II. Etheldred Taylor was devised land.
III. Harry Taylor (see later).
IV. Samuel Taylor was to receive land from his father's estate in case he returned to "Meherrin".
V. Elizabeth Taylor.
VI. Martha Taylor.

Harry Taylor, son of Samuel and Cecelia Taylor, moved to the part of Edgecombe County, N.C. which later became Nash County and in 1767 purchased land on Peachtree Creek from William Hill for 20 Lbs. (Edgecombe County, N.C. D.B. C, p. 529). His will is dated May 31, 1788, and was probated in the Nov. Court for that year (Nash County, N.C. W.B. 1, p. 46). His wife was named Sarah, probably Boykin. She married after the death of Harry Taylor, Howell Wrenn of Nash County.
Children of Harry Taylor and his wife Sarah (Boykin?):
I. Etheldred Taylor moved to Franklin Co., n.C. and died before Dec. 10, 1798.
II. Elizabeth Taylor m. Elijah Boddie who was b. 1765.
Children: (possibly others)
1. Elijah[6] Boddie (Elijah[5], Nathan[4], William[3], John[2], William[1]) born in 1788 and reared in Nash County, N.C. moved to Sumner County, Tenn., near Gallatin about 1815. He married Maria Platt Elliott of Sumner County,

Tenn., December 24, 1816. She died November 10, 1846.
Children born in Sumner County:

(1) Charles Elliott Boddie, b.Aug.14,1818; m.(1) Eveline Douglas; (2) Susan Haney.

(2) Elizabeth Blackman Boddie, b.Aug.26,1820; m.Wm. Robert Elliston.

(3) Mary Elliott Boddie, b.Feb.27, 1823; m.Rufus K. Cage.

(4) George Boddie, b.Oct.14,1825, d.Sept.1, 1846.

(5) Mourning Hilliard Boddie, b.Jan.26, 1828; m. Alfred Douglas. (No children)

(6) William Summerfield Boddie, b.May 4, 1830; d. June 11, 1833.

(7) Micajah Thomas Boddie, b.April 26, 1832; d. June 29, 1833.

(8) Gullieme Boddie, b.Nov. 26, 1834; d.June 13, 1835.

(9) Ella Douglas Boddie, b.June 15, 1836; m.Henry Craft of Memphis Tenn., Nov.5, 1856 and had several children, one of whom, Henry Craft Jr., born Feb.5,1856; m.21 June, 1891, Margaret Emma Galloway, b.July 1869, and had four children; daughter m. Henry Curtis Dewey.

(10) Van Buren Boddie, b.Dec.14, 1838; m.Anna Jewell

(11) Maria Boddie, b.Feb.5,1841, m. Carrington Mason.
(from Boddie and Allied Families, p.35)

III. John Taylor moved to Franklin Co., N.C.

IV. Samuel Taylor m. Sarah _____ . He died in Franklin Co., N.C. in 1831.
Children:
1. Harvey Taylor.
2. Elizabeth Taylor m._____ Lancaster and had issue.
(1) Olympia Lancaster.
(2) Alonzo Lancaster.
(3) Sarah Jane Lancaster.
(4) Mary Jamieson Lancaster.
(5) Samuel W. Lancaster.
(6) Ann Mariah Lancaster.
(7) Phillip P. B. Lancaster.
3. Nathaniel Macon Taylor moved to Madison Co., Miss. before 1838.

V. Hardy Taylor moved to Franklin Co., N.C. but died in Nash County, N.C. in 1809 after returning. (W.B.1, p.203). No issue.

VI. Boykin Taylor m. Rebecca _____. He died in Franklin Co., about 1826. His children were minors at his death.
Children:
1. Martha Taylor.
2. Catherine Taylor.
3. Francis Taylor.

VII. Harry Taylor m. Penelope_____. His land was divided in Nash County on Aug.14,1884 (D.B. 77, p.422).
Children:
1. Charlotte Taylor.

2. Jane Taylor m. Nero Mann.

VIII. Cecelia Taylor (b.ca.1784) m. about 1792 Benjamin Drake, son of James Drake, Revolutionary Patriot (See WHEELER'S HISTORY) and his wife Hartwell (Hodges) Davis, daughter of Benjamin Hodges and his wife Constance Goodrich (see Boddie: Southside Virginia Families, Volume I). At his death about 1833 Benjamin Drake was a man of means and owned 30 slaves. (Nash Co., N.C. D.B. 14, p.121)

Children:
1. John Adams Drake, b.1794.
2. Elizabeth Taylor Drake, m. James Harrison.
3. Nancy Boykin Drake,(b.Sept.24,1797; d.Nov.11,1862) m. William H. Mann (b.1796; d.Sept. 1846) on Feb.7, 1816. Children under father (see MANN).
4. James Bamphlyd Drake.
5. Henrietta Drake.
6. Temperance Drake.
7. John Quincy Drake
8. Hartwell Drake (See later)
9. _____.

Hartwell Drake, son of Benjamin and Cecelia (Taylor) Drake, married (1)_____.(2) Emaline Lewis in 1848.

Children:
I. William Drake, b.1865.
II. Benjamin Drake m. and had issue.
III. Ann Drake m. Daniel Collins.
IV. Martha Drake, m._____.

Children by second marriage:
V. Vashti Drake, m. Robert Compton and had issue.
VI. Shehayne Drake m. Cansada Curtis and had issue.
VII. Burrous Drake m. Melissa Curtis and had issue.
VIII. Esther Drake m. Alonzo Poole.

Children:
1. Christopher Augustus Poole m. Della Tear.
2. Eli Franklin Poole m. Nora Gay.
3. Benjamin Cicero Poole m. Laura Claridy.
4. Myrtle Ida Poole m. Luther Sinley.
5. Walter Shehayne Poole m. Margarie Locke.
6. Clyde Earnst Poole m. Elma Day.
7. Charles Alonzo Poole m. Emma Baker.
8. Emma Poole m. Walter Durham.
9. Effie Poole m. Henry Floyd Sherrod. Both are graduates of Peabody College in Nashville, Tenn. They reside (1955) in Decatur, Ala.

Children:
(1) Estalle Sherrod (b.July 2, 1921) m. Patrick Gardlin. Both are graduates of the University of Alabama.

Children:
a. Sarah Scott Gardlin, b.Aug. 30, 1950.
b. Sherry Ann Gardlin, b. Nov.21, 1953.
(2) Henry Floyd Sherrod, Jr., b.Jan.20, 1937.

DESCENDANTS OF EDWARD GURGANY
Member of
First General Assembly, 1619

Edward Gurgany, gentleman, arrived in Virginia on the "Phoenix", April 20, 1608. Capt. John Smith stated that on that day while they were busy at work hewing trees and setting corn, an alarm caused them all speed to take up arms expecting a new assault from the savages. Their doubts were presently satisfied with the happy sight of Master Nelson in the "Phoenix", then about three months missing after Captain Newport's arrival, being to all our expectations lost. Listed among the "Gentlemen" on that ship was Edward Gurgany. (Smith's Works, Arber Edition, pp. 33-34, 105, 108, 411).

It is evident that Edward was a member of the expedition of 1616, which was sent against the Chickahominies to collect much needed corn, for it is stated in Smith's Works, p. 529, that Smith's account was taken, in part, from the writings of Edward Gurgany.

It seems that Captain Argall had previously "conditioned" with the Indians before the expedition set forth, but had been treated with "much scorn and contempt." Captain George Yeardley commanded the expedition and upon reaching the Indian settlements, they dared him to come ashore and fight, "presuming more on his not daring than upon their own valor". They went ashore at "Ozinies" and marched along by the river bank, and the Indians "marched close along by us each threatening the other who should fi. t begin".

The next day they followed the Indians. Gurgany says that there were few places in Virginia that had such large fields and "more plenty of corn", which although it was but newly gathered had been hidden in the fields where we could not find it. "A good time we spent arguing the cause----. Our Captain caused us to make ready and upon the word to let fly amonge them." Also he commanded them to seize as many prisoners as possible. "The Captain gave the word, and we presently fired, when twelve lay, some dead, the rest sprawling on the ground; twelve we took prisoner. Near one hundred bushels of corn we had for their ransom". (Ib. 529).

Edward Gurgany was associated with Governor Argall in settling "Argall's Gift" and together with Captain Thomas Paulett, represented that place in the General Assembly in July 1619.

He and his wife, Anne, appear to have died within a year after the General Assembly, for she, a widow, in her will dated Feb. 11, 1619-20 bequeathed their land to Thomas Harris, who had evidently married their daughter Adrai. This is shown in a grant to Capt. Thomas Harris July 12, 1637 of 400 acres of land, "Due as followeth 400 acres being granted to Edward Gurgany by order of Court, being date Oct. 1, 1617 from the late Treasurer and Company and bequeathed by Ann Gurgany widow and relict of said Edward Gurgany to the said Thomas Harris by her last will bearing date Feb. 11, AD 1619-20 (C. p. 60).

Captain Thomas Harris was married twice. His first wife was ADRAI an ANCIENT PLANTER, proven by the following land grant to "Capt. Thomas Harris, 820 acres known by the name of "Longfield" Henrico Co., 26 Feb.1638---100 acres for his own personal adventure, 100 acres for his first wife ADRY HARRIS, as being Ancient Planters & 620 acres for the transportation of 13 persons. (C.P.101).

At a witchcraft trial held in Jamestown, Sept.11,1626, "Rebecca Gray was a witness against goodwife Wright" the suspected witch. She swore that "goodwife Wright did tell her that she told Thomas Harris he should bury his first wife, being then betrothed unto him, which came to pass" (Col.Surry-77). To indulge in such a prophecy in those days seems to have been very detrimental. Anyway Adrai Harris died sometime before September 1626.

Adrai was an Ancient Planter. This meant that she came to Virginia before November 1616, the time of the going away of Sir Thomas Dale. Now Edward Gurgany came over in 1608. Adrai, if his daughter, was married to Thomas Harris before the date of her mother's will, Feb.11,1619-20. At a minimum she would be probably 16 years of age at that date. She was married before that date, how long before is not known. Her birth was about 1604 or earlier. She would therefore be about four years of age at the time he came over in 1608 and Gurganey probably brought over his wife and daughter much later but at least before 1616 for her to be an Ancient Planter. Who else among the Ancient Planters but Edward Gurgany and his wife could have been the father and mother of "Ancient Planter" Adrai Harris?

Captain Thomas Harris, an Ancient Planter having come over in 1611, was a member of the House of Burgesses from Charles City in 1623/24 and from Henrico in 1639-47. Adrai Harris died about 1626, and Thomas Harris married apparently in 1626 a second wife whose first name was "Joan". There is no clue to her family name and it is positively unknown. (See V.H.G.-199)

The date of Thomas Harris' death is not known as his will has been destroyed. He had only three children, THOMAS, WILLIAM, and MARY. This is proven by the will of his son, Thomas, who died unmarried in Henrico in 1679. His will is as follows: "I give and bequeath unto my sister in law, LOUE HARRIS, my land at Ware according to the bounds set out in MY FATHER'S WILL. I give and bequeath to my cousin (nephew) RICHARD LYGON. all my horses, mares or foals, they not being given by my GRANDFATHER into the hands of his overseers, Feb. 10, 1678-79. Wits: Alice Harris, Mary Lygon Jr., Richard Lygon. Proved in Henrico County Court, june 2, 1679. Mary Lygon the younger.

William Harris, brother of Thomas, was not mentioned in the above will because he had died previously, his will being recorded in Henrico, Feb.1,1678. However, William's wife was named "Lucy" (last name unknown) who is referred to as "Loue" in Thomas Harris' will. Thomas" nephew, Richard Lygon, mentioned in the will, was the son of his sister, Mary Lygon, who had married Thomas Lygon Jr. (See later).

William Harris, son of Captain Thomas Harris and ONLY BROTHER of Thomas Harris Jr. who died in 1679, was born in

1629 according to a deposition. He was a Justice of Henrico, member of the House of Burgesses, 1652, 1653, 1656, 1658. In December 1656 he was appointed major of the Henrico and Charles City regiment. He married Lucy   , last name unknown, and and made his will April 20, 1678, probated Feb.1, 1678/9, as follows:

"Not knowing what the Lord hath ordained or at what tyme he he may take (torn) out this life I doe settle my estate of lands as followeth, I give & bequeath to my sonne Thomas all my land below the ward (ware?) to keep the ware/ward runn for his Bounds till ht shall come to ye spring at ye hed & then to follow a bottom on ye lower side of the clearing of John Rabon, to the hundred roade path, and then on a straight roade or course to the land of Seth Potter Ashbrooke but in no case to crofse porketts/perketts? path; to my younger sonnes WM & EDWARD HARRIS I give ye rest of my dividents, Wm. to have the plantason where I now live, & Edward ye land next Ashbrooke, But Wm. to extend Outwards one hundred yards beyond ye clearing of John Rabon on the path called perketts/porketts path, & Thomas on a straight course to ye redd? watter? & Edward the house next to Potter Ashbrooke's line as alsoe to ye Ashen swamp to them & their Heires; neyther to sell unlefs the one to ye other & if eyther did (died) without Ishow (issue) the land to come to ye Survivor, my two younger sons to live with their mother till of age of sixteen, if shee marry if not till 19 yeares of age; my will is that my wife live on the plantason during her life but not to hinder my sonne Wm. at the head of ye ward if he come (or rome?) for himselfe & I desyre my friends Mr. Tho: Cocke(?) & Mr. Wm.Randolph to see this my will performed. In Witnefsee of every (looks like L) to hereof I putt to my hand this 20th day of April, 1678." Wits: Rich.Lygon, Ann Stewart (Bk.1677-92, part 1, p.68)

Children:
I.   William Harris moved to New Kent County for on Aug.1, 1694, Hugh Lygon witnessed an acknowledgement of debt by William Harris, son of Major William Harris, decd. of New Kent Co. , to Sarah Knibb of Henrico (Bk.5, p.508).
II.   Edward Harris is said to have also been in New Kent in 1698 (Lygon-845)
III. Thomas Harris m. Mary   . His will was probated June 1730 in Henrico, and the will of his wife, Mary Harris, was probated Sept. 1745. They had eleven children. (For children see 4 V 249).

Col. Thomas Lygon Jr. died before March 16, 1675, as that is the date his wife Mary was appointed executrix of his estate (Will lost). Mary (Harris) Lygon was born in 1625 and died in 1704, aged 79. Her date of birth is known as she testified in 1689 that her age was 64. On Aug.29,1691, she deeded 200 acres of land at Curls in Henrico to her sons, Richard and Hugh Lygon, stating that it was part of a greater dividder "granted unto Capt. THOMAS HARRIS, decd. , and given by his will unto his DAUGHTER, Mary Lygon (Bk 2-352, 360a). Mrs. Mary Lygon made her will Mar.18, 1702-03, probated Feb.1,1703/4. She appointed her son in law ROBERT HANCOCK and daughter JOHAN HAN-

COCK executor and executrix of her will (BK 1697-1704, p. 366).

Robert Hancock (1659-1709), the son in law mentioned in Mrs. Mary Lygon's will, married her daughter Joan Lygon (1653-1726). Her date of birth is known because she stated her age as 30 years in a deposition made in 1683. Robert appears among the list of tithables in Henrico in 1679. He was the son of Sarah Hancock-Pigott, who mentions her son, Robert Hancock in her will in Lower Norfolk April 1, 1689 (McIntosh - 1-126). He held 860 acres of land in the Quit Rents Rolls of Henrico, 1704. In June 1708 he deeded his daughter, Joan Hancock and his son in law, Samuel Hancock, 200 acres of land.

Samuel Hancock, the above son in law, was a son of William Hancock who made his will in Lower Norfolk April 14, 1687, proven May 17, 1687. (Do. 113). Samuel was a grandson of Mrs. Sarah Hancock-Pigott and is mentioned in her will. She appoints her grandson Edward Moseley, overseer of her plantation and he is to keep "her grandsons, Simon, SAMUEL and George Hancock until they come of age according to their father's will (Do. 126) So it appears that Joan Hancock and Samuel Hancock were first cousins. Samuel's mother was Elizabeth Cockcroft, sister of William Cockcroft named in his father's, William Hancock's will. William Cockcroft in his will dated Jan. 20, 1686, makes his loving BROTHER IN LAW WILLIAM HANCOCK overseer of his Will (Do-103-104). Elizabeth Cockcroft, wife of William Hancock, was a daughter of William Cockcroft, Treasurer of the Merchant's Adventures at Rotterdam, Holland, in 1635. He was born in 1605 and died July 7, 1653. His wife, Elizabeth Burnet (1613-1653) was a daughter of Ralph Burnet and Magdalen Fox. (N. E. G. R. 100, p. 96) (See Corker S. V. L. Vol. 1)

Samuel[4] and Johan Hancock were married April 15, 1700. (History of Henrico Par. -227). In 1704 Samuel Hancock was the owner of 100 acres of land according to the Quit Rent Polls. In 1724, he and Arthur Moseley patented 500 acres in Henrico. On March 6, 1726, he and Arthur Moseley Jr. deeded part of this patent. Samuel sold 250 acres to Gilbert Bowman March 27, 1729. On Sept. 24, 1733, Samuel Hancock and Johan, his wife, for love' and affection, deeded their son, SAMUEL HANCOCK JR. one plantation, a tract of land containing 300 acres in Henrico except 45 acres of the tract of 200 acres lying on the south side of Spring Run that I sold to Robert Ferguson, which 200 acres was by deed of gift 1st day of June 1708 to me and my wife, JOHAN, by her FATHER ROBERT HANCOCK and afterwards in 1712 conveyed by deed to me by his son, Robert Hancock and the other 100 I purchased of my brother in law Robert Hancock and Robert, Sr. decd. and his son William. Wits: THOMAS JONES, John Branch, John Green (D. W. II, 1725-37, p. 414). Samuel's last transaction seems to have been a deed dated Dec. 24, 1734, wherein he sells 53½ acres to John Bowman (Id-501).

Samuel and Johan did not make wills, at least none have been found, so the dates of their deaths are not known.

Samuel and Johan Hancock had at least two children according to the deed of Robert Hancock in 1708, wherein he mentions "either of my daughter's Johan Hancock's children".

Samuel Hancock Jr., only known child of Samuel Sr. is said to have been born about 1701 or 1702 and died in 1760. He married about 1720, Elizabeth daughter of Elizabeth and John Jameson who died in 1760. Mrs. Elizabeth Jameson married secondly Arthur Moseley. This is proven by a deed made Feb. 27, 1747, by Elizabeth Moseley, widow, Samuel Hancock Jr. and Elizabeth, his wife, to Alex. Long "of a tract of 169 acres devised by John Jameson to his wife Elizabeth, now widow of Arthur Moseley, and at her death said land was to descend to his daughter Elizabeth, now wife of Samuel Hancock Jr. Arthur Moseley's will was dated Feb. 1728/9 and probated 1729 (33V 318)

Less than two months after the deed of gift of Sept. 24, 1733, Samuel Hancock Jr. and Elizabeth, his wife, sold on Nov. 1, 1733, their part of the tract of 200 acres, heretofore given them, to William Robertson as follows: "155 acres given by my grandfather Robert Hancock, in 1708 to my mother, Johan Hancock and my father, Samuel Hancock, and in 1719 deeded by my father, Samuel Hancock, to my uncle, Robert Hancock, except 45 acres conveyed and given me by deed of gift". (I.W.II, 1725-37, p.419).

Samuel Hancock, on May 3, 1736, bought from Thomas Jones 400 acres on Winterfork Creek patented by Richard Grills, deceased, and by him conveyed July 3, 1715, to Daniel Jones, father of Thomas Jones, same being part of 500 acres said Richard Grills sold to Daniel Jones on that date, the other 100 acres having been sold by him to John Read in 1731 (Deed Bk. 1736, p.543). Sarah wife of Thomas Jones, relinquished her dower rights. Their marriage occurred about 1736 as previous deeds were not signed by a wife (Ligon Bk. 555).

Samuel Hancock made his will in Chesterfield Sept. 1, 1760, same probated in that year (See will in full 33 V 319). Among his legatees was his daughter, Sarah Jones whom he gives "for and during her natural life the use, lent, and profit of a negro fellow named Dick and after her death I give said negro fellow to my grandson, Daniel Jones. (W.B.1-377).

Children:
I.   Simon made will in Bedford 1791, m. Jane Flournoy.
II.   John, made will in Chesterfield 1768.
III. Samuel Jr. moved to Prince Edward where Abraham Venable Jr. deeded him land April 1755 (O.B. 1754-58, p.35).
IV.   William, inventory filed in Befdord 1791.
V.   Johan, m. John Branch, will Chesterfield 1793.
VI.   Frances, m. Frances Osborne, will Chesterfield 1793.
VII. Sarah, b. 1719 or 1720, m. Thomas Jones and had Daniel Jones, mentioned in grandfather's will and Johanna who married William Reade and moved to Bedford. (See Reade V.H.G. p. 95 and Ligon Book 555-562 for descendants)

HARGRAVE
of
''''Oak Level", Sussex

The origin of this family is traced by Mr. G. Andrews Moriarity in an excellent article in the Virginia Magazine (Vol. 40, p.379). From the account he states that he hopes the Surry family will be able to connect with their ancestors in Lower Norfolk.

The first one of this family in Virginia was Richard Hargrave of Lower Norfolk who came from London in the "Bonaventure" sailing 2 January 1634-5. He then gave his age as 20 years (Hotten) and this age is afterwards confirmed by him in a deposition made 16 April 1672, when he gave his age as 60 years (N.E.G.R. Vol. 47, p.201). On 11 March 1652-3 he was granted 250 acres on Broad Creek, Elizabeth River in Lower Norfolk, 150 acres, part of patent granted to John Watkins 16 May 1644, and by him sold to said Hargrave 17 October 1646, and 100 acres for transporting 2 persons (C.P. 229).

He was evidently a Puritan for on December 15, 1654, he was one of a Grand Inquest that petitioned for a "Godly Minister", thus showing his Puritan leanings. In April 1674, he was granted 200 acres for transportation of four persons. He conveyed land to his son Benjamin Hargrave 12 August 1673, and again September 26, 1679. He made his will 21 November 1686, same proved 17 January 1686-7 (McIntosh Wills, Vol. I, p.100), and named children shown below and son in law Arthur Moseley.

Children:

I.   Richard born c 1645.
II.   Benjamin, born c. 1648. His will was dated March 15, 1704/5, proven 1710. He mentions an only daughter, Sarah; sister Ann Moseley, kinsman Charles Griffin.
III. Margaret, born c. 1650, m. Samuel Roberts.
IV.   Ann, born c 1653, m. as his third wife, before 20 Nov., 1686, Arthur Moseley, Burgess for Lower Norfolk, 1676, son of William and Susanna (Cockcroft) Moseley. The Moseley family was distinguished in Princess Anne County. Many of ther early portraits have been preserved. Arthur Moseley was married three times. His second wife was either a Guy or a Hancock, for she was a daughter of Sarah Pigott, whose first husband was a Guy and her second Simon Hancock (40 V 382) (Ligon-372)

By his third wife, Ann Hargrave, Arthur Moseley had Ames, Anthony, and Luke. Ames married Elizabeth, daughter of Tully Emperor, and had a son, Emperor, who removed to Nixonton, N.C. Emperor Moseley had two sons, Emperor who was a Master Mariner at Edenton, N.C., at the time of the Revolution, and Joseph who became a sea Captain and removed to Massachusetts.

Richard[2] Hargrave, eldest son of the above Richard, lived first in Lower Norfolk and later in Surry County. On August 17, 1682, as "Richard Hargrave Jr." he was brought before the County Court of Lower Norfolk for refusing to have a child baptized and may have been a Quaker dissenter. On 5 May 1693, he petitioned the court in right of his wife, Pembroke, one of the daughters of John Pead, dec., for a portion of her father's estate in hands of William Griffin who had married the said Pead's widow. He is shown as listed among the tithables in Surry on June 10, 1685, and on March 1699, he made his brother, Benjamin Hargrave, his attorney to acknowledge a deed for him in Norfolk (Norfolk Deeds 6, p.158) showing clearly that he formerly resided in that county.

John Pead patented 150 acres of land in Lower Norfolk, "beginning at a marked pine of William Beartines Creek on the south side of Winter Harbour near Point Comfort, Sept. 21, 1652. (C.P.265). He made his will Feb. 4, 1677/78, proved April 15, 1678. He gave his son, William Pead, first choice of his part of his lands and his son, Joseph, the other part. He divided his cattle between his wife and the other children inasmuch as William and John had cattle of their own. Wife executrix and neighbor, John Griffin, overseer. Wits.: John Griffin, James Pead (McIntosh 1-55).

Richard[2] Hargrave made his will 19 May 1704 and same was probated 4 July 1704. Samuel Thompson was the executor.

The children of Pembroke (Pead) and Richard Hargrave were: Bray, m. Mary (See later); Judith, m. James Lowrey; Lemuel (See later).

Lemuel[3] Hargrave, son of Richard[2] above, made his will 2 May 1740, probated 15 September 1742. He gave to his grandson, Jesse Hargrave, "that plantation where his mother now lives and all land on east side of Great Branch"*****100 acres and a mill to Samuel Hargrave when 21, son Jesse in possession of deceased son Benjamin's land on south side of Roanoke River in North Carolina. To grandson Samuel Hargrave, plantation where I lately lived on west side of Great Branch 100 acres. Legacies to son, Joseph Hargrave, and son in law, Anselm Bailey Jr. His children were: Jesse: Benjamin; Joseph; dau. m. Anselm Bailey Jr. (See Bailey).

Bray[3] Hargrave, son of Richard[2], served in the militia in 1687 (Col. Sur. -211). He, his brother, Lemuel, and his father, Richard, were tithables in Surry in 1688 (Id. 195).

Mary, wife of Bray Hargrave, was a daughter of Margaret and Augustine[2] Hunnicutt II. Augustine[2] made his will May 10, 1708, proven May 2, 1710. He bequeathed his plantation to his wife for Life then to his son, Augustine[3] Hunnicutt III. (BK. 6, p. 6) Margaret, wife of Augustine II made her will Aug. 23, 1717, probated July 16, 1718, and in it gave a legacy to her daughter MARY wife of BRAY HARGRAVE. Augustine[2] Hunnicutt II was the son of Augustine[1] Sr., who made his will May 30, 1682, probated March 6, 1682/3 and in his will added 40 acres to what he had already given his son Augustine[2], Jr. *(Bk. 2-325)

Bray lived in Lawne's Creek Parish where he died intestate in 1728. His wife, Mary, as administrator of his estate, filed an inventory of same in 1728. The appraisers were Robert Lancaster, Benj. Champion and John Holloman. His children were: Augustine[4] who married Mary (See later); Samuel[4] m. Martha Cheadle; Lemuel and Benjamin.

Augustine[4] Hargrave was a prosperous planter of Surry where he made his will which was probated June 21, 1763 (W.B. 1754-68). His legatees were his sons, William, Hartwell, Augustine, Thomas[5] (See later); and Hardy; daus. Katherine and Olive. (W.B. 1754-68).

Mary Hargrave, "sick and weak", made her death bed will Aug. 29, 1769, same probated Oct. 17, 1769. She mentioned all of the above children named by her husband except Hartwell and Katherine who were probably deceased. Katherine and her twin brother, Kesiah, were baptized March 23, 1743. Their Sponsors were Richard and Mary Murphy and Faith Judkins (Alb. Reg.)

Thomas[5] Hargrave, son of Augustine[4], lived in that part of Surry which later became Sussex. He was a Quaker and for reasons of conscience did not bear arms during the Revolution but is said to have served for a short time as a cook and died in 1781 or 1782. His wife, Letitia Lane, was a daughter of Joseph Lane (See Lane) and a descendant of Colonel John Flood, an Ancient Planter who came to Virginia on the Swan in 1610 and was Speaker of the House of Burgesses. Their children were: (1) William,[6] born Oct. 21, 1771, m. Sarah Ellis (See later); (2) Richard; (3) Lucy m. Pyland Travis; (4) Lemuel m. Letitia Lane (See Lane); (5) Sarah, m. William Turner.

William[6] Hargrave, son of Thomas[5] and Letitia Lane Hargrave, was born Oct. 21, 1771, according to the records of his son Rev. Richard Hargrave. The Albemarle Parish records of Sussex Co., Va., give his baptismal date as Nov. 21, 1771.

When a youth, William had witnessed the grief and consequent death of a Virginia slave whose family had been sold to Georgia Slave traders and it so affected him that he vowed that he would never take a day's service from a slave after he was legally competent to give him his freedom; and he kept his word.

William Hargrave had often listened to his father tell that he wished his son to be a preacher. He had heard, with a feeling of awe his father tell that on one occasion, while listening to Bishop Asbury preach, the Witness of the Spirit had been with him, saying "Your boy, William, will preach this gospel,""as clearly as though Bishop Asbury himself had spoken the words directly into his ear. It is not greatly to be wondered then, that after his father's death, influenced by the memory of his wish and the frequent prayers and psalm-singing of his widowed mother the lad felt continually oppressed with a yearning and a responsibility to make a definite avowal of religion. He said of that time, "I felt as though father's prayers were following me, wooing me to conversion and consecration." One evening when he was sixteen years of age, he went to his father's grave, and lying streached on the ground, full length beside the grave, prayed long and earnestly, not ceasing in his supplications for peace until he was wonderfully converted and blest. On becoming of age, several years later, his first act was

136

to give all his slaves their emancipation papers, feeling that slavery was contrary to the teaching of God's Word.

Opposition to Slavery caused the Hargrave family to move to Pike Co., Ind. in the year 1818. The country was new, and times exceedingly hard, and privations many and great. The people generally were poor and there were almost no schools then in the country.

Rev. William Hargrave and his son, Rev. Richard Hargrave were early Preachers in Pike County, Indiana, much loved and respected by the people they served.

William Hargrave was born Oct. 21, 1771; married Dec. 1, 1791, Sarah (Sallie) Ellis, the daughter of Elizabeth (Wright) and William Ellis, who was born at Richmond, Surry Co., Va., in 1769. When they settled in Pike Co., they named their home "Delectable Hill" near Otwell, Ind., where Sallie died April 28, 1840 and William on Feb. 8, 1849.

William Hargrave was a farmer and a local Methodist preacher.
Children:
I.   Lucy Hargrave, b. Oct. 29, 1792; m. Wesley DeBruler. (See later)
II.   Elizabeth Ray Hargrave, b. Nov. 2, 1795; m. Charles De-Bruler. (See later)
III.   Thomas R. Hargrave, b. Dec. 26, 1796; m. Martha Traylor
IV.   Martha Ellis Hargrave, b. Feb. 7, 1799; m. John Niblack.
V.   William Ellis Hargrave, b. Dec. 21, 1800, dsp.
VI.   Richard Hargrave, b. Dec. 5, 1803; m. Nancy A. Posey. (See later)
VII.   Lemuel B. Hargrave, b. July 13, 1806; m. Susannah W. De-Bruler.
VIII.   Sarah Hargrave, b. July 15, 1809; m. James Barnett.
IX.   Susannah Hargrave, b. Feb. 10, 1803; m. Andrew F. Kelso. (See later)

Lucy Hargrave, daughter of Sarah (Ellis) and William Hargrave, was born in Sussex County, Va., Oct. 29, 1793 and died at High Banks, Pike Co., Ind., Sept. 2, 1838. On Nov. 12, 1816 in Orange County, N.C. she married Wesley Debruler, the son of Mary (Hicks) and Micajah Greenfield DeBruler who was born in Granville County, N.C. Feb. 8, 1788; and died Nov. 9, 1863, in Boone Township, Dubois County, Ind.

Mr. DeBruler was a farmer.
Children:
I.   Lemuel Quincey DeBruler (twin), b. Sept. 21, 1817; m. Anna Condit.
II.   James Pressbury DeBruler (twin), b. Sept. 21, 1817; m. Sarah Graham.
III.   Thomas Franklin DeBruler, b. Jan. 5, 1820; m. Anna Baily.
IV.   John Hicks DeBruler, b. May 16, 1822; m. (1) Sarah Morgan; (2) Elizabeth A. Downey.
V.   Richard Ellis DeBruler, b. Feb. 6, 1828; m. Harriet McCristy. (See later)
VI.   Sarah Ann DeBruler, b. Feb. 3, 1830; m. Morris Sharp.

Richard Ellis DeBruler, son of Lucy (Hargrave) and Wesley

DeBruler, was born at High Banks, Pike County, Ind., Feb. 6,
1828 and died Dec. 6, 1906 at Otwell in the same county. On Sept.
6, 1848, in Boone Township, Dubois County, Ind., he married
Harriet Evaline, the daughter of Mary (Chapman) and John Mc-
Cristy, who was born in Boone Township Jan. 10, 1828, and died
there Jan. 25, 1897.

Children:

I.   Culvin Elbrige DeBruler, b. June 9, 1849; m. Elizabeth Mason.
II.   Lucy Adelaide DeBruler, b. Mar. 9, 1851; m. Robert Mitchell
       Craig. (See later)
III.   Mary Florence DeBruler, b. Dec. 12, 1852; m. Albert Rose.
IV.   Oliver Ellis DeBruler, b. May 12, 1856; m. Emma Davidson.
V.   Morris Franklin DeBruler, b. Oct. 30, 1859; m. Bell Hobbs.
VI.   Ella DeBruler, (twin) b. Oct. 25, 1862; m. Joseph Troyer.
VII.   Emma DeBruler, (twin) b. Oct. 25, 1862; m. Rev. M. L. Payton.

Lucy Adelaid DeBruler, daughter of Harriet E. (McCristy) and
Richard Ellis DeBruler, was born March 9, 1851 at Boone Township, Ind., and died in Otwell, Pike County, Ind., March 19, 1888;
on April 19, 1868 she married Robert Mitchell Craig, who was
born in Otwell, Pike Co., Ind., Nov. 17, 1843, and died there
April 25, 1930.

Mr. Craig was a community builder and was the first President
of the Otwell State Bank, a position which he held for 22 years. He
was a large land owner and business man. He was a member of
the Methodist Church, and served in every office that could be held
by a layman.

Children:

I.   Clement Ellis Craig, b. Feb. 13, 1869; m. Estella DeMotte.
       (See later)
II.   Harley Eben Craig, b. Oct. 19, 1872; m. Lula Abbott.
III.   Olive Frances Craig, b. Sept. 6, 1881; m. Walter Brinson.
       Children of second marriage to Emma Smoot:
IV.   Bernard Smoot Craig, b. Sept. 10, 1892; m. Emma Poth.
V.   Ethel Bernice Craig, b. Dec. 13, 1898; m. Clarence Whitehead.

Clement Ellis Craig, the son of Lucy Adelaide (DeBruler) and
Robert Mitchell Craig, was born in Otwell, Indiana, Feb. 13, 1869;
and married there on Feb. 8, 1909 Estella, daughter of Anna (Neihaus) and Dr. William Milton DeMotte, who was born April 28,
1887, in Haysville, Ind.

Clement Ellis Craig attended DePauw and Purdue Universities;
received his M. S. degree in Horticulture from the Virginia Poly-
technic Institute; he was with the Virginia Crop Pest Commission
for two years, where in addition to routine work he prepared a
bulletin on Pest Control; in 1908 he received his M. S. degree in
Agriculture from Cornell University, and taught at Purdue from
1909-12; he was Professor of Agronomia at the Institute de Agronomia, at Porto Alegre, Rio Grande du Sul, Brazil, S. A. from
1912-17; senior instructor in Agriculture in the U. S. Army at
Camp Dodge, in 1920. From 1920 to 1924 he was with the New
Mexico A. & M. College and Experiment Station where he taught
soils and prepared two bulletins on Soils. In 1924 he retired to
his farm near Otwell, Indiana.

There are no children.

Elizabeth Ray Hargrave, the daughter of Sarah (Ellis) and William Hargrave, was born in Sussex County, Virginia, November 2, 1705, and died at High Banks, Pike County, Indiana August 25, 1843. On Feb. 20, 1816, in Orange County, N.C. she married Charles DeBruler, son of Mary (Hicks) and Micajah Greenfield DeBruler, who was born at Granville, N.C. April 19, 1785 and died at High Banks, Pike County, Indiana, Dec.22, 1835.

Charles DeBruler was a Colonel in the Militia; and in 1820 a Justice of the Peace.

Children:

I.   William Greenfield DeBruler, b.Dec.2,1816; m.Rebecca Stubblefield.

II.   Jabes Milton DeBruler, b.Dec.11,1824, m.Eliza Payne.

III.   Susannah DeBruler, b.Feb.16,1827; m.John Banta DeMotte. (See later)

IV.   Eliza Ann DeBruler, b. April 13, 1828; m.(1) Wm.DeMotte; (2) M. Marshall.

V.   Charles Rufus DeBruler, m. Mahelia Stone.

Susannah DeBruler, daughter of Elizabeth Ray (Hargrave) and Charles DeBruler, was born at High Banks, Pike County, Feb. 16, 1827, and died at Boone Township, Ind., March 30, 1894. On Nov.10,1844 at Boone Township, she married John Banta DeMotte, son of Phoebe Banta and Lawrence DeMotte, who was born in Marion Township, Pike County, Ind., Aug.18,1823, and died in Boone Township, Feb.5,1898.

Children:

I.   William Milton DeMotte, b.Jan.5,1846; m.Anna Louise Neihaus. (See later)

II.   Mary Helen DeMotte, b.Mar.17,1847; m.James Nash.

III.   Eliza Ann DeMotte, b.June 22,1849; m. Jobe Chappell.

IV.   Hume Lawrence DeMotte, b.Jan.15,1852; m.Elizabeth Jane Green.

V.   Charles Albert DeMotte, b.Mar.10,1858; m.Ida Cordelia Wheeler.

VI.   Wesley Elsworth DeMotte, b.Nov.25,1862; m.Iva Brittain.

VII. Franklin E. DeMotte, b.Mar.23,1870; m.Arminta Nash.

Dr.William Milton DeMotte, the son of Susannah (DeBruler) and John Banta DeMotte, was born Jan.5,1846 at Boone Township, Ind. and died at Otwell, Ind., Mar.3,1931. On Jan.15,1873 he married Anna Louise, the daughter of Elizabeth (Miller) and Bernard L. Neihaus, at Huntingburg, Ind., where she had been born Dec.10,1852. She died May 3, 1923, at Otwell, Indiana.

Dr. DeMotte served in the Civil War in Company M, 10th. Indiana Cavelry. He attended the Collegiate Institute, Rockport, Ind. He graduated from the Cincinnati School of Medicine and Surgery on Feb.8,1871; and practiced his profession in Jasper, Haysville, and Otwell, where he continued until his death.

Children:

I.   Evaline DeMotte, b.Nov.19,1873; m.(1) Alexander Haury; (2) Ralph Boone Davidson.

II.   John Henry DeMotte, b.Nov.9,1875; m.Edith Hancock.

III.   Bernard L. (Ben) DeMotte, b.Sept.23,1879; m.Sallie Harris.

IV.   Lee DeMotte, b.Sept.6,1881; m. Martha Smith.

V.   Elizabeth Neihaus DeMotte, b.Oct.22,1883; m.Omer H. Stewart, M.D.

VI.   Estella May DeMotte, b.April 28,1887; m.Clement Ellis Craig. (See above)

Richard Hargrave, son of Sarah Ellis and William Hargrave was born at Yanceyville, Caswell Co., N.C. Dec.5,1803 and died at Attica, Ind. June 23, 1879. On March 10, 1829 at Bruceville, Knox County, Ind., he married Nancy A., the daughter of Richard Posey, Jr., and Frances (Allen), who was born at Bruceville,Ind., 1806 and died at Attica, Ind., June 12, 1871.

Richard Hargrave was a Preacher and District Superintendant of the Methodist Church, Indiana Conference.

Children:

I.   Sarah Frances Hargrave, b.Dec.24,1829; m.Rev.Noah Lathrop.

II.   William Posey Hargrave, b.June 1, 1832; m. Martha Erskin.

III.   Caroline Indiana Hargrave, b. April 18, 1834; m. Jonathan Campbell.

IV.   Richard Watson Hargrave, b.Sept.15,1836; m.Myra T. Hooker; d.1861; m. (2) Augusta Beacler, in 1864.

V.   Mary Elizabeth Hargrave, b.June 2, 1838, m. Elisha Little. (See later)

VI.   John Wesley Hargrave, b.Aug.11,1844; m.Charlotte Erskin. (See later)

VII.   Lucy Ellen Hargrave, b.Oct.26,1846; m.Elisha Little. (See Later)

VIII. Martha Ann Hargrave, d. in childhood.

Mary Elizabeth Hargrave, daughter of Nancy Anna (Posey) and Richard Hargrave, was born June 2, 1838 at La Porte, Ind., and died June 24, 1875 in Adams Township, Warren Co., Ind. On May 23, 1865 at Thorntown, Boone Co., Ind., she married Elisha Little, the son of Sarah (Oneall) and George Little, who was born Oct.13,1837 at Adams Township and died Aug.31,1918 at Williamsport, Ind.

Elisha Little graduated from Brown Academy in Thorntown, and entered the Union Army in 1862; served in Co.D, 10th Infantry Regiment until 1865. He was a farmer, and served in the Indiana Legislature.

Children of 1st. wife, Mary Elizabeth (Hargrave):

George Hargrave Little, and Anna Laura Little died in childhood.

I.   Carrie May Little, b.Dec.24,1871; m.Victor Howard Ringer. (See later)

II.   Leila Posey Little, b.Aug.20,1873, m. James M. Brink.

Children of 2nd.wife, Lucy Ellen (Hargrave):

III.   William Oneall Little, b.Feb.21,1878; m.Rose Ethel Brooks.

IV.   Richard Harrison Little, b.June 16,1884; m.Edna Ann Watkins.

Carrie May Little, daughter of Mary Elizabeth (Hargrave) and Elisha Little, was born in Adams Township, Ind., Dec.24,1871 and married June 16, 1926 in Indianapolis, Ind. Victor Howard

Ringer, son of Margaret (Schlosser) and Jacob Howard Ringer, was born Feb.13,1870 near Williamsport, and died there Oct.13, 1948.

Mr. Ringer was an attorney for over 53 years.

Mrs. Ringer graduated from De Pauw University in Greencastle, Ind., in 1901; studied in University of Wisconsin, Columbia Teachers College, University of California at Los Angeles. She was a member of Alpha Chi Omega Sorority at De Pauw. She was a teacher.for 33 years; seven years in Harrisburg Township High School, and fourteen years English teacher in Shortridge High School in Indianapolis. She is a member of the D.A.R. of Wm. Allen of N.C. line. Her present address is: 4 Center Street, Williamsport, Indiana.

No children.

John Wesley Hargrave, son of Nancy Posey and Richard Hargrave, was born Aug.11, 1844 at Crawfordsville, Ind., and died March 17,1915 at Kaw Valley, Kansas. On April 7, 1869 at Evansville, Ind., he married Charlott, daughter of Rev.John Erskin, who was born at McCutheonsville (later Evansville), Ind., Jan.31,1844 and died at Kaw Valley, Kansas, Feb.28,1915.

John Wesley Hargrave served in the Union Army in the 72nd. Volunteer Infantry in the War between the States.

Children:
I.   Martha Hargrave, b.Feb.21,1870; m.Charles E.Weeks.
II.   Richard Hargrave, b.Sept.10,1871; m.Grace Moralee.
III.   William Hargrave, b.Jan.17,1874; m.Dora Hinze.
IV.   Albion F. Hargrave, b.Jan.15,1875; m.Susanne Spuhler. (See later)
V.   Mary Hargrave, b.March 15,1878; m.Levi Erskin.
VI.   Caroline Hargrave, b.Nov.10,1876, d. in infancy.
VII.   Anna Hargrave, b.Feb.22,1881, d.Sept.10,1885.

Albion Fellows Hargrave, son of Charlotte (Erskin) and John Wesley Hargrave was born June 15, 1875 in Rensallear, Ind. On June 20, 1906, in Chicago, Ill., he married Susanne, daughter of Susanne (Winkler) and John Spuhler, who was born Sept.20, 1877 at Chicago and died Nov.30,1953 at Hinsdale, Ill.

Mr. Hargrave was educated at Kansas State College, Manhattan, Kan., and Northwestern University, Chicago. He has been an accountant in the Moody Bible Institue of Chicago since 1915.

Children:
I.   John Wesley Hargrave, b.July 18, 1907; m.Lucinda Hadsel. (See later)
II.   Albion F. Hargrave, Jr., b.Dec.8, 1911; m.Ione Safstrom.

John Wesley Hargrave, son of Susanne (Spuhler) and Albion F. Hargrave, Sr., was born July 18, 1907 at Chicago Ill., and married June 5, 1937 at Oxford, Ohio, Margaret Lucinda, daughter of Mary Lucinda (Perine) and Fred Latimer Hadsel, who was born Jan.28, 1912 at Oxford.

Mr. Hargrave received his B.S. in Architecture at the University of Cincinnati in 1929. He is a Registered Architect and Registered Professional Engineer. He was President of the University of Cincinnati Alumni Association, 1945-51; President

Architects Society of Ohio, 1953-54; Vice-President, Food Facil-
ities Engineering Society, 1955.

Mr. and Mrs. Hargrave now reside at 7070 Dearwester Dr.,
Cincinnati, Ohio.

Children:
I.   John Wesley Hargrave, Jr., b. May 30, 1942.
II.   Fred Hadsel Hargrave, b. May 23, 1945.
III. Lucinda Susanne Hargrave, b. March 11, 1948.

Susanna Hargrave, daughter of Sarah(Ellis) and William Hargrave, born in Caswell County, N.C., on Feb.10,1813 and died
August 26, 1889 at Ireland, Dubois Co., Ind.; married there Sept.
17, 1829 Andrew Foster Kelso, who was born in Spartanburg
County, S.C., July 20, 1807, and died at Ireland, Ind., July 12,
1872.

Susannah Hargrave and her husband, Andrew Foster Kelso
settled in Ireland, Dubois Co., Ind., in 1830, where he farmed
and operated a grist mill. Andrew served in the Civil War. He
was a trustee several years for the Shiloh Church in Dubois
County.

Children:
I.   William Hargrave Kelso, b. Feb. 26,1831, m. Nancy A. Chap-
       pel. (See later)
II.   Lemuel Locke Kelso, b. July 7, 1832, m. (1) Sarah T. Chap-
       pel; (2) Mary J. Coffman.
III.   James Lynn Kelso, b. 1834, m. Elizabeth J. McMurtery.
IV.   Sallie Ellis Kelso, b. Aug. 13,1835; m. Thomas Hill.
V.   John Foster Kelso, b. 1837, died young.
VI.   Martha Ann Kelso, b. 1839, d. Jan. 1,1857.
VII.   Elizabeth Jane Kelso, b. April 22, 1840, m. Charles Preston.
VIII. Benjamin Hall Kelso, b. March 19,1842, m. Mary Ellen
       Turner.
IX.   Lucy Angeline Kelso, b. 1843, d. young.
X.   Mary Caroline Kelso, b. July 11, 1845, m. Albert H. Stewart.

William Hargrave Kelso, the son of Susanna (Hargrave) and
Andrew Foster Kelso, was born Feb. 26,1831 in Knoxville, Dubois
Co., Ind., and died May 30, 1909, at Jefferson Township, Pike
Co., Ind. On Nov. 18,1852 he married Nancy A., daughter of
Jemima (Grayson) and Josiah Chappell. She was born April 13,
1833 at Jefferson Township, and died there Feb. 24,1892.

Children:
I.   Lelia Kelso, b. 1856; m. James Chew.
II.   Jemima A. Kelso, b. Mar. 4,1860; m. Elwood Capehart.
III. Andrew Homer Kelso, b. Sept. 5,1862; m. Mary Cowen.
IV.   Susanna A. Kelso, b. Dec. 15,1872; m. Alvin T. Capehart.
      (See later)

Susanna Kelso, who was born Dec. 15,1872, in Jefferson Township, and died April 23, 1921 at Algiers, Pike Co., Ind., married
at Jefferson Township, Aug. 21,1890, Alvin Thomas Capehart, the
son of Elizabeth (Thomas) and George Capehart, was born Oct. 20,
1866 at Jefferson Township, and died March 2, 1949 at Washington,
Daviss Co., Ind.

Children:
I.   Bessie Ann Capehart, b. June 24, 1891; m. Byron Haskins.
       (See later)
II.   Homer Earl Capehart, b.June 6, 1897 (U.S. Senator), m.
       Irma Mueller.
III.   William Paul Capehart, b. Sept.3, 1899; m. Lida Richey.
IV.   Ivan Elwood Capehart, b.Sept.20,1905; m. Ellen Young.

     Bessie Ann Capehart, who was born June 24, 1891 at Jefferson
Township, married Oct.1, 1909, at Otwell, Ind., Byron Haskins,
the son of Margaret Isabel (Wiseman) and Ellsworth Haskins, who
was born Aug.21,1890, in Boone Township, Dubois Co., Ind. Both
were educated in the township schools, and have engaged in farming
all their lives. Since 1936, Mr. Haskins has been the Manager of
the 2500 acre farm owned by his brother-in-law, Senator Homer
E. Capehart. This farm is located in Daviss County, Indiana, north
of the city of Washington.
       Children:
I.   Harry A. Haskins, b.May 12, 1910; m.Frances Kooper-
       schmidt.
II.   Robert Ellsworth Haskins, b. Mar.7,1913; m.Imogene Moore.
III.   Byron Cameron Haskins, b.Mar.7,1916; m.Julia White.
       (Divorced)
IV.   Ivan Ray Haskins, b.July 8,1919; m.Velma Beck.
V.   William Homer Haskins, b.Aug.1, 1923; m.Marie Kinniman.
VI.   Joseph Lee Haskins, b.Sept.6, 1926; m.Betty Bateman.
VII.   Jack Barnett Haskins, b.Jan.26, 1929.

     Lemuel Locke Kelso, the son of Susanna (Hargrave) and An-
drew Foster Kelso, was born July 7, 1832. He farmed in Dubois
County, Indiana until the Civil War, when he enlisted and eventu-
ally became a second lieutenant in Co. F., 10th. Indiana Calvery.
After the war, he increased his holdings of land in Boone Town-
ship, Dubois Co., to 440 acres. He was active in public affairs
until his death on April 19, 1919. He married first Sarah Turner
Chappell, and after her death Sept. 19, 1878 he married Mary
Jane Coffman.
       Children by first wife:
I.   Oscar Lynn Kelso, b.Oct.10,1854; m.Carrie Bolandbaker.
II.   Florence Elizabeth Kelso, b. July 24, 1856; m.James Corn.
       (See later)
III.   Erasmus Lee Kelso, b.Mar.23,1857; m.Gay Underwood.
IV.   Lincoln Phelps Kelso, b.Oct.25,1859; m.Sarah Glezen.
       (See later)
V.   Susannah B. Kelso, b.Feb.11,1861; m.Joseph H. Barr.
       (See later)
VI.   Benjamin Hall Kelso, b.July 11, 1863; m. Ida Flint.
VII.   Jemima Alice Kelso, b.Nov.8,1864; d. July 22, 1876.
VIII. Ulyssess Grant Kelso, b.July 20,1866; m.Dena Schrolring.
IX.   Edith Kelso, b.July 30, 1871; m. John Gude.
X.   Effie Kelso, b.Sept.5,1873; m.John Boyd.
       Children by second wife:
XI.   Zenas Cicero Kelso, b.June 9, 1882; m. Verda Brown.
       (See later)

XII.   Issac Howard Kelso, b. July 5, 1884; m. Maud Sulivan.
XIII. Harry Andrew Kelso, b. Feb. 4, 1887; m. Dove Haskins.
XIV. Clara Annetta Kelso, b. Feb. 5, 1890.
XV.   and XVI. Twins, died at birth.

Florence Elizabeth Kelso, the daughter of Sarah T. (Chappel) and Lemuel Locke Kelso, was born July 24, 1856; married James Corn and lived in Ireland, Dubois Co., Ind., where James owned 200 acres of farming land and ran a sawmill. In 1890 they moved to Jasper, Ind., where James served as postmaster, returning to the farm after four years. In 1900 they moved to Oklahoma, eventually settling in Faxon, Comanche Co.
    Children:
!.   Sarah Myrtle Corn, b. Oct. 21, 1880; m. Willis E. Betkin.
II.   Lawrence Mosby Corn, b. Aug. 18, 1882; m. Virginia Arnett.
III.   Lemuel Lock Corn, b. Feb. 7, 1884.
IV.   John W. Corn, b. Mar. 27, 1885; d. Dec. 23, 1922.
V.   Maud Margery Corn, b. Apr. 10, 1887; m. Henry Parker.
VI.   Everett Clyde Corn, b. July 19, 1889; m. Ann Marie Karr.
VII.   Elfa Beatrice Corn, b. June 19, 1891; m. Victor Lawson.
VIII.   Edna Grace Corn, b. Nov. 26, 1894; m. Noah Wesley Arring-
        ton. (See later)

Edna Grace Corn married in Lawton, Oklahoma, June 1, 1913, Noah Wesley Arrington, son of Priscilla Jane (Brisindene) and LeRoy Madison Arrington (See later) who was born in Reed Hill, Cocke County, Tenn., Nov. 30, 1889. Shortly thereafter they migrated to Twin Falls, Idaho, where Noah acquired 230 acres of choice irrigated land east of the city for his farming operations. He was also active in Civic affairs and in the Latter-Day Saints Church.

        Children:
I.   LeRoy Wesley Arrington, b. Jan. 15, 1914; m. Nov. 12, 1936,
        Mary Frances, daughter of Mary Frances (Taylor) and
        James Daniel Emanuel Pruit Nix, b. July 26, 1916 at Pirch-
        ard, Mobile County, Alabama. They are now farming east
        of Twin Falls.
        Children:
        1. Mary Drena Arrington, b. Jan. 1, 1938, at Ogden, Utah.
        2. Patty Jean Arrington, b. Feb. 2, 1943, at Twin Falls, Idaho.
II.   Thelma Eileen Arrington, b. Feb. 14, 1916; d. Jan. 23, 1917.
III.   Leonard James Arrington, b. July 2, 1917; was educated at
        the University of Idaho and the University of North Carolina,
        receiving the degree of Doctor of Philosophy in Economics
        from the latter institution in 1952. He is now Associate Pro-
        fessor of Economics at the Utah State Agricultural College
        in Logan, Utah. On Apr. 24, 1943, in Rawleigh, N.C. he mar-
        ried Grace, the daughter of Nina Haith (Cocke) and John
        William Fort, who was born Feb. 9, 1914, at Wake Forest,
        N.C. They reside at 754 N. 5th., E, Logan, Utah.
        Children:
        1. James Wesley Arrington, b. Dec. 17, 1948, at Logan, Utah.
        2. Carl Wayne Arrington, b. Sept. 13, 1951, at Logan, Utah.
        3. Susan Grace Arrington, b. Aug. 25, 1954, at Logan Utah.

IV. Marie Arrington, b. May 5,1919; m. Ezra E. Davidson. (See later)
V. Kenneth Richard Arrington, born Nov. 10,1923, m. Sept. 17, 1942 (divorced) Juanita Georgiana, daughter of Mary Francis (Taylor) and James Daniel Elemual Pruit Nix, b. Apr. 19,1923; m. (2) Doris Viola Baldwin, and at present is farming near Twin Falls, Idaho, on R.#3.
Children of 1st. wife:
1. Farlin Wesley Arrington, b. Aug. 15,1943.
Children of 2nd. wife:
2. Richard Baldwin Arrington, b. July 3, 1953.
VI. Asa Wayne Arrington, b. May 10, 1925.
VII. Doris Elaine Arrington, b. Sept. 23,1927.
VIII. Donald Charles Arrington, born July 25, 1929, at Twin Falls, Idaho, served 2 years in Occupation Army in Germany, m. Sept. 19,1952, at Logan Utah, Bella Cleene Baird, daughter of Florence Edith (Harris) and Ernest Wallace Baird, b. Jan. 19,1933 at Carey, Idaho; and at present is farming east of Twin Falls on R.#3.
Children:
1. Douglas Reed Arrington, born Oct. 20,1954, at Jerome, Jerome County, Idaho.
IX. Ralph Marvin Arrington, b. Dec. 11, 1930.
X. Ross Lamont Arrington, b. Feb. 7,1934.

Marie Arrington, daughter of Edna Grace (Corn) and Noah Wesley Arrington was born May 5, 1919 at Twin Falls; married Sept. 23,1937 in Salt Lake City, Ezra Earl Davidson, son of Lillian (Tucker) and Charles Earl Davidson, who was born in Oakly, Ida., May 6,1917; and served two years in the U.S. Navy during World War II; and was associated in business with his father.
Children, born in Twin Falls:
I. Milton Earl Davidson, b. Sept. 16,1938.
II. Deanna Marie Davidson, b. June 6,1940, d. June 10, 1952.
III. Charles Ezra Davidson, b. July 1, 1944.
IV. Jerry Dean Davidson, b. Jan. 10,1948.

The children of Leroy Madison Arrington and his wife Priscilla Jane Brisindine, were all born in Tennessee, either in or near Cocke County.
Children:
I. Bruce Sidney Arrington, b. July 6, 1880; m. Bessie Mae Emerson. (See later)
II. Le Anner Arrington, b. Apr. 3,1883; m. Willian O. Fisher. (See later)
III. Grover Nicholas Arrington, b. Sept. 5,1885; m. Katherine Hassenbalg. (See later)
IV. Jacob Frank Arrington, b. Oct. 9,1887; m. Annie M. Shields. (See later)
V. Noah Wesley Arrington, b. Nov. 30,1889, m. Edna Grace Corn, his cousin.
VI. Robert Glenn Arrington, b. June 6,1893, m. (1) Annie Lunnet Tuttle; m. (2), Bertha Workman Weatherman. (See later)
VII. Joseph Earl Arrington, b. June 21,1895; m. Genevieve Thornton. (See later)

Bruce Sidney Arrington, son of Priscilla J. (Brisindine) and Leroy Madison Arrington, was born at Newport, Cocke Co., Tenn., July 19, 1880; and married at Salt Lake City, Utah, Nov. 28, 1910, Bessie Mae, the dau. of Annie Louise (Crocker) and Chas. Perry Emerson, who was born at Yates Center, Woodson Co., Kansas, Sept. 1, 1887.

Mr. and Mrs. B. S. Arrington now reside at 801 Saturn, Idaho Falls, Idaho. Children:

I. Woodrow Emerson Arrington, b. Sept. 18, 1911, at Magna, Salt Lake City, Utah, m. Marjorie Darlene, dau. of Cecil Florence (Carstensen) and Ernest Clark Sherwood, b. Mar. 20, 1922 at Salt Lake, Utah, and m. Sept. 28, 1942 at Logan, Utah. Their address is now, Care Arrington Construction Co., Idaho Falls, Idaho. Children:
    1. John Sherwood Arrington, b. July 1, 1943.
    2. George Raymond Arrington, b. Aug. 13, 1943.
    3. Marwood Jeanette Arrington, b. Mar. 16, 1948.
    4. Howard Eugene Arrington.
    5. Barbara Arrington.
    6. Ronald Arrington, b. 1955.
II. Earl Monroe Arrington, b. Oct. 26, 1917, at Magna, Salt Lake, Utah; d. May 4, 1952 at Salt Lake City, Utah and was buried at Pocotello, Idaho. On Jan. 5, 1947 at Pocotello, he m. Maxine, the dau. of Katherin (Ebers) and Clerice Marchetti, who was born Oct. 27, 1923 at Pocatello, Idaho, where she now resides.

Le Anner Arrington, dau. of Priscilla Jane and Leroy M. Arrington was b. Apr. 3, 1883 at Parrotsville, Cooke Co., Tenn., and m. Mar. 1, 1908 at Lawton, Okla., William Orvil Fisher, son of Ida Irene (Sipe) and Samuel Brown Fisher who was b. Sept. 18, 1888 at Guthrie Center, Iowa.

Mr. and Mrs. W. O. Fisher now reside at Heyburn, Idaho. Children:

I.   Priscilla Irene Fisher, b. July 7, 1909, d. Dec. 17, 1916, Lawton, Okla
II. Alma Orvil Fisher, b. Elgin, Okla., Sept. 13, 1911, d. Jan. 17, 1933.
III. Newel Maroni Fisher, b. Jan. 14, 1914 at Twin Falls, Idaho, m. May 24, 1937 at Uale, Ore., Elma Elizabeth, dau. of Fannie Fern (Flake) and Ira N. Kelly, who was born June 3, 1917, at Ruper, Idaho. They now reside at Haywood, Idaho, R. #1.
     Children; born at Rupert, Mimiduke Co., Idaho.
     1. William Newel Fisher, b. Aug. 9, 1938.
     2. Walter Ira Fisher, b. Sept. 15, 1944.
     3. Kelly Marion Fisher, b. 1946.
     4. Jane Fisher, b. 1951, died in infancy.
IV. Ernest Arrington Fisher, b. Oct. 7, 1915, at Twin Falls, Idaho; m. Nov. 24, 1937, Hazel Virginia, daughter of Dorothy (Barger) and Louis Johnson, born March 21, 1919, at Preston, Idaho. Their present address is Terry Appliance Store, 9th. & State, Boise, Idaho. Children:
     1. Gordon Ernest Fisher, b. Apr. 1, 1939 at Preston, Idaho.
     2. Garth Johnson Fisher, b. Feb. 25, 1941, at Preston.
     3. Judith Fisher, b. 1947, at Boise, Idaho.
V.   Joseph Byron Fisher, b. May 4, 1918 at Wendall, Idaho; m. Maxine Cranney.
VI. Horace Eugene Fisher, b. May 5, 1922, at Heyburn, Idaho; m. Bette, the daughter of Ellen Lavera (Rawson) and John Carlton Fenton, b. Sept. 9, 1925 at Rupert, Idaho. Their present address is Pegg St., Boise, Idaho. Children, born at Rupert, Idaho:

1. Gerald Eugene Fisher, b.July 3, 1943.
2. Karla Kay Fisher,b. May 27, 1946.

Grover Nichols Arrington,son of Priscilla J.and Leroy M.Arrington,was born Sept. 5,1885 at Marshall,Madison Co. ,Tenn. ,and married June 4,1919 at Salt Lake City, Utah, Katherine, dau. of Clara Harrietta (Aherns) and Theodore Hassenbalg,who was born Aug.29, 1889 at Denver,Colo. They now reside on R.#2, Twin Falls, Idaho.
   Children:
I.   Harold David Arrington,b.Sept.2,1920 at Twin Falls,Idaho,m. Aug.26,1943,at Salt Lake City Billie Joyce,dau.of Bertha Isbel (Morgan) and Asa Morgan Bolton,b.Apr.21,1927 at Elmonita,Los Angeles Co. ,Calif. ,christened Apr.1927,at Baldwin, Calif. They reside at 830 Ash, Twin Falls, Idaho.
         Children, born at Twin Falls:
      1. Kathryn Joyce Arrington, b.June 6, 1944.
      2. Curtis David Arrington, b. Aug. 1, 1945.
      3. Ruth Rebecca Arrington, b.Dec. 2, 1946.
      4. Gary Theodore Arrington, b. March 9, 1951.
      5. Phyllis Marline Arrington, b.June 21, 1954.
II.   Ruth Arrington, b.Sept.7,1922; d.Oct.26, 1924.
III. Helen Mae Arrington (adopted), b.Feb.7, 1926, Boise, Idaho, m. Henry Matson.
IV.   Naomi Arrington (adopted),b.Mar.26,1930, Bosie, Idaho.

Jacob Franklin Arrington, son of Priscilla and Leroy M. Arrington,was born Oct.19,1887 at Reed Hill,Cocke Co. ,Tenn. , and m.May 1,1914 at Lawton,Okla. ,Annie Margaret,dau.of Mary (Jeneson) and Thomas Wm.Shields who was b.Aug.28,1893,at Taylor, Tex.Mr.and Mrs.Jacob Arrington now reside at 119 Tyler,Twin Falls, Idaho. Children, all born at Twin Falls:
I.   Annie Velma Arrington, b. May 3, 1915; m.July 27,1938, Franklin Cox,at.Cardston, Alberta, Canada. He was the son of Alice Charlotte (Erickson) and Franklin Saunders Cox. They now reside at 125 Buchannon, Twin Falls, Idaho.
         Children, all born at Twin Falls:
      1. James Stanley Cox, b.March 25, 1940.
      2. Charlotte Anne Cox, b. Oct.30, 1942.
      3. Richard Arrington Cox, b.June 28, 1947.
II.   Verda Louise Arrington,b. May 9, 1917; d. Feb.16, 1939.
III. Melvin J.Arrington,b.June 17,1923; m.Aug.19,1948,Norma Rae Lees,dau.of Frank E.Lees,in Salt Lake City,Utah.They now reside at 1494 W.3rd.W; Provo, Utah,and have one son, David Lees Arrington,b.in Provo May 1, 1955.
IV.   Margaret Valene Arrington,b.Oct.18,1929;m.June 21,1950, Gordon Linwood Crokett, the son of Anna (Hansen) and John A.Crockett,b.at Logan,Utah,Nov.11,1920.They now reside at 184 Taylor,Twin Falls. Children born in Twin Falls, Idaho:
      1. DeLana Lynn Crockett, b.June 16, 1951.
      2. John Arrington Crockett, b.May 5, 1954.
      3. Gordon Linwood Crockett, b.Aug.24, 1955.

Noah Wesley Arrington, the son of Priscilla and Leroy M.Arrington, was born at Reed Hill, Cocke C. ,Tenn, , Nov.30,1889. (For an account of his wife, Edna Grace Corn, and their children and grandchildren see CORN just before these Arringtons)

Robert Glenn Arrington, the son of Priscilla and Leroy M. Arrington, was born June 6,1893 at Reed Hill, Cocke Co., Tenn; he married, Sept. 20,1917, Annie Lunnet, daughter of Cynthia Estell (Jones) and Edgar Amos Tuttle, who was born June 14, 1895 at Menon Utah, and died at Twin Falls Nov. 20,1940 and is buried in the Twin Falls Cemetery. Mr. Arrington later married Bertha Workman Weatherman, and they now reside on R.#2, Twin Falls, Idaho.

Children of 1st wife:

I. Annie Belle Arrington, b.June 24,1918; d.June 1, 1921.
II. Mildred Flora Arrington, b.June 17,1919 at Magna Utah; m.Dec.23,1940 in Twin Falls, Joseph Earl Shrobe, the son of Lenora Forrest (Bennett) and John Leslie Shrobe, b. Sept. 8, 1913, at Filer, Idaho; they now reside on R.#2, Twin Falls, Idaho.
Children, born at Twin Falls:
1. Leslie Glenn Shrobe, b.Dec.12,1941.
2. Verna Gertrude Shrobe, b.Oct.15,1943.
III. Elsie Lea Arrington, b.Mar.19,1921, m.Aug.20,1941, at Salt Lake City, Francis Marion Egbert, Jr., son of Xenia LaVere (Hale) and Francis Marion Egbert, Sr., b.April 9, 1920. They now reside at 347 Sunrise Blvd. N., Twin Falls, Idaho.
Children, born in Twin Falls:
1. David Eugene Egbert, b.July 24,1942.
2. Le Larane Egbert, b.April 28, 1944.
3. Kendal Francis Egbert, b.Aug.28,1945.
4. Carol Anne Egbert, b.Dec.24,1946.
5. Merl Wayne Egbert, b.Feb.25,1949.
6. Myrna Louise Egbert, b. Oct. 5, 1950.
7. Loa Laree Egbert, b.Oct.30, 1954.
IV. Howard Glenn Arrington, b.Apr.12,1923; m.May 29,1946, at Idaho Falls, Idaho, Janell, daughter of Verona (Allen) and Frank Matthais Ravston, b. May 7, 1926. They now reside on R #2, Twin Falls, Idaho.
Children, all born at Twin Falls:
1. Susan Janell Arrington, b.Sept.26,1947.
2. Mary Lynn Arrington, b.May 7, 1949.
3. Glenn Steven Arrington. b.Feb.7, 1952.
4. Rita Calleen Arrington, b.July 13,1953.
V. Alden Carles Arrington, b. April 11, 1925; m.Sept.14,1949, Betty Jean Heth, b.1930 in Logan, Utah. They now live at 3955 S.2225 West, Roy, Utah.
Children, all born in Salt Lake, Utah:
1. Patricia Arrington, b.January 1951.
2. Katherine Arrington, b.July 26, 1953.
3. Dale Clayton Arrington, b.Oct.1954.
VI. Emma Irene Arrington, b.Mar.1,1927; m.Jan.8,1944 at Houston, Texas, (divorced) William Leslie Adams, son of Emma (Lynch) and David Renzie Adams, b.April 3,1922, in Houston, Tex. Mrs. Adams now resides at 21 Washington Cts., Twin Falls, Idaho.

Children:
1. Barbara Jeaĥ Adams, b. Sept. 9,1944 at Houston, Texas.
2. Terrance Ross Adams, b. Nov. 15, 1946 at Portland, Ore.
3. Eunice Elizabeth Adams, b. Mar. 12,1948, at Portland, Oregon.
4. Gail Irene Adams, b. Dec. 11,1949, at Vancouver, Wash.
5. Wanda Jane Adams, b. May 29, 1951, at Portland, Ore.
6. Richard Lee Adams, b. May 26,1953, at Portland, Ore.
VII. Lewis LaMar Arrington, b. Feb. 15,1929; m. Olive Louise, daughter of Hazel Amelia (Wells) and Frank Edwin Stevens, b. May 24,1929. They now reside at 1128 5th Ave., E., Twin Falls, Idaho.
Children:
1. Lydia Louise Arrington, b. Sept. 17,1952, at Twin Falls, Idaho.
2. Steven LaMar Arrington, b. Feb. 3,1954, at Monterey, California.
VIII. Gilda Lunnett Arrington, b. Feb. 14,1931; m. June 27,1948 at Twin Falls, Idaho, Harold J. Garrison, b. Feb. 1,1927 at Fiter, Idaho, son of Lillie (Barton) and Frank Garrison. Mr. and Mrs. H. J. Garrison reside at 42 Washington Cts., Twin Falls, Idaho.
Children:
1. Larry Lewis Garrison, b. June 20,1949, at Boise, Idaho.
2. Cynthia Jean Garrison, b. June 7, 1951, at Twin Falls, Idaho.
3. Sheila Marie Garrison, b. April 14, 1953, at Twin Falls, Idaho.
IX. Golden Elwyn Arrington, b. Jan. 15,1933.
X. Norman Eugene Arrington, b. Nov. 30,1935.
XI. Lee Orvıl Arrington, b. Feb. 1, 1939.

Joseph Earl Arrington, son of Priscilla and LeRoy M. Arrington, was born June 21, 1895, at Reed Hill, Cooke Co., Tenn., and married in Brooklyn, New York, Oct. 11,1932, Genevieve Thornton. They now reside at 8927-188 St., Hollis, N. Y., and have one son, Wendal Snow Arrington, who was born in Hollis, Oct. 3, 1936.

Lincoln Phelps Kelso, son of Sarah Turner Chappel and Lemuel Locke Kelso, was born Oct. 25,1859 in Ireland, Dubois Co., Ind. and died in Enid Oklahoma, Sept. 3, 1933. On Nov. 6, 1883, in Ireland he married Sarah Dillen Glezen, who was born in Ireland June 2, 1864 and died in Enid, Okla. Feb. 27, 1946.
Mr. Kelso was a farmer.
Children:
I. Mary Anna Kelso, b. Apr. 24,1885; d. Aug. 4,1914.
II. Sarah Turner Kelso, Jan. 20,1888; m. Porter W. Hopkins. (See later)
III. Edward Glezen Kelso, b. Apr. 8,1890.
IV. Lemuel Locke Kelso, b. Oct. 16,1891; m. Pauline Pierson.

Sarah Turner Kelso, daughter of Sarah Dillon Glezen and Lincoln P. Kelso, was born in Ireland, Ind., Jan. 20,1888, and married in Washington, D. C. on May 8,1918, Porter William

Hopkins, son of Alice Mathis and Frank Hopkins, who was born
August 6, 1880, in Ireland, Ind.

Dr. Hopkins was educated in Indiana and Kentucky as a phy-
sician and served as a Lieutenant in U.S. and France in World
War I. Mrs. Hopkins was educated in Indiana and is a graduate
nurse. They adopted two
> Children:
I.   Betty Jo Hopkins, b. Mar. 29, 1922; m. John Ewald Altenberg.
       Children:
       1. Terry Gene, b. 1945.
       2. Delira, b. 1949.
       3. Jimmy, b. 1952.
II.   Mary Lou Hopkins, b. March 4, 1924.

Susanna Bathsheba Kelso, daughter of Sarah Turner (Chappell)
and Lemuel Locke Kelso was born Feb. 11, 1861, near Ireland,
Ind., and died Feb. 1, 1943 at Bruceville, Knox Co., Ind. On Mar.
1, 1883 near Ireland, she married Joseph Hugh Barr, who was
born at Bruceville, Ind., where he died Feb. 1, 1922. He was a
farmer, stock raiser, banker and politician.
> Children:
I.   Hugh Lemuel Barr, b. Dec. 2, 1883; m. Clara Malinda Spel-
      burg. (See later)
II.   Sarah Kelso Barr, b. Dec. 24, 1884; m. Martin E. Linquest.
      (See later).
III.   Martha Baird Barr, b. Jan. 27, 1886; m. Don Douglas Slink-
      ard. (See later).
IV.   Oscar Lynn Barr, b. Sept. 14, 1887; m. Stella Walker Cham-
      bers.
V.   Charles Hollingsworth Barr, b. Apr. 17, 1892; m. Alice Belle
      Fox. (See later)

Hugh Lemuel Barr, son of Susannah Kelso and Joseph Hugh
Barr, was born in Bruceville, Knox County, Indiana on Dec. 2,
1883, and married Nov. 23, 1916 at Bicknell, Ind., Clara Malinda,
daughter of Rose Moore and Frank Spelburg, who was born Nov.
10, 1884 at Poland, Clay County, Indiana.

Mr. Barr was educated at Vincennes University, Vincennes,
Ind., and Indiana University, Bloomington, Ind. He was County
Attorney; Pauper Attorney; Proscecuting Attorney; Welfare Director; Member of State Committee for Prosecuting Attorneys of
Indiana. Head of several Lodges, including Royal Arch Masons
and Royal and Select Master Masons. He is now retired from the
law, and is a Real Estate Broker in Santa Barbara, California,
where they now reside at 1434 Bath Street. They have no children.

Sarah Kelso Barr, the daughter of Susanna Bathsheba (Kelso)
and Joseph Hugh Barr, was born in Bruceville, Indiana, Dec. 24,
1884, and married there, Oct. 26, 1915, Martin E. Linquest, who
was born at La Porte, Ind., April 20, 1890, the son of Emma
(Anderson) and Ernest G. Linquest, who was La Porte County
Recorder for many years.

Mr. Martin E. Linquest was Manager of Universal Atlas Ce-
ment Co.

Children:

I.   Ernest Barr Linquest, b. Dec. 3, 1919; d. April 12, 1953; m. June 11, 1949, Genevieve Thainer. He was a graduate of the University of Michigan and was a First Lieutenant in the in the second World War, serving in the European Theater; discharged July 4, 1946; recalled into service March 23, 1951; served in the Ordinance Dept. and served in Japan; discharged March 23, 1953.

Children:
1. Eric Barr Linquest, b. March 24, 1950 at Jackson, Mich.
2. Kurt Owen Linquest, b. June 24, 1953, at Jackson, Mich.

Martha Baird Barr, the daughter of Susannah (Kelso) and Joseph Hugh Barr, was born at Bruceville, Ind. January 27, 1886. On Dec. 25, 1905 she married Don Douglas Slinkard, who was born Nov. 27, 1882 at Edwardsport, Knox Co., Ind. Their address is Box 93, Bruceville, Ind.

Children:
1.   Susie Simonson Slinkard, b. Dec. 19, 1906 in Los Angeles, California where on Dec. 25, 1928 she married Virgil E. Williams, who was born in Indiana, Nov. 14, 1903. He was in the U. S. Navy for 8 years.

Children:
1. Virginia Sue Williams, b. Nov. 6, 1929 at Santa Barbara, Calif. m. July 12, 1946, at Chico, Calif., Joseph L. Dinnell, b. June 6, 1919 in California. He was in the Navy during World War II.
Children:
(1) Michael Lyle Dinnell, b. May 20, 1947 at Paradise, Calif.
(2) Jacqueline Sue Dinnell, b. July 17, 1949, at Paradise, Calif.
(3) Kathleen Diane Dinnell, b. July 6, 1951, at Paradise, Calif.
2. Walter Gayne Williams, b. June 23, 1935 is a recruit of the United States Navy at this time. (1955)

II.   Martha Ruth Slinkard, b. Jan. 30, 1910 at Bruceville, Ind.; m. Oct. 21, 1927 at Los Angeles, George E. Foley, b. Sept. 3, 1908 in Missouri. He was in the Marines before his marriage.
Children: both born in Los Angeles, California.
1. George Lee Foley, b. June 6, 1928; m. July 5, 1946 at San Francisco, Calif., Evelyn Schwartz, who was born Feb. 8, 1927 in California. He was in the Navy during World War II.
2. Richard Edward Foley, b. Aug. 25, 1931; m. Etta Faye Brewer, b. 1930 in Kentucky, in California, Feb. 5, 1955. He was in the Army, served in Korea, and is now a Sergeant, stationed at Petaluma, Calif.

III.   Joseph Wall Slinkard, b. Mar. 18, 1912, in Los Angeles; m. Sept. 20, 1932 at Nashville, Ind., Virginia Ruth McArthur, who was born Sept. 20, 1913, in Knox Co., Ind.

Children:
1. Donald Grant Slinkard, b. Sept. 8, 1933 in Indiana; d. Dec. 28, 1945 at Akron, Ohio.

IV.   Mary Alice Slinkard, b. Oct. 27, 1913, at Bruceville, Ind., m. there July 20, 1935, William E. Stedman, b. May 26, 1914, at New Lebanon, Ind.
Children:
1. Barbara Ann Stedman, b. Aug. 8, 1936, at Sullivan, Ind.
2. William Joe Stedman, b. Aug. 3, 1937, at Sullivan, Ind.
3. Joan Lynne Stedman, b. Dec. 5, 1942 at Greencastle, Ind.

V.   Alfred Barr Slinkard, b. Feb. 10, 1915, at Los Angeles; m. there Feb. 22, 1936, Alice Luella Hartka, b. July 11, 1917 at Los Angeles.
Children:
1. Rex Alfred Slinkard, b. Jan. 14, 1937 at Los Angeles.
2. Laura Luella Slinkard, b. Mar. 6, 1948, at North Hollywood, Calif.
3. Stephen Douglas Slinkard, b. Apr. 1, 1949, at North Hollywood, Calif.

VI.   Donna Douglas Slinkard, b. June 17, 1916, at Los Angeles; m. Oct. 29, 1938 at Bruceville, Ind., William Roger Ayers, b. June 15, 1913, at Logansport, Ind.
Children, all born at Gary, Indiana:
1. Douglas Roger Ayers, b. Sept. 30, 1940; d. same day.
2. Bruce Edward Ayers, b. Arp. 10, 1943.
3. Byron Lee Ayers, b. Dec. 17, 1946.
4. Cynthia Lynn Ayers, b. Dec. 5, 1948.

Charles Hollingsworth Barr of Bruceville, Ind., the son of Susanna Bathsheba (Kelso) and Joseph Hugh Barr was born in Bruceville April 17, 1892. He married, October 14, 1914 at Bicknell, Knox Co., Ind., Alice Belle Fox, who was born there June 6, 1894.
Children:
I.   Mary Lou Barr, b. April 29, 1917; m. Earl Edmund Faulkner.
II.   Charles Lee Barr, b. Jan. 6, 1924; m. Helen L. Morris.

Zenus Cicero Kelso, son of Mary J. (Coffman) and Lemuel Locke Kelso who was born June 9, 1882 was married at Pottsville, Ind., Aug. 10, 1902 to Nancy Lu Verda Brown, who was born April 20, 1880, and now lives at Willaims, Iowa. Zenus attended Culver Military Academy. After farming a few years in Indiana, he was Rural Mail carrier at Mountain Grove, Missouri for a time; then moved to Galva, Iowa. Their last move was to a farm near Williams, Iowa, about 1924. Zenus retired from the farm in 1930 and was employed by Hamilton County until his death. His hobby was working with his garden and flowers. They were married for a little more than 50 years.
Children:
1.   Vera Ruth Kelso, b. Dec. 24, 1903, near Ireland, Indiana, m. Feb. 9, 1927, Leslie A. Kolb, b. Jan. 14, 1892. Mrs. Kolb attended Iowa State Teachers College and taught school for a few years before her marriage. Her husband specialized in cattle feeding on their farm near Holstein, Ia., where all their children were born.

Children:
1. Joy Carmeen Kolb, b. Dec. 19, 1927, m. Wendall Everette Michaelson, b. Aug. 9, 1923. They live at Ida Grove, Iowa, where her husband is in the Automobile and Farm Implement business. Joy took a business course and was employed in an office before her marriage.
    Children:
    (1) Susan Key Michealson, b. Aug. 25, 1948.
    (2) Lorna Jean Michaelson, b. Feb. 25, 1951.
    (3) David Len Michaelson, b. July 10, 1953.
    (4) Melanie Ann Michaelson, b. April 24, 1955.
2. Jo Ann Mae Kolb, b. April 25, 1930; m. Feb. 7, 1953, Harley Sherman Nelson, b. Aug. 23, 1929; they reside at Aurelia, Iowa.
    Children:
    (1) Kimberly Jo Nelson, b. May 14, 1955.
3. Mary Lou Kolb, b. Oct. 14, 1934, attended Buena Vista College, Teachers.
4. Nancy Lu Verda Kolb, b. Oct. 18, 1941; attending school.

II. Irene Wilhemina Kelso, b. June 12 at Mountain Grove, Mo.; married June 4, 1934, William Jennings Bryan, b. May 17, 1907. She graduated from Iowa State Teachers College and taught school for several years. They reside at 607 N. Joslin, Charles City, Iowa.
    Children:
    1. Janet Nadine Bryan, attends the State University of Iowa where she is enrolled in the School of Nursing, and hopes to obtain a degree in Science along with her R.N.
    2. Gerald William Bryan, attends High School.

III. Russell Vaughn Kelso, b. April 25, 1913, at Mountain Grove. Mo.; married March 6, 1942, Veronica McLaughlin. They now reside at 2946 Iowa Street, Davenport, Iowa. He was a soldier in World War II.
    Children:
    1. Douglas John Kelso, b. June 5, 1944.
    2. Gerald (Gary) David Kelso, b. June 11, 1946.
    3. Barbara Ann Kelso, b. Sept. 18, 1943.

IV. Doyle Don Kelso, b. June 4, 1920 at Galva, Iowa; married in 1944 at Camp Gruber, Okla., Lenore V. Westwick; and they now reside at 1104 Marsden, Ames, Iowa.
        He served in World War II, first in the Aleutian Islands and later in Europe as a member of the Signal Corps. Was wounded in Europe and given the Purple Heart; attended Radio and T. V. School in Kansas City, Mo. Now a radio engineer and has own T. V. business in Ames, Iowa.
    Children:
    1. Dennis Doyle Kelso, b. Oct. 19, 1947.
    2. Sherilyn Kay Kelso, b. Aug. 6, 1952.

V. Marion Burdette Kelso, b. Feb. 7, 1925 at Williams, Iowa; married June 9, 1944 Norma Jane Tysdale and they now reside at 832 Home Park Blvd., Waterloo, Iowa.
    Children:
    1. Steven Lynn Kelso, b. Aug. 23, 1953.

HART of SURRY

Henry[1] Hart, first of his family in Surry, "on the last day of August, 1635, """ patented 350 acres "on the south side of the maine River over against Jamestown Island" called "Pynie Point", bounded by Capt. Powell's and John Long's land, 100 for his own and personal adventure of his wife, Rebecca Harte and 250 for transportation of 5 persons. (C. P. 31)

Rebecca Harte probably did not survive the seasoning period, for on Aug. 15, 1637, Henry patented 250 acres in James City, on the Surry side for the transportation of his wife Elizabeth Harte and four other persons. (C. P. 63) On May 6, 1638 he transferred his first patent of 350 acres to Edward Stephenson and Henry Cookeney. (C. P. 86) The bounds of this patent were mistaken and the patent was surrendered and renewed by Sir Francis Wyatt. (Id.)

John Kempe, on Oct. 24, 1639, patented 500 acres "on Grey's Creek, N. E. upon HENRY HART and S. W. upon Thomas Grey. (C. P. 115) This shows that Henry Hart was a neighbor of the Warrens and Shepards who lived in this locality and with whom his family intermarried. It was also adjacent to the land of Thomas, son of John Rolfe, which was later purchased by Thomas Warren. (C. P. 121)

Henry Hart was deceased before July 3, 1648, for "Thomas[2] Hart, son of Henry Hart, deceased, was granted 100 acres at Smith's Fort. (C. P. 176) Thomas Hart married Anne Sheppard, daughter of Major Robert Sheppard (1604-1654) of Surry. Major Sheppard was a lieutenant, captain and major of militia, Justice of Surry and Burgess in 1646-47-48. Major Robert Sheppard married Elizabeth, daughter of William Spencer, Burgess of Mulberry Island 1624-32-33. William Spencer, Ancient planter, is noted as a member of the first expedition which arrived at Jamestown in 1607. (See Colonial Surry pp. 47-48.) Mrs. Elizabeth Shepard, widow of Major Robert Shepard married, secondly, Thomas Warren, builder of the famous "Warren House". (Id. 66-72. V. H. G. 244-46)

Thomas Hart was listed among the Tithables of Surry, June 10, 1668, but he was dead one year later by June 10, 1669, when the "Widow Hart" only was listed. Mrs. Hart married secondly, William Newson, between June 10, 1669 and Jan. 4, 1669/70, when as the wife of William Newson, she deeded land to their sister Alice Rawlings. (48 V. 268, Article by Dr. Holtzclaw)

William Newsom presented an account of the estate of Thomas Hart, decd., Nov. 4, 1674, mentions "my wife's third part" and the rest due to the three orphans of Thomas Harte, decd., vis.; HENRY, THOMAS, and ROBERT HARTE. William Newsom died in 1691, aged 43 years. His widow then married George Foster (1639-97) by whom apparently she had no children. However, George Foster had children by his first wife, Elizabeth, and two of his daughters by his first marriage married their step-brothers: Mary Foster married Henry Hart and Elizabeth Foster married Thomas Hart.

Children of Anne (Sheppard) and Thomas[2] Hart.

I. Henry[3] Hart, on Nov. 6, 1683, acknowledged to have received of "My father and Guardian William Newsum my full due and part of my decd. Father and Uncle John Sheppard's estate, due unto me by will or otherwise." (D&W. 1671-84, p. 338) On May 4, 1703, Henry Hart planter, of Lawne's Creek Parish, deeded to his brother Robert Hart, 1000 acres of land lying on main Blackwater, which land "the said Henry Hart should and ought to have after the expiration of 99 years the said land being granted to the said Robert Hart and to him and his heirs by the last will and testament of John Sheppard, decd., dated Feb. 3, 1668. This land was granted to "Capt." Robert Shepard, Oct. 8, 1650, "Upon ye main Blackwater". (C.P. 204) Henry Hart "as eldest son and heir of Anne, who was Anne Shepard, sister and heir of John Sheppard" deeded away his right of revision in a tract of land left to Thomas Hart, late of Isle of Wight, decd., for a term of 81 years by will of John Sheppard (D&W 1715-30, p. 40). Henry Hart, as related above, married Mary, daughter of his step-father, George Foster. Henry made his will in Surry, Nov. 8, 1734, probated Nov. 21, 1739. He mentions sons: JOSEPH and HENRY; wife MARY; daughters LUCY and LYDIA and SIX ELDEST DAUGHTERS, not mentioned by name. (48V 270) Lucy Hart married John Champion. (Vol. I - 128)

II. Thomas[3] Hart was born about 1664-5, as he first appears as a tithable in William Newsum's household in 1681. He moved to Isle of Wight by 1709 as he made a bond to Samuel Cornwell in that year and was dead by Nov. 20, 1716, when his eldest brother, Henry Hart, who would be his heir, if no wife and children, deeded away the land left to him by their Uncle, John Shepard.

III. Robert[3] Hart was born 1666-7 as he appears as a tithable in 1683. He married Priscilla, daughter of Captain Charles Barham. (See Barham) He made his will June 23, 1720, probated July 20, 1720. He mentions sons: WILLIAM, THOMAS, (under 18) and ROBERT (See later); daughter ANNE and her sons; daughters: ELIZABETH, SARAH, MARY and PRIS-CILLA, (last two under 16 years of age); wife PRISCILLA; grandson Robert Harte. An account of his estate dated Sept. 16, 1724, shows that Anne was married to a WARREN. This was ANNE HART married to her cousin ALLEN WARREN, Jr. (See Warren, V.H.G.) The account shows that THOMAS FOSTER, not mentioned in the will, was paid a legacy. Elizabeth is not mentioned in the account whereas Sarah, Mary and Priscilla are. This indicates that the unmentioned Elizabeth was the one who married Thomas Foster.

Robert[4] Hart, (Robert[3], Thomas[2], Henry[1]) born c. 1703, died 1770, married c. 1724, Mary Washington, daughter of Richard Washington (1659-1724). His will dated June 25, 1770 and proved

Sept. 13, 1770 in Southampton County, Virginia. By 1739 they were living in that part of Isle of Wight County which later became Surry.
Children:

I. Thomas Hart (untraced) was left land in Southampton in his father's will. One Thomas Hart left a will in Nash County, in 1794 (N. C.).

II. Robert Hart, died 1797 in Southampton County, Va. married Sarah_____, living in 1789.
Children:
1. Averilla Hart, m. 1790, Jesse Hart.
2. John Hart, living in 1810 in Southampton Co. One John Hart m. 1805 in Sussex Co., Va., Martha C. Hall.
3. Robert Hart, b. 1777, living in 1850 in Southampton, m. 1803, his first cousin, Charity Hart, b. 1782. (3 daughters, a son, John C. Hart.)
4. Drury Hart, m. 1804, Cynda Hargrave.
5. Sylvia Hart (untraced).
6. Sarah Hart (untraced).

III. Jesse Hart, d. 1796 in Southampton Co., m. Nancy_____, living in 1790.
Children:
1. Richard Hart, m. 1794, Lucy Clarey.
2. Olive Hart, m. 1787 John Atkins.
3. Sarah Hart.
4. Mary Hart, m. 1795, Joshua Womble.
5. Moses Hart, m. 1796 Sally Clary.
6. Mildred Hart
7. William Hart
8. Jane Hart
9. Charity Hart, b. 1782, living 1850, m. 1803 her first cousin, Robert Hart, b. 1777.

IV. Elizabeth Hart, dsp. 1770 in Southampton.

V. Lucy Hart (untraced)

VI. Mary Hart (untraced)

VII. Sarah Hart (untraced)

HARVIN of SOUTH CAROLINA

Richard Harvin is the traditional ancestor of this family and he is said to have arrived in South Carolina about 1740. However, his place of residence is not known as he apparently did not leave any record of his whereabouts.

The family is said to derive from De Harvin, a family originally of Norman descent long established in the north of England.

Richard Harvin had two sons, Richard and John. Here we are on firmer ground as there are records of both sons.

Richard Harvin II served in the Revolution as one of Marion's men (See Marion's Men by Wm. Willis Boddie, page 12; Stub Indent Q, No. 500). He is said traditionally to have been General Marion's Commissary and to have had his negroes gather supplies and take them into swamps where Marion could get them. The traditionary date of his birth is said to have been 1746. This seems incorrect as he would have been about 40 years of age before he married and had children.

Richard's son, Samuel, was a manufacturer of shoes and harness. His old vats in Clarendon County are said to be in good condition now and were used for the Confederate Army 1861-64. His first home "Blackwood" in Clarendon County was burned by Sherman.

Children of Richard Harvin II.

I.   James Edward Harvin, b. May 17,1776, m. Miss White
II.   Richard III, b. Jan. 10,1778, m. Elizabeth Nowell
III. Charles, b. Oct. 12,1779, m. Miss Burgess
IV.   Nancy, b. April 17, 1781, unmarried
V.   John, b. Oct. 15,1783
VI.   William Washington, b. Mar. 29,1785 m. (1) Singleton, (2) Wells (children by Wells)
VII. Tabitha Lucy Elizabeth, b. May 19,1789, died in infancy
VIII. Thomas J. b. August 27,1790, d. June 11, 1809.
IX.   Samuel, b. Jan. 1, 1793, m. Sarah A. Spears
X.   Sarah, b. Jan. 1, 1796, m. Thomas Davis
XI.   Agnes, m. Charles Spears

John Harvin, second son of Richard I, served in the Revolutionary Army. Pursuant to an act of the General Assembly passed on March 16,1783, the Commissioner paid John Harvin the sum of twenty nine pounds, one shilling and eight pence for the delivery of 35 Gallons of Rum to Sumpter's Brigade and 51 days Militia duty as Lieutenant in 1781-1782 as per account audited (Rev. War Papers Historical Com.)

On Oct. 15, 1784, Gov. Benjamin Guerard for Ł 2/6/8 issued a grant to John Harvin for 100 acres in Craven County surveyed June 12, 1761 on Black River Swamp. (Grant Bk. 2, p. 18) Now this has been interpreted to mean that it was surveyed for John

Harvin in 1761. Therefore he was supposed to be 21 years of age
and born in 1740. Now when John Harvin made his will on April 4,
1805, all of his four children were young and under age which hard-
ly agrees with the above. He was then probably about 45 years of
age.

John Harvin received a grant of 749 acres on Dec. 6, 1802, surveyed for Thomas Carson on Feb. 16, 1801, on Halfway Swamp of
the Saluda River adjoining lands of Thomas Carson and John Pool.
(G. B. 49-151). On Oct. 13, 1804, John Harvin sold to Gabriel Jones
for $100.00, 118 acres, being taken from 749 acres tract and 237
acres taken from older grants. (D. B. 25-248).

John Harvin made his will April 4, 1805 in Edgefield District,
S. C. probated July 1805. He desired that "his male negroes be
placed in an equal manner as possible as my children, ELIZABETH
WHITEHEAD, JAMES HARVIN, REBECCA HARVIN, and WILLIAM
HARVIN come of age x x desires/children be schooled and raised
in a decent manner x x when my youngest child comes of age there
is to be a final division of my estate. John Gayle, William Whitehead, extrs; and wife Rebecca Executrix. (W. B. "B"-311).

John Harvin married Rebeckah Naomi Nowell of Edgefield.
Their children were:
I.   Elizabeth Harvin, m. before 1805, William Whitehead.
II.   Rebecca Harvin, m. James Barlow (See later)
III. James Harvin, m. Miss Campbell
IV.   William Harvin.

Rebecca Harvin, daughter of John Harvin and wife, Rebecca,
was born 1794, Laurens Co., Georgia, died Dec. 19, 1830, Laurens
Co., Ga., m. Dec. 19, 1810, Laurens Co., Ga., James Barlow,
born Feb. 18, 1791, Wake Co., North Carolina, died Sept. 19, 1855,
Laurens Co., Ga.
      Children:
I.   Dr. William Barlow, m. Elizabeth ?
II.   Dr. Wade Barlow
III. Amelia Barlow, m. Windsor
IV.   John Harvin Barlow, b. Feb. 9, 1816, m. (1) Louisiana C.
      Davis, (2) Louisiana Deats Butler. (See later)

John Harvin Barlow, born Feb. 9, 1816, son of Rebecca (Har-
vin) and James Barlow, married first Louisiana Carolina Davis,
daughter of Benjamin and Martha Taylor Davis, on Dec. 22, 1841.
He was born in Laurens Co., Ga., but moved to Lowndes County,
Ala., where he died Oct. 9, 1871. He married secondly in 1864,
Louisiana, daughter of James Deats, and widow of William Archer
Butler. She was born Dec. 2, 1832 and died Jan. 3, 1878 in Houston,
Harris Co., Texas. After the death of her husband she removed
to Texas with her children and several of their half brothers and
sisters (See V. H. G. 259).

      Children of first wife:
I.   Martha R. Barlow, b. 1844, never married.
II.   Thomas Wade Barlow, b. 1846, never married.
III. William Franklin Barlow, b. 1847, d. 1865, never married.
IV.   Robert Merritt Barlow, b. 1849, never married.
V.   Mary Emma Barlow, b. 1854, m. Jessie Dean Boring.

VI. James Jackson Barlow, b.1855, never married.
VII. Ella Aurelia Barlow, b.1857, m.(1) Will Buchanan, (2) Jessie D. Boring.
VIII. John D. Barlow, b.1859, d.1942, m.1883, Josephine Erwin. Children by second wife:
IX. Janie Lanier Barlow, b.1865, m.B.C. Morrison.
X. Laura Harvin Barlow, b.June 18,1867, m.William Jefferson Suggs. (See later)
XI. Joe Foster Barlow, b.1869, m.Hattie Rokar.

Laura Harvin Barlow, b.June 18, 1867, Pleasant Hill, Lowndes Co., Ala., m. March 18,1888, Spring Creek, Jones Co., Texas, William Jefferson Suggs, b.Aug. 6, 1863, Columbus, Colorado, d.Aug.14,1941, Victoria, Texas, educated in Allen Private School, Moulton, Gonzales Co., Texas. He was a farmer and cattleman in Gonzales Co.
Children:
I. John Harvin Suggs, b.Dec.30,1888, m.Ceceal Massey.
II. Joseph Jefferson Suggs, b.Dec.15,1890, m.Pearl Powitzky.
III. Richard Davis, b.Mar.16,1892, m.Margaret Swann.
IV. Nanette Suggs, b.Nov.13,1895, m.Thomas Bunyan Robinson. (See later)
V. Frank Barlow Suggs, b.Aug.16,1898, never married.

Nannette Suggs, b.Nov.13, 1895, Cleburne, Jones Co., Texas, m.Thomas Bunyan Robinson, b.July 7, 1884, Arlington, Tarrant Co., Texas, son of Allen and Sue S. (Wyman) Robinson.
Mrs. Robinson graduated at the University of Houston with degrees of Bachelor and Master of Science. She is a charter member of the Fort Bend Chapter of D.A.R. Mrs. Robinson resides in Missouri City, Texas, where she has been a teacher in the schools for a number of years. She is a member of the Delta Kappa Gamma, an honorary society for women teachers.

SUPPLEMENT TO HARVIN FAMILY
by
Mr. B.J. Kincaid

Richard Harvin m.8/3/1775, Frances Ragan "In Sumter District" (N.& S.Car.Mar.Rec. - Wm.Montgomery Clemons). Here is the record in family Bible of his son,James Edwin Harvin: (This is a bona fide copy taken from a fly leaf of the Bible of James E.Harvin). Edward Dickey was married to Mary McGill 24 March 1761. Sarah Dickey was born 5 January 1762; James Dickey born 21st October 1763. Mary Dickey Senr. Departed this life 4th December 1765 aged 27 years. Mary Dickey Junr.Departed this life 22nd. December, 1765. Edward Dickey was married to Anne Neilson 19th Aug. 1766. Elizabeth Dickey born 9th May 1767 Died 15th March 1772. Mary Dickey born 17 February 1769. Esther Dickey born 25th Mar. 1771. Died 13th September 1775. Edward Dickey Junr. born 7th May 1773. Anne Dickey Junr.born 5 December 1775. William Neilson Washington Dickey born 7th April 1778. William N.W. Dickey was married to Mary Atkinson 15th March 1798. Sarrah Dickey was born February 24th 1799. Anne Dickey was born Sep-
(Continued on Page 389)

HERBERT OF COLEBROOK CO., Monmouth, England
and Prince George County, Virginia

The first of the name in Virginia was John Herbert who settled on an estate called "Puddledock" in Prince George County,
Virginia, then Charles City. The site of "Puddledock" is on the
south bank of the Appommattox River, a few miles north east of
the present city of Petersburg. He appears to have been for some
years agent for Richard Buller, a London merchant. As John
Herbert named his two sons Richard and Buller some relationship
may be indicated.

The tombstone of John Herbert was formerly at "Puddledock"
but has now been moved to Blandford Churchyard in Petersburg.
According to the epitaph thereon, John Herbert was the son of
John Herbert, apothecary of London, and grandson of Richard
Herbert, citizen and grocer of London and was born in 1659 and
died March 17,1704. The arms and crest on the tombstone are
the same as those of George Herbert, the poet. (Slaughter,
Bristol Parish, pp.107-167).

In the Visitations of London for 1634 there is a pedigree which
includes a Richard Herbert who seems to be the same mentioned
on the tombstone. From this pedigree and from the will of Henry
Herbert of Colebrook, dated 1656, this family is as follows:
(V.M.18, p.18, 36, p.230, 8W (1) 147). (22 V 176)

I.   Mathew Herbert of Colebrook married＿＿＿＿ Herbert, the
        sister of Sir William Herbert of Swansea Co., Glamorgan.
        They had issue.
II.   William Herbert of Colebrook married Katherine, the
        daughter of Thomas Morgan of Tredeger in Co. Monmouth.
        They had issue.
        1. William Herbert - of whom later.
        2. Thomas Herbert - no further record.
        3. Mathew Herbert, citizen and draper of London, married
           Elizabeth, daughter of James Rudyed.
        4. Richard Herbert, of whom later.
        5. John Herbert, mentioned in his nephew's will in 1656.
        6. Cecil Herbert, no record.
        7. Dorothy Herbert, no record.
        8. Jane Herbert married＿＿＿＿ Lewis.
        9. Margaret Herbert, no record.

William Herbert of Colebrook, Co. Monmouth. The name of
his wife is not known. Issue, according to the will of his son
Henry:
I.   William Herbert, no record.
II.   Thomas Herbert, no record.

159

III. Henry Herbert of Colebrook, Co. Monmouth married Mary Rudyed, apparently a sister of the wife of his uncle Mathew. His will, dated March 14, 1654 and proven July 23, 1656 mentions his father, the above brothers, wife Mary, son James, daughters Katherine, Priscilla and Elizabeth, his uncles Mathew and John and his aunts Katherine Powell, Anne Pownall and Jane Lewis. (V.M. 32, p.176)

4. Richard Herbert, citizen and grocer of London, and seemingly son of William Herbert of Colebrook. As Richard Herbert of St. Catherine's Creekchurch, grocer of London, he married Anne Shuttleworth, spinster, the daughter of Henry Shuttleworth of Wedford, Co. Essex, yeoman on Jan. 31,16 , at St. Martin's Outwick, London. (London Marriage Licences, Foster,) Only known issue, John Herbert, apothecary of London, the father of John Herbert of Virginia.

The will of Elizabeth Gramer, widow, of Gerrard Street, parish of St. Ann Westminister, Co. Middlesex, dated July 6,1772 and proved Mar. 31,1773, directed that she be buried in the vault in the parish church of Islington, Co. Middlesex, in which her parents and other relatives were buried. Among the legacies were two thousand pounds to cousin Mary Claiborne, wife of Augustine Claiborne of Virginia and thirty pounds a year to Ann Mitchell of Virginia, daughter of late cousin Martha Cocke. Also mentioned in the will were late uncle William Cooke of Chatham, Kent, and the Rev. Charles Shuttleworth. Her lands in Stepney and Lambeth were devised to Mary Claiborne. As the descendants of John Herbert (1659-1704) appear to have been the only surviving relatives of Mrs. Grammer and received the bulk of her estate, she was undoubtedly a descendant of Richard Herbert above, or of his son John Herbert, the apothecary.

5. John Herbert - apothecary of London. Only known issue:
I. John Herbert, b. 1659 of Virginia.

6. John Herbert of Virginia, b.1659, d.1704. The date of his arrival is not known. He was in the colony by Dec.13,1682 at which time the Council condemned him for shipping out deerskins on the ship "Dolphin" contrary to the act of 1680 prohibiting the exportation of such skins (V.M.18-252). On April 21, 1690 he received two large grants in Charles City County, 2870 acres on the south side of the Appomattox and 1215 acres at or near Monksneck. (P.B. 8-74, 75). He married in Virginia Frances Anderson. Her parentage is not known. The will of John Anderson, dated Prince George Co. Mar. 13,1718 mentions brother William Anderson, "Nephew" Martha Cock, wife to Jame P. Cocke, "nephew" Ann Herbert, nephew Buller Herbert, the plantation given me by his father John Herbert and nephew Richard Herbert. John, William, and Frances Anderson may have been the children of one Rinson Anderson who obtained judgement in Charles City as guardian of his four sons Mathew, William, John and Henry Anderson, legatees of Thomas Symons, decd. against George Downing, executor of Symons. (Charles City Court Minutes 1687-1695-276).

On Aug. 7, 1752, the following notice appeared in the Va. Gazette. "If any of the descendants of Mr. John Herbert, late merchant on James River, will apply to the printer hereof, may hear of something to their advantage.

N.B. He formerly married Mrs. Frances Anderson of the said place and died in the year 1704 or 1705 and what arms he bore is said is cut on his tombstone. He left two sons, Buller and Richard, and one daughter named Martha who married one James Powell Cocke.

This notice was probably placed by Mrs. Gramer, see will, in an attempt to locate her Virginia relatives.

Frances Anderson, widow of John Herbert m. (2) Peter Wynne of Prince George County but had no issue by him. (V.H.G. -181). She made her will on Oct.16,1725 and mentioned her daughter

Martha Cocke, son Richard, son Buller and daughter-in-law
Mary Herbert. To the latter was left a slave with the provision
that the slave be freed when 21 years of age. The will was probated March, 1726.

John Herbert and Frances Anderson had issue:
I.   Ann Herbert, died young.
II.   Martha, married prior to 1718 James Powell Cocke and
       left issue.
III.   Buller Herbert, of whom later.
IV.   Richard Herbert, Vestryman of Bristol Parish in 1726.
       (Chamberlayne-29) His will, probated in Henrico in 1731
       mentions wife Phoebe, daughter Frances and son John.
       In 1740-41 John Herbert was the ward of his uncle James
       Powell Cocke. He died in 1760 without issue. The will of
       John Herbert, probated in Chesterfield, left his property
       to his "brother" William Anderson and Herbert Claiborne,
       son of his cousin Mary Claiborne. The inventory of his es-
       tate, dated Chesterfield County, July 15, 1760 lists a li-
       brary of almost five hundred volumes. Interestingly enough,
       among the books was a collection of the poems of George
       Herbert, who used the same coat of arms as the Virginia
       family and appears to have been a remote relative. (8W(1)-
       145).

7. Buller Herbert. He inherited "Puddledock" and resided there.
He was Captain of the Prince George Co. Militia and a vestryman
of Bristol Parish in 1721. (Chamberlayne Bristol Parish, p. 6).
He is last mentioned in the vestrybook in 1729 and in 1730 reference
is made to Instance Hall, executor of Buller Herbert, decd. According to family tradition Buller Herbert married Mary Stith, the
daughter of Capt. Drury Stith of Charles City Co. and his wife Su-'
sannah Bathurst. However, the will of Drury Stith has been mutil-
ated and the portion remaining lists only his sons, William Byrd
of "Westover" in his diary makes several references to Drury
Stith's two daughters (April 14, 1720 & March 6, 1721) and on Aug.
18, 1720 he recorded that he went to Capt. Drury Stith's for the
marriage of his daughter Mary. On Aug. 31, 1720 he noted that he
walked from Maj. Mumford's (who lived on the south side of the Appommattox) to Mr. Herbert's who had just brought his wife home
the day before.

Buller Herbert and Mary Stith had issue:
I.   John Herbert, b. April 4, 1724, died young.
II.   Ann Herbert, b. March 21, 1726, died young.
III.   Mary Herbert married Col. Augustine Claiborne of "Windsor"
       Sussex Co., Va. by whom she had many descendants. (V.H.G.
       40). She died Aug. 17, 1801.
       Children of Mary Herbert and Augustine Claiborne named
       on page 40, V.H.G.
       1. Mary Herbert Claiborne, b. 1744, d. 1776, m. 1761 Char-
          les Harrison, b. 1740, d. 1796, the son of Benjamin Har-
          rison of "Berkeley" Charles City County, Va. and his wife
          Anne, the daughter of Robert "King" Carter. Charles Har-
          rison was Colonel of the 1st Continental Artillery in the

Revolution. They had issue among others, Mary Herbert Harrison, b. 1776, d. 1833.

2. Elizabeth Claiborne, b. 1756, d. 1794, m. Thomas Peterson of Prince George Co., Va., Sussex Co. M. B. dated 6-15-1775. He was born circa 1751 and died 1789, the son of John Peterson and Martha Thweatt. They had issue, among others, a son, John Herbert Peterson. (See later)

John Herbert Peterson, b. 1776, d. 1829, m. 4-9-1795 his first cousin Mary Herbert Harrison, see above. John Herbert Peterson wrote an interesting history of the Claiborne, Peterson and Harrison families which was published in W(2) 2. They had issue, among others, John Augustine Peterson of Prince George County, b. 4-15-1798, d. 1879 m. (1) 1-10-1822 Virginia Ann Thweatt, b. 1805, d. 12-11-1824, and (2) in 1828 Eliza Frances Thweatt. (S. V. F. -390). He had issue by his first marriage, John A. Peterson, Jr. and Virginia Ann Peterson who married Nathaniel Colley Cocke (S. V. F. p. 155). Their daughter Virginia Peterson Cocke married William Edward Smith of "Magnolia", Halifax Co., N. C., and had issue among others Elizabeth Herbert Smith who married Dr. Kempton P. A. Taylor.

HILL of SURRY

Robert[1] Hill and his wife, Mary, emigrated to Virginia in 1642, when they were listed as head rights of Francis England of Isle of Wight County ("Cavaliers and Pioneers", p. 140). They had several children, including:

Sion[2] Hill (1654-1705), of Surry County, Va. On Feb. 9, 1679/80, Sion Hill of Surry County confirmed to Edmond Wickins land sold to the latter in Isle of Wight County by "my father, Robert Hill decd.", said land having been assigned the latter in 1653 by George Archer. This was also signed by Elizabeth Hill. Witnesses were Richard Tibbot and Robert Kae (Isle of Wight Will and Deed Book 1, p. 427). In 1679 administration was granted Sion Hill on estate of Mrs. Mary Davis (b. 1620); his securities were George Williams and George Foster; witnesses were Robert Ruffin and William Edwards. (Surry County Deeds, etc. #2, p. 13). In 1679 Sion Hill administered estate of John Spiltimber; his securities were Joseph Rogers and John Phillips; witnesses were William Edwards and Benjamin Harrison. In 1679 Peter Deberry, the orphan of Peter Deberry, chose Sion Hill as guardian. In 1680 Sion Hill of Surry County witnessed a sale of land to Major Samuel Swann of Surry, by Ralph Hill of Isle of Wight, son of Lt. Col. Nicholas Hill decd. (Isle of Wight W. & D. Bk. 1, p. 435). In 1681 Sion Hill patented 420 acres in Surry County (Land Office Book 7, p. 111). In 1685 he sold this land to William Gray (Surry County Deed Book 2, p. 39). In 1689, Sion Hill, in a deposition, stated that he was then 35 years of age. Sion Hill is recorded in Surry County Tithable Lists as paying taxes in 1699 for himself and Sion Hill Jr.; Robert Hill paid for himself; In 1700 and also 1702 Sion Hill paid for himself, Sion Hill Jr., and Richard Hill; in 1703 he paid for himself and Richard Hill while Sion Hill Jr. paid for himself. In 1704 Sion Hill and Robert Hill were listed in the Virginia Quit Rent Rolls for Surry County. William Browne Sr. in his will dated Dec. 4, 1704 instructed his executors to make conveyance of land sold to Sion Hill. (See Coker)

Sion[2] Hill married 1677 Mrs. John Spiltimber, nee Elizabeth (Green?).

Children:
I.   Robert[3] Hill (1678-1765), m. ca. 17--, Tabitha, 9 children. (See later)
II.   Sion[3] Hill (1682-17--), m. ca. 1707, Elizabeth Marriott (dau. Mathias Marriott).
III. Richard[3] Hill (1684-1723). (See later)
IV.   Capt. Thomas[3] Hill (1686-1737), m. 17--, Priscilla (Gray?), children.
V.   Michael[3] Hill (168_-1755), m. 17--, Elizabeth_____. (See later)

164

Richard[3] Hill (1684-1723) lived in Surry County, Va. On Feb. 21, 1721 he witnessed a sale of land to Henry Browne by Robert Hill; deed was also signed by Tabitha Hill (Surry County Book 1715-30, p. 391). On Feb. 20, 1722/23 a land patent previously applied for, was granted Richard Hill for 200 acres on the south side of the Main Blackwater Swamp on the corner tree of his old land (Land Office Book II, p. 316). The estate of Richard Hill was appraised March 20, 1722/23 by James Wall, Henry Browne and Edward Harris; Hannah Hill, administratrix, this was examined by William Gray Jr., and John Newsum.

Richard[3] Hill married, ca. 1713, Hannah Briggs (1692-17--), daughter of Henry Briggs (1662-1739) and his wife, _____ Howell.

Children:

I.   Green[4] Hill (1714-1769), m. 1739, Grace Bennett (1726-1772). (See later)

II. Mary[4] Hill (ca. 1716-17--), m. 17--, William Malone. Children.

III. John[4] Hill (ca. 1718-1765), m. 1742, Mildred Gilliam (dau. of John Gilliam), 10 children.

IV. Richard[4] Hill (1720-1775). (See later)

Capt. Richard[4] Hill (1720-1775) lived in the southern section of Surry County, Va., which in 1753 became Sussex County. On Nov. 16, 1742, William Gilliam of the Parish of Albemarle, "for love and good will to my daughter Margery and her husband, Richard Hill", gave them 200 acres of land beginning at a tree between John Gilliam and Lewis Green, adjoining Col. Bolling and the Miery Marsh, with reversion, if no issue, to his son William Gilliam. Witnesses were William Green, Peter Green, and William Green, Jr. (Surry County Deed Book 4, p. 64). On July 17, 1749, Nathaniel Green of the Parish of Albemarle released to Richard Hill for £ 11 all claims he had on the plantation the sd. Hill lives on, which sd. plantation was sold by Lewis Green of Prince George County to William Gilliam Sr., and by the sd. Gilliam conveyed to sd. Richard Hill and Margery Hill and their heirs. (Surry County Deed Book 5, p. 436). In 1755 inventory of the estate of Michael Hill returned by William Gilliam, Richard Hill and William Gilliam Jr. (Sussex County Will Book A., p. 34). In 1755 Richard Hill bought of Thomas Chambers of Edgecombe County, N. C. a tract of 100 acres on the Nottoway River in Sussex County, Va. (Sussex County Deed Book A, p. 92). In 1762 Richard Hill bought of William Gilliam for 700 £ a tract of 700 acres on the north side of the Nottoway River on the sd. Hill, the Southwesters Swamp, William Winfield, and John Tyus. (Sussex County Deed Book b, p. 322). On May 4, 1763 "Martha Gilliam of Brunswick to Richard Hill of Sussex County, for divers good causes, but more especially for the better maintenance of the said Richard Hill and his wife, Margery, all my estate, being what kind soever". (Sussex County Deed Book C, p. 12). The will of Richard Hill, dated Oct. 3, 1774, codicil Jan. 23, 1775, proved Aug. 17, 1775, was witnessed by John Chamblis, William Winfield, and Burrell Green. Executors were his wife, Margery, son-in-law, William Ruffin, and son, Green Hill. The inventory of his estate, filed by the executrix, Margery Hill, in 1775, showed 58 negroes, 11 horses, 66 cattle, 240 hogs, 50 sheep, 50 geese, etc.

Capt. Richard Hill married 1742 Margery Gilliam (ca.1726-178), daughter of William Gilliam (ca.1704-1764) and his wife, Susanna Green (daughter of Lewis Green). Capt. Hill died July 9, 1775.

Children:

I. Sarah[5] Hill (1743-ca.1813), m.1st.1762, William Ruffin (1735-1781), 2nd.ca.1785?, Capt. James Smith (d.1811). No children.

II. William[5] Gilliam Hill (1746-1764).

III. Hannah[5] Hill (1748-17--), m.1764 Ephraim Parham. In his will in 1793 he mentions a gift of two negroes from Richard Hill made to him in 1766.

IV. Green[5] Hill (1752-   ), m.1773 Mary, dau. of George Booth. Green Hill's will, dated July 3, 1800 in Sussex, mentions children: Henry, William and Martha. If children die, properties to go to nephews Richard and Nicholas Long and Richard Hill, son of brother Richard. He gave his Stony Creek plantation to Green Hill Booth, now living in Georgia. (Bk.K-199)

V. Richard[5] Hill (1754-   ).

VI. Thomas[5] Hill (1757-   ).

VII. Mary[5] Hill (1760-1761)

VIII. Henry[5] Hill (1762-1763) Twin.

IX. Howell[5] Hill (1762-1763) Twin.

X. William Gilliam[5] Hill II (1765-   )

XI. Rebecca[5] Hill (ca.1768?   ), m. 1788 Nicholas Long.

Green[4] Hill (Richard[3], Sion[2], Robert[1]) of Surry County, Va., inherited 300 acres of land (of which 100 was originally bought of Col. William Browne by Sion[2] Hill, and 200 were patented by Richard[3] Hill just before his death). As soon as he came of age Green Hill sold this land and moved to Bertie County (later Northampton County) in N.C. The sale of the 300 acres by Green Hill to William Evans for Ł 40, on Dec.17,1735, witnessed by James Washington, Robert Webb Jr., and Charles Gee, is recorded in Surry County Book 1730-38, p.541. In 1736 Green Hill of Bertie County, N.C. bought of Nicholas Thompson of Surry County, Va., 330 acres in Bertie for Ł 20. This is recorded in Bertie County Book E, p.89.

This Green[4] Hill (1714-1769), m.1739, Grace Bennett (1726?-1772). He named his eldest son Henry Hill after his grandfather Henry Briggs, and he named his first daughter Hannah after his mother; his son Green[5] Hill named a son Richard Hill as well as a daughter Hannah Hill. (See 17 C, p.311)

Incidentally, the sale of 300 acres in Virginia for forty pounds and the purchase of 330 acres in North Carolina for twenty pounds affords some indication of the reason for many moving across the border. (For Green Hill family see 17C)

Michael[3] Hill (Sion[2], Robert[1]) married Elizabeth, daughter of John Mitchell. On March 9, 1748/49 Michael Hill Sr., deeded his son, Michael Jr. 120 acres on the north side of the Nottoway River, on Bolling's line, Isarel Pickens and Thomas Chambers, part of a tract formerly granted John Mitchell by patent in 1723.

Wits: Thomas and William Oliver, William Welborn. (Surry D.B. 5-435). Inventory of the estate of Michael Hill was filed Oct.13, 1755, by William Gilliam, Sr., and Jr. and Richard Hill. John Hill was administrator.

Michael[4] Hill, the son of Michael and Elizabeth Hill, was born Feb.20, 1721. (Bristol Par.Reg.p.312). He married Susannah, dau. of Wm.Cook about 1740 (Bk.1738-56, p.446).

Children of Michael[4] Hill Jr. and Susanna (Brist.Par.Reg.):
I.   Elizabeth, dau. Michael and Susanna Hill, born July 18, 1743 (p.318).
        Elizabeth Hill, a child, dies Sept.28,1758,reported by Michael Hill (APR).
II.   Anne, dau. of Michael & Susanna Hill,born April 27,1746 (p.319).

There was another Michael Hill whose family is reported in the Albemarle Register. Inasmuch as he seems to have been married about 1755, he could not have been the son of Michael[4] Hill who was married about 1740 and had children born in 1743 and 1746. This Michael Hill married about 1755 Mary probably a Malone and had children born as follows: (APR)
I.   Elizabeth, born Oct.15,1756, Sponsors, William and Mary Malone, Lucy Hill.
II.   Michael, born May 3, 1759, Sponsors, Geo.Robertson, Richard Hill, Francis Threewats.
        He probably married secondly, Nancy Tyus, Security John Tyus.
        Their children were:
        1. Isaac, born Aug.31, 1763, Sponsors, Wm. & Sarah Welborn, John Brown.
        2. Mary, born March 28, 1765, after father's death. Sponsors, Peter Winfield, Francis Threewats, Betty Wynne.

Inventory of the estate of Michael Hill was filed 1766 by George Booth, Richard Jones and Richard Hill. Ann Hill executrix. (W. B. "B"-219). In 1770 an account of his estate was returned by John Hill and Anne, his wife, late widow of Michael Hill (Id.266).

In 1778, the will of Michael Hill, orphan of Michael Hill, decd. was proven. His legatees were: Cousin George Bell, son of James Bell; Cousin Rebecca Bell, daughter of James Bell; Cousin James Bell to be executor. Wits.Nathan Barker, George Rose, John Willie (W.B."C"-309).

(The foregoing pages were kindly compiled by Mr. W. A. Graham Clark of Washington, now deceased.)

Robert[3] Hill (Sion[2], Robert[1]) is shown with a wife, Tabitha, in 1721 when he made a sale of land to Henry Browne (Ante). He patented 145 acres in Isle of Wight, Jan.23,1724 and deeded this land on the south side of Fountain Creek to Arthur Jordan "plantation where I now live." He was styled "Junior" because his uncle Robert was residing nearby. Fountain Creek evidently ran into Northampton for on May 22, 1725, he was granted 160 acres on south side of Fountain Creek in Northampton Co., N.C. This may be about the time that a 25 mile strip along the border of Virginia and North Carolina was found to be in North Carolina and ceded by Virginia.

Robert Hill patented 700 acres at different times in Edgecombe County which became Halifax in 1758. He made his will in Halifax June 18, 1762, probated April, 1766. as follows: to son GREEN HILL a negro called Simon; to son SION HILL the plantation we now live on south side of Blue Marsh, after decease of my wife, to son ABNER HILL a negro called Peter; to son THOMAS HILL fifty pounds Virginia currency; to daughter TABITHA CHAPMAN and daughter AGNES ARRINGTON a negro each; to daughter LEW-WRAINA CHAPMAN two pounds, 10 Shillings; daughter ANN STEED a negro; daughter MARY BRYANT land on both sides of Red Bud Creek below mouth of Crab Tree; and daughter MILBRY all land above Crab Tree. Cattle to grandson, John Chapman. Sons Abner, Sion and Green Hill exrs. (B K 1-159)

Children:

I.   William C. made his will in Halifax in 1803 and mentions wife Sarah, and three children: Martha, James and Henry. He provided that certain negroes be hired out to support his aunt LURANCY ARRINGTON.

II.   Green.

III.   Sion. His will was dated and probated 1782 in Wake Co. Mentions wife Sarah, and children: Shadrack, Green, William and Thomas.

IV.   Thomas, (c1725-1789) m. Sarah. (See later) Other children of Robert and Tabitha are mentioned in the will.

Thomas Hill, son of Robert and Tabitha Hill resided near Scotland Neck in Halifax, formerly Edgecombe, where he patented 220 acres in 1742 and 500 acres in 1743. He was a Regulator in 1768 and may have participated in the battle of Alamance. He was paid 222 lbs. of tobacco by the state in 1787 for some service rendered during the Revolution but the type of service was not stated. (Clark's State Record) His will was dated Nov. 27, 1787, and probated Aug. 1789 as follows: to wife Sarah Hill 1040 acres of land with manor plantation east side of Fishing Creek and 470 on west side......After wife's death to be divided between sons THOMAS, BENJAMIN and ROBERT HILL and daughters ELIZABETH JONES and MARY JONES. Other legatees were daughters: ANNA LONG, FANNY MACNEAL and SALLY ALSTON; JAMES LONG, HENRY HILL LONG, HILL JONES, WALLACE ALSTON, son of SALLY ALSTON; Granddaughters: SALLY LONG and SALLY MASON ALSTON; son RICHARD HILL. Exrs.: son Robert Hill, Edward Jones, and wife Sarah Hill. (WB 3-172) This was the will of a wealthy man. He bequeathed 80 negroes and much land.

Benjamin, son of Sarah and Thomas Hill was born Dec. 13, 1761 in Halifax Co., and died in Greene County, Alabama before 1851. He married Nov. 28, 1787, Mary, daughter of Jesse Wooten (1750-1808) and granddaughter of Capt. James Wooten of the Revolution, both from Johnston County, N.C. Jesse Wooten served as a private in the 10th Regiment of the N.C. Continental line under the command of Col. Abraham Shepard. He served for two and one half years, enlisting on April 4, 1776 and was discharged Oct. 30, 1778. (N.C. Roster, p. 172) His father, James Wooten, was a Captain of Militia in Johnstone Co. 1754-55 and served until the General Muster in 1774. (N.C. Co. L Rec) Thomas Wooten, immigrant ancestor of this family probably came here from the town of Castor in Northamptonshire, for in his will dated March 15, 1669, probated Nov.1670, he stated: "After my son's (Richard) decease, he leaving no issue, I give plantation to my NEXT OF KIN OF MY NAME in Northamptonshire, at a town called Castor near unto Peterborough". (See S.V.F. Vol.I)

Benjamin Hill applied for a pension in Greene County, Alabama and stated that his age was 71, that he had entered into service March 1, 1780 in Chatham County, N.C. under Captain Ase Bryant in Col.Dudley's Regiment that they marched from Ramsey's Mill to Camden S.C. where they were engaged in battle near that place; that on or about May 13, 1780, Col.Dudley discharged the regiment. Benjamin lived in North Carolina until 1827 when he moved to Greene County, Ala., and bought land there Jan.12, 1828. His will was dated Oct.29,1831 and probated Dec.19,1842. Children named in the will were: WOOTEN, SHERWOOD, BERRY, (See later) JAMES and JESSE, MARY HILL married JOHN MOORE (BK C-15).

Berry Hill, son of Benjamin, was born Feb.7, 1807, in Johnston Co., N.C. and died in Caddo Parish, La., Sept.23, 1888. He married Elizabeth Reach, born Jan.19, 1807, in Wake Co., N.C., died June 26, 1885. They were married Oct. 3, 1827 in Wake Co,, N.C., and had nine children. (See Roach History, p.222).

John Berry Hill, their son, born 1833 in Green Co., Ala., died in Caddo Parish, La., married April 25, 1857, Rachel Lucy Wynne Ridgeway, born June 26, 1836, died at Mansfield, La. Feb.15, 1918. Their daughter Mary Jane Hill married Douglas Fair Roach. (See Cato Family, Vol. I)

GREEN HILL of GEORGIA

Green B. Hill was born in Virginia about 1775, and married Martha, daughter of Winifred and Lot Ivey, who was born about 1774, also in Virginia.

Children:
I.   Mary Hill, b.ca.1805, in Jasper Co., Ga.
II.   William Hill, b.ca.1807 in Jasper Co., Ga.: dsp. before 1850 in Fayette Co. m.(1) Sophronia Milner; m.(2) Mary Ann Kelley.
III.   Ivey Hill, b.Nov.6,1810; d. Aug.22,1886; m.Oct.27,1830, Lucy Jones. (See later).
IV.   John Hill, b.ca.1816, in Jasper Co., Ga., m.Mary Howland.
V.   Rev.Martin Hill, b.ca.1813, in Jasper Co., Ga.; m. Ann Tomlin.
VI.   Benjamin Hill, b. ca.1825 in Jasper Co., m.Rebecca Overton

Ivey Hill, the son of Martha (Ivey) and Green B. Hill, was born June 6, 1810 in Jasper County, Georgia, and died August 22, 1886 in Cass County, Texas; married the 27th of October, 1830, in Jasper County, Lucy Jones who was born In Jasper Co., Ga., June 3, 1813, and died the 16th of June, 1900, in Cass Co., Texas. They had eighteen children; however eight died in childhood.

Children:
I.   Martha Emily Hill, b. Dec. 10, 1831, Fayette Co., Ga., m.

Daniel F. Hyatt. (See later)
II.   Green Berry Hill, b. Oct. 9, 1836, Fayette Co., Ga.; m. Senilla _____ .
III.   T. Amelia Permelia Hill, b. Oct. 1, 1838, Fayette Co., m. Josiah Waits.
IV.   Seaborn Ivey Jones Hill, b. Jan. 11, 1840, Fayette Co., m. Martha Jane Clark.
V.   Miranda E. Hill, b. Sept. 10, 1841, a surviving twin, dsp.
VI.   Francis Patterson Hill, b. Nov. 18, 1845; m. Rachel Witt.
VII. John Simon Hill, b. June 14, 1843; m. Charity Daniel.
VIII. Abner Mattison Hill, b. Dec. 20, 1846.
IX.   Nancy Emaline Hill, b. Mar. 30, 1848; m. Harris Daniel.
X.   Queen Victoria Hill, b. Mar. 2, 1852; m. John Daniel.

Martha Emily, the daughter of Lucy (Jones) and Ivey Hill, was born in Fayette County, Georgia, Dec. 10, 1831, and died at Ruth, Marshall County, Ala., Feb. 26, 1904. On February 6, 1847, in Fayette County she married Daniel Franklin Hyatt, who was born Sept. 25, 1829, in Anson, N.C. and died in Cass County, Texas, Sept. 15, 1897.

Children:
I.   James Pleasant Hyatt, b. Oct. 16, 1848, in Fayette Co., m. Ruth Ann Hadley.
II.   Joseph Woodard Hyatt, b. July 31, 1850 in Randolph Co., Ala., m. Nancy E. Burden.
III.   Mary Ann M. Hyatt, b. Mar. 22, 1852, m. David E. Brown. (See later
IV.   William Martin Hyatt, b. May 10, 1854; m. Missouri Jester.
V.   Daniel Greenbury Hyatt, b. Mar. 3, 1856; m. Nancy Ann Elizabeth Briscol.
VI.   Seburn Ivy Hyatt, b. Apr. 5, 1858; m. Sadie Gilly.
VII. Lucy Jane Hyatt, b. Apr. 5, 1860; d. Mar. 29, 1917.
VIII. Francis Marion Hyatt, b. June 24, 1862, m. Fanny Briscol.
IX.   James Robert Hyatt, b. Aug. 6, 1865; m. Ophelia Crawford.
X.   Martha Elizabeth Hyatt, b. June 28, 1868; m. Smith Williams.
XI.   Jessie Young Hyatt, b. Jan. 1, 1870; m. Annie Bell.
XII. John Henry Hyatt, b. Feb. 23, 1872; m. Mary Briscol.
XIII. Samuel May Hyatt, b. May 3, 1874.
XIV. Nancy Ann Luella Hyatt, b. July 11, 1876, m. Herbert Mullins.

Mary Ann Amanda, daughter of Martha Emily (Hill) and Daniel F. Hyatt, was born March 2, 1852, in Randolph County, Alabama. (After 1852 Cleburne County was formed from Randolph, and the Hyatt land fell in Cleburne.) She died in Cedarview, Uintah County, Utah, on Feb. 27, 1919. On October 28, 1870, in Caroll County, Georgia she was married by her Uncle, Martin Hill, a Baptist Minister, to David Emanuel Brown, who was born in Caroll County, April 4, 1851, and died in Ontaria, Idaho, Jan. 1, 1927. They had thirteen children, of whom four died in childhood.

Children:
I.   Emily Caroline Brown, b. May 11, 1872; m. Benjamin O. Johnson.
II.   Mary Elizabeth Brown, b. Oct. 28, 1874; m. Phillip E. Scogings.

III.   Emanuel Franklin Brown, b.June 10,1877; m.Amelia Jane Marratt.
IV.   Martha Jane Brown, b.June 27,1883; m.Thomas A.Hunt. (See later)
V.   Sarah Delila Brown, b.Feb.15,1885; m.Joseph Merrell.
VI.   Candus Genett Brown, b.Oct.1,1888; m.Edward Moroni Hunt.
VII.   John Henry Brown, b.Dec.27,1891; m.Fay Campbell.
VIII.   Lexie Bell Brown, b.March 24,1893; m.Jesse Labrun.
IX.   Neta Rosette Brown, b.Nov.20,1895;m.Alva Leo Labrun.

Martha Jane, daughter of Mary Ann Miranda (Hyatt) and David Emanuel Brown, was born June 27, 1883 at Monroe, Sevier County, Utah, and on Oct. 4,1910 married Thomas Alvin Hunt, who was born at Monroe Dec.15,1881 and died Aug.1,1941 at Salt Lake City, Utah.

Mrs. Hunt taught school in her early marriage, while her husband attended th University of Utah, and received his legal training. He was a practising Attorney, and served for a time as Richfield City Attorney, and was for many years Sevier County Attorney until his death.

Children:
I.   Ina Mattie Hunt, b.Oct.7,1911; m. Max Swain Tuft.
II.   Lela V. Hunt, b.Feb.9,1914; m.Weldon Peterson. (See later)
III.   Alvin Carlyle Hunt, b.Dec.21,1915; m.Alta Berthelson.
IV.   Lila Fae Hunt, twin, b.Aug.14,1918; m.Melvin D.Christiensen.
V.   Ila May Hunt, twin, b.Aug.14,1918,m.(1) LaFae Busenbark; (2) Thomas A. Hawkes.
VI.   Thomas David Hunt, b.Feb.7,1921; m.Alta Nielson.

Lela V., the daughter of Martha Jane (Brown) and Thomas Alvin Hunt, was born Feb.9,1914 at Salt Lake City, Utah, and married there Dec.2,1935, Weldon Peterson, who was born Sept.10, 1912 at Richland, Sevier County, Utah.

Mrs. Peterson attended Snow College and the University of Utah. Her present address is, Mrs. Weldon Peterson, Bo⁻ 207, Monroe, Utah.

Children:
I.   Lawrence Peter Peterson, b.Nov.14,1936.
II.   Wendy Elizabeth Peterson, b.July 10,1938.
III.   James Weldon Peterson, b.Aug.8,1942.
IV.   Suzanne Peterson, b.Dec.18,1943.
V.   Margaret V. Peterson, b.March 1, 1946.
VI.   John Daniel Peterson, b.Feb.18,1949.
VII.   Mark Hunt Peterson, b.April 16, 1951.
VIII.   David Alvin Peterson, b.July 1, 1954.

Hilliard
of Virginia and North Carolina

The extensive material on the Hilliard Family, included on
pages 172-274 of the first edition,
has been reprinted with corrections in Volume IX of
HISTORICAL SOUTHERN FAMILIES.

HOLT of SURRY

The first of this family in Surry was Randall Holt who came over in William Ewen's ship "The George" in 1620 when he was thirteen years of age. His age is known because when the Census of 1625 was taken he was then residing in the household of Dr. Potts on the Main and was eighteen years of age.

At a Court held March 20, 1625, it was ordered that Randall Holt, "upon his petition, shall serve and remain with Doctor Pott until Christmas next, and that Doctor Pott was to deliver up his indentures and make him free, also give him one suit of aparell from head to foot and one barrel of corn."

He founded the fortune of his family by marrying Mary, daughter and sole heiress of John Bailey. On October 26, 1626, Edward Grendon, Burgess for the south side, presented a power of attorney from Richard Bailye, guardian to Mary, only daughter and heir of John Bailye, late planter in Virginia. The Court approved the lease of her lands on Hog Island for three years. Mary Bailey lived in Jamestown at that time and Dr. Potts residence was not far away.

On September 18, 1636, Randall Holt patented 400 acres of land at the head of Lower Chippokes Creek, near John Dunston, for the transportation of eight persons (C.P. 48). He was granted 400 more acres of land next to her former patent July 20, 1939. (C.P. III).

Randall died before August 1, 1636, for on that date his son Randall Holt patented 710 acres as "Son and heir of Mary Bayley, late of Hogg Island, sole daughter and heir of John Bayley of said Island. 700 acres called Hogg Island lying over against Archer's Hope on the Tappahanna side of the river, and 10 acres in James Island adjacent the late dwelling house of Robert Evers, towards Goose Hill, North towards land lately belonging to Jenkins Andrews. 490 acres being expressly granted to the said Mary Bayley, orphan, February 20, 1619***. If the said Island does not amount to 490 acres, then so much as wanteth shall be supplied to her elsewhere, and if the said Island does contain over 490 then the said Mary shall purchase the surplus from the Company. The surplus being 210 acres is now due by transportation of 5 servants in the ship William and Thomas August 24, 1618."

It seems that John Bailey may have perished on the ill fated William and Thomas in its voyage to Virginia in 1618 with the Puritans of the Ancient Church of Amsterdam. (See 17th Cent. p. 24) This ship was blown off its course and it was six months before its passengers saw the Virginia Capes. From the above patent, it appears that Mary Bailey was an orphan when she received the patent of 1619.

2. Randall Holt, only son of the first Randall, married Elizabeth Hansford, daughter of John Hansford of York county and widow

of Christian Wilson. Her father's will was dated and probated
in 1661 in York county and therein she is referred to as under 16
years of age and unmarried. She could not have been married to
Christian Wilson very long. for in October 1663, Randall Holt,
newly wedded, receipted for her portion of her father's estate
to Edward Lockey. Her mother, Mrs. Elizabeth Hansford, was
then married to Mr. Lockey, formerly a wealthy merchant of
London. (York Bk. I, pp. 67, 90, 96, 97).

One of Mrs. Holts brothers was Colonel Thomas Hansford,
executed by Berkeley for his part in Bacon's Rebellion. In the
report of John Berry, one of the High Commissioners, sent over
by Charles II to inquire into the causes of the Rebellion, Mr.
Berry says "Captain William Digges, a gallant brisk, young gentleman, who in a single dispute betwixt him and Charles Hansford,
one of the chiefest champions of the Rebels side, cut off one of
Hansford's fingers, forced him to fly, and maintained the Governor's cause with great vigor till forced to fly to Maryland."
(V.M.V. p.68). (This is Digges' story to the Commissioners).

Thomas Hansford was the first native born Virginian to die on
the scaffold. He pleaded passionately with Berkeley to have him
shot like a soldier and not hanged like a dog. Berkeley told him
he was not condemned for being a soldier, but as a rebel taken in
arms against the King and must suffer the death the law prescribes
for treason. So he became one of the first martyrs to the cause of
American freedom. (Tyler 1, p.249)

Randall Holt was appointed a Justice in Surry December 22,
1668. In 1675, the Reverend Robert Parke arrived from England
and was a guest of Randall's at his home on Hog Island. While
there, the Reverend Parke became engaged in controversy with
the Reverend William Thompson, rector of the Lawne's Creek
Church. (See Col. Surry, Chapter XIV).

Randall made his will in Surry April 26, 1679, and same was
probated September 26, 1679. (B2, p.223). He gives all of his
land to his eldest son, John, and if John dies without issue then to
his son William, and if William die likewise, to son Thomas. His
wife, Elizabeth, was to have all of his personal property "for the
maintenance of my six children". Children were to have benefits
of their labors at 17 and son John to have assigned to him a "good
plantation in my Island at 21, rest of the Island to be at disposal
of wife during her life".

John Goring, a Cavalier officer of Charles I, escaped to Virginia and in his will provides that if his son Charles Goring dies
before 21, his estate was to go to William and Thomas Holt, sons
of Mr. Randall Holt, deceased. What relationship he was to the
Holts does not appear.

Mrs. Elizabeth Hansford Holt made her will March 4, 1708-09,
same probated May 3, 1709, Legatees: To Charles Holt, son of
"my son John Holt", deceased; cows, to Joseph Holt, son of above
mentioned John Holt; feather bed, to Benjamin Holt, son of said
John Holte; cows, to granddaughter Mary Seward: Bequests to
son Thomas Holt and daughter in law Frances Holt; to Thomas
Edwards, sons William and Thomas Holt, daughter Jane Hancock,
wife of John Hancock, and Lucy, wife of Joseph Mountfort. Sons
William and Thomas, Executors. (Bk.5, p.111)

Children:
I.   John, d. 1705, m. Mary, dau. of Thomas Binns. (See later No. 3)
II.   William, m. Elizabeth, dau. of William Seward. (See later No. 4)
III.   Thomas, m. Frances, dau. of Francis Mason. (See later No. 5)
IV.   Jane, m. John Hancock.
V.   Lucy, m. Joseph Montford (Mumford).
VI.   Elizabeth, m. Thomas Edwards.

3. John Holt, born about 1664, d. 1705. In 1687 he was in the Cavalry Militia of Surry Co. He m. Mary Binns, dau. of Thomas Binns and his wife Elizabeth Alston. (W. M. XX 89-91). In 1703, he petitioned the House of Burgess to be Keeper of the Ferry across the James to Archer's Hope Creek.

Elizabeth Binns, his mother in law, widow of Thomas Binns, m. secondly, about 1673, Col. Francis Mason, of Surry, and in her will, dated Sept. 22, 1712, she mentions her dau. "Mary Holt". But her husband, Col. Francis Mason in his will (1696) does not name her, but names her "daughter Frances Holt, wife of Thomas Holt," showing that Mary was probably not a Mason, but a Binns, child of Thomas Binns, her first husband, who died intestate.

John Holt of Hog Island died 1705. His mother, Mrs. Elizabeth Holt, named three of his sons in her will in 1709. (Ante). His children were: John (see later #6); David, Charles, Joseph and Benjamin.

6. John Holt, like his father, also lived on Hog Island. In 1720 he petitioned the House for permission to keep a ferry at Hog Island and for the building a bridge over the creek which divided Hog Island from Mainland.

He made his will July 19, 1723, same probated Dec. 18, 1723. Legatees: Son, Thomas Holt, land on South side of Nottoway River and Ł100 when 21 years of age. Daus., Mary and Elizabeth when 21 years old or married. Rest of estate to son, John. Brothers, Thom. Holt and Charles Binnes to assist the executor "my son John Holt." (Bk. 7, p. 49)

Charles Binns was a son of Thomas Binns, brother of John Holt's wife, Mary Binns.

7. John Holt succeeded his father John at Hog Island and like his father and grandfather petitioned the House of Burgesses in connection with the ferry at Hog Island Creek. In 1732 and again in 1744, he presented a petition that the bridge he kept up be a public charge, but it was rejected.

He is said to have married Elizabeth Wilson. His will was dated September 21, 1759, and probated October 16, 1764. In 1769, Mrs. Elizabeth Holt deeds Hamilton Usher St. Goerge "lower land that I hold on Hog Island assigned to me by my son Randolph Holt, deceased." Randolph Holt, to whom his father had given land on Hog Island, was a student at William and Mary in 1754. He died unmarried and in his will dated October 4, 1765, he gave his brother Joseph the plantation called "Grays" adjoining Hog Island, and leaves legacies to his sisters, Anne and Mary Holt.

Children of John and Elizabeth Holt were: Randolph, will probated 1770, John, will probated 1783 (see later #12); Joseph; daus. Kezia, Elizabeth, Mary and Anna; Grandson John Randolph Williamson.

4. William Holt, second son of Elizabeth (Hansford) and Randolph Holt (2) married Elizabeth, daughter of William Seward, who made her will March 16, 1702-03 and names her daughter Elizabeth Holt. (B. 5, p. 274). Thomas Holt was executor July 6, 1703. (B. 5, p. 281).

278

William Seward in his will probated May 4, 1703, gives his daughters, Mary Bruton and Elizabeth Holt, each a pewter dish. (BK. 5, -274)

Robert Caufield of Surry in his will probated in 1691, mentions "Mrs. Mary Holt", and his niece Elizabeth Holt, wife of William Holt.

William Holt's will was probated May 16, 1726 (B.7, p.637). He gave his son, William Holt, "my Trooper's Arms". To son, Thomas Holt, "all my land on south side of Nottoway River, where he now lives;" to daughter Sarah five shillings; son Charles and daughter Tappahanes NEWSOM. Elizabeth, Ann and Mary, remainder of estate to be equally divided. Wife, Elizabeth, executrix. (Bk.7, p.637).

Elizabeth Holt's will was probated September 21, 1737. Legatees; daughters, Tappahanes NEWSOM. Anne, and Mary Holt, son Charles.

Children:

I.   William made his will March 1753, names wife Mary, and children: Benjamin, will probated 1770, (see later #13); William, inventory filed 1778; Francis, will probated 1769 (see later); Martha; Mary, Hannah and James, will probated 1782.

II. Charles married Elizabeth, daughter of Richard Presson. He made his will in Surry October 9, 1767, probated April 27, 1773. Children: 1. Henry, 2. Charles, 3. Samuel; 4. William. (William may have been the William Holt whose will was probated 1801. He names wife Becky, daughters Hannah B. Thompson; Catherine; sons. Francis and William Holt) 5. Lucy, m. Wall; 6. Anne; 7. Hannah; 8. Sarah, m. John Clanton.

III. Thomas made a deed January 1764, to his son in law Henry COCKE. (V.M. 5, p.453) Inventory of Thomas' estate was filed 1775.

IV. Tappahanes, m.   NEWSOM.

V.   Elizabeth

VI. Anne

VII. Mary

5.   Thomas Holt, third son of Elizabeth (Hansford) and Randall Holt (2) of Hog Island was a Justice in 1697, a Burgess in 1699, and a sheriff in 1702-1705-1706. He married Frances, daughter of Francis Mason who mentions his daughter Frances Holt in his will. Also James Mason, son of Colonel Francis Mason, mentions his "sister Holt" in his will, probated 1702, and his "niece" Mary, daughter of Captain Thomas Holt. He also referred to his "brother" (half brother) Thomas Binns, deceased.

Mrs. Elizabeth (Aston) Binns-Mason, widow of Colonel Francis Mason, in her will dated September 1713, probated February 17, 1713-14, after certain bequests, leaves the remainder of her estate to grandchildren; Eliza, Mary, Katherine, Martha, Lucy, Frances, and Thomas Holt, Jr.: names John Allen, to whom she leaves 20 shillings, executor. (B.6, p.173).

In 1701, Mrs. Elizabeth Mason, gave her grandson Francis Holt, one half of 777 acres patented by her as Mrs. Binns, 18

Oct. 1669, and the other half to her grandchildren, Francis Mason and Charles Binns.

In 1701, Thomas and Frances Holt "administrators of Thomas Binns, decd." receipted Ethelred Taylor and Elizabeth his wife, administrators of James Mason, deceased. Ethelred Taylor had married James Mason's widow. (See "Descendants of Ethelred Taylor)

In 1704, in the Quit Rents, Thomas Holt held 950 acres for Thomas Binns' orphans. Thomas Holt's will was probated in Surry County March 17, 1730. (B.8, p.86). He names wife, Mary, and following children:

I.   Elizabeth, m. Nicholas COCKE.
II.   Mary, m. William Hansford, who died in York, 1733, and left a son, Lewis, who moved to Norfolk and married Mrs. Anne Taylor, a widow in 1753. Mary Holt Hansford married secondly - Steele, and in her will probated in York, July 20, 1767, leaves her property to her "son" Lewis Hansford, and if he dies to his four children.
III.   Katherine, m. Thomas COCKE.
IV.   Martha, m. John NEWSOM.
V.   James, m. Anne (Boush) O'Sheal. He was born 1710, died 1779, moved to Norfolk before 1752; married Anne O'Sheal, daughter of Samuel Boush, Sr. His will was dated January 5, 1779, and he describes himself as "James Holt, son of Thomas Holt, born at Hog Island in Surry County, Virginia at present in Norfolk, attorney at law". He was a Burgess from Norfolk, 1772 and 1774; member of the Conventions of 1775-1776; Judge of the Admirality Court 1776; and member of the first State Senate, 1776-7.

He left no children. In his will he gave a legacy to his brother Henry's daughter, Clarimond, "provided she did not marry a Scotchman". He also willed property to James and Henry, sons of his brother Henry, and to Leander, Sarah, and Thomas, children of his brother Henry, "by his last wife." (Tyler 7, p.283, V.M. 5, p.454).
VI.   Henry, m. twice, wives unknown, and died in 1813, His son, James, was a midshipman in States Navy in the Revolution. He married Martha, daughter of William COCKE of Surry and had an only child, William Cocke Holt, born in Norfolk 1783, died 1832, aged 49. He was a member from Norfolk in the House of Delegates 1807-1813 and in the Senate 1817-1832, being president thereof the last ten years. (Tyler 7, p. 283). On March 17, 1832, Mrs. Cocke made an affidavit concerning the heirs of Henry Holt, decd., who served three years in the Virginia State Navy. She stated that James Holt, eldest son and heir at law was deceased and that William Holt was the only surviving child and heir at law of James Holt. (Burgess-1468.)

The following pages were written
by Thomas M. Mann, Jr.

6. Thomas Holt, son of William Holt and his wife Elizabeth Seward, was born about 1700. He was devised by his father "all my

Land on the South Side of Nottoway River whereon he now lives".
This Thomas Holt is identical with the Thomas Holt who died in
Southampton Co., Va. in 1788 for at his death that Thomas Holt
owed 310 acres on the south side of Nottoway River. On August
9, 1750, Thomas Holt sold to his son Thomas Holt for 10 Lbs. a
plantation in Surry and Southampton Counties where on "Thomas
Holt Junr. now liveth", it being land "granted to ye said Thos.
Holt Senr." Jan. 12, 1747. (D.B. 1, page 155). Thomas Holt was
born probably about 1700 and was too old to have been Thomas,
son of John. Thomas Holt, son of Thomas, remained in Surry.
The name of the wife of Thomas Holt (d. 1788) is not known but it
is thought that she was Ann Newsom, sister of William Newsom
who married Tappanas Holt.

Children of Thomas Holt:
I.   Charles Holt, living in 1786.
II.   Thomas Holt (see later no. 7)
III.   Jesse Holt, who died in Southampton County before August 9,
1776 (Minute Book 1775-78) when the guardian for his daugh-
ter was appointed. He married_____Kirby, daughter of
William Kirby (d. 1772).
IV.   Amy Holt m.____Martin.
V.   Sarah Holt m. _____ Land.
VI.   a daughter m. _____ Rawlings.
VIL   Frederick Holt.

7. Thomas Holt (b. 1725-29) m. ca. 1750 Ann Arrington, daughter
of John Arrington (see ARRINGTON). He was given land in 1750
by his father which land he sold Dec. 13, 1770 (D.B. 4, p. 317)
and Feb. 19, 1771 (Hal. N. C. D. B. II, p. 300). His father devised
him "the plantation whereon I now live". On Apr. 10, 1789 "Thomas
Holt and Ann his wife of County of Hallifax State of North Carro-
lina" sold this plantation to Etheldred Taylor of Southampton Co.,
Va. (D.B. 7, p. 272). His will was dated Dec. 14, 1793 and probated August 1794 (Hal. Co. N. C. W. B. 3, p. 230). His wife survived him. He sold provisions to the Continental Army. (see
HOLT vouchers).

Children:
I.   Joseph Holt (b. ante 1755) m. (1) Nancy_____ (2) Rebecca
_____, He lived in Halifax County where he died in 1833-
34 (W. B. 4, p. 107). During the Revolutionary War he also
sold provisions to the Continental Army. (see HOLT vouch-
ers). Nancy was the mother of all his children.
       Children:
      1. Temperance Holt m. (1) Jesse Holt (children under father
         herein); (2) Joseph Parker. (See later No. 8)
      2. Mary Holt m._____ Holt (see below).
      3. Harvey Holt. No issue.
      4. a daughter m. _____ Cook and had issue Eli Cook who
         m. Christianna Dickens (see DICKENS herein).
II.   Rebecca Holt m. _____ Read.
III.   Thomas Holt m. Elizabeth and died before 1800.
IV.   James Holt was living in 1800. The census of that year shows
him as the only "Holt" in the county with a son possibly the
correct age to be the Jesse Holt who married Temperance

Holt above. James Holt died before 1810.
Children (possibly others):
1. Jesse Holt m. Temperance Holt. (For children see No. 8 below).
2. a son Holt m. Mary Holt above and had issue: Eagly Holt who m. 1857 Elias G. Neville and Hezekiah N. Holt who m. and had issue.

V. Arrington Holt m. Patsey_____. Not in Census of Hali-
VI. Patience Holt m._____ Johnston.
VII. William Holt m. Polly_____ .

8. TEMPERANCE HOLT (b.1780), daughter of Joseph and Nancy Holt, was twice married. Her first husband was her cousin, Jesse Holt, who was probably son of James Holt. Temperance Holt married second Joseph Parker (b. Jan. 18, 1761, d. in Hal. Co., N.C. 1834-5) on May (8 ?) 1822. She died on Jan. 27, 1852.
Children:
I. Joseph W. Holt (see later 9)
II. Hilliard Holt m. Emily Reid in 1849. No known descendants.
III. Eaton Holt. died unmarried.
IV. Nancy Holt m. James Parker (see later 10)
V. Hilby Holt m. William T. Wood (see later 11)
VI. James Harvey Parker, son of Joseph Parker and his wife Temperance Holt, m. Mary Crosby Scott (see later 12)

9. Joseph W. Holt (b. December 15, 1811, died May 26, 1884) m. Harriet A. Daniel (b. Jan. 1, 1808; d. Feb.14, 1882) March 25, 1830.
Children:
I. Lavinia Ann Holt (b. May 4, 1835) m. Joseph J. Fletcher.
II. Etha Linda Elizabeth Holt (b. Mar. 2, 1838; d. Dec. 10, 1928) m. Joseph Daniel Wood (b. Dec.11, 1832; d. June 12, 1901) Dec. 29, 1867.
Children:
1. Joseph Daniel Wood Jr., b. April 17, 1870; d. Jan. 5, 1872.
2. Isaac Thomas Wood (b. April 1, 1872) m. (1) Bessie Bristow Feb. 21, 1897 in Dillon, S.C. and (2) Rosa Wilhelmina Worrell (b. April 11, 1884, d. Feb. 10, 1935) Sept. 18, 1902.
Children:
(1) Joseph Columbus Wood, b. Dec. 4, 1897, m. Emily Louise Moore. Res. Dillon, S.C.
Children:
a. Elizabeth Kay Wood.
b. Emily Louise Wood.
c. Margaret Carolyn Wood.
d. Josephine Wood.
e. Joseph Columbus Wood Jr.
Children by second marriage:
(2) Margaret Raeburne Wood (b. June 28, 1904) m. Edgar Rivers Lafferty Jr. of Richmond, Va., June 11, 1941. Res. Lester Manor, Va.
Child:
a. Edgar Rivers Lafferty III, b. May 24, 1943.

        (3) Grace Carolyn Wood, b. Dec. 28, 1907, m. James Edwin Hughes (died 1952) in 1934. Res. Marion, S.C.

Children:

a. Robert Stuart Hughes.

b. James Edwin Hughes Jr.

        (4) Samuel Perrin Wood II (b. Feb.12, 1910) m. Elise Troy Cross on Dec. 19, 1932. Res. Mullins, S.C.

Children:

a. Elise Troy Wood.

b. Samuel Perrin Wood, Jr.

        (5) Ivan Thomas Wood (b.Sept. 7, 1912) m. Margaret Evans. Res. Marion, S.C.

Children:

a. Ivan Thomas Wood, Jr.

b. Rosina Wilhelmina Wood.

        (6) Francis Edgar Wood, b. Aug. 5, 1919; d. Mar.11, 1952.

3. Samuel Perrin Wood, b. Jan. 25, 1876, m. Mary Martin on June 29, 1933. Res. Selma, N.C. No issue.

4. Ira David Wood, (b. July 13, 1878; decd.) m. Lucy Della Savage (b.May 2, 1878; res. Enfield, N.C.) Nov. 23, 1904, daughter of William Henry Savage and Martha Ellen Merritt his wife.

Children:

        (1) Evelyn Ray Wood (b. Dec.31, 1905) m. Robert Edward Shervett Jr. March 24, 1935. Res. Enfield,N.C.

Children:

a. Ira David Wood III, b. Nov. 19, 1948.

b. Carol Winstead Wood, b. August 28, 1918; died in France August 1, 1944, of wounds received in battle near St. Lo.

III. Jane Catherine Holt, daughter of Joseph and Harriet Holt, was born Feb. 11, 1846; d. June 10, 1910.

10. Nancy Holt (d. June 7, 1884), daughter of Jesse and Temperance Holt, married James Parker (d.Aug. 1851) on March 28, 1847.

Children:

I.   James Watsob Parker (b.Feb.26, 1852; d. June 12, 1904) m. June 11, 1874 Mary A. Stallings (b.Sept.18, 1852; d. June 12, 1922) daughter of Etheldred and Martha Stallings.

Children:

1. Mary Allena Parker (b.June 28, 1876) m. W. H. Howenton. No issue.

2. George Lauther Parker (b. April 25, 1880) m. (1) Ella Stallings and (2) Virla Cobel. Res. Enfield, N.C.

Children:

        (1) Benson Parker m. Merdith Parks. Issue: Ella Fay Parker.

        (2) Gilbert Parker, died unmarried.

        (3) Lauther Parker, killed in World War II.

        (4) Robert Earl Parker, m. Nora Lewis. Issue: Lauther Earl Parker Jr.

By second marriage:
(5) Shelly Pickett Cobel Parker, unmarried.
3. James Loyd Parker (b. June 21, 1882) m. Nora Willie.
Res. Engield, N.C.
Children:
(1) Dorois Parker m. Paul Chester Fisher. Issue: Paul Chester Fisher, Jr.
(2) James Roscoe Parker, m. Julia Ray Harper. Res. Enfield, N.C. Issue: James Lee Parker.
(3) Thelma Parker m. Lacy Barkley of Virginia. decd. Res. Enfield, N.C.
Issue: James and Ferdy Cary Barkley.
(4) Fred Parker, unmarried.
(5) Willie Parker married Frances Thomas.
Issue: Thomas, Susan, Frances and Nancy Parker.
4. Fletcher Parker, b. May 13, 1886, d. Feb. 21, 1903.
II.   Hilby Holt, daughter of Jesse and Temperance Holt, m.
on Dec. 2, 1841 William T. Wood (b. Feb.11, 1811 in Virginia)
son of Daniel and Margaret Wood.
Children:
I.   Neomy Pantheer Wood (b.Sept.24, 1844) m. Throne Wallace.
Issue: 3 children.
II.   Temperance Mariah Wood (b.Aug.4,1846) m. Carter Fletcher.
Issue: 5 children.
III.   Elizabeth Goodwin Wood (b. Mar.19, 1848) m.Solomon Britt.
Issue: 6 children.
IV.   Matthew Thomas Wood (b. May 1, 1854) m.Lulu Gunter. They
reside in Enfield, N.C.
Children:
1. Blanche Wood m. Bryant Sherrod and had issue: Earl, Mildred, Daphne and Rom Sherrod.
2. Raymond Wood m. Carrie Sherrod. She and her sons reside in Enfield, N.C. Issue: Raymond Wood, Dr. Sherrod N. Wood, and Matthew Thomas Wood.
3. Marion Wood died unmarried.
4. Ruth Wood m. Watson Sherrod. Res. Enfield, N.C.
Issue: Watson Sherrod Jr. unmarried.
5. Eugene Wood m.   . Res. Hal. Co., N.C.
Issue: Eugene Wood Jr.
V.   William Cary Wood, a daughter (b. June 10, 1849).
VI.   Clarinda Amanda Henretter Nicholson Wood, b. May 29, 1852, m. John Brown.
VII.   Buchanan Wood (b.Nov.6, 1859) m. Mattie Goodrich.

12. James Harvey Parker, son of Joseph Parker and wife Temperance Holt, was born in Halifax County, N.C. on Jan.19, 1823 and died at his home in Enfield, N.C. on June 16, 1899. On Dec.21, 1841 he married Mary Crosby Scott who was born in Topcliff, Yorkshire, England on Jan. 26, 1819 and died in Enfield, N.C. on Aug. 13, 1902. She was the daughter of William Scott (b.Oct. 10, 1797; d. July 20, 1852) and his wife Rebecca Whitehead (b.Apr.14,1798; d.June 11,1863). They were born in Darlington, Durhamshire, England and were married there April 16, 1818. They came to the United States between 1821 and 1825, settling first in Orange County,

N.C., then in Halifax County, N.C. They, however, moved to St.
Charles Co., Missouri in the 1840's where they died. William H.
Scott, brother of Mary Crosby (Scott) Parker, was in the Gold
Rush of 1849.

Before the War Between the States, James Harvey Parker moved
from his home "Sandy Hill" to a plantation of his located near Whitaker's Chapel which he named "Rose Hill". This is now owned by
the Lawrence family. The Census of 1860 shows that he had property
evaluation of $60,000.00, making him one of the largest "planters"
in the county. However, he suffered greatly from the effect of the
war, but these reverses could not long hinder a man of his abilities.
Within a few years he was again sufficiently able to send his children to college. His obituary states that he was the largest land
owner in the county and that "most of Enfield belonged to him".
James Harvey Parker did not fight in the War Between the States
but rather was appointed to supervise the collection of food and supplies from his section of the county.

Children of James Harvey Parker and his wife Mary Crosby
Scott:

I.   William Fletcher Parker, born Nov.6, 1842, died Dec. 2,
        1909) married on January 3, 1865 Elizabeth Jane Herring
        (born August 26, 1847, died October 24, 1922) at Kenans-
        ville, N.C. (for her ancestry see Whitfield, Bryan, Smith
        and Related Families). He was a Lieutenant in the CSA.
        Their home "Branch Grove" near Enfield, N.C. is now
        owned by their granddaughter, Caroline Alston Mann. Wil-
        liam Fletcher Parker represented his county in the House of
        Representatives for two terms after 1900.
        Children:
        1. William H. Parker, an infant son, born September 6,
           1865, died September 7, 1865.
        2. Mary Elizabeth Parker (b. at "Rose Hill" October 6, 1866)
           married Benjamin Denton Mann, son of Benjamin Denton
           Mann and his wife Caroline Matilda T. Williams. Children
           under father (See MANN herein).
        3. Kittie Parker, born March 2, 1869, died June 9, 1870.
        4. James Horner Parker, born December 22, 1870, died
           June 8, 1871.
        5. Henry Herring Parker, born December 22, 1870, died
           June 8, 1871.
II.   Ann Mitchell Parker (born October 20, 1843. died April 6,
        1878) married (1) June 27, 1867 John H. Godwin and (2)
        Feb.7, 1872 Dr. F. M. Garrett.
        Children:
        1. Myra C. Garrett, born May 6, 1875.
        2. Annie M. Garrett, born April 3, 1878.
III.   Joseph John Parker, born December 24, 1844, died June 4,
        1845.
IV.   Samuel Watts Parker (born May 3, 1848) married (1) Mary
        Hunt, April 16, 1873 (2) Mrs. Loula Currin Tignor. No issue.
V.   Mary Jane Parker (born October 29, 1849, died May 24, 1875)
        married May 24, 1875 Algernon Barbee of Chapel Hill. No
        issue.
VI.   James Watson Parker born December 13, 1850, died April
        29, 1851.

VII.   William Rebecca Parker (b.September 26, 1852) m. Nov.3,
       1875, W. R. Bulluck.
          Children:
       1. James Parker Bulluck (born Feb. 11, 1879) m. Mary
          Eaton Avent, daughter of Thomas Vernon and Mary Spen-
          cer (Hart) Avent (see Alstons and Alstons of North and
          South Carolina for ancestry).
             Children:
          (1) Mary Elaine Bulluck m. Edward Tillery. Res.:
               Scotland Neck, N.C.
                  Children:
               a. Janacy Elaine Tillery m. Myrle Worrell.
               b. Cornelia Bulluck Tillery.
               c. James Edward Tillery.
          (2) James Parker Bulluck, Jr., m. and resided in Louis-
               ville, Ky. in 1953.
          (3) Rebecca Routh Bulluck, died young.
       2. Mary Mag Bulluck (b. August 3, 1880, d. Aug. 9, 1903)
          m. William Willis Ward.
             Child:
          (1) Hazel Rebecca Ward (b.June 30,1905) m.Garland L.
               Taylor. Res.: Enfield, N.C.
                  Child:
               a. Scott Garland Taylor, b.June 21, 1930.
       3. Routh William Bulluck (b. Aug.25, 1883) m. April 1, 1912
          Claude Norwood Kimball, decd., Res: Enfield, N.C.
             Children:
          (1) Gertrude Fleming Kimball, died young.
          (2) Rebecca Parker Kimball, born Nov.9, 1919. Res.
               Enfield, N.C.
          (3) Claude Norwood Kimball, died May 21, 1944 in World
               War II.
       4. Mary Scott Bulluck, born September 25, 1885, married
          Charles Allen Cochran June 30, 1910.
             Children:
          (1) Robert Bulluck Cochran (b.March 21, 1916) m. Mary
               Emma Brown. Residence: Rocky Mt., N.C.
                  Children:
               a. Mary Carroll Cochran.
               b. William Charles Cochran.
          (2) Mary Routhe Cochran (b.Mar.8, 1919) m. Robert
               Brumbrock Adams. Residence: 1955,Huntsville, Ala.
                  Children:
               a. Jo Ann Adams.
               b. Charles Scott Adams.
       5. William Fletcher Bulluck, b. Feb.3, 1888, died young.

VIII. Laura Walke Parker, daughter of James Harvey Parker
       and his wife Mary Crosby Scott, (b.Sept.19, 1853; d.April
       28, 1887) m.Jan.29, 1879, A. W. Bracey of Mecklenburg
       Co., Va.
          Children:
       1. Cary A. Bracey (b.Dec.3, 1879)
       2. Mary S. Bracey (b. May 10, 1881).

3. Algernon S. Bracey.
4. Ann Laura Bracey (b. Oct. 1, 1886) m. William Thomas Person.
  Children:
  (1) Laura Frances Person m. John Picto. Residence: Littleton, N.C.
  (2) Mildred Ashton Person.
  (3) Annie Daphine Person.
  (4) Vivian Parker Person.
  (5) Julius Watkens Person.
  (6) Ann Randolph Person.
  (7) Virginia Thomas Person, died young.

IX. Romulus Bragg Parker (b. June 3, 1856, d. July 31, 1939, Sunday night 12:15, which would be really Aug. 1, 1939) m. (1) June 8, 1881 Victoria Hunt (b. Nov. 10, 1857, d. July 12, 1912) of Oxford, N.C.; m. (2) Sarah Myrick of Littleton, N.C. (for her ancestry see THE STORY of the MYRICKS, by Bowden). She resides in Enfield, N.C. It is to her that the author of this chapter is indebted for much of the information on the Parker line.
  Children:
  1. James Harvey Parker, died young.
  2. Robert Hunt Parker (b. Feb. 15, 1892) m. Nov. 28, 1925 Rie Alston (Williams) Rand (for her ancestry see: ALSTONS and ALSTONS of NORTH and SOUTH CAROLINA). He is a justice of the Supreme Court of North Carolina. Residence: Raleigh, N.C. No issue.
  3. Romulus Bragg Parker (b. Nov. 23, 1917) m. June 29, 1945, Marysue Edmondson of Birmingham, Ala. They reside in Enfield where he practices law.
    Children:
    (1) Romulus Bragg Parker III, b. Sept. 12, 1946.
    (2) Adah Reuben Parker, b. Feb. 22, 1952.
  4. Walter Myrick Parker (b. Feb. 13, 1923) who resides in Enfield, N.C. and manages the family farm, "Oak Hill".

X. Cary Scott Parker (b. Apr. 3, 1861; d. Nov. 25, 1928) m. Oct. 6, 1880, Z. H. Hunt of Oxford, N.C.
  Children:
  1. W. Scott Hunt (b. June 30, 1881) m. Mammie
    Children:
    (1) William Hunt m. Mary Taylor and resides in Oxford, N.C. Issue: 2 children.
    (2) James Hunt.
    (3) Elder Hunt, died young.
  2. David Alexander Hunt, m. Alma Fleming. No issue.
  3. Mary Elizabeth Hunt, died without issue.
  4. Samuel Parker Hunt, died without issue.

JUDKINS of SURRY

by

Dr. B. C. Holtzclaw

The progenitor of this family was Samuel Judkins whose will dated 1671 was probated in Surry County May 7, 1672. It mentions his eldest son, Samuel, sons, Robert and Charles, and wife, Lydia Gray. The widow, Lydia Judkins, married (2) Capt. Thomas Pitman and was dead prior to March 4, 1678/9 (Bk.2.p.201). Lydia may have been a daughter of Capt. William Gray (1661-1719) whose will was witnessed by Nicholas Maget, Robert Judkins and Saml. Maget, all connected with this family.

I.   Samuel Judkins, eldest son of Samuel and Lydia, was born 1657-8, as he was a tithable in 1674. He married Elizabeth, daughter of Edward and Elizabeth PETWAY of Surry Co. and died in Surry in 1705, his inventory being dated May 18, 1705 (Bk.3, p.339). He had two sons, namely:

1. Samuel Judkins, b. 1683-4 (tithable first 1700), m. Ann   , and died in Surry Co. 1740, his will dated April 13, 1740, and probated October 15, 1740, mentioning son Samuel, daughters, Ann Champion and Sarah Holt, granddaughter Lucy Champion, and wife Ann. (See CHAMPION, Vol I, p.128)

2. John Judkins, b. about 1686-90, m. Martha   , and died in Surry Co. 1760. His will dated Dec. 12, 1758 and probated May 20, 1760. His wife, Martha, died in 1772, her will being dated Jan.19, 1767 and probated November 19, 1772. The two wills show the following children:

(1)   Nicholas Judkins, born about 1710-12 (first appears in the records in 1733, D.&W.1730-38, p.306), m. Elizabeth   , died in Surry County 1765. His will, dated May 20, 1763 and probated in Surry June 18, 1765, mentions sons, John and Jacob, daughters Mary, Martha, Ann and Elizabeth Judkins, and wife Elizabeth.

(2)   William Judkins, died in Surry County in 1760. His will, dated Dec. 10, 1760 and probated Dec.16, 1760, mentions sons, Joes, Thomas, Jordan and Mark, daughters, Hannah, Rebecca and Sarah Judkins; brothers, Joseph and Samuel Judkins, executors.

(3)   Joseph Judkins, died in Surry County in 1779. His will dated October 3, 1778 and probated Feb.23, 1779 was as follows:

" To my daughter, Sally Lane, 1 negro & 250 pounds cash to Sally Lane for her and John Lane to buy land; said land to go to her death to my grandson, Judkins Lane.

To my son, James Judkins and to my daughter Sally Lane all the rest of my estate to be equally divided between them.

Executors: John Lane, James Judkins and Sally Lane" (W. B. II)

(4) Samuel Judkins, probably identical with a Samuel whose will was probated in 1782 in Surry Co.

(5) Jesse Judkins whose will was probated in Surry in 1781.

(6) Charles Judkins.

(7) John Judkins, will probated in Surry 1794.

(8) Mary Judkins, m. a BARHAM (probably Robert Barham Jr. whose wife's name was Mary).

(9) Ann Judkins m.   Mouring.

(10) Sarah Barham. m. probably Charles BARHAM. John Judkins' will mentions not only his daughters, Mary and Sarah Barham, but also leaves bequests to Charles Barham and to his grandson, Robert Barham.

(11)   Judkins (probably) m. William Thompson. John Judkins' will leaves a bequest to William Thompson and legacies to his grandchildren, Philip, Frederick, Rebecca and Patty Thompson.

II.   Robert Judkins, second son of Samuel and Lydia, was born 1660-1661, as he first appears as a tithable in 1677. He married Elizabeth   and died in Surry County in 1693, his will, dated May 19, 1693 and probated Jan. 2, 1693/4 mentioning his sons, William and Robert, daughters Elizabeth and Sarah and wife, Elizabeth (Book 3, p. 343). The son William m. Margaret Harris and died in 1721, leaving two daughters, Elizabeth who married John Berriman and Hannah. The widow Margaret married (2) Bartlett Morland by Aug. 16, 1721; she m. (3) by 1729 James Vaughan. (cf. Va. Mag. 46, p. 360, D&W 1715 - 30, p. 971).

Robert Judkins, son of Robert and Elizabeth, married Faith, daughter of Nicholas Maget and moved to Sussex Co. where he died 1761. His will, probated Feb. 20, 1761 (Sussex Bk. A, p. 188) mentions his wife, Faith, sons, William, Robert and John, and daughter, Sarah Judkins. Robert's and Faith's son, William, is probably identical with a William Judkins who died in Sussex Co. in 1790, his will, dated October 10, 1786, and probated Sept. 2, 1790, mentioning wife, Sarah, sons, James, John and Nicholas. Three of the children of William and Sarah Judkins are mentioned in the Albemarle Parish Register as follows: William, b. Oct. 22, 1748; John, b. Oct. 3, 1746; Mary, b. Nov. 29, 1750. Robert Judkins, the other son of Robert and Faith, married Sarah   and had the following children recorded in the Albemarle Parish: Elizabeth, b. Jan. 5, 1759 and Susannah, b. May 2, 1761.

III.   Charles Judkins, son of Samuel and Lydia, was born in 1670

289

or 1671, as he first appears as a tithable in 1687. He married
Jean or Jane   , and died in Surry in 1710, his will
mentioning his wife, Jane, and sons, James, Charles,
Thomas and William. His widow was married (2) to William
Williams prior to Sept. 12, 1711 (Va. Mag. 48, p. 360). The
son, Thomas Judkins died unmarried in Surry in 1732. His
will leaving his property to his brothers, William, James
and Charles. Of the other sons, William Judkins is probably
identical with a William Judkins with wife, Catherine, the
birth of two of whose children is recorded in the Albemarle
Parish Register, namely, William, born March 22, 1739/
40, and James, b. March 5, 1742. Charles Judkins, son of
Charles and Jane, married Sarah GRAY, lived in Albemarle
Parish, and died in Sussex Co. in 1774. His will dated Nov.
6, 1773 and probated in Sussex June 16, 1774, mentions
sons, John, Charles and Gray; daughters Sarah and Mary
Judkins and Frances Hobson; son-in-law Amos Atkinson;
grandchildren, Margaret Drake, Sarah and Jemina Atkinson, Allen, Berney and Mary Dunn; and son-in-law Thomas Dunn. The births of the following of Charles and Sarah
Judkins' children are recorded in the Albemarle Parish
Register: 1. John, b. Dec. 19, 1737; 2. Frances, born
about 1740; 3. Susannah, b. July 14, 1740; 4. Charles, b.
Feb. 16, 1742; 5. Gray, b. Aug. 28, 1748. The Register records the death of Charles Judkins as Feb. 24, 1774. It also
records the births of the children of two of his sons as follows: (1) children of John and Mary Judkins: Charity, b.
Jan. 14, 1764, Martha, b. Dec. 4, 1765, Gray, b. April 11,
1770, and Howell, born Oct. 28, 1772; (2) Lucy, daughter
of Charles Judkins Jr. and Martha, was born Oct. 2, 1769.
(Charles Judkins, who married Sarah Gray, above, may have
been a son of John Judkins, d. 1760, and wife, Martha, but
it seems more probable that he was son of Charles and Jane).

LANE of SURRY and SUSSEX, VIRGINIA

Lane is an illustrious name in American annals, for Sir Ralph Lane established the first English colony on Roanoke Island, N.C. in 1585.

Sir Francis Drake, on his way back to England from the sacking of St. Augustine in Florida visited the Colony of Governor Ralph Lane and offered him a ship, a pinnace, and a months stores for his colony of 103 persons if he wished to remain, otherwise he would take them all back to England. Lane chose to stay; but the ship on which the stores were laden foundered suddenly in a storm. Drake had no more stores to give so Lane had to go home.

It is said that Sir Ralph Lane was the first Englishman to smoke tobacco, and introduced the practice to Sir Walter Raleigh.

Sir Ralph Lane was the son of Sir Ralph Lane and his wife Maud, daughter and co-heir of Lord William Parr of Horton, Northampton. Sir Ralph Lane of the Virginia venture died in Dublin, Ireland in 1603, and is buried in St. Patrick's Church. No mention of wife or child appears in his will and it is improbable that he was married. His property was bequeathed to two nephews, William and Robert Lane. (D.N.B. 32, p.77) This particular Lane family was numerous and the pedigree of it appears in Blair's History and Antiquities of Rutland, page 167.

The first of the Lanes in Virginia appear in the muster of Lieutenant Edward Waters at Elizabeth City in 1624. They were Thomas Lane, aged 30, who came in the "Treasurer" in 1613, and Alice Lane who came in the "Bona Nova" in 1620. No further record of these people is found (Hotten, p.253).

Richard Lane, aged 38, Alice Lane, aged 30 and Jo., Samuel and Oziel, their children, aged 4, 7, and 3, were licensed in England to go beyond the seas to the Island of Providence April 16, 1635 in the ship "Expectation" (Hotten). This ship was apparently one of a fleet bound for Providence, New England.

None of the people named appear in the Virginia patent records before 1665, either as patentees of land or as transported persons.

A Thomas Lane patented 1000 acres of land in Northumberland 26 July 1665, (C.P.463) and married Martha, widow of Nicholas Morris, in Nov.1651 (C.P.211). As Thomas and Martha Lane they made a deed to land Jan.18, 1670 (V.M.25,p.193).

The first of the family in Surry were Robert Lane with one tithable and Thomas Lane with two tithables, who appear in the tax list of 1668.

Robert Lane married Hannah, daughter of Thomas Culmer, for on November 6, 1662, Thomas Culmer, surgeon, gave his daughter Hannah, wife of Robert Lane, 300 acres of land at Upper Sunken Marsh, "formerly belonging to William Jennings, cooper. If daughter Hannah die land to go to Robert Lane" (Bk. 1, p.198). This patent was renewed in the name of Robert Lane 18

March 1662 (C.P. 326). On 2 May, 1666, Robert Laine and Hannah, his wife, sold this land to "Thomas Taylor, of Martin's Brandon, Charles City, mariner - reserving to Nathaniel Knight one half of the land purchased by him from heirs of Colonel Flood", called "Broad Neck".

A Richard Lane made his nuncupative will in Surry, 18 March 1686-7. He gave his wife (not named) his whole estate, if she marry the estate to go to two sons (not named). The first appearance of this Richard Lane in Surry records was on 28th of the 9th month, 1679, when he witnessed a deed between John Bynum and Richard Jordan.

Thomas[1] Lane, born 1634, is the first of the family in Surry from whom this family is traced. On June 11, 1667, as "Thomas Lane of Surry, planter", he made a marriage contract with Elizabeth Jones, widow, of the same, which provided that he, Thomas Lane, should pay to Elizabeth Jones, her daughter, out of her deceased father's estate, when she came of age or marries", the Plantation which was her deceased father's called "Sheepsheads", worth 1000 lbs. tbco. with cows etc. (Bk.1,p.184).

Thomas[1] Lane, (spelled "Laine") deposed on January 3, 1670 that he was 36 years of age (Bk.1, p.1380). On 1st day, 7th month, 1674 he was summoned with John Price to appraise the estate of Thomas Taylor. They met at Arthur Long's house. Thomas Lane made a deposition as to what occured there before Captain Charles Barham, justice, and stated he was aged 39. In 1682 Thomas Lane patented 400 acres in Surry (P.B. 7-184).

Thomas[1] Lane, Thomas[2] Lane Jr. and Joseph[2] Lane appear in the militia list of 1687, the only ones of the name who appear on this list.

Thomas[1] Lane and Thomas[2] Lane Jr. each held 200 acres in the Quit Rent rolls of 1704. Thomas[1] Lane made his will 5 January 1708, probated 3 January, 1709, and desired that his land be divided between his sons, Thomas[2] and Joseph[2] Lane. He made them executors and desired that the land be processioned between them by their neighbors (Bk.1694-1709, Part 2, p.440).

Children:
I. Thomas[2] Lane m. Jane Flood. (See later)
II. Joseph[2] Lane m. Julian   . (See later)

Thomas[2] Lane inherited 200 acres from his father in 1709 and on Sept. 5, 1710 he bought the other half of his father's lands from his brother Joseph Lane who was then residing in Isle of Wight county (D.B. 5, 1709-15, p.37).

In 1693, Nicholas Smith and Elizabeth, his wife, Thomas Lane and Jane, his wife, daughters of John Flood, deceased, conveyed 150 acres of land near plantation of Mrs. Arthur Jordan and the late Colonel John Flood, now in possession of Walter Flood. (For Flood, see V.H.G.-301)

On March 7, 1709, Thomas Lane and Jane, his wife, sold to William Newsom of Surry all the tract where Thomas Lane lately lived in Lawne's Creek Parish containing 50 acres between the College Path and the path that led to Phillip Clark's. Wits. Wm. Chambers, Robert Lancaster. (D.B.1694-1709, part 2, page 445).

On April 15, 1715, Thomas Lane and wife, Jane, sold 100 acres of land on head of Sunken Marsh part of the patent of 400 acres to Thomas Lane in 1682 near William Holt's line. Wits: Thomas Hart, Thomas Lane Jr., William Hart. (D.B. 5, 1709-1715, p. 325).

Thomas Lane and Henry Hart of Lawne's Creek Parish sold to John Cocke of Southwark 100 acres where Thomas Hart now lives for twenty three pounds sterling paid by said John Cocke. (D.B. 1715-30, part 2, p. 373.)

Thomas Lane Jr. predeceased his father, dying in 1721. Thomas Lane Sr. made his will Oct. 8, 1733, probated Nov. 2, 1734, as follows:

"Grandson, Thomas Lane Plantation that his Father lived on, with the land belonging to it. According to bounds held by his father, being as I suppose One hundred acres". Grandson, Joseph Lane, fifty acres of land beginning at Mouth of the First Branch so up to both branches and joining on both his brother's land. Gives Rebecca White a gray mare "Bonny". Daughter MARY HART his horse "Tuck". Appoints his daughters, Mary Hart, and Rebecca White Exors. (D.B.1730-38, p.428).

Thomas[3] Lane, Junior, who died previous to May 12, 1721, had his personal estate appraised on that date by his wife, Mary Lane, at 39 pds. 16s. 7 pence after payment of debts. (Id.333) His two sons, mentioned in their grandfather's will bore the familiar names of THOMAS and JOSEPH.

Thomas[4] Lane, son of Mary and Thomas[3] Lane, was probably the Thomas Lane of Surry who made his will in Surry March 5, 1770 as follows:

"Well of health. To loving wife, Mary, negroes & 1/3 of the 100 acres I now live on including dwelling house and orchard for life.
To daughter, Sally Lane, negro after her mother's death.
To son, Ethelred, 100 acres being the same land purchased by my brother John - also household goods.
To son Thomas 100 acres being the other part of the land I now live on.
To Sally, household goods.
All rest to my wife Mary"
Exors. Wife, Mary, son, Ethelred.
Witnesses: Thomas Bailey, John Bailey, Wm. Bailey.
Proved March 19, 1771. (Bk.II, p. 140)

Joseph[4] Lane, son of Mary and Thomas Lane, married Lucy, last name unknown. On Oct.7, 17--, Joseph Hart of Surry sold him as "Joseph Lane of Albemarle Parish, Sussex" 100 acres in Sussex (D.B.-"A"-248). Wits: Joseph Ellis, Hartwell Hart, William Cocks and Jane Lane. On April 20, 1763, George Briggs sold him 100 acres called "Lightwood Lands" (B-386).

Joseph Lane, Oct. 17, 1771, sold THOMAS HARGRAVE, late of Surry, 200 acres north side of Lightwood Swamp in Sussex. Wits. Joseph Ellis and John Phillips (D-413).

Joseph made his will in Sussex Dec. 4, 1774, proven Sept. 28, 1775 and mentions wife, "Lucy" and following children: JOSEPH;

DRURY; JESSE; LETITIA, m. (1) Mr. Butler, (2) THOMAS HARGRAVES (see HARGRAVES); LELAH, m. Mr. Phillips; LUCY; SARAH; MOLLY, m. Richard Andrews; THOMAS.

Jesse Lane, son of Joseph[4] Lane and wife Lucy, was baptized Oct. 3, 1751; married Anne   and had the following children baptized in Albemarle Parish:

I.   Samuel, June 29, 1766. Sponsors: Joseph and Thomas Lane; Mary Johnson.
II.   Peter, June 21, 1768. Sponsors: John Blow, Jr., Nath Felts, Jr., Eliz. Nix.
III. Rebecca, Dec. 15, 1772. Sponsors: Wm. and Mary Birdsong, Anne Cleary.

There was a contemporary Joseph Lane in Surry whose wife, Rebecca, was the daughter of a John Lane who died in Surry in 1777, leaving a will as follows:

Surry Will Book 1768-1779, Book II, Page 479

Will of John Lane, sick. To my son, William Lane, the land on which he lives 150 acres, being part of the land I now live on divided by marked trees.

To my son, Benjamin Lane, land and a negro.

To my son, John Lane, land I bought of William and James Gordon, also 10 pounds casy and a negro.

To my son, Frederick Lane, the plantation where I now live.

To my son, Micajah Lane.

To my daughter-in-law, Rebecca, wife of Joseph Lane, deceased, the use of the land I bought of Benjamin Little and John Judkins, this tract to be divided among the children of the said Joseph Lane. Micajah to have his legacy when 21 years.

To my daughter, Lucy Smith.

To my granddaughter, Martha Judkins 10 S.

To my grandson, William Judkins 10 S.

To my daughter, Sally Lane 80 pounds.

Residue to all my children, William, Benjamin, John, Frederick, Micajah, Lucy and Sarah.

Executors: William and John Lane Junior.

Signed November 11, 1777. John Lane Senior.

In presence of Jesse Cocks, William Cocks and Henry Smith.

Proved Dec. 23, 1777 by Wm. and John Lane Jrs.

Joseph[2] Lane, son of Thomas[1], was a tithable in Surry in 1688-94-98 and 1702. He was living in Isle of Wight county Sept. 5, 1710 when he sold 200 acres in Surry inherited from his father, Thomas[1] Lane, to his brother, Thomas[2] Lane, Jr. of Surry as follows: "Joseph Lane of Isle of Wight and Jilian, his wife, for valuable consideration sell to Thomas Lane of Surry 200 acres given me by my father in his last will, co-heir of the aforesaid Thomas Lane, half of a patent of 400 acres bearing date of 1682 (D.B. 5-1709-15, p.37).

Jilian is a very unusual name. It is very probable that she was the widow of William Alderson who made his will in Surry, Jan. 24, 1683; probated March 4, 1683/4. He provided for his estate to be divided into two parts between his wife Jilian and daughter Elizabeth. If daughter should die her part to go to her mother if she be living, if not to her next of kin. Wife to be executrix.

Wits.: Robert Ruffin, William Newsum. (B.K. 2-348)

Joseph Lane Sr., his son Joseph Jr. and his daughter, Mary Howell, were executors of the will of Joseph's son-in-law, Matthew Howell. Matthew made his will Jan.11, 1719, probated April 25, 1720, as follows: Legatees, sons, Thomas and Joseph Howell, unborn child; to wife moneys due me from John Gent, Richard Braswell, John Edwards, and Henry Flowers. Father Joseph Lane Sr., Joseph Lane Jr. and wife, Mary Howell, to be extrs. Wits.: Thomas Jarrett, Arnale Pew. (S.B-26).

Joseph Lane patented 1400 acres in Isle of Wight June 16, 1714. He moved to Albemarle County, Chowan Precinct, N.C. where he was residing on Aug.24, 1721, when he sold 250 acres on the south side of the Nottaway River out of the patent to John Thomas of Isle of Wight. Wife, Jilian, signed the deed. (Gr.B. p.446).

Joseph Lane probably died intestate as his will does not appear in the records. The Joseph Lane who died in Edgecombe was Sheriff of Edgecombe 1751-52 left a will but does not mention any children. This Joseph's will was dated Dec.6,1757 and probated November Court 1758 as follows: Legatees, brother William Lane, sisters, Faith Bynum, Drusilla Bryant. Other legatee, Winifred Pope. Executors: John Bradford and Henry Pope. Wits: Benjamin Merryman, Barnabas Lane, David Dickson (Grimes-207). He died before Nov. 27, 1758 for on that day his executors were allowed his salary as former Sheriff of Edgecomb for the years 1751-1752 (Col.Rec.) He was a Justice in Edgecombe 1748-49 and Boundary Commissioner in 1749 (N.C. Rec.Vol.4,pp. 521-22-24-966). He evidently had no descendants as he mentioned only a brother and two sisters.

This Joseph was evidently a son of Benjamin Lane. In the abstract of his will shown on page 333, N.C.H.G. Register, it shows that he mentions BROTHERS. William Lane and NEWITT. Joseph was the "grandson Joseph Lane" mentioned in the will of Edward Drew of Southampton Co. who made his will Nov.24,1745, probated March 8, 1749. Among his legatees he mentioned son, NEW-ITT. grandson, JOSEPH LANE: granddaughter, FAITH LANE, dau. of Benjamin Lane and dau. Ann Lane.

Faith Lane is evidently the sister, Faith Bynum, mentioned in Joseph Lane's will of 1758.

Joseph's brother, William Lane, made his will in Halifax Jan.22, 1786, proved Nov.1788. He mentions wife, Elizabeth; daus. Jane Eelbeck, Patty Battle, Ann Flewellen, Elizabeth Hill and Tabitha Lane: sons, William and Joseph Lane, FATHER BENJAMIN LANE. Exrs. Jetho Battle and Abner Flewellen. (Bk. 3-106).

Benjamin Lane, father of Joseph and William, was living in Edgecombe Co., Dec.12, 1748, when he deeded Thomas Pope 240 acres in Halifax "part of a patent granted Benj. Lane". Wits: Wm. Bryant, Joseph Lane.

Joseph Lane[3], evidently son of Jilian & Joseph[2] Lane Sr., married Patience, daughter of Major Barnaby McKinnie Sr. of Halifax, N.C. in 1730 (N.C.Col.Rec.11.317,519). Joseph's eldest son, John Lane had a daughter named "JILIAN".

Major McKinnie married Mary, widow of Jacob Ricks and daughter of Jeremiah Exum, Justice of the County Court of Isle of Wight (27W (1) - 60). Mourning McKinnie, sister of Patience McKinney, married John Pope and there was a close association between the Pope and Lane families. They later migrated together to Georgia.

Barnaby McKinnie was a Justice of the Peace in Bertie April 19, 1724, He was commissioned a Judge of the General Court of N.C. Oct. 6, 1725 and served as a Member of the General Assembly from Edgecombe January 15, 1735 (27W (1) 60). His will was dated Aug. 31, 1727. A codicil to his will dated Dec. 3, 1739 is of record in Halifax (D.B. 1-312)

Joseph[3] Lane and Patience, his wife, sold to John Hardy, gent., 200 acres of land in Edgecombe for 200 pounds. (Except two acres sold to his Majesty's Justices) This land was patented by Benjamin Hill and by him conveyed to Joseph Lane, April 1, 1743 (Halifax Bk. 3-213). The sale of these two acres was confirmed Aug. 20, 1747. Joseph Lane for 10 sh. conveyed the two acres for a court house to the Justices of Edgecombe Co. Wits: John Lane, Barnabas Lane, Nathan Cooper (Bk. 5-159).

On Feb. 19, 1755, Joseph[3] Lane made a deed of gift to his grandchildren: "daughters of my son, John, viz: Ann Lane, Mary Lane and Patience Lane, daughter-in-law Mary Lane. Wits.: Joseph Lane, James Lane (Bk. 2 - 211)

Joseph[3] Lane of Halifax Co., N.C. made his will Nov. 29, 1773 "sick and weak" to sons, JOSEPH, JAMES and JESSE he gave negroes; to grandson, Henry Lane, one negro named "Hercules"; to son, JOEL LANE all remainder of estate, real and personal; and made him executor. Wits.: THOMAS HOWELL and Henry Holt. Probated Feb. 1777 (W.B. 2, p. 35).

Children of Patience and Joseph Lane:

I.   John was evidently the oldest son for on August 12, 1755 as heir at law of his mother, Patience Lane, he deeded a half interest in land left by will of Col. Barnaby McKinnie, decd., to his daughters, Patience Lane and Mourning Pope, to her father, Joseph Lane, for 400 pounds- land in Edgecombe. Wits.: John Haywood, Henry Pope, Theo. Haywood (Halifax B 2-319). John Lane predeceased his father. His will was dated Feb. 13, 1774, probated Jan. 1776. He named sons, DAVID LAND, grandson, David Lane, daus. OLIVE JOYNER, ANN EVERARD, KEZIAH McKINNIE, PATIENCE JOYNER, MARY PITTMAN, MOURNING LANE, JILIAN LANE. Wts: McKinnie Howell, David Summers (Bk. 2-351).

His wife, Mary, predeceased him (Bk. 2-32). Also his son, John. (Bk. 1-204).

David Lane, eldest son of John, was made executor of his father's will. David, as David Sr., made his will Nov. 12, 1789, probated August 1790. He named son, DAVID: dau. ANN SHELTON; gr. daus. Martha Shelton and Elizabeth Barnes (orphans). Exrs. son, David, and son-in-law, Burwell Shelton.

II. Barnabas died before his father. He made his will as of Edgecombe Parish, Halifax Co., June 1762, probated Sept. 1762. He mentions wife (not named); sons, MARTIN and BARNABAS;

friend Martin Middleton; all my children. Exrs.: Joel Lane, Benajah Saxon, John Bradford. (Bk.1-83). Martin Lane, his son, is said to have served in the militia in the Revolution and died in Giles County, Tenn.

III.   JESSE, born July 3, 1733, m. Winifred Aycock. (See Later)

IV.   JAMES, m. Lydia Speight and died in Wake Co., in 1805.

V.   JOSEPH, m. Ferribee Hunter, daughter of Isaac Hunter. Joseph was a Justice of the County Court held in Wake on June 4, 1771. He died in Wake in 1798. His will mentions sons: JOHN, HUGH, daughters SARAH McCULLERS; MARY BALL; PENELOPE POWERS; TABITHA O'KELLY; grandson Henry A. McCullus. (Olds Abstracts)

Isaac Hunter, (father of Ferribee) and his brother Theopelius, settled in Hohnston County in that portion that afterwards became part of Wake. Isaac kept a famous tavern of its day on a 600 acre tract there three and a half miles north of Raleigh on the road to Warrenton. Theopelius was a delegate to the Hillsborough Covention of 1775, and Lt. Col. of Wake militia regiment in that year. (Wheeler 2-416) Isaac's first wife was Rebecca Hart and his second, Charlotte, daughter of John Giles Thomas. (N.C. Booklet)

VI.   JOEL. m. (1) Martha Hinton; (2) Mary Hinton, her sister. They were daughters of Col. John Hinton of Wake County and his wife Grizelle Kimbrough. Joel was a member of the Provincial Congress which met at Hillsborough August 20, 1775. (N.C. Roster 503) He also represented Wake County in the State Senate from 1782 to 1792. (Wheeler-422). Col. Hinton, his father-in-law, was Colonel of the militia of Wake County and his son John Jr., was 1st. Major on Sept. 9, 1775. (N.C. Roster 503). Joel Lane was the founder of Raleigh as he deeded the city 1000 acres for the present site April 4, 1792. His will was probated in Wake in 1795.

Children:
1. Henry Lane, b. March 6, 1764, m. his cousin Mary Hinton; d.1797 and left descendants.
2. James Lane, b. Oct. 7, 1766.
3. William Lane, b. Oct.15, 1768.
4. Nancy Lane, b. July 22, 1773.
5. John Lane, b. March 6, 1775, m. Sarah Elizabeth Jones.
6. Martha Lane, b. Feb.19, 1778, m.(1) Dugah McKeithin; (2) Jonathan Bricknell; died in Raleigh, May 20, 1852.
7. Elizabeth Lane, Aug.6, 1780, m.Stephan Haywood; left several children.
8. Mary Lane, b. January, 1783.
9. Thomas Lane, b. Sept.12, 1785, m. Nancy Lane, daughter of Martin Lane; moved to Giles Co., Tenn.; and died there March 29, 1832, leaving issue.
10. Dorothy Lane, b.Dec.13,1787, second wife of Dr. Allen Gilcrist; m. May 1806, moved from N.C. and left descendants.
11. Joel Hinton Lane, b. Oct.11, 1790, m.Mary Freeman; moved to Giles Co., Tenn.; served in war of 1812 with volunteers from Wake Co., N.C.

12. Grizelle Lane, b. June 3, 1793; m. George Lillington
Ryan; d. in Raleigh, 1868, leaving no descendants.

Jesse[4] Lane, son of Patience (McKinnie) and Joseph[3] Lane,
was born July 3, 1733. He married Winifred Aycock Dec.16,1755.
She was the daughter of Rebecca Pace, formerly the widow of
John Bradford), and William Aycock. Rebecca Pace was the daughter of Richard Pace of North Carolina. (see Pace family, p.168,
V.H.G.) He was a descendant of Richard Pace who saved Jamestown in the Massacre of 1622, by warning its inhabitants of the
coming Indian attack. (See Barker-Bradford-Taylor, V.H.G. p.
154)

Mrs. Barton Lane of 1118 West Magnolia Street, San Antonio,
Texas, kindly forwarded the following quotation from a letter
written by Winifred Aycock:

"My mother's name was Rebecca Pace. She was born in the
Colony of Virginia. She was married to John Bradford when she
came to North Carolina after her husband died, she was married
to my father, William Aycock.

"I was born within ten miles of Raleigh. I had two brothers,
James and Richard Aycock.

"My grandfather came to North Carolina in the year 1784.
Grandfather Pace's father was named Richard Pace. He lived in
Virginia. Great grandfather Pace had four brothers and three
sisters and all of them married and every one of them had a son
named Richard because that is a family name. He spelled his name
Pase sometimes. I know my mother came to Chowan in Albemarle
County, North Carolina, and she told me that they lived on a river
near a creek in Virginia that was next to her grandmother's house.

"My mother was born in a county in Virginia where five coun-
ties meet. She was the oldest girl, and her sister Mary was next.
Mother knew of (great) grandfather's brothers -- Uncle Thomas,
John and George, but never knew of Uncle James; he moved away.
She said her Aunts had been to North Carolina and visited them.
Elizabeth lived in the old home place but Aunts Ami and Sarah
moved to South Carolina. My grandfather was Richard Pace, Jr.
I married and moved in Johnson County, North Carolina in 1784-
My mother died before, ---here."

Jesse Lane with his father-in-law William Aycock and his
relatives the Popes and Bradfords, moved to Wilkes County, Ga.,
about 1784. In 1788 he lived on Long Creek, three miles below
Lexington on a large plantation which was afterwards bought by
Col. Hardin. This was on the Oconee River below Athens. When
Jesse came there the Indians and Tories were still troublesome.
Winifred, his wife, only lived ten years after they arrived. Wini-
fred Lane, her daughter was only fourteen when her Mother died.

Winifred Aycock Lane was born April 11, 1741 and died Dec.
16, 1794, from pneumonia contracted when she was driven from
her home by the Indians. She is buried in the "Old Cemetery" at
Athens, Clark County, Ga. Her parents belonged to the Church
of England of which she was also a member until converted to
Methodism by the Reverends Humphries and Major.

These two preachers held a great revival at Jesse's home.
They built an arbor and placed benches for the congregation and

at night had torch lights arranged on stands which were called
"Rush Light". Many people were converted and the new doctrine
soon spread through that portion of Georgia.

Jesse Lane had a long and distinguished career in the Revolutionary Army. On March 1, 1777, he enlisted for three years
service as a private in Captain Jacob Turner's company, 3rd.
N. C. Regiment, commanded by Col. Jethro Sumner. (Clark's
State Record, Vol. XVI, p. 1101) (Roster N. C. Soldiers, p. 68)

What Jesse did individually, we do not know, but we can follow
the fortunes of his company and regiment. The 3rd. N. C. Continental Line (the Regular Army soldiers of the Revolution), marched
northward to join Washington's Army on March 15, 1777. (N. C.
Booklet 17, p. 117) In the journal of Hugh McDonald, a soldier in
the N. C. Brigade he stated that as they passed through Virginia
they scarcely marched two miles at a time without being stopped
by ladies and gentlemen with presents and flowers. (Id.)

The Brigade arrived at Philadelphia on July 1st. and participated in the Battle of Germantown Oct. 4, 1777, where Gen. Nash,
the brigade commander was killed and Jesse's company heavily
engaged. Capt. Turner was killed and several others in his company. A monument was erected over their graves, bearing the
following inscription: (Wheeler, 2-143)

> "Hic jacet in pace
> Colonel Henry Irwin of North Carolina,
> Captain Turner
> Adjutant Lucas and six soldiers killed
> Killed in the Battle of Germantown
> One cause, one grave."

The North Carolina Brigade spent the winter of 1777-1778 at
Valley Forge enduring the terrible sufferings of that season. On
the last day of 1777, there were present for duty 572; sick 425;
absent on duty 137. (Id. 126)

They participated in the Battle of Monmouth, June 29, 1778.
Col. Jethro Sumner was promoted to Brigadier General Jan. 9, 1779,
and after his promotion his regiment was consolidated with the 1st.
of which Hal Dixon was Lt. Colonel. The regiment fought in the
Battle of Stono, June 20, 1779.

The N. C. Line was reorganized into battalions. Jesse Lane
was number 10 on the list of "Returns of Soldiers of the 2nd. Battalion N. C." reinlisted during the War, agreeable to Resolution of
Congress, and general orders, at Paramis, March 12, 1779 under
Col. Pattons command in Lt. Col. Harney's Company. On expiration of former enlistment, March 1st., 1780, he was paid $100.
(Vol. 13, State Rec., N. C. p. 327).

This payment of $100 on expiration of enlistment identifies him
as the same Jesse Lane who enlisted March 1st., 1777. This is
about as far as we can follow Jesse's career in the Continental
Army. Both Lt. Col. Harney and Colonel Patton were taken prisoner
with their command at Charleston, S. C. May 12, 1780. (N. C. Roster, pp. 37, 44.) Nothing is now remembered among his descendants about his capture at Charleston. It is stated by many of his
his descendants that he fought at the Kings Mountain with his son
John Lane, but John was born on Sunday, Christmad day, 1769,

and Kings Mountain was fought in Oct. 7, 1789. Jesse's name is not on the Roster of King's Mountain Soldiers.

However, it appears that two of his sons did serve in the Revolution, Charles and Richard-- they were old enough to serve.(N.C. Roster, p.617).

It is also stated that Jesse fought at Cowpens, Eutaw Springs and Guilford Court House. These were the battles in which the Continental Line was engaged. Anyway, Jesse was in the Army 7 years, for he received a grant of 640 acres within the limits of the land alotted soldiers of the Continental Line, May 14, 1784. This grant may have been in Georgia. (N.C. Roster, p.251)

Jesse Lane visited his children in Kentucky and Illinois and died in the last named state in 1806.

Children of Winifred (Aycock) and Jesse Lane.

I.   Charles Lane, born Oct.2, 1756, m. Elizabeth Mallory; served in the Revolution; descendants moved West or South.
II.   Richard Lane, born Feb.8, 1759; m. Mary Flint; descendants lived in Oxford, Ga., Texas, California, and Florida. Revolutionary service. (See later)
III.   Henry Lane, born May 28, 1760, died in infancy.
IV.   Caroline Lane, born May 26, 1761; m.(1) David Lowery, (2) George Swain. (See later).
V.   Rhoda Lane, born May 21, 1763; m. John Rakestraw.
VI.   Patience Lane, born March 6, 1765, m. John Hart, son of Nancy Hart of Revolutionary fame; moved to Kentucky. (See later).
VII.   John Lane, born Sunday, Christmas Day, 1769; m.Elizabeth Street; father of General Joseph Lane of Oregon and others. (See later)
VIII. Jonathan Lane, born April 3, 1767; m.(1) Patience Rogers; (2) Mary Colley.
IX.   Simeon Lane, sixth son of Jesse Lane, born March 10, 1771, married Judith Humphreys, father of William Lane, who married Miss Bailey, parents of Mrs. Parmelia Lane Campbell, mother of Mrs. Quince Nolan, of McDonough, Ga., who is mother of the two gifted orators, Colonel T. and Jack Nolan. Other descendants are Rev. Lon Campbell (missionary to China); Rev.John Lane, of Mississippi, who married Miss Vick, for whom Vicksburg was named. Senator Joseph Bailey, of Texas, and Mrs. M.J. Miller also belonged to this line.
X.   Rebecca Lane, March 5, 1773, who married James Luckie, was mother of Mrs. General Williamson and Colonel Richard Luckie, father of Mrs. Oliver Jones, of Atlanta, and Mrs. Lizzie Moss, of Athens.
XI.   Joseph Lane, March 28, 1775, seventh son of Jesse Lane, was born the year before the Declaration of Independence. Married Elizabeth Hill. Father of Ann Lane (or Nannie) who married the illustrious Georgian, Judge Walter T. Colquitt, father of General Alfred H. Colquitt, Peyton Colquitt, Emily Colquitt Carter, and Elizabeth Colquitt Ficklin (moved to Illinois). General Alfred Colquitt was governor of Georgia and senator at the time of his death. Colonel Peyton Colquitt, "the bravest of the brave", met his death at the front during

the battle of Chickamauga. Left no descendants. Governor Colquitt's children are Mrs. Captain Newell, of Milledgeville, Mrs. Marshall, Mrs. Preston Arkwright, of Atlanta, Miss Dorothy Colquitt, and Judge Walter T. Colquitt. Colonel I. W. Avery, in his "History of Georgia" says of General Colquitt: "Coming from a blood renowned in Georgia annals, the inheritor of eloquence and ability for the administration of public affairs, a gentleman of rare Christian character, with manner singularly simple and hearty, reflecting a temper uniformly genial, General Colquitt had such a hold upon the respect and affection of the masses as few men have enjoyed."

XII.   Mary Lane, born January 18, 1777.
XIII. Sarah Lane, born January 18, 1777 (Twins and married brothers, Thomas and John Kirkpatrick; moved to Illinois).
XIV.   Winifred Lane, born October 11, 1780, m. James Peleg Rogers.
XV.   Jesse Lane, born June 12, 1782, m. Rhoda Jolley.
XVI.   Elizabeth Lane, born September 6, 1786, m. William Montgomery', moved to Mississippi.

Richard Lane, the second son of Jesse Lane and Winifred Aycock Lane, was born February 9, 1757, married about 1779, Mary Flint, daughter of David Flint of Wake County, who made his will March 13, 1775, proven June 1775. He mentions his daughter "Molly" in his will and appointed Joseph Lane one of the executors. Wits., Jesse Lane, Martin Lane.

Richard Lane and his brother Charles Lane served as soldiers in Capt. Woods Horse, Col. Malmedy's regiment in 1780-81. (N. C. Roster, 617). Richard moved to Georgia and settled near his father on Long's Creek. This part of Wilkes later became Oglethorpe, where he made his will July 6, 1793. He stated: "I lend my wife Mary my whole estate, real and personal, until my son Samuel arrives at 21 when the estate is to be divided amonge my dear wife and my children: Mary, Samuel, Henry, ---Lane and child my wife now carries, be it boy or girl. Wife Mary, executrix. Wits., Jesse Lane, Alex Hawkins, Wm. Tillman.

The will was torn, but the missing child and the unborn child were Joel Lane and Richard Quinney Lane; for on Jan. 30, 1804, In Clarke County, Ga., Hope Hull was appointed Guardian for Joel Lane and Richard Quinney Lane, with William and Josiah Freeman as surities.

Children:
I.   Mary, born c. 1780-81; m. William Freeman. (See later)
II.   Rev. Samuel Lane, born c. 1782; m.   . (See later)
III.   Henry Lane, born Aug. 31, 1784, m.   . (See later)
IV.   Joel, resided in Troup County, Georgia and had several children.
V.   Richard Quinney m. Martha Burge. (See later).

Mary[6] Lane, (Richard[5], Jesse[4]), born about 1780-81, married Aug. 6, 1794, in Oglethorpe County, Georgia, William Freeman. He died July 7, 1817 in Jasper County, Ga. She made her will in Monroe County, Ga., Nov. 16, 1841, probated Nov. 17, 1842. Her legatees were: daughter-in-law Mary, widow of son Josiah; daughters, Cynthia Pendergrast, Elizabeth Ellison; son William Freeman, Jr.; grandson, William Capers Freeman, son of Josiah;

Grandchildren, Francis, Eliza, Tarpley and Josiah Herring; children of daughters Sarah; Cynthia; Elizabeth, and son, William; and grandaughters Amanda F. and Mary Freeman.

Their children were: Josiah, m. Mary   ; Sarah m. Arthur Herring (See later); Cynthia, m. Hiram Pendergrast; Elizabeth, m. J.B. Ellison; and William.

Sarah Freeman, married November 7, 1814 in Jasper County, Ga., William Arthur Herring, who was born in Lunenburg Co., Virginia about 1792, and was killed in the Mexican War, 1847. He was a Justice of the Inferior Court, Troup Co., Ga., 1827.

Their children were: Francis; Elizabeth C.; William Tarpley, born Feb. 29, 1818, m. Sarah Jane Ford (see later); Josiah, m. 1823, Rebecca Ford.

William Tarpley Herring, born Feb. 29, 1818, married Jan. 28, 1841, Sarah Jane Ford, born March 3, 1823, died April 24, 1885 In Russell County, Alabama. Mrs. Herring was educated at Wesleyan College, Macon, Ga.

Children:

I. Charles Henry Herring, born Nov. -1842; m. Louisiana Tucker.
II. William Arthur Herring, born 1844, killed in War.
III. Warren J. Herring, born 1845; m. Ophelia Sykes.
IV. Mary Frances Herring, born July 13, 1847, m. Wyatt Chadwick. (see later)
V. Lena Herring, m. Henry Dudley.
VI. Jane Herring, m. George Williams.
VII. Joseph Tarlpey Herring, m. (1) Victoria Ramsey, (2) Lizzie Edwards.
VIII. James Lewis Herring, m. Sally Sykes.

Mary Frances Herring, who was born in Zebulan, Pike Co., Ga., July 13, 1847, and died June 21, 1931, married Nov. 15, 1866, near Phenix City, Ala., Wyatt Holmes Chadwick, who was born November 8, 1844 in Russell County, Ala., and died Jan. 28, 1844 in Oneonta, Blount Co., Alabama. He served in Company K 7th. Ala. Regiment, C.S.A. through the War.

Children:

I. William Chadwick, born Nov. 6, 1867; m. Estella Browning.
II. Princia Elmira, born 1869; m. William Buckner.
III. Berdie, born 1871, died young.
IV. Alonzo Euell, born April 18, 1873, unmarried.
V. Julian Wesley, born April 20, 1875, unmarried.
VI. Ada Evelyn, born Feb. 12, 1877; m. (1) Dan Chapman; (2) Sam Williamson.
VII. Eddie Leone, born July 27, 1879, m. John William Wilson. (See later)

Eddie Leone Chadwick, who was born in Oneonta, July 27, 1879, married January 14, 1903, at Columbus, Ga., John William Wilson, who was born near Buena Vista, Marion County, Georgia, Feb. 18, 1875 and died August 4, 1928, at Columbus. He was educated in Buena Vista and Atlanta, Georgia schools, and was a Transfer Clerk in the U.S. Postal Service.

Children:

I. Florence Julien Wilson, born November 30, 1908, m. C.A.

Harris. (See later)

Florence Julien Wilson, who was born Nov. 30, 1908, at Columbus, Ga., married there, Nov. 24, 1931, Charles Ansley Harris,
who was born Sep†. 8, 1909, at Warwick, Worth County, Ga. They
now reside at 2745 Foley Drive, Columbus, Ga. Mr. Harris received his education at Locust Grove Military School and was a
member of the Civil Air Patrol during World War 2. Mrs. Harris
attended the Womans College of the University of N. C.; active in
U. D. C. and D. A. R.; new Regent for the second time; also active
in Church and School groups.
        Children:
I.   Charles A. Harris, Jr., born March 3, 1936.
II.   Wesley Fields Harris, born July 8, 1941.

The Reverend Samuel Lane, second child of Mary (Flint) and
Richard Lane, married Mary Matilda Carter. The Reverend Lane
was a noted pioneer preacher of the Methodist Church in Georgia.
He died in Corinth, Georgia, in 1848.
The Reverend George Wesley Yarborough, his grandson, on
July 8, 1920, placed a memorial on the Walls of the Corinth Methodist Church in his own handwriting in which he stated, among other
things, as follows:
"While under his care in my childhood, he led me by the hand to
the House of God that stood near the spot on which the present church
now stands.....
"To this saintly man, more than any other, I am indebted for
the first and deepest impressions of my religious life ..... written
by my own hand in my 82nd. year."

The children of Mary (Carter) and Rev. Samuel Lane were:
1. Mark; 2. Sarah, m. John Trigg Leftwich of Bedford, Va., 3.
Winifred; 4. Matilda, m. Rev. John D. Lewis; 5. Amanda Ellen,
m. Rev. John Wesley Yarborough. (See later); 6. Jefferson.
A family Bible contains the birth, death and marriage dates
of these children. It is regretted that information was not furnished.

Amanda Ellen Lane, who was born February 25, 1817, married
Dec. 1, 1836, in Corinth, Heard County, the Rev. John Wesley Yar-
borough, who was born May 20, 1813, in South Carolina. She died
March 8, 1891, in Oxford, Newton County, Ga., where her hus-
band had predeceased her, Dec. 16, 1879. They are both buried
in the Haywood-Yarborough lot in the Cemetery.
Their children were: 1. Rev. George Wesley, (See later); 2.
Samuel: 3. Walter; 4. Wilbur Fiske; 5. Dabney Penn; 6. Mary
Fletcher, m. Bishop Atticus Greene Haygood, (See later); 7. Emma
Harris; 8. Claudia Graves; 9. Martha.

The Rev. George Wesley Yarborough was the father of the Rev.
J. Francis Yarborough, Methodist Minister of Decatur, Ga., who
died October 30, ----. The Rev. J. Francis Yarborough was edu-
cated at Emery College and entered the North Georgia Methodist
Conference in 1899. He married Miss Martha Humphries. Their
children are: Dr. John Francis Yarborough, Jr., of Augusta,
Georgia; Mrs. L. S. Kelly; Mrs. Thomas W. Thornton of Elberton,
Georgia; and Misses Margaret and Elizabeth Yarborough of Atlanta.

Mary Fletcher Yarborough, daughter of the Rev. John Wesley Yarborough, was born at Corinth, Heard County, Ga., November 2, 1839; married June 6, 1859, Bishop Atticus Greene Haygood and died in Decatur, Ga., April 13, 1913. Bishop Haygood was born in Watkinsville, Clarke County, Ga., on Nov. 19, 1839, and died Jan. 19, 1896, in Oxford, Ga. He graduated from Emory College, class of 1859, and served as Chaplin of the 15th. Georgia Regiment, Col. Thomas Thomas commanding in the Army of Northern Virginia during the War Between the States. He was president of Emory College, 1875-1884, and a memorial tablet has been erected there in his honor. The Bishop and his wife are buried in the Oxford Cemetery. Their children were: Wilbur Fletcher, (See later); Mary; Atticus Greene, Jr.; and Laura Haygood.

Wilbur Fletcher Haygood was born Jan. 15, 1864, In Atlanta, Ga., and died Feb. 5, 1940, at Decatur, Ga. He married Dec. 15, 1887, at Savannah, Ga., Mary Richardson Rogers, born June 19, 1864, daughter of Mary Jane (Wood) and Osborn Thorn Rogers, at Covington, Ga. She died July 17, 1950, at Las Vegas, Nevada, while on a visit to her youngest son.
Children:
I.   Paul Haygood, born July 14, 1889, married (1) Lulu Helm; (2) Loretta Fitzgerald.
II.   Wilbur Rogers Haygood, born July 15, 1890, m. Alberta Gans.
III. Atticus Claud Haygood, born March 7, 1894, m. Mary C. Hankins.
IV.   Osborn Rogers Haygood, born June 25, 1905, m. Viola Foremaster.
V.   Mary Louise Haygood, b. June 28, 1892, m. Hugh H. Trotti (See later)

Mary Louise Haygood, born June 25, 1892, in Sheffield, Ala., married June 25, 1914, in Pawhuska, Oklahoma, Hugh Hubbard Trotti, who was born July 13, 1889, in De Kalb County, Ga., son of Ella Evans (Cozart) and Lawrence Jefferson Trotti. They live at 230 Wilton Drive, Decatur, Georgia.
Mr. Trotti entered the service of the Atlanta Constitution on Feb. 14, 1910 as assistant cashier. He became Cashier 10 years later and Treasurer in 1927, then in 1934 he was made business manager and in 1937 Vice-President of this noted southern newspaper of which Mr. Clarke Howell is Editor. Mr. Trotti is now retired, but is still active as a trustee of the First Methodist Church; Secretary and Treasurer of the Decatur Board of Education.
Mrs. Trotti was in charge of the Y. M. C. A. Hut at the Remount Depot at Camp Gordon, Ga., during World War I and received a silver vase bearing the inscription:
Mrs. Louise Trotti,
With deep appreciation for her faithful services,
From Officers and enlisted men of Auxiliary Remount
Depot 316, Camp Gordon, Ga., March 15, 1919.
Children:
I.   Mary Louise Trotti, born July 17, 1916, graduated from Brenau College, Gainsville, Ga. She obtained a Library

Science Degree at Emory University, and is now assistant librarian on the staff of the Decatur-De Kalb Regional Library.
II. Hugh Hubbard Trotti, Jr., born June 11, 1933, entered the U.S. Army Sept., 1954.
III. Lawrence Jefferson Trotti, born November 16, 1935, is a student at Davidson College.

Henry Lane, son of Mary Flint and Richard Lane was born Aug. 31, 1784, in Wilkes County, Ga. He died in Mississippi of injuries received by being thrown from a buggy by a run-away horse; when he was seventy-four years old. He was en route west with his son Iverson, and many of the Pope family who were going to Texas. He died within the hour, on November 9, 1858. The site of his grave is not known.

On Jan. 1, 1809, Henry Lane was married to Miss Martha Herring in Clarke County, Ga. Reverend Hope Hull performed the ceremony. (Book A Marriage Records of Clarke County) Henry Hull married a second time, late in life. This marriage was not successful.

Martha (Herring) and Henry Lane were the parents of ten children. These were listed in the Bible of his daughter, Eliza, who married John Jefferson Finley:
I.   William Herring Lane, born October 28, 1809; m. Susan Ponder, November 3, 1834; he was a physician, died Jan. 4, 1836.
II. Rebecca Littleton Lane, born November 23, 1811, m. Rev. Soloman Graves April 3, 1828, died June 12, 1831, leaving two children:
     1. Francis L. Graves, born Dec. 29, 1830.
     2. Martha H. Graves, born March 22, 1829.
III. Eliza Lane, born January 22, 1814, died March 15, 1847; m. John Jefferson Finley, Feb. 28, 1839, died at the birth of her fifth child: she and the infant daughter buried in the Conchardie graveyard on the Chocoloca River in Talledega County, Alabama.
IV. Rev. Richard Lane, born Jan. 21, 1816, m. Margaret Pope; d. 1900, buried at Jefferson.
V.   Rev. James Sterling Lane, born February 27, 1818, died Dec. 8, 1883; m. Sophronia Audos, one of three wives.
VI. Mary Ann Stokes Lane, born August 30, 1820, m. James Madison Finley in 1839.
VII. Henry Capers Lane, born January 18, 1823. d.s.p.
VIII. Francis Asbury Lane, born Feb. 4, 1825; m. had a family, moved to Arkansas.
IX. Egbert Summerfield Lane, born May 11, 1827. d.s.p.
X.   Iverson Wesley Lane, born October 22, 1829, m. Martha E. Pope.

Caroline Lane, eldest daughter of Winifred (Aycock) and Jesse Lane, born May 26, 1761, married first David Lowry who was killed in a battle with the Creek Indians September 16, 1787; married second George Swain of Ashville, and moved from Elbert, Ga., back to North Carolina.
Children by first husband:
I.   James Lowry, m. Esther Siler. (See later)

II. Mary Lowry, m. Hanson (no children).
III. Patience Lowry, m. Irwin.
Children by second husband:
IV. George Swain Jr., father of Mrs. Dr. Crawford Long of Georgia, and grandfather of Mrs. A.O. Harper of Elberton, Georgia, and others.
V. Governor David Swain of North Carolina, afterward president of Chapel Hill University. Grandfather of Mr. Grant of Asheville.
VI. Cynthis Swain, married William Coleman. Her son, David Coleman, was Colonel Thirty-Ninth Regiment North Carolina (C.S.A.). Always wore the Confederate gray and asked to be buried in it.
VII. Althea Swain, married William Siler.
VIII. Matilda Swain, married Jacob Siler.
IX. Caroline Swain, married J. Hall.

James Lowry, son of Caroline Lane and David Lowry, married Esther Siler and had the following children:
I. Caroline Lowry, married Rev. David E. Cumming, grandfather of Linton N. Robson, Ginn Book Co.
II. Margaret Lowry, married C. B. Weaver (1) and P. Roberts (2).
III. Elizabeth Siler Lowry, married Dr. S.B. Gudyer, living in Candler, N.C.
IV. Matilda Lowry, married James Robinson, parents of Lieutenant Governor Robinson; (2) married J. K. Gray.
V. Harriet Lowry, married B.K. Dickey, living near Murphy, N.C.
VI. Louisa Lowry, married James Patton, Lafayette, Ga.
VII. Lorena Luckie Lowry, married Newman Henry, Candler, N.C.
VIII. James Lowry, Lieutenant Colonel Thirty-Ninth North Carolina Regiment, C.S.A., 5 sons, 2 daughters; James, the eldest, living in Prescott, Ariz., Charles and John in Nevada.

Patience Lane, third daughter of Winnifred (Aycock) and Jesse Lane, was born March 28, 1765. In 1785 she married John Hart, son of Benjamin Hart and Nancy (Ann) Morgan of N.C. John Hart and associates founded Watkinsville, County seat of Clarke County, Ga. John and Patience lived on Long Creek in 1788, three miles from Lexington. In 1803 they moved to what is now Henderson County, Ky., seven miles south of Henderson. His will was proven in Henderson County, 1821 and names eight children. (W.B. A-346)

General Joseph Lane of Oregon stated that his father, John Lane, Uncle John Hart and Uncle David Lowery were in a battle with the Creek Indians Sept.16, 1787, when David Lowery was killed.

Rebecca Hart, daughter of Patience (Lane) and John Hart was born Feb.28, 1797, in Georgia; died August 15, 1866 in Dallas, Texas. She married in Henderson, Ky., 1817, Dr. Thomas Worthington, born May 27, 1786 in Berkeley Co., Va.; died 1852 in Kentucky. They had nine children, among whom were: Martha,

who married William Caruth, and Ann Amamda, who married
Capt. Walter Carruth.

Ann Amanda Worthington, youngest child of Rebecca (Hart)
and Dr. Thos. Worthington, was born July 2, 1841; married
March 5, 1865, Capt. Walter Carruth, who was born Feb. 1, 1826,
in Allen County, Ky., died February 3, 1897 in Dallas County,
Texas. He was Quartermaster of the Confederate Army, stationed
at Tyler, Texas, during the war of 1861-65, in Col. W. H. Dar-
nell's regiment and Col. Stone's regiment until the end of the war.
Mrs. Carruth died May 16, 1932, in New York City.

Raymond Percy Carruth, the son of Anne Amanda (Worthing-
ton) and Capt. Walter Anderson Carruth was born Jan. 27, 1885,
at Dallas, Texas, died Jan. 30, 1945, at Miami, Florida; married
June 12, 1912, Margaret Anne Scruggs, daughter of Mary Isabella
Hasting (Dial) and Major James Briscoe Scruggs, who was born
February 18, 1892.

Mrs Scruggs-Carruth was educated at Bryn Mawr; received
at B. A. degree in 1943 at the Southern Methodist University in
Dallas, and an M. A. degree in 1944; majored in psychology and
was honored by the national Psi Chi Society for scholarship; she
was on the staff of S. M. U. 1945-49; and has held or holds national,
state or local offices in many of the leading patriotic societies,
art organizations and garden clubs. She is a writer, lecturer,
illustrator and co-author with her mother of "Gardening in the
South West"; was a citizen-member of the State Roadside Commission of Texas Highways; and is active manager of Scrugs,
Price & Co., Insurance Agents in Dallas, Texas.

Children:
I.   Walter Scruggs-Carruth, born July 15, 1914; m. Feb. 27,
       1942, in Dallas, Margaret Louise Wilson, born May 16, 1920.
       No children.
II.   Marianne Worthington Scruggs-Carruth, born September 20,
       1917; died December 6, 1918.

Joseph Lane, son of Elizabeth (Street) and John Lane, a Delegate and a Senator from Oregon; born in Buncombe County, N. C.,
December 14, 1801; moved with his parents to Henderson, Ky., in
1810; attended the common schools; moved to Vanderburg County,
Indiana, in 1821; member of the State house of representatives
in 1822, 1823, 1831-33, 1838, and 1839; served in the State senate
1844-1846; during the Mexican war was commissioned as colonel
of the Second Indiana Volunteer Regiment on June 25, 1846; promoted to brigadier general on July 1, 1846; and brevetted major
general October 9, 1847, "for gallant and meritorious conduct in
the Battle of Huamantla, Mexico", honorably discharged July 20,
1848; appointed by President Polk Governor of the Territory of
Oregon and served from March 3, 1849, to June 18, 1850, when
he resigned; elected as a Democrat Delegate to the Thirty-second
and to the three succeeding Congresses and served from March 4,
1851, until February 14, 1859, when the Territory became a
state; during the interim between the sessions of the Thirty-second
and Thirty-third Congresses was appointed Governor of the Territory by President Pierce and served from May 16 to 19, 1853,
when he again resigned; upon the admission of Oregon as a State

into the Union he was elected to the United States Senate and served from February 14, 1859, to March 3, 1861; did not seek re-election in 1860, having become a candidate for Vice-President; nominated for Vice President of the United States on the Democratic ticket of Breckinridge and Lane in 1860; died in Roseburg, Oregon, April 19, 1881; interment in Masonic Cemetery. (Biographical Directory of the American Congress, 1774-1948, U.S. Government Printing Office, 1950 - page 1434)

His children were:
I. Mollissa Lane, married Barlow. Died at Jacksonville, Oregon.
II. Nathaniel Lane, died at Portland, Oregon.
III. Joseph C. Lane, living at Ruckles, Oregon.
IV. Simon R. Lane, living at Roseburg, Oregon.
V. Colonel John Lane, C.S.A., living in Lewiston, Idaho.
VI. Colonel Lafayette G. Lane, died 1896, Roseburg, Oregon. (See later)
VII. Mrs. Mary V. Lane Shelby, San Jose, California.
VIII. Mrs. Emily Lane Floed, San Jose, California.
IX. Simeon Lane, living at Roseburg, Oregon.
X. Mrs. Winifred Lane Mosher, Portland, Oregon.

Lane, La Fayette (son of Joseph Lane and uncle of Harry Lane), a Representative from Oregon; born near Evansville, Vanderburg County, Indiana, Nov.12, 1842; attended the public schools at Washington, D.C., and at Stanford, Conn.; studied law; was admitted to the bar and commenced practice in Roseburg, Oregon; member of the State house of representatives in 1864; code commissioner in 1874; elected as a Democrat to the Forty-fourth Congress to fill the vacancy caused by the death of George A. La Dew and served from October 25, 1875, to March 3, 1877; unsuccessful candidate for re-election in 1876 to the Forty-fifth Congress; resumed the practice of law; died in Roseburg, Oregon, on November 23, 1896; interment in the Catholic Cemetery. (Same ref., p.1434)

LANE, Harry (grandson of Joseph Lane and nephew of La Fayette Lane), a Senator from Oregon; born in Corvallis, Benton Co., Oregon, August 28, 1855; attended the public schools, and was graduated from Willamette University, Salem, Oregon, in 1876; received the medical degree from the same university in 1878; took postgraduate work in the College of Physicians and Surgeons of New York City; commenced practice of medicine in San Francisco, California, returned to Oregon and settled in Portland, where he resumed the practice of medicine; superintendent of the Oregon Insane Asylum 1887-1891; mayor of Portland 1905-1909; elected as a Democrat to the United States Senate and served from March 4, 1913 until his death in San Francisco, California, May 23, 1917; interment in Lone Fir Cemetery, Portland, Oregon. (Same ref., p.1433)

LUCAS of SURRY

In 1628, William Lucas of Saltashe Co., Cornwall, merchant, was recorded as owner of the ship "Supply", which sailed to Virginia in January 1625/6 (Va. Mag. Vol. 15, p. 318). On August 16, 1644 provision was made by the Virginia Council for William Lucas and his family (Minutes of the Council, p. 502) and William Lucas was granted 800 acres in the Lower Norfolk Co. Va., Aug. 22, 1647, having married the relict of Caesar Hugget. It is doubtful whether these men were identical and uncertain what, if any, was their relation to William Lucas of Surry Co. The latter was born in 1629, and appears briefly in the records with his wife, Anne (b. 1630) in testimony in a law-suit June 3, and 11, 1659. (Surry D. &W., 1645-71, pp. 133-4).

William Lucas of Surry was probably related to Roger and Walter Lucas, who appear in the records of Charles City Co. (Charles City Co. O. B., 1655-65, pp. 117, 121; Wm. and Mary Quarterly, ist Series, Vol. IV, p. 168). Apparently, William and Anne Lucas had only one son, William Lucas, who was born in 1654 (D. & W. 1671-84, p. 183). William Lucas Sr. probably died soon after 1659, and there is some reason to think that his widow, Anne, married (2) Robert Dennis of Surry. Robert Dennis died between 1670 and 1671, and his widow, Anne Dennis, on March 1, 1671/2 deeded 50 acres of land out of a large tract she had bought from John LeGrande to her son-in-law, Abraham Evans, having previously sold half of the total tract to William Lucas (D. &W. 1671-84, p. 264). William Lucas was witness to the deed from LeGrande to Anne Dennis (Id., p. 13), and on Nov. 1, 1688, was deeded more of the land by Nathaniel Dennis, son and heir of Robert and Ann Dennis (D. &W. 1687-94, p. 92). William Dennis appears in William Lucas' household in the tithables of 1687, and Nathaniel Dennis is shown with Lucas in 1690. Ann Dennis also deeded land to her son-in-law, John Harris, about the same time that she made the deed to Abraham Evans (D. &W. 1671-84, p. 87). If the identification of Anne Dennis and Ann Lucas is correct, William and Ann Lucas probably had two daughters in addition to William Lucas, Jr., one of whom married Abraham Evans and the other, John Harris.

William[2] Lucas (William[1]), b. 1654, lived in that part of Surry County which was very close to Charles City (later Prince George), and died there in 1717. He married Grace Beckwith, daughter of Marmaduke and Maudlin (Creed) Beckwith of Surry Co. (See Creed Family). She died 1720. The will of William Lucas was dated Oct. 1, 1716 and probated December 18, 1717 (D. &W. 1715-30, p. 79), that of Grace Lucas was dated December 22, 1719 and probated February 17, 1719/20 (Id., p. 249). Among other bequests Grace

Lucas left the major part of her estate to be divided between her son, William, and "my daughters Ann, Grace, Hannah and Elizabeth if She recovers of the present fitt of Sickness she Laboureth under, but if she does not recover then Henry Briggs to have no part of my estate", thus showing the marriage of the daughter, Elizabeth, to Henry Briggs. There is no indication in the wills as to whom the other daughters married, though Grace made a bequest to Valentine Williamson and made John Collier one of her executors, which may indicate that one daughter married a Williamson and another a Collier. Elizabeth Lucas was probably the eldest child of William and Grace. Her father acknowledged receipt of a bequest to her from her god-mother (and aunt), Elizabeth Beckwith, on March 6, 1687/8 (D. &W. 1687-94, p. 38).

Children:

I. Elizabeth Lucas, married Henry Briggs. (See Briggs Family)

II. William Lucas, m. Martha , and moved to Brunswick County, where his will was dated February 25, 1739 and probated March 5, 1740. It mentions his son, John, and the latter's two eldest daughters, sons, William, Charles, Samuel and Daniel, grandson William Lucas, and wife, Martha; Moses Johnson and John Irby, trustees.

III. Ann Lucas.

IV. Grace Lucas.

V. Hannah Lucas.

VI. Mary Lucas.

VII. Charles Lucas, m. Mary, daughter of Benjamin Evans of Prince George Co. (Prince George D. &W. 1713-28, p. 787). Mary Lucas died in Isle of Wight Co. in 1734, her will leaving her property to her sons, William and John.

DESCENDANTS of THOMAS and ELIZABETH MANN

of Isle of Wight

by

William Marion Mann, Jr.

The English ancestry of Thomas Mann has not been absolutely established, but is probable that he was descended from John Mann of Kent who during the reign of Henry VIII married a member of the House of Cornwall. His great-grandson, William Mann of Kent, married Frances Blanderhasset and has issue two sons: Sir Charles Mann and George Mann. Since Thomas Mann, the emigrant, named his eldest son Charles Mann it is possible that either Sir Charles Mann or George Mann was his grandfather. It is only in the Kent family of the name that the given name Charles appears (The Visitations of Kent, 1619-p. 23). Furthermore Thomas Mann came to Virginia during a period of great political unrest in England and at a time when many persons of quality came to America. In support of this is the fact that Thomas Mann never used his mark but always signed his name which shows that he was a person who had had the advantages of some education. The arms and crest of the Mann family of Kent are recorded as follows: "ARMS:-Or, a chevron ermine between three lions rampant guardant sable: impaling, ermine. six escallops gules, three two and one. CHREST:-Five Spears argent issuant from the top of a tower or".

1. Thomas Mann, the ancestor of this family, was born in England about 1626 and emigrated to Virginia and settled in Nansemond County about 1648. On March 22, 1650, John Garwood was granted 1,000 acres of land in Nansemond County lying on the north side of the head of Indian Creek for transporting twenty persons to the colony. Among these twenty persons was this Thomas Mann (C.P. p. 205). It was this same Thomas Mann who moved to Isle of Wight County, Virginia, and was assigned land by Richard Booth in 1681. However, since the records of Nansemond County have been burned, nothing of the early life of Thomas Mann in America is known.

On April 20, 1680, Richard Booth obtained a patent of 560 acres of land in Isle of Wight County on Corowaugh Swamp for transporting twelve persons into the colony. (W.D. 1, pp. 473; D.B. 1, pp. 53-54). On November 8, 1681 he assigned his interest in this land to Thomas Mann and his wife Elizabeth with John Rogers and Charles Mann as witnesses (D.B.1, p. 473). On that same day Richard Booth sold to his sister's husband, John Rogers, 100 acres on Beaver Dam Swamp; and on the next day, November 9, 1681, he gave 100 acres adjacent to his sister, Mary Rogers

(Ibid, p.473). On Nov. 8, 1681, just after being assigned the grant by Richard Booth of Isle of Wight "Thomas Mann of ye County of Nansemond & Elizabeth" his wife gave to their son, Charles Mann, 200 acres of land "lying & being upon ye Branch of Curawaugh Swamp in ye Lower Parish of the Isle of Wight" with John Rogers and Richard Booth witnessing the deed (Ibid., p.474). This tract of 200 acres was part of the land that had been assigned to Thomas Mann that same day by Richard Booth, and the numerous transactions on the same day may indicate a close kinship between the parties, it probably being that Thomas Mann married Elizabeth Booth, sister of Richard Booth.

Thomas Mann soon afterward moved to Isle of Wight County where he lived the rest of his life on his Corowaugh Swamp plantation, for on June 9, 1683, "Thomas Man of Isle of Wight County & Elizabeth his wife for 2050 Lbs. of Tobacco" sold to Theophilus Joyner of the same county 150 acres of land, part of a tract of 300 acres which was granted to Thomas Mann, September 22, 1682 (D.B. 1, p.303). On this deed as on the others which Thomas Mann signed, he wrote his own name which proves that he was a man of some education and was probably the younger son of some landed gentleman in England.

Thomas Mann sold or bought no more land after he sold the 150 acres to Theophilus Joyner in 1683, and his name does not appear on the records of Isle of Wight County until he died in 1689, at which time appraisement of his estate was recorded in Isle of Wight County (W.D. vol.II, p.307). It was undated but the date has been ascertained from records near it in the same book and from the fact that his son Thomas Mann sold 100 acres of land on Corowaugh Swamp to Henry Hearne in Feb.1690 (D.B.1, p.24). Elizabeth (Booth) Mann, the wife of Thomas Mann, survived him and was living the 9th of February 1693 (Ibid. pp.53-54). She was born about 1628, probably in England.

Children of Thomas Mann and his wife Elizabeth (Booth?):
I. Charles Mann (b. ca.1660; died ca.1688 in Isle of Wight County) was given 200 acres by his father in 1682. In the deed it was stated that if Charles Mann should die without issue the land was to revert to the heirs of Thomas Mann (W.D.B.1-pp.473-474). Charles Mann died without issue and without a will since Thomas Mann II after 1688 is shown selling land which description shows it was the land once owned by Charles Mann.
II. Sarah Mann m. ca.1684 Francis Davis who was living in Isle of Wight County in 1704 (D.B.1, p.120: Quit Rent List 1704)
III. Thomas Mann b. ca. 1666. (see later number 2)
IV. a daughter who m.   Crawman and had issue a son William Crawman.

2. Thomas Mann, son of Thomas Mann and his wife Elizabeth (Booth?), was born in Nansemond County, Virginia, before 1669, probably about 1666, as he was at least 21 in 1690 when he sold 100 acres of land on the north east side of Corowaugh Swamp to Henry Hearne (D.B. 1, p.24). In that year he was also granted 200 acres with Hodges Councill, the younger, adjacent John Brown

312
and Kinsale Swamp for transportation of four persons into the
colony. Hodges Councill and Thomas Mann assigned their right to
Kerle on September 9, 1691 (Ibid., pp. 40-41).
   In 1693, Thomas Mann, "planter", gave to his sister Sarah
Mann. the wife of Francis Davis, 100 acres on Corowaugh Swamp.
On September 13, 1694, he sold to James Curley 150 acres on the
north side of the same swamp, adjacent to the said Thomas Mann's
line, James Johnson, and Charles Mann's old field. William Duck,
William Bull, and Edward Bryan witnessed the deed (Ibid. p.122).
   In 1692 Thomas Mann discovered an illegal flaw in the assign-
ment which Richard Booth had made his father, Thomas Mann, on
November 8, 1681, for that year he went to court and brought action against Richard Booth to make a "good and sufficient" deed of
sale for the land to him Thomas Mann, Junr., heir of Thomas
Mann, Senr., deceased. Richard Booth was compelled to do so,
and on Feb.9, 1692/3 made another deed to Thomas Mann, Junr.
(Ibid.pp.53-54). On Nov.8, 1696 Thomas Mann sold the remainder
of this land, then 200 acres, to Nicholas Tyner (Ibid.p.218). He
sold the land as "Thomas Mann, Jr., and heir of Tho: Man late of
ye Isle of Wight County Deceased". The last record dealing with
Thomas Mann is Isle of Wight County is dated February 9, 1697/
98 and states:
   "Know all men by these presence that I Thomas Mann do assigne
   & make over all my right, title & interest of ye within mentioned
   patten to William Butler-his heirs & assignes forever, witness
   my hand & seal this 9th day of February 1697/98. Wit: Richard
   Reynolds, Joyner Reynolds (Id.pp.234-235).
It was for his last remaining interest in the patent which had been
granted to his father on September 22, 1682.
   In 1698 or 1699 Thomas Mann followed the tide of migration down
the Chowan River to North Carolina and settled in Chowan Precinct.
In 1699 he applied for his first grant of land in North Carolina and
640 acres was surveyed for him March 30, 1700. It was recorded
April 9, 1713 (G.B.96-A, p.142). On April 1, 1701, the Surveyor
General or his Deputy was ordered to lay out for Thomas Mann another tract of 640 acres and this was done April 7, 1701. This
grant was formally issued December 17, 1716 (G.B. III, p.144).
This was some twenty years after Thomas Mann was actually in
possession of the land, for on March 2, 1702/3 Charles Griffin
and his wife, Mary, sold to William Hooker for 15 lbs. 100 acres
"lying & being on Wicacon Creek in Chown Prest beginning as by
a Surver bearing date April the 7th, 1701, at a markd pine in Thos
Manns Line where he now lives and running into the Woods along
the sd line". (Chowan D.B.W., p.41). On the tax list for Albemarle County, N.C. taken March 25, 1717 Thomas Mann is shown
paying taxes on 1140 acres (Albemarle Early Records 1715-1730,
p.10).
   Thomas Mann married about 1708 Bridgett Hooker, daughter of
William Hooker and his wife Ann, who came to Chowan County,
N.C. in 1694 with her parents from Surry County, Virginia. Thomas Mann died in either October or November, 1735, in what was
then a part of Bertie County but what is now a part of Hertford Co.,
N.C. (G.B.4, will no.7). His wife survived him.
   Children of Thomas Mann and his wife Bridgett Hooker:

I. (Elizabeth?) Mann (born ca. 1709) m. ca. 1727 Richard Williams, son of George Williams Senr. of Bertie Co., N.C. and his wife Joan.
    Child:
    1. George Williams (b. ca. 1728).
II. Bridgett Mann m.   Griffin.
III. John Mann (b. ca. 1715) sold the land which he heired from his father (Bertie D.B.E. pp. 236, 354, 485: D.B.F. p. 332) and moved to Edgecombe County, N.C. about 1738 where he bought land from William Walker in 1743. He sold this land in 1745. No further record.
IV. Thomas Mann (see later number 3)
V.   Mary Mann.

3. Thomas Mann, son of Thomas Mann and his wife Bridgett Hooker, was born about 1718 in what is now Hertford County, N.C. He died in Nash County, N.C. in 1792 on his "Manor Plantation" on Swift Creek and Short Swamp (W.B.I, p. 83). This plantation was first granted to Thomas Mann on September 17, 1744. It was re-granted some years later and was recorded in Nash County in 1789. (D.B. 2, p. 1).

Since his father's will did not meet some legal technicality, "not being duly witnessed to convey lands from heirs", John Mann, Thomas' brother, gave him 490 acres of land on the south side of Wiccacon Creek adjacent to the lands of Friddle Keef, William Downing, Joseph Watsford, and John Wynns (Bertie D.B.D. p. 287). Within a year after giving his brother land John Mann moved to Edgecombe County, N.C.

In 1740 Thomas Mann followed his brother to Edgecombe County and on Feb. 8, 1741, sold his lands in Bertie to "Mary Speight widow of Thos. Speight Late of Perquimonds" (D.B.F.p. 330). After coming to Edgecombe County Thomas Mann acquired numerous tracts of land through purchases and land grants. In 1783 his holdings amounted to nearly 4,000 acres (Tax List of 1783). This land lay in the newly formed county of Nash. In Thomas Mann's will, dated June 6, 1792, there were mentioned 41 slaves which were devised to his children and grandchildren.

Thomas Mann's wife was Elizabeth, probably the daughter of James Denton of Hertford County, N.C. whom he married before May 18, 1752 (Halifax Co., N.C. D.B. 4, p. 252). She was born about 1725 and is mentioned in his will.

Children of Thomas Mann and his wife Elizabeth (Denton?):
I. John Mann (b. 1744-55; d. 1781). No issue.
II. William Mann, mentioned as brother in the will of John Mann in 1781 but not mentioned in the will of his father in 1792 and not on census of 1790. No issue.
III. Mary Mann (v. 1758-61) m. ca. 1778 Edmund Drake, probably as his second wife. She died 1793-1803 (Nash Co. W.B.1, p. 142).
    Children:
    1. Henry Drake.
    2. Caswell Drake.
    3. Mary Drake.
    4. Penelope Drake.

     5. Sarah Drake.
IV. Penelope Mann m. John Nicholson (see later no. 4).
V. Elizabeth Mann, m. Joseph Wright Nicholson (see later no. 5)
VI. Allen Mann (b. ca. 1765) m. Elizabeth Ann Nicholson, daughter
of Thomas and Ann Nicholson. Thomas Nicholson was the
son of Lemuel Nicholson and during the Revolutionary War
served in the 2nd. Co. from Halifax Co. After the death of
Allen Mann, Elizabeth Ann Nicholson m. John Arrington and
had issue: Samuel, Elizabeth A. N. and Archibald Arrington.
    Children of Allen Mann and his wife Elizabeth Nicholson:
    1. Thomas Nicholson Mann died in 1824 while "en route" to
       Central America to fill his post as foreign minister. No
       issue.
    2. James Nicholson Mann (d. 1853) represented Nash County
       in the House of Commons in 1827. No issue.
VII. Denton Mann m. Sarah Wheeless (see later no. 6)

4. Penelope Mann, daughter of Thomas Mann and his wife Eliza-
beth (Denton?) was born about 1752. She married John Nicholson of
Nash County, N. C., son of Lemuel Nicholson, in Nov. 1770. John
Nicholson (d. 1799) served as a lieutenant and then as a captain in
the Revolutionary War (Loosing, vol. II, p. 638). On Jan. 3, 1787,
he was appointed Lt. Col. in the Edgecombe County Militia (Turner:
History of Edgecombe County, p. 90).
    Children:
I. Letitia Nicholson m. Samuel Crowell.
    Children:
    1. Samuel Crowell.
    2. Asbury Crowell.
    3. Peggy Crowell m.   Wooten.
    4. Letitia Crowell m. Dr. Alexander Jelks.
II. Matilda Nicholson.
III. Timothy Mann Nicholson (d. 1808) m.   Exum.
    Child:
    1. Sally Nicholson, under 21 at father's death.
IV. Penelope Nicholson m.   Whitfield. She died 1861.
    Children:
    1. Matilda Whitfield m.   Joyner.
    2. Eliza N. Whitfield.
    3. Mary Philips Whitfield.
V. Mary Nicholson m. Dr. Robert Jelks (see later no. 7)
VI. Pherby Nicholson m.   Shelton.
    Child:
    1. Calvin Shelton.
VII. Elizabeth Nicholson.
VIII. Ann Nicholson.

7. Mary Nicholson, daughter of John Nicholson and his wife Pene-
lope Mann, married Dr. Robert Jelks of Edgecombe Co., N. C.
She died before March 4, 1836.
    Children of Dr. Robert Jelks and his wife Mary Nicholson:
I. Dr. John Alexander Jelks.
II. Martha Jelks (b. ca. 1841) m. (1) Green Drake; (2) William
    Threadgille of Alabama.

Children:
1. Mary Elizabeth Drake m.   Phillips of Hawkinsville, Ga.
2. William Green Drake.
3. Louisa Drake.
4. Sarah Temperance Drake m. Col. Fred Tate.
5. James Threadgille, killed C.S.A.
6. Rebecca Bolivar Threadgille m. James Gray Sills, her first cousin. Children under father.
7. Thomas John Threadgille m. Sallie Graves.
8. George Threadgille.

III. Louisa Marish Penelope Mann Nicholson Jelks m. Dr. Gray Sills (see later number 8)
IV. Capt. James Williams Dorest Jelks died June 1862 C.S.A.
V. Marcellus Bolivar Jelks

8. Louisa Maria Penelope Mann Nicholson Jelks (b. Aug. 2, 1815; d. Dec. 19, 1886) m. on Nov. 18, 1834 Dr. Gray Sills (b. Jan. 19, 1804; died April 23, 1891) son of Davis Sills (born April 5, 1774, died June 13, 1833) and his wife Mary Justice (born March 18, 1774; died Nov. 1, 1818) m. May 25, 1798, daughter of John Justice of Halifax County, N.C. Dr. Gray Sills attended medical school at Jefferson in Philadelphia. The name of Dr. Gray Sills' plantation in Nash County was called "Belford".
Children:
I. David Nicholson Sills (b. April 20, 1836, died Oct. 19, 1897) m. Nov. 26, 1879 Eloise Williams of Warren County, N.C. He studied medicine at the University of Maryland and served as a lieutenant in the C.S.A.
Children:
1. Annie Louise Sills, m. Dr. David Brooks.
2. David Nicholson Sills, m. Helen Nelson of New York. They resided in Maryland and Delaware.
Children:
(1) David Nicholson Sills m. Norma   . He studied at the University of Maryland.
(2) Nelson Sills.
3. Robert Williams Sills, m. Oma Clutz of Salisbury and resided in Winston-Salem, N.C.
Children:
(1) Robert Sills
(2) George Sills
(3) Baird Sills
II. Mary Louise Sills, born April 13, 1838, d. Feb. 19, 1918.
III. Martha Sarah Sills (b. Dec. 26, 1840, d. Oct. 1, 1919) m. Nov. 20, 1866 William Joseph King of Franklin Co., N.C.
Children:
1. Temperance Lou King m. Capt. Philip Alston of Louisburg, N.C.
2. Gray Richmond King m. his cousin, Beverla Pierce. They resided in Nashville, N.C.
Children:
(1) Mable Gray King.
(2) William Joseph King.

3. Pattie L. N. King m. Herbert Boone of Franklin Co.,
N. C.
    Children:
    (1) William Boone m. Millie Braswell of Nash County,
        N. C.
        Children:
        a. Charlotte Boone m.   Jennings.
        b. Martha Boone m.   Burgess.
        c. Daniel Boone m.
    (2) Richard Boone m. Marguerite   of Kingston,
        N. C. Res. 1953, Nashville, N. C.
        Child:
        a. Gray Boone.
    (3) Robert Boone m.
    (4) Louise Jelks Boone, unmarried.

IV.   Lucy Susan Sills, born June 29, 1843, died 1896.
V.   James Gray Sills, son of Dr. Gray Sills and his wife Louisa
Jelks, was born August 13, 1845 and died October 16, 1919.
He married his first cousin, Rebecca Bolivar Threadgille
(above) in January 1870. He was in the C. S. A., Register of
Deeds for Nash County and a state senator.

    Children:
1. William Gray Sills was a graduate of West Point. During
   World War I he was wounded in action and died in France.
   He was a colonel. He m. Carolyn Jones of San Francisco.
    Children:
    (1) William Gray Sills m. Dorothy Draper. He gradu-
        ated from West Point and died while stationed in
        Hawaii.
        Child:
        a. William Gray Sills.
    (2) Caroline Sills m. Col. Branner Perdue.
    (3) Betsy Arrington Sills m. Robert Porter who was
        killed in the Battle of Midway.

VI.   Robert Alexander Sills (born Jan. 5, 1848; d. April 28, 1884)
m. July 7, 1880 Nannie Harrison. He was in the C. S. A. and
later studied medicine at the University of Maryland. He
died in Rocky Mt., N. C.

    Children:
1. Mattie Sills m. Charles Overman of High Point, N. C.
    Child:
    (1) Robert Overman.
2. Robert Alexander Sills m. Emily Harney of Plymouth,
   N. C. He was a merchant.
    Children:
    (1) Walter Harney Sills.
    (2) Nancy Hope Sills.
    (3) Emily Roberta Sills.

VII.   Thomas Alfred Sills, son of Dr. Gray Sills and his wife
Louise Jelks, was born at "Belford" March 7, 1850, and
died in Nashville, N. C. Nov. 11, 1914. On Nov. 16, 1882
he married his first cousin Martha Scott Thompson of
Crawford, Miss. He served as Register of Deeds and in

1898 was elected Clerk of the Superior Court of Nash Co.,
N.C.
  Children:
1. Scott T. Gray Sills m. Lulu Carden.
2. James Nicholson Sills m. Pattie Marie Smith. In 1913 he
   was appointed·to fill his father's position as Clerk of the
   Superior Court when his father resigned. He has held this
   position since that date and has never had opposition. He
   resided in Nashville, N.C.
     Children:
   (1) Lorraine Sills m. Hubert E. May of Nashville, N.C.
   (2) Pattie Sills graduated from Duke University having
       studied medicine and interning there. She married
       Dr. Edward Hale Thornhill of Bluefield, Va. Res.
       Raleigh, N.C.
         Children:
       a. Patricia Thornhill.
       b. Barbara Thornhill.
3. Louise Jelks Sills, daughter of Thomas Alfred Sills and
   his wife Martha Scott Thompson, has for many years
   served in the capacity of secretary to the Clerk of the
   Superior Court for Nash County. She is a member of the
   Daughters of the American Revolution having joined under
   her ancestor THOMAS MANN. It is to her that the author
   of this chapter is indebted for the material on the Nicholson and Sills families herein. Res. Nashville, N.C.
4. Isa Rebecca Sills m. Thomas Barker Dameron of Warrenton, N.C. Res. Goldsboro, N.C.
     Children:
   (1) Isa Sills Dameron m. Edgar E. Barton.
   (2) Marth Scott Dameron m. Maj. M. E. Perry.
   (3) Thomas Barker Dameron, M.D. m. Nancy Jane
       Henry.
   (4) William Henry Dameron.
5. Mary C. Sills m. Peter Hines Bunn.
     Child:
   (1) Thomas Sills Bunn.
VIII. Rebecca Isa Sills, daughter of Dr. Gray Sills and his wife
      Louise Jelks, was born June 22, 1852 and died July 27, 1853.
IX.   William Bolivar Sills, born October 23, 1854; d. Oct. 13, 1856.

5. Elizabeth Mann, daughter of Thomas Mann and his wife Eliza-
beth (Denton?), was born about 1760 in what is now Nash County,
N.C. then a part of Edgecombe. About 1778 she married Joseph
Wright Nicholson (b. ca. 1740; d. 1807), son of Lemuel Nicholson.
Joseph Wright Nicholson is said to have commanded a company
of Regulators during the Revolution.
   Children of Joseph Wright Nicholson and his wife Elizabeth
   Mann:
I.   James Mann Nicholson (b. ca. 1780; d. ante Oct. 1811) m.
      Mary Arrington, who, after his death, m. Joseph Arrington,
      sherrif of Nash County. They moved to Alabama in 1832-3.
        Children:
      1. Eliza Ann Nicholson m.   Tyson.

Child:
(1) Ellen Tyson.
2. a daughter.

II. Guilford Nicholson m. Sallie Lee Wiggins of Martin Co. He was a private in the 1st Co. Halifax troops in War of 1812. He died Feb. 26, 1834.
Children:
1. Thomas Willis Nicholson, m. Martha E. Thorne. Several of their children moved to Alabama.
Children:
(1) Henry W. Nicholson.
(2) Guilford Nicholson m. Bettie Winter.
(3) Ed Thorne Nicholson.
(4) Thomas W. Nicholson.
(5) Edmund P. Nicholson.
(6) Sarah M. Nicholson m.   Hobson.
(7) Samuel Thorne Nicholson
(8) Joseph W. Nicholson m. Alice Eudore Clark.
(9) Mason Wiggins Nicholson.
(10) James M. Nicholson.
(11) Anna Thorne Nicholson.
2. Sarah Ann Nicholson, daughter of Guilford Nicholson and his wife Sallie Lee Wiggins, m.   Hardeman. She moved to Texas and carried with her the Nicholson family Bible.
3. Martha M. Nicholson m. Dr. James B. Yellowby.
4. Eveline E. Nicholson, died in 1849.

III. Thomas Wright Nicholson, son of Joseph Wright Nicholson and his wife Elizabeth Mann, married Temperance Winifred Wiggins, sister of Sallie Lee (Wiggins) Nicholson.
Children:
1. Winnie Wiggins Nicholson m.   Matthews.
2. Mary W. Nicholson m.   Harrison.
3. Laura Nicholson m.   Jones of Mississippi.
4. Dr. John L. Nicholson.
5. Joseph James Nicholson.
6. Blake Baker Nicholson m. Lucy E. Thorne.
C Children:
(1) Temperance Nicholson m.   Daniel.
(2) Samuel Thorne Nicholson m. Ann Lucas. He was a doctor.
Children:
a. David Lucus Nicholson.
b. Blake Baker Nicholson.
c. John Nicholson.
d. Lucile Nicholson.
(3) John T. Nicholson.
(4) Ida Mabbett Nicholson.
(5) Thomas Nicholson.
(6) Blake Baker Nicholson.
(7) Plummer Nicholson.
(8) Willie Nicholson.
(9) Lucille E. Nicholson.
(10) Kate Nicholson.

7. Samuel Timothy Nicholson.

6. Denton Mann, son of Thomas Mann and his wife Elizabeth (Denton?), was born about 1765 on his father's "Manor Plantation" in what is now Nash County, N.C. About 1788 Denton Mann married Sarah Wheeless, daughter of Benjamin and Mildred Wheeless. Before his father's death Denton Mann purchased several large tracts of land on Swift Creek (D.B. 3, p.349; D.B.4, pp.64, 74; D.B.6, p.557). However, his home was on the plantation given him by his father, the gift being confirmed in his father's will (W.B. 1, p.83) Through marrying Sarah Wheeless Denton Mann also acquired possession of her inheritance from her father in a division of his estate which took place before Oct.18, 1798 (D.B.6, p.370). Denton Mann died before 1812 for in that year his estate was divided between his children. His wife had predeceased him and the lands which she heired from her father were given to her children but no distinction was made between them and those of Denton Mann (D. B. 9, p.47).

   Children of Denton Mann and his wife Sarah Wheeless:
I.   John Mann (b.1790/91) was mentioned in the will of his grandfather, Thomas Mann, in 1792. Before May 25, 1822, John Mann moved to Monroe County, Alabama (D.B.10, p. 384).
II.   Benjamin H. Mann (b.ca.1794) was living in Monroe County, Alabama on May 25, 1822 (Ibid).
III. William H. Mann (b.1796) m. Nancy Boykin Drake. (See later number 9).
IV.   Penelope Mann (b.ca.1789) died without issue before Sept. 13, 1821 when her borther William H. Mann sold his interest in her land (D. B. 10, pp.330, 384).

9. William H. Mann, son of Denton Mann and his wife Sarah Wheeless, was born in 1796 and died September 1846. On Feb.7, 1816 he married Nancy Boykin Drake (Sept.24, 1797; died Nov. 11, 1862), daughter of Benjamin Drake and his wife Cecelia Taylor (see TAYLOR herein). William H. Mann lived at Ransom's Bridge, Franklin County, N.C. where he owned land and operated a store.

   Children of William H. Mann and his wife Nancy Boykin Drake:
I.   Sally (Sarah) Ann Mann (b.Nov.16, 1816; d. in Tennessee in 1869) m. 1844 Simm Joseph Jones (b.Aug.15, 1807; died in Tennessee in 1876). They were the parents of at least one daughter, Lenor Jones (b.Cotton Grove, Madison Co., Tenn.) who married Benjamin R. Donelson, M.D.
II.   Benjamin Denton Mann (see later number 10).
III. Penelope Elizabeth Mann, born Jan. 30, 1822.
IV.   James Thomas Mann, born Nov.16, 1824. No issue.
V.   Henretta Mann, born June 2, 1827.
VI.   Martha D. Mann, born July 30, 1829, m.   Brandon. She died Jan.5, 1852.

10. Benjamin Denton Mann, (b.March 13, 1819, died October 21, 1863) married (1) May 9, 1844, Mary Muranda Taylor (died March 22, 1849) and (2) on Jan.4, 1853 Caroline Matilda T. Williams (b.Jan.27, 1833, died Jan.20, 1900), daughter of John Allen Wil-

liam·s and his wife Charlity Dawson Alston of Warren Co., N.C.
(see ALSTONS and ALSTONS of NORTH and SOUTH CAROLINA
by Grove for ancestry of Caroline Matilda Williams) The name of
Benjamin Denton Mann's plantation was "Elm Lane" and at the
time of his death in 1863 he was one of the county's largest plant-
ers.
Children:
I.   Mary A.C. Mann (born August 20, 1848) m. Hardy Wheeless.
       Child:
       1. Mary (Millie) Wheeless, died unmarried.
II.   John H. Mann, born Nov. 5, 1853, died March 22, 1855.
III.   Oliver DeWitt Mann (see later no. 11).
IV.   Lilla Dale Mann, born Feb. 11, 1857; m.J.P. Ellinor, Feb.
       20, 1873; died April 28, 1873.
V.   Peter D. Mann (twin) b. Oct. 5, 1858, died young.
VI.   Elizabeth Whitmel Mann (twin) (see later no. 12).
VII.   Virginia Dare Mann, born Jan. 5, 1860, died June 6, 1861.
VIII. Benjamin Denton Mann (see later no. 13)
IX.   William Rosser Mann (see later no. 14).

11.   Oliver DeWitt Mann (b. Dec. 25, 1854, died July 2, 1934) m.
Dec. 17, 1879 Mamie Smith Green (born Aug. 6, 1854, died July 25,
1920), daughter of Zeno Holstire Greene of Pitt County. He attended
Louisburg Academy, Franklin County, N.C. In 1883 he moved
with his family to Whitakers and served that town as Mayor, alder-
man and clerk-treasurer. He and his family were Methodists.
Children:
I.   Lilla Davis Mann (b. March 21, 1881, died April 24, 1949)
       m. June 28, 1911 Dr. Andrew Ebenezer Bell (born Nov. 18,
       1887, died Nov. 24, 1948) of Rowan County, N.C., son of
       Walter Monroe Bell and his wife Sarah Elizabeth Parks.
       Children:
       1. Mary Parks Bell (born April 30, 1912) married August
          8, 1946 Carroll Wayland Weathers (born Oct. 18, 1901 in
          Cleveland Co., N.C.). Carroll Wayland Weathers is
          Dean of the School of Law of Wake Forest College. Res.
          1955, Raleigh, N.C.
          (1) Jane Bell Weathers, born March 21, 1948.
          (2) Mary Katherine Weathers, born March 18, 1950.
       2. Lilla Mann Bell (born April 30, 1913) m. October 8,
          1948 Jacob Winstead (born Oct. 23, 1905). Res. Rocky
          Mt., N.C.
          Children:
          (1) Margaret Bell Winstead, born August 18, 1950.
          (2) Andrew Jacob Winstead, born Feb. 8, 1952.
       3. Louise Davis Bell, born April 13, 1915, m. Alfred
          Moffitt (b. Dec. 3, 1911) of Guilford Co., N.C.
          Child:
          (1) Hugh Alfred Moffitt, born Dec. 10, 1949.
       4. Ralph Monroe Bell, born Sept. 3, 1916. He is a doctor.
       5. Helen Bell (b. Dec. 30, 1917) m. Henry Hand Rankin
          (b. Jan. 6, 1909) of Gaston Co., N.C.
          Children:
          (1) Louise Bell Rankin, born Nov. 13, 1945.

(2) Henry Richard Rankin, born February 21, 1950.
6. Eleanor Harris Bell (born Oct. 16, 1919) m. Oct. 8, 19--
   John Wilson Alexander (b. July 5, 1919).
   Children:
   (1) John Wilson Alexander, born October 24, 1950.
   (2) Ann Kemp Alexander, born March 2, 1952.
II. Zeno Greene Mann (born March 8, 1883, died Oct. 10, 1951)
   m. on Aug. 27, 1913 Matie Christain Brown (b. Feb. 27,
   1889, died May 5, 1955), daughter of Hezekiah Brown and
   his wife Susan Elizabeth Hooker, of Martin County, N. C.
   He was a merchant. engaged in farming, and a Methodist.
   They resided in Whitakers, N. C.
   Children:
   1. Oliver DeWitt Mann (born May 3, 1915) m, Aug. 20,
      1949, Susan Elizabeth Whitfield (born July 14, 1919),
      daughter of Lewis Evander Whitfield of Clinton, N. C.
      (for her ancestry see WHITFIELD, BRYAN, SMITH
      and RELATED FAMILIES by WHITFIELD, Vols. 1 and
      II.). Res. Whitakers, N. C.
      Children:
      (1) Susan Elizabeth Mann, born Sept. 29, 1950.
      (2) Matie Christian Brown Mann, born March 26, 1955.

III. Annie Estelle Mann (born Dec. 26, 1885, died Oct. 18, 1951),
   daughter of Oliver DeWitt Mann and his wife Mamie Smith
   Greene, m. on Nov. 25, 1908 Richard Speight Cutchin (b.
   October 26, 1884, died September 29, 1914). He was a
   dentist.
   Children:
   1. Annie Lee Cutchin (b. April 10, 1911) m. on June 28,
      1940, Benjamin Holland Neville (b. Dec. 12, 1911). He
      is a lawyer. Res. Whitakers, N. C.
      Children:
      (1) Mary Anne Neville, born Nov. 20, 1942.
      (2) Benjamin Holland Neville, born June 25, 1946.
      (3) Elizabeth Cutchin Neville, born Oct. 15, 1954.
   2. Richard Speight Cutchin (born April 12, 1914) m. on
      June 10, 1939, Katherine May Houston (b. Aug. 27, 1918)
      of St. Petersburg, Fla. Res. Whitakers, N. C.
      Children:
      (1) Frances Houston Cutchin, born Sept. 22, 1943.
      (2) Katherine Mann Cutchin, born Jan. 7, 1948.

12. Elizabeth Whitmel Mann, daughter of Benjamin Denton Mann
and his wife Caroline Matilda T. Williams was born Oct. 5, 1858
and died Dec. 18, 1937. In March 1875 she married Joseph E.
Carter, son of William Dallas Carter and his wife Polly Hawks.
   Children:
I. Myrtie Carter (born July 12, 1877) m. on Dec. 29, 1897,
   Dr. John T. Strickland (born Jan. 27, 1866, died Nov. 27,
   1946). She is a Methodist, a member of the United Daugh-
   ters of the Confederacy, National Society Daughters of the
   American Revolution, and National Society Magna Charta
   Dames. She resides in Nashville, N. C.

322

Children:
1. John Allen Strickland (b. Nov. 15, 1898; d. 1944) m. Erma Christine Horton. No issue.
2. Madeline Matilda Strickland (b. Jan. 21, 1900) m. Harold D. Cooley. He is a congressman from his district.
   Children:
   (1) Roger D. Cooley (b. Sept. 20, 1924) m. Barbara Smith of Raleigh, N. C.
   (2) Harriet Cooley m. Dr. Benjamin J. Lawrence, Jr. of Raleigh, N. C.
       Child:
       a. Benjamin J. Lawrence III.
3. Gorman Hearst Strickland (born Sept. 16, 1904, died April 15, 1927 unmarried).
4. Horace Gilmore Stricland (born Feb. 22, 1906) m. Agnes Seek.
   Children:
   (1) Carter Strickland, born Nov.   , 1941.
   (2) Jane Carroll Strickland, born Sept. 19, 1943.
5. Elizabeth Strickland (born June 6, 1909) m. (1) R. L. Vaughan (2) Edward Thomas Garnett of England.
   Child:
   (1) John Strickland Vaughan.
6. Milton Mann Strickland (twin) born April 23, 1913, m. Catherine Griffin.
   Children:
   (1) Catherine Strickland.
   (2) Matilda Strickland.
   (3) Ann Lyon Strickland.
7. Mattie Carter Strickland (twin) born April 23, 1913, died Oct. 22, 1913.
8. Rosco Conkling Strickland (born December 9, 1918) m. Margie Freeman of Sanford, N. C.
   Child:
   (1) John Thomas Strickland, born September 20, 1952.
II. Leyta Roberta Carter, daughter of Joseph E. Carter and and his wife Elizabeth Whitmel Mann, was born Dec. 2, 1880 and died Dec. 13, 1951. In 1939 she m. Robert L. Lofton. No issue.
III. Mattee Carter, born Sept. 13, 1882, died Dec. 1904, d. s. p.
IV. Hubert Carter, born Sept. 24, 1886, died Dec. 8, 1945, d. s. p.

13. Benjamin Denton Mann, son of Benjamin Denton Mann and his wife Caroline Matilda T. Williams, was born at "Elm Lane" May 12, 1861, and died at Duke Hospital, Durham, N. C., Sept. 8, 1934. He received his education at Davis High School which he attended until 1884. Benjamin Denton Mann was twice married - first on Nov. 11, 1891, to Mary Elizabeth Parker, daughter of William Fletcher Parker and his wife Elizabeth Jane Herring (see HOLT herein), in Enfield, N. C. Mary Elizabeth Parker was born at "Rose Hill", her grandfather Parker's home, on Sept. 12, 1865 and died in Enfield on Oct. 6, 1908. Benjamin Denton Mann was engaged in farming and related occupations. He made his home in Enfield, N. C. after 1895. He and his wife were

Methodist.

His second wife was Annie May Spruill (b. May 12, 1875; d. Oct. 1, 1944) of Columbia, N.C. There was no issue by this marriage.

Children of Benjamin Denton Mann and his wife Mary Elizabeth Parker:

I. Benjamin Denton Mann (born Aug. 27, 1892) is a graduate of Trinity Park School and of the Atlanta Dental College. He m. (1) Myra Fleming (2) Mrs. Thelma S. Gilmore. He resides in Columbus, Ga. No issue.
II. Fletcher Parker Mann (twin) born Aug. 28, 1894, d. May 12, 1895.
III. Bettie Herring Mann (twin) born Aug. 28, 1894, d. Aug. 13, 1895.
IV. William Marion Mann (see later number 15)
V. Caroline Alston Mann (born February 25, 1900) is a graduate of Greensboro College for Women. For a number of years she taught in the public schools of North Carolina and then worked in the Bank of Samings, New York City. She returned to Enfield, N.C. in 1954 where she has resided since and is engaged in farming and related occupations. She is a Methodist and a member of the United Daughters of the Confederacy, the National Society Daughters of the American Revolution, the National Society Magna Carta Dames, the Society of Descendants of Knights of the Most Noble Order of the Garter and the Colonial Order of the Crown.
VI. Rachel Herring Mann, born July 9, 1903, died July 12, 1904.
VII. Solon DeWitt Mann, born June 27, 1905, died June 19, 1906.

15. William Marion Mann, son of Benjamin Denton Mann and his wife Mary Elizabeth Parker, was born in Enfield, N.C. Oct. 1, 1896. On June 5, 1927, he married Teressa Hope Dickens of Latta, S.C., daughter of Robert Patrick and Margaret Ann Dickens (see DICKENS, GREEN and BRANCH families herein for her ancestry). She was born Oct. 6, 1902, and graduated from Coker College for Women in Hartsville, S.C. in 1923. After receiving her B.A. degree there, she taught in the public schools in North Carolina until her marriage. She is a Methodist and a member of the National Society Daughters of the American Revolution, the United Daughters of the Confederacy, and the National Society Magna Carta Dames.

William Marion Mann graduated from Trinity Park School at Durham, N.C. in 1918. On June 4, 1918 he volunteered for the navy and was on his way to Europe when peace was declared Nov. 11. He was released from active duty Jan. 23, 1919 and later was given his honorable discharge papers Sept. 30, 1921. On May 27, 1921, he received his L.L.D. degree from Wake Forest, N.C. For the past thirty years he has been engaged in farming and related occupations.

Children of William Marion Mann and his wife Teresa Hope Dickens:

I. William Marion Mann Jr., the author of this chapter and several others herein, was born in Enfield, N.C. on Jan. 7, 1931. He graduated from the Enfield Public School in 1949 and received his B.S. degree from Wake Forest College June 1, 1953 with the distinction of "Cum Laude". While at Wake Forest College he was a member of the Alpha Sigma Phi Social Fraternity and was elected by that chapter as its most outstanding pledge of the pledge class of 1949-50. He was also a member of the Alpha Epsilon Delta Honorary Premedical Fraternity, Beta Chemical Fraternity. William Marion Mann, Jr., is at present studying medicine at the Bowman Gray School of Medicine for Wake Forest College and is a member of the Phi Chi Medical Fraternity. He is also a Methodist and a member of the National Society Sons of the American Revolution, the Society of Colonial Wars, and the Somerset Chapter Magna Carta Barons. Through his aunt, Caroline Alston Mann, he has successor membership in the Society of Descendants of Knights of the Most Noble Order of the Garter and in the Colonial Order of the Crown.

II.   Robert Fletcher Mann was born in Enfield, N.C. on Nov. 7, 1932, and graduated from the Enfield Public School in 1951. On May 30, 1955, he received his B.S. Degree from Wake Forest College with the distinction of "Summa Cum Laude" and at present is studying medicine at the Bowman Gray School of Medicine for Wake Forest College. He was also a member of the Honorary science fraternities at Wake Forest College, Alpha Epsilon Delta, Beta Beta Beta, and Gamma Sigma Epsilon. He is a Methodist and a member of Phi Beta Kappa Society and the National Society Sons of the American Revolution and the Kappa Alpha Social Fraternity.

14.   William Rosser Mann (b. at "Elm Lane" August 31, 1863; died Whitakers, N.C. August 15, 1926), son of Benjamin Denton Mann and his wife Carolina Matilda T. Williams, married on June 10, 1908, Sarah Chesson (Brown) Howard (born February 27, 1879), daughter of Hezekiah Brown and his wife Susan Elizabeth Hooker of Martin County, N.C. On May 2, 1901, J.O. Hearne, W.T. Hearne, W.R. Winstead and William Rosser Mann formed a joint Stock Company to manufacture and sell coffins, caskets, etc. This company was located in Whitakers. A few years after its formation William Rosser Mann bought out all the other stock holders and became sole owner. He was also engaged in farming and his son is the present owner of "Elm Lane". He was mayor of Whitakers for two terms.

Children of William Rosser Mann and his wife, Sarah Chesson (Brown) Howard:

I.   Chesson Matilda Mann (b. Aug. 12, 1912, Whitakers, N.C.) m. Richard Spencer Pindell, Jr., on June 9, 1934. They now reside at Raleigh, N.C.
    Children:
1. Richard Spencer Pindell, III, born October 2, 1935.
2. Jack Mann Pindell, born October 30, 1937.

II.   William Rosser Mann (born October 3, 1914 Whitakers, N.C.) m. Aug. 8, 1949 in the "Little Church Around The Corner", New York City, Carolyn Elizabeth Van Ness.
    Children:
1. William Rosser Mann III, born Sept. 22, 1950.
2. James Grantham Mann, born Dec. 10, 1951.
3. Mark Van Ness Mann, born April 5, 1954.

MACON of NEW KENT and NORTH CAROLINA

Gideon Macon, the ancestor of this distinguished southern family was in New Kent County as early as January 9, 1674, at which time he was Sub-Sheriff of New Kent. (20V31)

The family name is derived from the town of Macon in France, and it has been stated that he was of the family of Gabriel de Macon, Siegneur de Sauzet in the County of Auvergne in France. (33V85)

The family evidently fled from France to England. A clue to their English home is found in the will of ANNE MACON of St. Botolphe, Aldgate, London, widow, which was dated Sept. 9, 1699, and proven on August 3, 1700. Consistory Court of London, Redman, fo. 94, (1670-1720) (10V412).

She bequeathed to "Mr. Gideon Macon, now living in Virginia and to his wife to each of them a ring of 20 s. apiece. To Gideon Macon, his son, my silver tankard... to Anne Macon daughter of Gideon Macon, the elder, my silver porringer; to Martha my six silver spoons; to Mary Elwenn, Spinster, all my wearing linen... to Sarah Freckelton a silk petticoat which was her sisters.... Rest to son-in-law Robert Freckelton; executor and to my friend Mr. John Baldwin to see this will executed. Wits., John Shaw, John Goodyear, Ath. Lake.

Gideon Macon served as Burgess from New Kent Oct. 10, 1693, and in 1698. (15V-439,441) He died in 1703 and his widow Martha married Captain Nathaniel West. (See West Vol. I and V.H.G.)

Children of Gideon Macon:
I.   Gideon, born June 20, 1682.
II.   Anne, born December 15, 1684.
III. William, born November 11, 1694.
IV.   John, born December 17, 1695.
V.   Martha, married January 31, 1703, Orlando Jones of King William County; died May 4, 1716. Their daughter, Frances Jones, born August 6, 1710, married Colonel John Dandridge and was the mother of Mrs. Martha Washington.

John Macon[2] son of Gideon[1] and Martha Macon was born Dec. 17, 1695. He married Anne, daughter of William Hunt. "This is confirmed by a deed recorded in Surry County, dated April 1, 1714, wherein William Hunt and Tabitha his wife of Charles City County, conveyed land on the Nottoway to William Hamlin. This memorandum states that they had two daughters, Mary, born May 15, 1695, who married Robert Minge, and another daughter who married John Macon". (2T113, 278)

This is a different version from what is shown in Tyler's Magazine Vol. 13, p. 18, but the above Hunt marriage seems correct. The William Hunt mentioned in Tyler's Vol. 13, made a will dated March 20, 1711, and probated June 20, 1715. His wife was named Sarah.

JOHN MACON, on November 8, 1717, witnessed the will of
William Jones, together with Edward Harper and Matthew Edlee.
William Jones will was probated in Surry County May 21, 1718.
He bequeathed to his brother, Edmund Hubbard his plantation at
Meherrin and an account due from Abraham Saul.... to kinswoman
ANN HUNT a horse had of John Stevens and all jewels, gold silver
goods and chattles....my Kinsman GEORGE HUNT, he to be exe-
cutor. (Bk.7-121)

George Hunt of the Parish of Weynoke in Charles City, on Nov.
4, 1719, deeded to Edward Goodrich of Parish of Westover in
Charles City, 280 acres patented by William Jones, decd., in Surry, who by his last will gave same to George Hunt. (Surry DB "B"
1715-30, p.238) This land was granted William Jones in 1714.
(See Col.Surry, p.180; G.B.10)

In 1719, Francis Mayberry, Elinor his wife, and George Hunt
of Charles City sold 100 acres of land in Surry which had been
bought by Major William Hunt of William Wyche. (D.B. "B" 237)

From these deeds it appears that George Hunt may have been
a son and heir of Major William Hunt and that one of Major Hunts
daughters married Francis Mayberry. Major William Hunt held
3130 acres in Charles City in the 1704 Quit Rents. As "Major
William Hunt" he patented 140 and 190 acres in separate grants
in 1711. (Col.Surry-180)

The date of John Macon's death is not known. He evidently
lived in Charles City County where nearly all of the records are
destroyed. His only known child was GIDEON MACON of Warren
County, N.C., who named his first child and daughter ANNE
HUNT MACON. (See later)

Gideon[3] Macon (John[2], Gideon[1]) son of John Macon and his wife
Ann Hunt moved to Granville County, N.C. where he married Priscilla Jones, daughter of Abigal (Sugars) and Edward Jones of Granville. Abigal Sugars was the daughter of John Sugars, or Shugars,
of Isle of Wight who married about 1680, Elizabeth, relict of Thomas Clay of Surry and possibly the widow of Col. James Mason.
(V.H.G. 226)

Gideon Macon made his will in Granville Dec.20, 1761, proven
Feb.1762 as follows: "to son HARRISON MACON, 400 acres on
North side of Tar River; son JOHN MACON tract of land on both
sides of Shocko Creek; to GIDEON MACON plantation where I dwell;
in case any of my above mentioned sons die without lawful issue
lands to be divided among sons then living; to daughters ANN ALSTON,
SALLIE, MARTHA, MARY MACON......(Seven children are under
age); loving wife PRISCILLA to have use of manor plantation during
life and certain negroes; to be divided at her death between seven
youngest children. Wife Priscilla, son-in-law John Alston and friend
William Johnston, extrs." Priscilla Mason married secondly, James
Ransom and had six children.

Children of Priscilla (Jones) and Gideon[3] Macon;
I. Anne Hunt Macon, m. (1) Capt. John Alston; (2) William
   Green. (For children see Alston History, p.116)
II. Sallie Macon, m. Col. John Hawkins, son of Col. Philamon
   Hawkins. (For children, see Alston History, p.272)
III. Martha Macon, m. Joseph Seawell. (Id. p.512)

IV.   Harrison Macon, m. Hannah Glenn and had: (1) Gideon; (2)
Polk Fuller; (3) Nathaniel; (4) Priscilla; (5) Nancy Macon.
V.   John Macon, born June 17, 1755, m. (1) Johanna Tabb; (2)
Elizabeth Williams; (3) Mrs. Joyce. (See later)
VI.   Nathaniel Macon, born 1757; died June 29, 1837; m. Hannah
Plummer. (V.H.G. p.) Mr. Macon was at Princeton
College when the Revolution closed the college. He returned
to Warren County and enlisted as a private in his brother
John's Company. In 1791 he was elected to the U.S. House of
Representatives, where he served until 1815. He served as
Speaker of the House from 1801 to 1806. In 1815 he was e-
lected to the U.S. Senate and served until 1828. In 1825-26-
27 he was chosen President pro tem. of the Senate. Wheeler,
in his History, devoted eight pages to his biography. (Vol.II,
432-439.)
   Children:
   1. Plummer Macon. (1786-1792)
   2. Elizabeth Kemp Macon, born September 12, 1784; m.
William John Martin and had several daughters. (See
S.V.F. p.356)
   3. Seignora Donald Macon, m. William Eaton. (See V.H.G.
-183)
VII.   Mary Macon, m. James Johnson.
VIII.   Gideon Hunt Macon, m. (1) Mary Green; (2) Mary Hartwell.
   Children of first wife:
   1. Nathaniel Green Macon.
   2. William Green Macon, m. Charity Dawson Alston.
   3. Ann Hunt Macon.
   4. Priscilla Mary Macon, m. (1) Mr. Morse; (2) Micajah
Hawkins.
   Children of second wife:
   5. Lucy Macon, m. Mr. Haughton, moved to Wetumpka, Ala.
   6. Martha Macon, m. Guston Alston.
   7. Elizabeth Green Macon.
   8. Albert Gallatin Macon.
   9. Arthur Macon.
   10. Henry I. Macon, m. Arabella Atherton Macon. (see later)

John[4] Macon (Gideon[3], John[2], Gideon[1]) was born in Warren
County, N.C., June 17, 1755, and died there April 28, 1808. He
married first, Johanna Tabb; second, Bettie Williams (1761-1814);
and third, Mrs. Joyce. He served as a Captain in the 7th. Regiment of the Continental Line, Col. Hogun, commanding, from
Dec.12, 1776 to Jan. 1778 and received 1097 acres of bounty for
24 months service. (N.C. Roster pp.94, 236.) He retired from the
Army to enter the House of Commons from Warren where he
served from 1779 to 1784 and succeeded his brother Nathaniel Macon in the Senate serving there until 1795. (Id. 615; Wheeler 11-
441) His children by Johanna Tabb, first wife, were: 1. George;
2. Priscilla J.; 3. William H.; 4. Mary; m. (1) M. HUNT, (2)
Thomas Craighead; 5. John T.; 6. Saphrenia; 7. Gabriel. Children
of second wife, Bettie Williams, were: 8. Thomas J.; 9. Nathaniel;
10. HENRY[5] HARRISON, born December 13, 1796, married Margaret Brooks. (See later)

Henry[5] Harrison Macon, born Dec. 13, 1796, and died in Warren County, Tenn., April 20, 1851. He married in 1822, Margaret Brooks, born in North Carolina December 27, 1800, died Feb. 3, 1860. They moved to Warren County, Tenn., where their children were born. They had three sons whose birth and death dates are unknown. Their other children were:

I.   John Macon, born 1829, died 1906; m. 1855 Martha Ann Ramsey, born 1838, died 1906.

II.   Nancy Macon, born April 6, 1833, married Sept. 26, 1852 Joseph Humphrey Cunningham, born April 11, 1830. (See later).

III.   Mary Macon, born March 11, 1837, died Feb. 4, 1901; m. Fielding O. Gravett, who died April 14, 1865. Their son, Thomas B. Gravett was born Sept. 26, 1864. Franklin Gravette, their eldest son, birth date unknown, moved to Oklahoma with his mother, where after several years she married Mr. Duckworth.

IV.   Gideon Macon, born December 25, 1838.

V.   Henry Harrison Macon, Jr., born Sept. 11, 1839; m. Fannie Smith. He served in the War Between the States and on the way to camp enroute by train a bouquet was thrown to him by a pretty girl. After the war he returned to the place where the bouquet was thrown, found the girl and married her.

Nancy Macon, daughter of Margaret (Brooks) and Henry Harrison Macon, Sr., who was born April 6, 1833, married Sept. 26, 1852, Joseph Humphrey Cunningham, born April 11, 1830, died May 31, 1891. Mrs. Cunningham died Jan. 26, 1911. They are buried in the Tullahoma, Tenn. Cemetery.

Children: (from the Cunningham family Bible now in the possession of Mrs. Clarence B. Kirby)

I.   Margaret Brooks Cunningham, born August 1, 1853, m. James M. Davis Wilson of Lincoln County, Tenn. Their chilwere: 1. Mary Catherine, born Oct. 12, 1879, living in St. Louis, Mo.; 2. Nannie Lou, born October 28, 1877, m. William W. Whitman of Chattanooga, Tenn. Mrs. Whitman died in February, 1938, in St. Louis.

II.   Nancy Josephine Cunningham, born November 11, 1855, married as his second wife, Isaac Newton Bynum, who died Sept. 1924, and is buried in the Bynum family plot at Tupelo, Tenn. Nancy Bynum died June 19, 1932. (No children)

III.   Romulous Calhoun Cunningham, born July 14, 1858, in Warren County, Tenn., died March 31, 1908, at Larkinsville, Ala.; married 1886, Susan Elizabeth Jones. born Jan. 30, 1865, died December 20, 1950, buried in Greenwood Cemetery, Chattanooga.

Children:

1. Willie Hal Cunningham, born Jan. 11, 1887, died at Larkinsville, Alabama, Dec. 13, 1906.

2. Ava Beatrice Cunningham, born May 3, 1890, now living at 746 Vine Street, Chattanooga, Tenn.

3. Grover Cleveland Cunningham, born November 9, 1892; died in infancy.

4. Venton O. Cunningham, born June 6, 1896; lives in Chattanooga.

329

5. Opie Read Cunningham, born Feb.9, 1901, lives with her brother and sister in Chattanooga.
6. Joseph Humphry Cunningham, born Jan.27, 1904, m.Oct. 2, 1926, Gertrude Agnes Hasty of Chipley, Ga. They live in Knoxville, Tenn. Their son, Joseph Hal Cunningham, born Jan.17, 1928.
IV. Harrison Macon Cunningham, born Jan.17, 1861. (See later)
V. Sarah A. Cunningham, born April 30, 1863; married Sept. 5, 1895, as his second wife, Marion Dale Swift, born Sept. 20, 1841; lived in Caddo, Okla. Mrs. Sarah A. Swift, died Nov. 20, 1925. Their son, Edward C. Swift, live in St.Paul, Minn.
    Children: (Edward C. Swift) (1) Dolliver, born Oct.6, 1930; (2) Darwood Carlisle, born May 5, 1935; (3) Eleanor Rose, born March 29, 1937.
VI. Mary C. Cunningham, born Sept.20, 1865, died July 11, 1867.
VII. William James Cunningham, born Aug.14, 1868; m. April 25, 1895, near Scottsboro, Ala., Mary Jane Hill. They moved to Bowie, Texas.
    Children:
    1. Eldrige J. Cunningham, born November 17, 1897, lives at Lubbock, Texas.
    2. and 3. Eula and Beula Cunningham, twins, born July 8, 1900, died in infancy.
    4. Mary Hill Cunningham, born May 11, 1902, lives in Lubbock, Texas.
    5. Elizabeth Cunningham, m. Guy Burkhalter, lives at Snyder, Texas.
    6. Edna Cunningham, m. Woodrow Webb of 320 Ave. G, Lubbock, Texas.
    7. Margaret Cunningham, m. Mr. Grimes, of 309 Ave. R, Lubbock, Texas.
VIII. Joseph Wilson Cunningham, born Feb.13, 1871, died November 2, 1876.

Harrison Macon Cunningham, son of Nancy (Macon) and Joseph Humphrey Cunningham, was born January 17, 1861, at Hickory Creek, Warren County, Tenn. At an early age he and Capt. Andrew Card came down Elk River and operated a saw mill near Athens, Ala. There he met Sarah Margaret Card, the lovely niece of Capt. Card, daughter of Mariah (Holland) and Benjamin Franklin Card. She was born Jan.24, 1866 and died March 27, 1900. They were married at the Old Holland Homestead near Scottsboro, where William Holland, a soldier of the Revolution, and James Holland, of the War of 1812, lie buried. Benjamin F. Card was born Jan. 27, 1839, died Oct.11, 1904. He served in the 35th Tenn. Volunteers C.S.A. His wife was born July 6, 1846, and died Sept. 22, 1918.

Children of Sarah (Card) and Harrison Macon Cunningham:
I. Inez Cunningham, born June 7, 1889, near Athens, Ala.; m. William Isaac Floyd, of Flat Creek, Tenn.
    Children:
    1. William Isaac Floyd, Jr., born Jan.26, 1910, Tuscaloosa, Ala.

    2. Margaret Long Floyd, born March 22, 1912.

    3. Jane Ann Floyd, born Sept. 23, 1915, at Marion, Ala.

II.   Lorene Cunningham, born Sept. 8, 1892; m. Virgil Van Buren Cornelison, born Sept. 10, 1892, near Scottsboro on Dec. 17, 1914.

    Children:

    1. Thomas Hal. Cornelison, born Sept. 14, 1915.

    2. Virgil Van Buren Cornelison, born Mar. 5, 1917.

    3. Robert Blaine Cornelison, born March 24, 1919.

    4. Anderson Card Cornelison, born November 8, 1920, died May 8, 1921.

    5. Billie Barton Cornelison, born November 6, 1922.

    6. Philip Kyle Cornelison, born Feb. 24, 1925.

III.   Bertha Cunningham, m. Clarence Barton Kirby. (See later)

Harrison Macon Cunningham married secondly, August, 1903, Mary (Bynum) Proctor, born July 6, 1873, the widow of William Proctor.

    Children of second wife:

IV.   Rita Cunningham, born November 10, 1905.

V.   Vula Pearl Cunningham, born April 22, 1907; m. Clyde Sutton Matthews, born June 25, 1930.

VI.   Harrison Macon Cunningham, Jr., born Feb. 8, 1909. He was engaged to be married in June 1930, but on April 5, while standing in a drug store on the square he was stabbed to death by a drunken woman and her accomplice. They did not know him, but were looking for a man in a Navy blue suit, so struck an entirely innocent man, whom they had never even seen before because of the color of his suit. His father dispersed the mob which quickly formed to hang them.

Mr. Cunningham, Sr., died December 29, 1945, and is buried beside his only son. His wife, Nancy (Bynum) Proctor Cunningham died June 13, 1932. All three are buried in Goose Pond Cemetery.

Bertha Cunningham, daughter of Margaret (Card) and Harrison Macon Cunningham, born June 11, 1897, and Clarence Barton Kirby, born Feb. 28, 1891, were married by the Rev. U.S. Bridges at Scottsboro, Ala. They reside on a farm near Scottsboro.

    Children:

I.   Clarence Bennett Kirby, born Feb. 28, 1923, m. Oct. 14, 1951, Mary Jane Harrison, daughter of Mae and Percy Harrison of Shreveport, La., who was born Aug. 19, 1931. He served in World War II as a P-51 pilot (Mustang) and a Jet pilot in the Korean War. They have two children, Scott Harrison Kirby, born November 23, 1952 at Mather Air Force Base, Sacramento, Calif., and Nancy Beth Kirby, born August 29, 1955, at 11:39 A.M. Mr. Kirby is a Chemical Engineer and is employed by Allied Dye and Chemical Co., Atlanta, Ga.

II.   James Macon Kirby, born July 17, 1925; m. Una Faye Houk, born July 9, 1924, daughter of Virginia (Hudsheth) and William Houk. J.M. Kirby served in World War II as a private in Co. B, 184th Regiment, 7th Division, and was wounded at Okinawa, May 25, 1944; entered Alabama Dental College and is now a dentist in Birmingham.

III. Hugh Harry Kirby, born February 6, 1930; entered the Air Force July 17, 1950, and spent 28 months at West Dayton Air Base near London. He visited Macon, France, the home of the Macons.

NORWOOD of NORTH CAROLINA

(Continued from page 335, V.H.G.)

George[2] Norwood of Northampton County, N.C., was a son of William[1] Norwood of Surry County, Virginia, whose will was probated there in 1703. (V.H.G. 334)

Mr. Fairfax Harrison says, in his article on "Henry Norwood, Virginia Treasurer", that William Norwood was "An authenticated member of the Norwood family of Leckhampton, Gloucestershire, England" (33V-4).

Smith, the noted English antiquary, in his "Lives of the Berkeley's" Vol. II, says: "Thomas, fifth Lord Berkeley, in 20th. year of King Henry VII - married Alienor, daughter of Sir Marmaduke Constable of York, Kt., then the widow of John Ingelby, Esq., son and heir of Sir Wm. Ingelby, Kt. (p.228) (See chart V.H.G. p. 340)

"This Lord Thomas by his first wife, Alienor, had two sons, Thomas and Maurice and two daughters, Muriel and Jone. (p.229)

"Muriel, eldest daughter of this Lord Thomas, was in the 18th. year of King Henry VIII, married at Yate to Robert Throckmorton of Caughton of Warwick, (afterwards Kt.), son and heir of Sir George Throckmorton and Kath. his wife, daughter of Nicholas, Lord Vaux. (p.230)

"Muriel Berkeley and Robert Throckmorton had issue: Thomas, Mary, Emme and Kath. in order. (p.231)

"Kath. fourth child of Muriell and Robert married Henry Norwood of Leckhampton in Gloster by whom they had William and Jane. (p.234)

"The said William Norwood (who yet liveth, 1618) by Eliz. his wife, daughter of William Ligon, Esq., had issue:

"Richard (Norwood) by his wife Eliz., daughter of Nicholas Stuard, D.C.L. hath issue: Augustine, Francis, John, William, (Surry, Virginia) Richard, Edward, Thomas, Eleanor and Dorothy. Ao. 1618.

William, brother of Richard, died sp.

Henry third brother of Richard, by Eliz. his wife, daughter of Sir John Rodney hath issue: Charles, (Clerk of Virginia Assembly 1654-56), Henry, (Treasurer of Virginia, 1661-1673.) and Jane 1618.

Ralph, 4th brother liveth a soldier in the Low Countries, 1618.

Thomas, 5th. brother hath yet no issue.

Maurice, 6th. brother is dead without issue.

Eleanor, married George Blunt of Sellington Worcester.

Elizabeth married Richard Moore, Esq., by whom she had divers children.

Jane, married Mr. Bracebridge who hath no issue".

Elizabeth Norwood, daughter of William Norwood of Surry,

married Francis Branch. She is mentioned as "my daughter Elizabeth Branch" in his will. He also mentioned his granddaughter Elizabeth Branch. (See Branch.)

George[2] Norwood, son of William[1] Norwood of Surry, made
his will in Northampton County, N.C. April 21, 1749, same probated August Court, 1749, as follows: Sons: SAMUEL (300 acres
of land on the River; "one third part of my still, one-half of my
Quince orchard, one-third part of the fruit of my apple orchard,
one of the three Pare trees, that which stands nearest the river
called Norwood's Pare and four of the Catteron Pare trees",)
WILLIAM, (Cattle at "Nutbush" and one negro). Grandsons:
GEORGE NORWOOD, son of NATHANIEL (240 acres of land, one
horse, one negro girl), NATHANIEL son of NATHANIEL (310
acres of land at the mouth of Green's Creek, and one negro), JOHN
NORWOOD. son of WILLIAM (160 acres of land on Green's Creek
and one negro girl). Granddaughters: ELIZABETH, MARY, and
SARAH. daughters of NATHANIEL NORWOOD. "I give Ten Pounds,
Twelve shilling and Six pence Virginia Money to be made into rings
with the first letters of my name engraven of them for each grand-
child I have." Executors: WILLIAM, NATHANIEL and SAMUEL
NORWOOD (sons). Witnesses: John Justis, William Wooten.
(Grimes Abstract of Wills 1690-1760-p.271)

        Children of George[2] Norwood.

I.   Samuel[3] Norwood received 300 acres on the River from his
father. He married Mary, the daughter of Robert Smith of
Surry as proven by a deed that Samuel Norwood and wife Mary
and Thomas Bradford and wife Elizabeth made on Feb.18,
1739 to John Jones of Prince George, Va., for a parcel of
land in Surry on the north side of Blackwater which land was
formerly owned by Robert Smith, father of said Mary and
Elizabeth. Wits.: Holmes Boisseau, James Jones, James
Glover. (Surry, BK 3-p.125)

    Robert Smith bought 150 acres on the Morratuck River
adjoining the land of the Widow Molton, Sept. 30, 1718, from
William Reeves. Wits.: Thomas Smith, John Molton. (Hath.
I-623) On the same day Reeves sold William Love 140 acres
adjoining the land of Robert Smith. Wits.: Thomas Smith,
John Green. Also he sold to Elizabeth Molton 150 acres
adjoining Philip Jones. Wits.: John Smith, John Molton.

    Robert Smith made his will Jan.26,1726,probated May
Court,1726 in Bertie County. He gave one plantation to son
ROBERT and legacies to daus. ELIZABETH and MARY. Wife
MARY was executrix and Barnaby Melton executor. Wits.:
William and John Low,John Werham.(Grimes 347) Appraisal
of the estate was made by Barnaby Melton,and legacies were
distributed to the widow; eldest dau. Elizabeth; youngest dau.
Mary and son ROBERT. (Bertie BK B.-201)

    A Robert Smith proved his rights in North Carolina Feb.
8, 1742, for the transportation of the following persons,
viz: Robert Smith, Mary Smith, John Smith, Elizabeth Smith,
JAMES SMITH, Annie Smith, William Smith.

    James Smith's will (not dated) was probated in Halifax,
June 1762. He gave legacies to James, son of John Smith;
to MARY NORWOOD. wife of Samuel Norwood; to James,
son of Jeremiah Smith; to James son of William Killingsworth;

334

Sarah Spann, wife of John Spann; Rebecca Bundy, daughter of said wife FRANCES; sons and daughters of William Smith; decd.: late of Northampton County; rest and residue to be divided between MARY NORWOOD. daughter of SAMUEL NORWOOD and BETTY or ELIZABETH BRADFORD. Exrs.: Wife Frances and James Smith, son of John Smith.(BK 1-70.)

II. Nathaniel[3] Norwood had a family of five children mentioned in his father's will as grandsons and granddaughters to wit: 1. George; 2. Nathaniel; 3. Elizabeth; 4. Mary; 5. Sarah. A Nathaniel Norwood made his will in Granville in 1783 and mentions children: 1. John; 2. Gilliam; 3. Jordan; 4. Mary; 5. Benjamin; 6. Glover; 7. Penelope. Nathaniel Norwood patented 400 acres in Edgecombe 1743. (Vol. IV-634)

III. William[3] Norwood was given cattle at "Nutbush" and William's son John was given 160 acres on Green's Creek. (See later)

William[3] Norwood, son of George [2], patented 600 acres in Bertie in 1742. (N.C. Col. Reg. IV-619) He is said to have married Mary, daughter of John Wall, Burgess of Brunswick Co., Va. The date of William's death is not known. His on John was the only son mentioned in his grandfather, George[2] Norwood's Will.

John[4] Norwood, son of William[3] served in Granville county militia, in Capt. Glover's Company of Col. Wm. Eaton's regiment in 1754. (State Rec. vol. II. -371); served on the Committee of Safety in the Halifax Dist. in Sept. 1775. (Wheeler 1-74) John[4] Norwood witnessed the will of Henry Edwards, and that of George Williams in Edgecombe in 1758. (Grimes)

There were several John Norwoods in the Revolutionary Army. The John Norwood who served in the Continental Army from Warrenton in the Halifax District was probably his son. (N.C. Roster, pp. 354, 546.) As a member of the Committee of Safety he was too important and probably too old to have served as a private in the Continental Forces. He was also a member of the State Convention of 1788. (N.C. Record, Vol. 22.)

John[4] Norwood, born September 1, 1728, married first, Jan. 14, 1755, Lydia Hackney Ledbetter, born Aug.17, 1732, widow of the Rev. George Ledbetter. She died Feb. 24, 1764, and John Norwood married secondly, Dec. 17, 1765, Mrs. Leah Lenoir Whitaker, (Leah Crawley Lenoir), widow of William Whitaker, born Dec. 18, 1737.

John Norwood's will was dated Nov. 13, 1802, probated Dec. 1802, as follows: "I, John Norwood of Franklin County, N.C. ......having before this date given my son JOHN NORWOOD as much of my property as I then intended for him, I now further give him 5 pounds of Virginia money, in full of what he shall receive of my estate.".....to son, GEORGE NORWOOD Ł 15; to sons WILLIAM and THOMAS NORWOOD, negroes and cattle; to son WASHINGTON NORWOOD 328 acres by George Norwood and Whitaker's lines; to daughters: ELIZABETH BRANCH, LEAH NORWOOD and MARY NORWOOD, negroes; to wife LEAH NORWOOD my main plantation of 600 acres on condition that she support my youngest son, JOHN WALL NORWOOD; if she refuses or neglects to support him I hereby authorize trustees I shall hereafter appoint to take possession of sufficient property to support my said

son, JOHN WALL NORWOOD...... After decease of my wife
Leah, my youngest son John Wall Norwood shall enjoy during life
the whole of my manor plantation; after his decease it shall be
equally divided among all of my children by my wife Leah. Wits.:
Jordan Hill, Jordan Thomas, G. Hill, (Rec. BK. D)
    His widow, Leah Norwood, made her will Dec. 18, 1819, pro-
bated in Franklin County, Dec. 1831. (BK. J-176). Her legatees
were: daughter ELIZABETH BRANCH, one negro, Ipse, and
whatever may be due me on bond of her late husband, John Branch
to settle certain payments; daughter, LEAH GANT. widow of William Gant.....; daughter WINIFRED and husband Edwin Cook.....;
daughter MARY NELSON; and mentions her late husband Joseph
Outerbridge; to sons William and Robert L. Whitaker, 5 shillings
each, together with what I have already given them; residue of estate to Elizabeth Branch and her husband. Wits.: John Norwood,
John Gill.
    Surviving children of first wife, Lydia Ledbetter:
I.   John Norwood, born May 11, 1759; m. 1788, Clara Ferral.
        He served as a private in N.C. Militia and died in 1830. (N.
        C. Roster, pp. 354, 546.)
II.   George Norwood, born April 23, 1763.
        Children of second wife, Leah Lenoir Whitaker:
III.   Judge Wm. Norwood, born Jan. 15, 1767, at Hillsborough,
        N.C., died 1842, married Robina Hogg, daughter of James
        Hogg, born 1722, died 1860.
IV.   Thomas Norwood, born May 8, 1768.
V.   Elizabeth Norwood, born March 17, 1770; m. Col. John
        Branch.
VI.   Leah Norwood, born Sept. 9, 1772, m. (1) Wm. Gant; m.
        (2) Mr. Webster.
VII.   Winifred Lenoir Norwood, born April 1774; m. (1) Wm. Tom-
        linson; (2) Edwin Cook. (See later)
VIII.   Washington Norwood, born Oct. 19, 1776, m. Mariana Gant.
IX.   Mary Norwood, born 1780, died 1862; m. (1) Joseph Outer-
        bridge; (daughter Mary m. Joseph Johnson); (2) Col. Joseph
        Nelson.
X.   John Wall Norwood, born November 24, 1781, too late for
        his disability to have been war caused.

    Evelina Roe Tomlinson, daughter of William Tomlinson and
his wife, Winifred Lenoir Norwood, was born in Greensville, Va.,
June 30, 1798 and died Nov. 4, 1834, at New Bern, Craven County,
N.C. She married in New Berne, August 3, 1819, Lucas Jacob
Benners, Jr., who was born in New Bern, June 19, 1791, and died
there Dec. 31, 1836.
    Mr. Benners was a planter, and served in the State Legislature
(Wheeler, Vol. II, p.128)
    Children:
I.   John Norwood Benners, born May 20, 1820, d.s.p.
II.   Sarah Frances Benners, born Dec. 9, 1821; m. James Hogg
        Norwood, son of Robina Hogg and Wm. Norwood.
III.   Joseph Nelson Benners, born July 8, 1823; m. Sarah Green;
        no issue.
IV.   Lucas Jacob Benners, born Sept. 3, 1825, d.s.p.

V. Washington Benners, born July 4, 1826, d.s.p.
VI. Julia Matilda Benners, born September 7, 1827, m. John
Asa Beal Fitzgerald.
VII. Elizabeth Lovick Benners, born Feb. 21, 1829; m. David
Steele Willis. (See later)
VIII. Mary Winifred Benners, born April 14, 1830. d.s.p.
IX. Robena Ann Benners, born June 12, 1831; m. James Joseph
Hines.
X. Nancy Pettigrew Benners, born April 30, 1833, d.s.p.
XI. Isaac Henricus Benners, born Oct. 5, 1834; m. Harriet
Hatch.

Elizabeth Lovick Benners, daughter of Evelina Roe Tomlinson
and Lucas Jacob Benners, was born in New Bern, Craven Co., N.
C. Feb. 25, 1829, and died there Feb. 25, 1868; also at New Bern,
April 27, 1847, she married David Steele Willis, who was Secre-
tary and Treasurer of the North Carolina Railroad, and State Grand
Master of North Carolina Masons.
Children:
I. Fanny Willis, born Feb. 14, 1849, m. Clarence W. Miller.
II. Evelina Tomlinson Willis, born August 20, 1850, died in
infancy.
III. Alonzo Thos. Jenkins Willis, born Dec. 20, 1851, died in
infancy.
IV. Robina Norwood Willis, born Aug. 7, 1853, m. Lucius Tate.
V. David Steele Willis, Jr., born Dec. 24, 1854, m. Carrie
Richton.
VI. Jenkins Willis, born July 7, 1856, m. Emma Smathers.
VII. Elizabeth B. Willis, born August 27, 1857, m. James Robt.
Hyatt. (See later)
VIII. John Whitford Willis, born March 27, 1859, d.s.p.

Elizabeth Benners Willis, daughter of Elizabeth Benners and
David Steele Willis, was born Aug. 27, 1857, in New Bern, N.C.
and died March 7, 1926, at Waynesville, N.C. On Dec. 24, 1883,
at Waynesville, she married James Robert Hyatt, who was born
April 12, 1853, at Whittier, Jackson Co., N.C. and died Jan. 6,
1932 at Waynesville.
Children:
I. David Edward Hyatt, born May 14, 1885, m. Aurora Glen
in 1909.
II. Josepha Benners Hyatt, born Jan. 2, 1887, m. Willis Micaga
Burwell, Dec. 1909.
III. James Ellis Hyatt, born August 27, 1888, m. Mary Pauline
Jones, Dec. 26, 1912.
IV. Buel Hyatt, born Sept. 3, 1891, d.s.p. August 18, 1931.
V. Elizabeth (Betty) McCall Hyatt, born Oct. 6, 1893, m. Regi-
nald V. Arnold. (See later).

Elizabeth McCall Hyatt, daughter of Elizabeth Benners Willis
and James Robert Hyatt, was born in Waynesville, N.C. on Oct.
6, 1893 and was married there Sept. 17, 1921, to Reginald Vlademar
Arnold, son of Helen Higgins and Dr. Royce M. Arnold, who was
educated in Vienna and Berlin. Mr. Arnold was born in New Orleans, La., June 10, 1891.

Mr. Arnold was trained in Architectural Offices in New Orleans, working while he went to school, and attended classes in the atliers of European teachers. He attended Tulane, and in 1921 he passed the Board of Louisiana Architects; he is on the Accredited list of School Architects of America; Member of American Institue of Architects, State chairman of Tennessee Chapter; Past Commander of Knights Templer; Past Commander of American Legion. He served as 1st. Lieutenant in World War I, spending 18 months overseas. He trained Home Guard in World War II, serving as Captain.

Mr. and Mrs. Arnold reside at 539 Alabama St., Bristol, Tennessee.

PERRY of ISLE of WIGHT
and
NORTH and SOUTH CAROLINA

A Perry family was among the earliest settlers of Virginia. Captain William Perry came over in the "Starr" in 1611. He later married Isabella, widow of Richard Pace, and came to live at " "Pace's Paines". Captain Perry represented Pace's Paines in the House of Burgesses, Oct. 1629 and March 1630. In February 1631-32 he was Burgess for the territory "from Captain' Perry's downward to Hog Island". He was a member of the Council 1632-34. (Col. Surry, p. 53)

"He later moved to Charles City County where he died in 1637 and was buried at the old Westover Church. His tomb is still there but the epitaph is now illegible. It was copied by Campbell the Historian:

'Here lyeth the body of Captaine
William Perry who lived neire
Westover in the Collony
Who departed this life the 6th day of
August, Anno Domini 1637' " (Col. Surry, p.53)

Captain Henry Perry, son of William and Isabella, married fhe daughter of Captain George Menefie, Member of the Council and the owner of "Buckland" a large estate which adjoined "Westover". Captain Perry eventually became possessed of the whole of "Buckland". He was a Burgess in 1652 and a Member of Council 1654-1661. (Tyler's "Republic", p. 229) Captain Perry married secondly, Edy, widow of Jeremiah Clements who was Burgess in 1641, for the Surry side of James City. This marriage was before March 17, 1657, for on that date "Captain Henry Perry, Esq., Member of the Council who married the Executrix of Jeremiah Clements of Upper Chippokes now sells 250 acres to Edward Oliver on Upper Chippokes part of a patent of 350 acres formerly granted to the aforesaid Jeremiah Clements" . (Surry BK. 1-160) Captain Perry left two daughters as co-heirs, Elizabeth, who married John Coggs of Rainslipp, Middlesex, England, and Mary, who married Thomas Mercer, a stationer of London. (Tyler-229)

A very wealthy firm of Merchants in London was that of Perry and Lane, composed of Micajah Perry and Thomas Lane. They conducted an extensive trade with Virginia and several relatives of Micajah's settled there.

Micajah Perry, the head of the firm, died in London in 1720. His will was dated Sept. 27, 1720, and probated Oct. 3 of that year. (17W (1)-266). His principal legatees were his daughter-in-law, Sarah Perry, and her two children, Micajah Perry who became Mayor of London in 1728, and Phillip Perry, a member ...

Peter Perry, brother of the first Micajah Perry was the firm's Virginia representative. He made a deposition in York County in 1679 and stated that he was 28 years of age (BK.1675-84 folio 214) On Nov. 24, 1681, as attorney for Micajah Perry of London he was appointed trustee for Margaret Fellows, widow of William Fellows, decd. (Id. folio 353) Peter Perry was Burgess for York in 1688 and is said to have left descendants in Charles City County.

Mary Perry, sister of Micajah and Peter Perry, married a Mr. Lowe, who settled in Charles City. Their children were: 1. Micajah Lowe who married Sarah Hamblin. After his death in London in 1703, Sarah Hamblin Lowe married secondly, William Edwards of Surry and was the mother of Micajah and Sarah Edwards; (15W (I) 80, 196) 2. Susanna Lowe; 3. Mary Lowe; 4. Johanna Lowe who married John Jarrett and had Elizabeth Jarrett who married John Tyler of Charles City, ancestor of President Tyler. Elizabeth Jarrett was the only child mentioned in the will of their uncle, Micajah Perry, and both were single in 1720.

Phillip Perry, who bought 100 acres from Nicholas Aldred Sept. 10, 1655, in Ise of Wight, is seemingly the ancestor of this family. (17c.-528) He made his will in Isle of Wight County, Nov. 20, 1667, probated Oct. 9, 1667, "aged 70 years". His legatees were his eldest son Phillip, not 21, youngest son, John, wife, Grace. Overseers: Ralph Channel; Wits.: Anselm Bailey, James Bagnell. (Book 2-77)

On October 9, 1669, Ralph Channel, in right of Grace, his wife, relict of said Perry, requested probation of will. His surities were Richard Penny and James Bagnall. (ADMN., p. 22)

The eldest son, Phillip, disappears from the records and may have moved to Nansemond.

John Perry, youngest son, on August 10, 1674, requested administration of the estate of John Young who died intestate, he having married Elizabeth Young, daughter and heir of John Young. His surities were John Marshall and Francis Ayers. (Admin., p. 34)

Phillip Perry was called "Phillip Perry of Whitemarsh" for in 1673, John Perry, son of "Phillip Perry of Whitemarsh", decd., sold the land he inherited from his father to Colonel Joseph Bridges of "Whitemarsh" who had a large estate nearby.

John Young was probably the son of Richard Young who patented land in Isle of Wight in 1635. John Young was mentioned in the will of Edward Chetwine, Sept. 27, 1649.

John[2] Perry (Philip[1]) and his wife Elizabeth of the Upper Parish of Nansemond, on May 26, 1675, sold to Nathaniel Bacon 70 acres in the Lower Parish of I. of W., bought of John Young and Robert Butts. (17c.572) A John Perry held 870 acres in Nansemond in the Quit Rents of 1704. John Perry on Jan.15, 1727/28 witnessed the will of Richard Bond of Nansemond which was probated in North Carolina. (Hathaway, Vol. 1, p.133)

PERRY of NORTH CAROLINA

Isaac Perry was born about 1760 in Halifax Co., N.C.: married about 1785-90 in Raleigh, Wake Co., N.C., Sarah Whitaker, born 1766 Halifax Co., N.C.; died near Augusta, Ga.; said to be a daughter of Robert and Sarah Whitaker. Isaac Perry served in the Revolutionary War in the Continental Army. See army account No. 1443 of the North Carolina Line. Amount paid him Ł 186.12.8 and see also N.C. Roster, p. 410. The heirs of Isaac Perry received a grant of land for services in Continental Line. The number of acres is not known, but apparently was 640 (Id 291). A Hardy Perry also served in the Militia (Id. 410).

Isaac Perry of Wake County, on Sept. 6, 1796, deeded Robert Jones 340 acres in Franklin County on the waters of New Creek, beginning at a line formerly Norwood's to Rose's line at Nelson corner...etc. Wits.: Wash. Norwood, John Norwood, Wm.Webb. (D.B. 1797-99, p. 137). Isaac Perry was a bondsman for Hugh Whitaker at his marriage to Margaret Perry in Wake in 1797. It is possible that Margaret was a sister of Isaac Perry and that Hugh Whitaker was a brother of Sarah Whitaker, the wife of Isaac Perry.

Inasmuch as the name "Hardy" appears among the descendants of Isaac Perry, the following theory is suggested concerning the derivation of the name.

The will of a John Hardy was probated in Halifax May 1774. His legatees were his son Benjamin Hardy and his grandchildren, Elizabeth, Mary, Penelope and Tabitha, daughters of his deceased son HUGH HARDY. It appears that his grand daughter Elizabeth Hardy had married a Whitaker by Dec. 6, 1773, for in a codicil dated Dec.6, 1773, he mentions his grand daughter ELIZABETH WHITAKER, her three sisters, blind brother-in-law Benj. Greeb, and Martha, daughter of son Benjamin. (BK 1-345) Hugh Hardy, deceased son of John Hardy, in his prior will in Halifax, dated Nov.20, 1761, probated Jan. 1763, mentions wife, Bethea, brother Samuel, and "all my children" (Id. 95)

The husband of Elizabeth (Hardy) Whitaker is not named. However having married about 1773 it is possible that she was the mother of Hugh Whitaker who married Margaret Perry in 1797 and Sarah Whitaker who married Isaac Perry.

A theory concerning the derivation of the name "Isaac" in the Perry family is also advanced. Isaac Hunter made his will in Chowan, April 17, 1752, probated April 1753. His legatees were his sons: Elisha Jesse, Daniel and Jacob. His daughters were: Sarah Hunter, Hannah Riddic, Rachel Walton; he gave daughter ALICE PERRY, a negro named Tobey; to ELIZABETH PERRY a negro girl; to grand children, the daughters and sons of JOAN PERRY, decd., namely, JESSE, PHILLIP, MARY PERRY and SARAH FIELD five pounds each. (Certified copy of will and Grimes -177)

Phillip Perry was evidently the husband of deceased Joan (Hunter) Perry. Phillip made his will July 5, 1751, probated Oct. 1751. In addition to the above four children he mentions Rachel, Jude and Mirium. Executor was Jacob Perry, son of Jacob Perry. Wits.: Moses Field, Benj. Perry, Elizabeth Perry. (Grimes- 177)

Mr. R. C. Champion of Albany, Georgia, advances the above theories and also states that it is possible that Elizabeth Hunter was the wife of John Perry of Edgecombe who, in his will dated Jan. 27, 1752, probated Sept. 1758, names wife "Elizabeth" and

sons John and William. (Halifax 1-54) Alice Hunter may have
married Joseph Perry, brother of Phillip, John and Jacob Perry.
An Isaac Perry was deputy Surveyor of South Carolina in
1765 and probably was the Isaac Perry who was living in Wilkes
County, Ga., in 1784. Another Isaac Perry was in Perquimans
in 1758 and in Bertie in 1770; and another one was a Revolutionary
soldier in Halifax and moved to South Carolina. These three Isaac
Perrys may have been the sons of the three daughters of Isaac
Hunter who married Perrys.

     Children of Isaac Perry:
I.   James Perry.
II.   Alfred Perry.
III. Edwin Perry.
IV. Henry Hardy Perry, born November 3, 1795; m. (1) Mary
    -----------; (2) Martha Halstead. (See later)
V.   Margaret (Polly) Perry.

     Henry Hardy Perry, son of Isaac and Sarah (Whitaker) Perry,
was born Nov. 3, 1795; died 1876, Marion, Twiggs Co., Ga.;
m. (1) Mary--------; (2) Martha Halstead, widow of John Church-
well. Henry Hardy Perry was educated in common schools and
served as a private in the War of 1812.
     Children of 1st wife, Mary---- who was born Aug. 20,1797,
    died July 18, 1837:
I.   Samuel Whitaker Perry, born Nov. 17, 1817, died in Miss.
    about 1905.
II.   Henry Saxon Perry, born July 26, 1822, died Oct. 30, 1826.
III. Elizabeth Ann Perry, born Oct. 15, 1824.
IV. David Marion Perry, born August 10, 1826.
V.   Elizabeth Sarah Perry, born December 9, 1830; died March
    7, 1836.
VI. John Randolph Perry, born December 6, 1834, died of wounds
    at Richmond, Va., June 29, 1862.
VII. James Calhoun Perry, born Feb. 9, 1837, died 1849.
VIII. Henry Harrison, born May 15, 1840, died Jan. 31, 1844.
    Children of 2nd. wife, martha Halstead:
IX. Martha Margaret Perry, born March 1, 1844; m. David
    Champion. (See later)
X.   Latamore Perry, born Feb.19, 1846, died March 1, 1846.
XI. Cynthia Cornelia Perry, born Feb.11, 1847; died July 28,
    1848.

     Martha Margaret Perry, daughter of Henry Hardy and Sarah
(Whitaker) Perry, was born March 1, 1844, in Marion, Twiggs
Co., Ga.; died February 28, 1916, Doles, Worth County, Ga.,
married Oct. 1, 1868, Twiggs County, Ga., David Fort Champion,
born Oct. 10, 1834, Bullock County, Ga.; died Oct. 1, 1915,
Albany, Dougherty County, Ga.
     Children of Martha Margaret Perry and husband David
Champion:
I.   Lula Eudora Champion, born July 4, 1869, m. 11/19/1885
    Benj. Gleaton, born March 12, 1864 died June 21, 1935.
    Children:
    1. Henry Perry Gleaton, born Feb. 17, 1887, died March 9,
      1949, m. Eliza E. Scruggs of Hahira, Ga., Sept. 12,1913.

342

Children:
(1) James Perry Gleaton, born Sept. 12, 1914.
(2) Margaret Elizabeth Gleaton, born Aug. 1916, died May 30, 1918.
2. Mattie Emmie Gleaton, born Aug. 1, 1888, m. Dr. C.T. Amason, Jan. 23, 1907. Died Nov. 12, 1918.
Children:
(1) Charles Curtis Amason, born Nov.10, 1908, died Feb. 26, 1910.
(2) William Clifford Amason, born April 7, 1910.
(3) Randolph Emmett Amason, born Sept. 14, 1911.
(4) Elleighfare Amason, born Sept. 27, 1913.
(5) Charles Thomas Amason, born March 5, 1917.
3. Clarence Edgar Gleaton, born Sept. 20, 1890, died Sept. 13, 1891.
4. David Benjamin Gleaton, born Jan. 10, 1892, m. Clara A. Giddens July 18, 1917.
Children:
(1) Edna Jay Gleaton, born August 2, 1921.
5. Elmer DeWitt Gleaton, born Feb. 28, 1894, m. (1) Mary Keen Nov. 11, 1917. m. (2) Vivian Afton Snyder May 25, 1929.
Children by first wife Mary Keen.
(1) Peggy Lou Gleaton, born Nov. 12, 1924.
Children by second wife Vivian Afton Snyder.
(2) Joseph DeWitt Gleaton, born June 2, 1930.
(3) Junita Afton, born Jan. 6, 1932.
(4) Benjamin Newell Gleaton, born Jan.15, 1941.
II. Martha Emma Champion, born May 20, 1871, m. Aldrich Partin Fuquay December 29, 1891, born March 25, 1861, died July 16, 1946.
Children:
1. Ethlyn Fuquay, born Nov.15, 1893, m. Rev. W.A. McKee.
Child:
(1) Emma Jane McKee born April 23, 1915, m. Kurt Sepmeier.
2. Aldrich Perry Fuquay, born April 15, 1897, m. (1)------- m. (2) Eloise Wilkinson.
Child by first wife:
(1) Dora Jim Fuquay, born Dec.2, 1919, m. Leland Culligan.
Child by second wife:
(2) Judith Aldrich Fuquay, born Sept. 10, 1937.
3. Margaret Ruth Fuquay, born Nov. 12, 1900, died ----.
4. Janice Partin Fuquay, born Feb. 7, 1903, m. Dr. A.M. Collingsworth.
5. Martha Fuquay, born Dec.12, 1906, m. ------ Peacock.
III. Cora Elizabeth Champion, born Jan.20, 1876, m. J.T. Corley.
Child:
1. Dorothy Corley born about 1904, m. ------ Hewson.
IV. David Emmett Champion, born June 9, 1878, died Dec.25, 1900.
V. Thomas Edwin Champion, born July 9, 1880, died Nov.15,

1952, m. Annie Jay Robson, Evergreen, Ala. 1909.
Child:
1. Elizabeth Champion.
VI. James Perry Champion, born March 31, 1883, m. Eloise Stewart. (See later)
VII. Randolph E. (Fort) Champion, born Oct. 26, 1887, m. Katherine Muse. (See later)

Randolph E. Champion, of Albany, Georgia, born October 26, 1887, Worth County, Ga., m. Nov. 2, 1916, Albany, Dougherty County, Ga., Katherine Muse, born December 10, 1895, Albany, Georgia, Dougherty County, Ga., dau. of Augustus Wynn Muse and Sarah Tucker. Education: High School and Eastman Business College, N.Y. He and his brother own and operate the Albany Warehouse Company and are engaged in fertilizer manufacturing and the operation of a cotton warehouse in Albany, Ga.
Children:
I. Katherine Champion, born August 13, 1921, m. James M. Meadors.
Children:
1. Katherine Meadors, born Aug. 22, 1943.
2. James McWhorter Meadors, Jr., b. March 17, 1946.
II. Randolph E. Champion, born April 24, 1930, unmarried.

James Perry Champion, born March 31, 1883, married Eloise Stewart, who died Dec. 30, 1929.
Children:
I. Anita Champion, born June 14, 1916, m. James E. Reynolds.
Children:
1. Anita Reynolds, born February 10, 1939.
2. James E. Reynolds, Jr., born Sept. 7, 1944.
II. James Perry Champion, Jr., born Sept. 26, 1918, m. Jane Luthy and had 3 children:
1. James Perry Champion, 3rd., born Nov. 11, 1943.
2. Elizabeth Hollis Champion, born April 29, 1945.
3. Wendy Frederick Champion, born Aug.19, 1954.
III. Eloise Stewart Champion, born August 5, 1921, m.Charles Heinemann, and had 2 children:
1. Ann Eloise Heinemann, born March 31, 1945.
2. Jean Marshall Heinemann, born March 11, 1949.
IV. Joseph Stewart Champion, born Jan.17, 1926, married Elizabeth Hollingsworth, had 3 children:
1. Joseph Stewart Champion, born June 9, 1949.
2. Kathleen Hollingsworth Champion, born Dec. 2, 1950.
3. Elizabeth Hollingsworth Champion, born May 29, 1952.

DESCENDANTS OF BENJAMIN PERRY OF KERSHAW CO.S.C.
by
John Ben Perry, Jr.

1. Benjamin Perry died 1794/5 in Kershaw County, S.C. and left two wills, one dated 1779 named a wife Mary, the other dated 1789 named a wife Sarah. The wills are by the same man, as the same children and slaves are named in both wills. He had a brother James who died in 1806 in Kershaw County, S.C. who also left a will. It is believed they were originally from Bertie County, N.C. as Colonial Records of N.C. Vol. 9, p.804/6 show two brothers of this name signed a petition at Windsor, N.C. on Cushy River in 1768. There is presently no proof however that these are the same two men.

Benjamin Perry bought lands of William Simpson who had patented same in Kershaw County in 1771/72. In 1787 Benjamin Perry patented 1,000 acres in Camden District. Indents of military service are on record in Columbia, S.C., signed both Benjamin Perry and Benjamin Perry Jr.

    Children of Benjamin Perry, believed to have been by his wife Mary were:
I.   Rigdon Perry, believed to have died between 1779 and 1789.
II. Benjamin Perry. (See later)
III. Zadock Perry. (See later)
IV. Mary Perry married Sion Coates and died by 1789.
V.   Sarah Perry married Jesse Tillman and died ca 1811, Kershaw Co.
VI. Elizabeth Perry.
VII. Wineford Perry.
VIII. Ruth Perry, who married   Rhodes and died by 1779 and left three children:
    1. Perry Rhodes.
    2. Alcey (Alice?) Rhodes believed to have married Edwards.
    3. Henry Rhodes.

2. Benjamin Perry, Jr., son of Benjamin, married Mary Starke, daughter of Maj. Thomas Starke of the Revolutionary Army originally from Virginia. Benjamin died 1813 in Lancaster Co., S.C. Their children were:
I.   John Stark Perry married Sarah
II. Wilmott Stark Perry born 1809 died 1888 at Wilwood, Fla. and married her cousin Jacky Perry (son of Josiah?)
III. Molsie (Mary) Perry married James Jonathan Douglas and he was dead by 1835 and she then married Dr. Pomeroy Bush.
IV. Elizabeth Perry married Dr. James Massey.
V.   Madison Stark Perry born 1814 moved to Florida in 1847, married Martha Peay Starke (his cousin?) and was Governor of Florida and an officer in C.S.A. He died in 1865.

VI.   Thomas Perry.

2. Zadock Perry, son of Benjamin Sr. was born Nov. 10, 1754 and died January 18, 1815 in Lancaster County, S.C. and is buried near Rich Hill. He married ca 1785 Tabitha Tillman b. ca 1765 and died 1830/35 Lancaster County, S.C. Zadock's tombstone reads "Who was Engaged in Arduous Duties for the Defense of His Country in the Revolution of '76. Hark to the Tomb, a Doleful Sound", but no record has been found of his army service. Their children were:

I.   Zadock Perry, Jr. (See later)
II.   Rigdon Perry, believed to have married Frances Hammond and moved to Alabama.
III.   Isaac Tillman Perry, married Agnes   , died by 1829 and left two children: 1. Janes and 2. Tabitha.
IV.   Ruth Perry, married Robert Douglas (see later).
V.   Comfort Perry died 1829 Lancaster Co., S.C., married Nathaniel Barber.
VI.   Sarah (Sally) Perry married Francis Tillman Ingram.

3. Zadock Perry Jr., son of Zadock, born March 8, 1795, Lancaster County S.C. married ca. 1821 Dorcas Clance Duren (1801-72) daughter of Thomas Duren of Kershaw County, S.C. Zadock and family moved to Mississippi in 1845 but before leaving made his will dated at Liberty Hill, S.C. in 1844. This will recorded in Yalobusha County, Miss. Zadock and his wife Dorcas are buried on his plantation in Mississippi in what was then Yalobusha County but now Grenada County. Their children were:

I.   Oliver Hazard Perry. (See later)
II.   Thomas Duren Perry, born 1824 Lancaster County, S.C. married Henrietta Louisa Dye of Lancaster January 20, 1846. Died Mississippi 1853 and buried on the old Perry plantation.
III.   Zadock Elmore Perry, born 1829, buried beside his grandfather Zadock Sr. near Rich Hill, S.C.
IV.   Mary Ann Perry born October 12, 1823, Lancaster County, S.C., died February 5, 1884, Grenada County, Miss.; married Benjamin Williams Jr. who was born April 26, 1824, Kershaw County, S.C. and died July 27, 1894, Grenada Co., Mississippi.
V.   Dorcas Rebecca Perry, born Lancaster County, S.C. 8-25-1830, died 2-18-64 in South Carolina, married 10-23-1851 George F. Ingram who was born 4-22-1829, Kershaw County, S.C. died 7-7-1902 Grenada County, Miss.
VI.   Reuben Rufus Perry, born 1-20-1836, Lancaster County, S.C., died 11-1-1890, Grenada Co., Miss. Married 12-10-1872 Mary G. Smith in Grenada County.
VII. Sarah Elizabeth Perry, born 8-24-1832, died 8-22-1872, Grenada County, Miss,, married January 1852 Dr. John J. Gage in Grenada County, Miss.
VIII. Ellenor Tabitha Perry, born 1-6-1838 Lancaster Co., S.C. and died 7-6-1918 Grenada County, Miss. Married 3-9-1856 Kershaw Williams who was born in Kershaw County, S.C. 1826 and was killed at the Battle of Murfreesboro, Tenn. She married a second time to Dr. James B. Gage, Sr.
IX.   Louisiana Perry, born 1-14-1834, Lancaster County, S.C.,

died 2-15-1869, Yalobusha County, Miss. Married June 10, 1857, Dr. A. A. Powell.

4. Oliver Hazard Perry, son of Zadock Jr., was born September 29, 1822, in Lancaster County, S.C. He married first, Elizabeth Williams, daughter of Benjamin Williams and his wife Tabitha who were originally from Kershaw County, S.C. The first wife Elizabeth died in childbirth as did the child, and O.H. Perry married a second time another Elizabeth Williams, daughter of John Williams, his first wife's cousin.

Children of O.H. Perry and his second wife were:

I.   Thomas Duren Perry, born 5-29-1853, Yalobusha County, Miss., died an infant.
II. John Calhoun Perry. (See later)
III. Oliver Hazard Perry, Jr., born 6-27-1854, Yalobusha Co., Miss., and married Louisiana Elizabeth Williams in 1878 and died Grenada Co., Miss., 2-18-1937.
IV. Robert Edwin Perry, born 1-12-1868 married first, Allie Smith, 2-15-1894, second Jesse Parker, 12-17-1913 and he died 5-14-1939.
V.   Charles Elmore Perry, born 5-20-1856 Yalobusha County, Miss., and died March 9, 1936, Grenada County, Miss. He married Lelia Williams.
VI. Mary Lurana Perry, born November 26, 1861, married William P. Williams, Feb.7, 1878, and died April 6, 1954, Grenada County, Miss.
VII. Tabitha Elizabeth Perry, born December 21, 1863, Grenada County, Miss., married 1. John Williams; 2. John Thompson; 3. F. L. Rawls.

5. John Calhoun Perry, son of Oliver Hazard, was born September 14, 1851, in Yalobusha County, Miss., married Susan Ann Johnson 11-14-1873 and died at Grenada, Miss., Jan.19, 1929. Susan Ann Johnson was the daughter of Benjamin Franklin Johnson and his wife Mary Elizabeth Sledge and the Sledge and Johnson families were originally from Sussex County, Va. and North Carolina. (See South Side Va. Families, Vol. I, by J.B. Boddie). Their children were:

I.   John Ben Perry. (See later)
II. Lillian Estelle Perry, born 10-27-1876, married Rice Pressgrove in Grenada, Jan. 19, 1898, and died in Grenada March 16, 1943.
III. Mary Elizabeth Perry. (See later)
IV. Claud Augustine Perry, born Nov.15, 1879, married Willie Mai Lee, Holmes County, Miss., December 23, 1908. Died Grenada, Nov. 11, 1942.

6. John Ben Perry, son of John Calhoun, was born Oct. 3, 1874, in Grenada County, and married on November 2, 1897, Sarah Gertrude Ray, the daughter of Dr. Henry Jonathan Ray and his wife, Elizabeth Wood Stokes. He died April 5, 1947, at Grenada, Miss.

Their children were:

I.   Henry Ray Perry, born Grenada, Miss., March 26, 1899, married Jan. 1, 1926, Lucille Rimes of Tylertown, Miss. Now living Albequerque, N.M.

II. Louise Perry, born August 5, 1900, at Grenada, Miss.,
married Donald French Brower October 24, 1945, now
living at Rumson, N.J.
III. John Ben Perry, Jr. (See later)
IV. Thomas Moore Perry, born July 25, 1904, at Grenada,
Miss., married Lillie Killebrew in Holmes County, Miss.,
April 13, 1935, and died August 7, 1941, and is buried at
Goodman, Miss.
V. Mary Lillian Perry, born December 23, 1908, Grenada,
Miss., married Orley Radcliff Lilly, Feb. 16, 1931, now
living at Grenada, Miss.
VI. George Covington Perry, born March 1, 1915, married
Julia Marie Guidry, June 9, 1948 and now living at Jackson,
Mississippi.

7. John Ben Perry, Jr., son of John Ben, born June 26, 1902,
at Grenada, Miss., married Lena Webb Catoe of Tallahatchie
County, Miss., April 16, 1923. She was the daughter of Earl
VanDorn Catoe and his wife Mary Jane Coggins, of Webb, Miss.,
and E. V. Catoe was originally from Chester County, S.C. J.B.
Perry, Jr., presently living at Grenada, Mississippi, 750 South
line St.
Their children:
I. Mary Jane Perry. (See later)

8. Mary Jane Perry, daughter of John Ben Jr. was born July 2,
1928, at Grenada, Miss., married Guy Ragan Green, Jr., Jan.
28, 1949, and now living in Wertheim, Germany, where her hus-
band is a Lieutenant in the U.S. Army.
Their children:
I. Guy Ragan Green, III, born September 10, 1950, and died
Sept. 6, 1954, at Grenada, when struck by an automobile.
II. Mary Lillian Green, born Aug.25, 1955, at U.S.Army
Base Hospital, Wurzburg, Germany.

6. Mary Elizabeth Perry, daughter of John Calhoun Perry[5] was
born Grenada County, Miss., April 22, 1882, married Joseph
Meaders Brown, Feb. 14, 1901, and now living in Grenada, Miss.
They had one child:
I. Susan Ann Brown, who married T. B. Revell, Jr., and
they had two children: 1. Theodore Bryan Revell, 2. Joseph
Thomas Revell.

3. Ruth Perry, daughter of Zadock Perry Sr. (2) was born ca.
1781, in Lancaster County, S.C. and died ca 1828 in Lancaster
Co. She married Robert Douglas who was born in Antrim County,
Ireland, December 21, 1779, and died October 1846 in Lancaster
County, S.C. Their children were:
I. Robert Douglas Jr. who came to Mississippi with his first
cousin Zadock Perry Jr.
II. Zadock Perry Douglas was born in Lancaster Co., S.C.,
1-8-1811, came to Mississippi with his cousin Zadock Perry,
Jr., and died March 5, 1853, and was buried on Zadock
Perry's plantation near Grenada, Miss, which was at that
time in Yalobusha County, now in Grenada Co. His estate
was administered in Yalobusha County and 1/5 share went to

each of his brothers and sisters herein named.
III. Sarah Tabitha Douglas, died in 1850. She had married Henry C. Horton and moved to Shelby County, Ala.
IV. Elizabeth Douglas. (See later)
V. James Klancey Douglas, born Lancaster County, April 25, 1805, and died March 27, 1890, near Eupora, Miss., buried in the old LaGrange Cemetery.
VI. Mary Comfort Douglas, married John C. Bell and moved to Pickens County, Ala.

4. Elizabeth Douglas, daughter of Ruth Perry and her husband, Robert Douglas, married ca 1831, Andrew Jackson Mackey in Lancaster County, S.C. and their children were:
I. Sarah Ann Comfort Mackey. (See later)
II. Lyttleton Perry Mackey, married Amanda Bruce.
III. Mary Elizabeth Mackey, born 1837 and died 1908 in Lancaster Co., S.C., married April 6, 1862, William Ruffin Bennett, as his second wife.

5. Sarah Ann Comfort Mackey, born 1832 and died 1861, Lancaster County, S.C., and married first   Lambeth, second, William Ruffin Bennett.
    Children of William Ruffin Bennett and Sarah Ann Comfort Mackey:
I. Andrew J. Bennett, born May 1, 1856, died November 30, 1893, married Ella Crowell.
II. William Perry Bennett. (See later)
III. Robert Simon Bennett, born Dec.19, 1860; died September 10, 1931. Unmarried.
    Children of William Ruffin Bennett and Mary Elizabeth Mackey:
IV. Ruffin Thomas Bennett, born July 19, 1865, died July 10, 1937; m. Nancy Hunter Bailey.
V. James Kernay Douglas Bennett, born January 29, 1866; died August 7, 1867.
VI. Charles Davis Bennett, born Feb.17, 1868; died July 25, 1908; married Mamie Clifton.
VII. Mary Lenora Bennett, born October 17, 1870, died Oct.11, 1951; m. M. Judson Beckham.
VIII. Edward Martin Bennett, born Feb.15, 1873; died July 2,1939; m. Vadie Moore.
IX. Sarah Elizabeth Bennett, born April 18, 1876; living in 1955. married Walter Terry.
X. Lucie Amanda Bennett, born April 12, 1879; living in 1955; m. M. Judson Bell.
XI. Daisy Bennett, born Feb.25, 1882; living in 1955; married Richard Baxter Robinson.

6. William Perry Bennett, born January 28, 1858; died Feb.13, 1943; m. Leila Josey, born August 3, 1866; died February 7, 1950.

    Children:
I. Carl Ganson Bennett, born December 14, 1892; died August 13, 1941; m. Estaline McCain.
    Child:
    1. William Carl Bennett, born April 9, 1939.

II.   Lucius Martin Bennett, born December 14, 1894; m. Mary Costner.

        Child:

        1. Lucius Martin Bennett, Jr., born July 21, 1942.

III.   Perry Belle Bennett, born Feb. 16, 1898. m. Benjamin Clyburn Hough. No children.

        (See Southside Virginia Families, Vol. I, by J. B. Boddie)

PHILIPS of SURRY

The Philips family of Edgecombe County, N.C. , descends from one William Philips whose will was recorded in Surry Co. , Va. , in 1721. The parentage of this William Philips is unknown. In 1681 two persons by the name of William Philips died in Isle of Wight County, one of whom was styled "William Philips of "Blackwater". This is of interest as William Philips of Surry, died 1721, owned a plantation on the Blackwater River. David Philips, John Philips, Jno. Philips and William Phillips appear on the Surry Co. tithable lists in 1678. (Col.Surry, p.189). Their relationship, if any, is not known. John Philips appears on the rent rolls of Surry in 1704 with 270 acres of land and William Philips with 300. (Ibid: p.214). The Philipses in Surry and Isle of Wight probably descend from one Thomas Philips, born 1599, who came to Virginia in the "William and Thomas" in 1618 and who was living at Basse's Choice at the time of the muster in Feb.1625. His wife Elizabeth, born 1602, came to the colony in the "Sea Flower" in 1621. (17th Cent. p.88). Thomas Philips was granted 300 acres of land in James City County July 9, 1635, on the south side of the Chickahominy River, 150 acres for the personal adventure of himself, Elizabeth his wife and Elizabeth his daughter. (Nugent-p.26). On May 29, 1638 Peleg Buck was granted 500 acres in James City " "near land lately in the tenure of Thos. Philips. (Ibid: 83). One Elizabeth Philips made a deposition in Surry in 1672 giving her age as 72. (Col.Surry, p.216). Thus, she could have been the wife of Thomas Philips, above, who was born in 1602.

1.   William Philips, first known ancestor, married Mary Swann, daughter of Mathew Swann, a prominent early citizen of Surry. (Col.Surry-107). The will of William Philips, dated 2-14-1721, probated 4-19-1721 mentioned wife Mary, sons John, William, Swann, and Mathew Philips, the last three being under the age of 16 years, and daughters: Anne; Mary; and Elizabeth Philips. The inventory of William Philips, signed by Mary Philips in April, 1721, listed personal property on the Blackwater plantation, the Round Hill plantation and the "Home" plantation. As Mary Philips, widow of William Phillips, she made her will in Surry 3-28-1727. The will mentions daughter Mary, wife of John Edwards, daughter Ann, niece Mary Crafford, daughter of Carter Crafford, daughter Elizabeth, wife of William Hancock, sons William and Swan Philips and grandaughters Ann Hancock and Mary Edwards. Carter Crafford was appointed executor. (Surry Wills 1715-1730, 697).
     Issue of William Philips and Mary Swann.
I.   John Philips - of whom later - mentioned in will of Mathew Swann.
II.   Mary Philips m. John Edwards - untraced.
III.   Elizabeth Philips m. William Hancock - untraced.

351

IV. Ann Philips - no record.
V. William Philips, untraced. On 9-19-1738 he sold to Wm.
George land that his father Wm. had bought 11-5-1694. Hence
he is not the William Philips whose will was probated in
Surry in 1734, as stated in V.H.G. - p.308.
VI. Swann Philips - no record.
VII. Mathew Philips - no record.

2. John Philips, born circa 1698, mentioned in the will of his
grandfather Mathew Swann in 1702. On 2-19-1719 he purchased
265 acres on the Main Swamp of Lawnes Creek from Lovelace Savidge. (Surry B.1715-255). His will was dated 8-11-1758 and probated the following year. He devised his land in Southampton and
on the "Bold Robbin" Branch in the county of Surry to son Hartwell
who appears to have been the youngest. Son Hartwell and kinsman
Carter Crafford were appointed executors. Only daughter Mary
Warren was married when the will was made but the final division
of his estate 1-19-1762 among the heirs suggests the names of his
other sons-in-law. The estate was divided among the heirs. Arthur
Philips; Joseph Philips, Hartwell Philips, Allen Warren, Moses
Bennett, Joshua Wood, Joshua Proctor and Micajah Exum. The wife
of John Philips is uncertain. Hannah, daughter of John Fort of Sur-
ry was married to a John Philips in 1721. (S.V.F.-196). Martha,
the youngest daughter of Robert Crafford of Surry married a Phil-
ips and a similarity of names suggests that it might have been this
particular John Philips. (V.H.G.-296).
John Philips, of course, may have married twice.
Issue:
I. John Philips - untraced.
II. Joseph Philips, m. Sarah Exum. See later.
III. Arthur Philips - He moved to Edgecombe County, N.C.,
where he purchased land on Fishing Creek in 1751. (Hali-
fax D.B. 4-131)
IV. Hartwell Philips m. (1) Jane Hancock; (2) Feraby Jones.
V. Elizabeth Philips - untraced.
VI. Lucy Philips - untraced.
VII. Ann Philips - untraced.
VIII. Sarah Philips - untraced.
IX. Mary Philips m. Allen Warren III of Surry County, Va. In
Volume 2, p.3, Surry County Deeds, Allen Warren conveyed
to his step-father John Little, his lands in "Philips Pocoson".
Allen Warren III was the son of Allen Warren Jr., and his'
wife Anne Hart.
Issue of Mary Philips and Allen Warren III. (See V.H.G.-
251)
1. William Warren, died 1804.
2. Arthur Warren
3. John Warren
4. Jesse Warren
5. Martha Warren m. Mr. White
6. Mary m. Mr. Murphee

Joseph Philips, son of John Philips (2). Joseph Philips married Sarah Exum, Southampton M.B. dated 1-19-1759. She was

the daughter of John Exum of Isle of Wight Co. He moved to Edgecombe County, N.C. before his death. The will of John Exum was
probated in Edgecombe in 1775 and mentions daughter Sarah Philips. It is erroneously stated in "17th Century Isle of Wight Co.
p. 455, that this daughter Sarah m. Etheldred Philips. Joseph
Philips appears to have moved to North Carolina in 1750. On
11-20-1750 he purchased 162 acres on the south side of Swift
Creek from Thomas Exum, Edgecombe D.B. 4, 204. From 1760-
61, he received several grants (Book D, p. 461, 463, 466) and in
1763 purchased a tract from Jesse Nichols. (Book C, p. 5). The
will of Joseph Philips, dated 11-6-1779 and probated 1783, Edgecombe W.B. "B", p. 147, mentions sons Etheldred, Exum, Mathew, Benjamin, and Joseph, daughters Sarah and Martha and his
lands and mill on Swift Creek and his lands on Tar River.

Joseph Philips and Sarah Exum had issue:

I. Joseph Philips, born 10-31-1763, died 5-22-1822 m. 1785
    Milberry Horn (1764-1851) of Edgecombe Co. Descendants
    given in The Battle Book, p. 341. The removed to Tennessee
    and settled a plantation called "Sugar Tree Grove" 6 miles
    from Nashville.
II. Benjamin Philips - settled near Nashville, Tenn. - untraced.
III. Mathew Philips - no record.
IV. Sarah Philips - untraced.
V. Martha Philips - untraced.
VI. Exum Philips, died November 1802. His will probated Edge-
    combe W.B. "D", p. 152 mentions daughter Polly, sons
    Mathew, James, Joseph, and Thomas Philips and directed
    that his brothers Joseph and Benjamin Philips, then in Ten-
    nessee, settle his sons Mathew and James in that state. Jo-
    seph Philips, son of Exum Philips, m. Anne Taylor and left
    a will in Edgecombe in 1822 leaving an only child Mary Phil-
    lips.
VII. Etheldred Philips, son of Joseph. The will of Etheldred Phil-
    ips, dated 12-15-1791, and probated May, 1795, bequeathed
    his water grist mill on Swift Creek to his sons Exum and
    Eaton Philips and mentioned "Other sons and daughters" but
    not by name. He married Jane Lewis, the daughter of Col.
    Exum Lewis of Edgecombe County and his wife Elizabeth Fig-
    ures. They had issue three children who reached maturity:
    1. Charlotte Philips m. (1) Mr. Gray, (2) John L. Jackson
       and (3) John D. Ward. She left no living issue.
    2. Figures Philips, m. and left descendants who are untraced.
    3. Exum Philips. He m. Sally Nicholson, sister of Timothy
       M. Nicholson whose will, probated Nash County, May,
       1808, mentions sister Sally Philips and brother-in-law
       Exum Philips. However, Sally is not mentioned in the
       will of John Nicholson, father of Timothy. Exum Philips
       and Sally Nicholson had issue four children: John Philips,
       died Savanna, Ga., 1854; Timothy Miles Philips, died
       unmarried, Griffin, Ga.; Penelope Philips m. Robert H.
       Halstead of Ga.; and Dr. Etheldred Philips, born Nash
       County, 1801, died Marianna, Florida, June 29, 1870,
       attended U.N.C. and practiced medicine in Florida where
       he married Susan Gautier and had issue three sons. His

interesting correspondence with his cousin Dr. James J.
Philips of Edgecombe is preserved in the Southern Historical Collection at Chapel Hill, N.C.

3.   Hartwell Philips, youngest son of John Philips (2) of Surry.
As Hartwell Philips of Surry County, Va., he m. (1) Jane Han-
cock, daughter of John Hancock, Sussex County, M.B. dated
2-24-1762. (Col. Surry-p. 230). He m. (2) in N.C. Pheraby Jones.
The will of James Jones of Halifax County, N.C., probated Nov.
1778, W.B. w, 86, mentions wife Sarah, sons John, Frederick and
Albrittain and daughters Feraby Philips and Ann Hancock. Soon
after his first marriage Hartwell Philips moved to Edgecomb Co.,
N.C. On 10-11-1763 he purchased land on the north side of Swift
Creek and Tar River. (Edgecombe D.B. "C", p. 82.) On 5-19-
1764 Hartwell Philips and Jane his wife of Edgecombe County,
N.C. sold 230 acres of land in Surry to Anthony Diggs. (Surry
D.B. 1760-1769, p. 212). On 3-20-1764 Hartwell Philips sold to
John Warren 265 acres originally granted to Robert Savidge in 1682
and transferred to John Philips 2-16-1719, the father of sd. Hartwell and devised to Hartwell by will. Hartwell Philips acquired large
holdings of land in Edgecombe County and died in Oct. 1801. His will
was probated in Nov. 1801, Edgecombe W.B. "D", p. 133. The executors were sons Frederick and two kinsmen Exum Philips and
Exum Philips, Jr.

      Issue of Hartwell Philips. It is very probable that his daugh-
      ter Mary was by his first wife.
I.   Mary Philips. She m. Benjamin Clary of Sussex County, Va.,
      who was related to the Hancock family. As Mary Clary of
      Sussex County, Va., she deeded her share in her father's
      estate in 1815. (Edgecombe, D.B. 15, p. 200).
II.   Rebecca Philips m. John Hancock and d. August 1809. No
      record of issue.
III. Frederick Philips - of whom later.
IV.   Olive Philips, born 1779, died March 15, 1848. She married
      a Mr. Weeks of Edgecombe County and died without issue.
V.   John Hartwell Philips, died Feb. 2, 1804 while a student at
      the University of N.C.
VI.   Benjamin Philips, died unmarried March, 1800.
VII. Jean Philips, died unmarried March, 1816.
VIII. Elizabeth Philips, m. John Evans. Only issue: Frederick
      Philips Evans, m. February 13, 1834, Arabella, daughter
      of Gen. Joseph ARRINGTON and moved south.

4.   Frederick Philips, born 5-2-1772, only surviving son of Hartwell Philips. He resided at "Manor Hill", Edgecombe County. He
represented Edgecombe in the General Assembly in 1797 and was
at times a school teacher and county surveyor. According to Bishop Cheshire's Book, "Non Nulla", Frederick Philips suffered fi-
nancial reverses and had to sell his last remaining slave to edu-
cate his son at the University of Pa. Medical School, thinking this
the best way to equip him for a career. Frederick Philips married
Sally Tart, died January 23, 1816. Her parentage is unknown but
she was seemingly the grandaughter of Jonathan Tart whose will
was probated Edgecombe County May, 1789. Frederick Philips
Philips died 10-1-1837 at "Mount Moriah", the home of his son,

James J. Philips.
  Issue of Frederick Philips and Sally Tart:
I.   James Jones Philips, born March 12, 1798. (See later)
II.   Margaret B. Philips, born 1799, died 4-22-1844, m. Michael
      K. Parker of Edgecombe. They moved to Sumpter County,
      Ala. No further record.
III. Pheraby Philips, born Jan. 4, 1802, died unmarried Nov. 1880.
IV.   Eliza J. Philips, born Jan. 21, 1804, died June 9, 1887,
      m. October 15, 1851 John Parker of Edgecombe County
      and Mobile, Alabama. No issue.
V.   Pennina Philips, born 1806, m. (1) Henry Horne (1807-1833)
      and m. (2) June, 1837, Dr. John A Missis, who advertised
      in the Tarboro paper as a "Thompsonian Botanical Physician
      residing at the Falls of Tar River". They later moved to
      Tennessee.

5. Dr. James Jone Philips, born 1798, died April 10, 1874,
M. D. University of Pa., successful physician and planter. About
1828 he purchased a plantation in the northwestern part of Edgecombe County, 7 miles from the original Philips settlement on
Swift Creek, which he called "Mount Moriah". He married April
23, 1834 Harriet Amanda Burt, born August 4, 1817, died Sept.
28, 1890, the daughter of William Burt and his wife Susan Sims of
Hilliardston, Nash County, N.C. Dr. Philips and his wife are
buried in the family graveyard at "Mount Moriah".
  Issue of James Jones Philips and his wife Harriet Burt.
I.   Sally Tart Philips, born March 22, 1835, m. December 7,
      1851 Col. Francis Marion Parker, C.S.A., son of Theophilus
      Parker of Tarboro and his wife Mary Toole.
      They had issue:
      1. Mary Parker m. Joseph John Battle. (Battle Book)
      2. James Philips Parker, born 1855.
      3. Theophilus Parker, born 1857, died 1920 unmarried.
      4. Harriet Burt Parker, born 1860, m. Peter Arrington
         Spruill. They had issue:
         (1) Peter A. Spruill, died France 1918.
         (2) Mary James Spruill, d. s. p.
         (3) William E. Spruill, m. (1) Florence Chalk; (2) Mary
             Ann Battle.
         (4) Frank Barker Spruill, married Frances Philips, of
             whom later.
      5. Haywood Parker, born 1864 of Ashville, N.C., m. Jose-
         phine Patton .
      6. Francis Marion Parker, born 1867, died unmarried 1913.
      7. Sally P. Parker, born 1870
      8. Kate D. Parker, born 1873.
      9. Frederick M. Parker, born 1875.
II.   Susan Sims Philips, born March 6, 1836, died in infancy.
III. Frederick Philips, born June 13, 1838, prominent lawyer
      and judge, Tarboro, N.C. died June 14, 1905, m. 1864 Mar-
      tha S. Hyman, 1840-1925, daughter of Henry Hyman and
      Martha E. Porter. They had issue:
      1. Anne D. Philips, born May 16, 1866, m. October 22, 1890
         Herbert Worth Jackson of Richmond, Va.

2. Mary Philips, married Hal. Wood of Edenton.
3. James Jones Philips, born 1869.
4. Martha Hyman Philips, married Dr. Woodward.
5. Josephine Philips, born October 26, 1878, married April 27, 1905, Albert Pike of Rockbridge County, Va.
6. Lela Burt Philips, married James D. Gillam.
7. Frederick Philips.
8. Henry Hyman Philips, married Ethel Skinner.

IV. Susan Sims Philips, second of the name, born September 15, 1842, m. Feb.19, 1861, Joseph John Battle as his first wife.
V. William Burn Philips, born March 26, 1844, died Jan.29,1856.
VI. Joseph Battle Philips, born Jan.8, 1848, m.(1) Pattie Battle; (2) Mary Marriott. See Battle Book for descendants of both marriages.
VII. John Ward Philips, born Jan.31, 1850, of whom later.
VIII. Harriet Amanda Philips, born October 18, 1851, m. Nov.7, 1870, Hon. Benjamin Hickman Bunn, Member of Congress and prominent in local civic affairs. He was the son of Redmond Bunn of "Benvenue", Nash County, N.C., and his wife Mary Bryan.

Harriet Philips and Benjamin H. Bunn had issue:
1. Mary Bryan Bunn m. George Lewis of Wimberly, M.D. and had issue.
2. Harriet Amanda Bunn, d.s.p.
3. James Philips Bunn, atty in Rocky Mount, N.C. m. Ella Lee Moorman and had issue.
4. Elizabeth Bunn - unmarried.
5. Redmond Bunn, d.s.p.
6. Benjamin H. Bunn m. Mavis Lindsey and had issue.
7. Laura Maud Bunn m. Kemp Davis Battle. (See S.V.F. p.   )
8. Katherine Bunn m. William Coleman Woodard of Rocky Mount. 5 children.

IX. Laura Maud Philips, born July 1, 1853, m. 1873, John Peter ARRINGTON.
X. Elizabeth Jane Philips, born May 4, 1855, m. George Cullen Battle on November 10, 1875. See Battle Book for descendants.
XI. Martha Parker Philips, born Jan.18, 1857, died in infancy.
XII. Walter Everett Philips, born July 17, 1860, died unmarried May 2, 1939.

6. John Ward Philips, son of Dr. James J. Philips, born 1850, died October 30, 1902, Rocky Mount, N.C., m. Feb.28, 1877, Katherine Hart Wimberly, born 1859, daughter of George L. Wimberly (1836-1924) and his wife Frances Jane Whitfield.

John Ward Philips and Katherine Wimberly had issue.
I. John Ward Philips, born 1878, died unmarried.
II. Frances Philips, born 1880, m.(1) Augustus M. Shaw, (2) Frank Parker Spruill, see above, grandson of Sally Tart Philips.
Issue of 1st marriage:
1. William Shaw, President Peoples Bank, Rocky Mount, N.C. m. Burt Perry, daughter of Elijah Boddie Perry.
Issue of 2nd marriage:

2. Frank Parker Spruill, born 1910, attorney in Rocky Mount, N.C., m. Polly Irby Easley and has issue: Anna Easley Spruill, born 1940; Harriet Burt Spruill, born 1943: and Frank Parker Spruill, born 1952.
3. Edward Muse Spruill, born 1912, an Episcopal Clergyman and rector of Grace Church, Plymouth, N.C. M m. Florence Estelle Eagles and has issue: Florence Estelle Spruill.
4. Katherine Wimberly Spruill, born 1916, m. William B. Harrison of Rocky Mount and has issue: Frances Wimberly Harrison, born 1942; William B. Harrison, born 1943; Frank Spruill Harrison, born 1946, and Katherine Curtis Harrison, born 1950.
III. Maude Philips, born 1882.
IV. Harriet Philips, born 1884.
V. George Wimberly Philips, born 1886, m. Mattie Grimes.
VI. Robert Diggs Philips, born 1889, m. Mrs. Lillian Atkinson.
VII. Walter Everett Philips, born 1891.
VIII. Katherine Wimberly Philips, of whom later.

7. Katherine Wimberly Philips, daughter of John Ward Philips, born August 12, 1898, m. October 6, 1923, in the Church of the Good Shepherd, Rocky Mount, N.C., Hassell Howard Weeks, born October 11, 1894, died Dec.29, 1953, the son of George Weeks and Elizabeth Legett of Edgecombe County, N.C. They had issue:
I. Hassell Howard Weeks, Jr., born June 26, 1925, Rocky Mount, N.C.; attended the University of N.C.; m.June 6, 1953 at Nashville, Nash County, N.C. Helen Williams Bachelor of Nashville.
II. John Philips Weeks, born June 20, 1931, Rocky Mount, N.C.

ROGERS of SURRY
by
Dr. B. C. Holtzclaw

Beside the family of John Rogers treated below, there were two other Rogers families living in Surry County in the latter half of the 17th Century. One was that of Joseph Rogers of Lawnes Creek Parish, who disappears from the records toward the end of the century and apparently left no issue. The other was that of Richard Rogers of Southwark Parish, who lived at Cabin Point, near the Charles City line. Richard Rogers died in 1678, his will, dated March 27, 1678 and probated in Surry May 7, 1678, mentions his sons John, Richard and William, and his daughter Mary. His widow, Mrs. Grace Rogers, was granted probate on his estate June 22, 1678. The daughter Mary Rogers married John Rivers, and they made the inventory and were appointed administrators of John Rogers in 1697 (D. & W. 1693-1709, pp. 138, 140). William Rogers, son of Richard Rogers, died in Surry in 1701. His will, dated Feb. 1700, and probated Sept. 2, 1701, mentions his wife Elizabeth, sister Mary Rivers, and "nephews" Grace, Mary and John Rivers (id. pp. 215, 225). As Richard Rogers, son of Richard, does not appear in the records, it would seem that this family died out in the male line.

John Rogers of Southwark Parish, Surry County, ancestor of the Rogers family which follows, was perhaps identical with a John Rogers, aged 18, who came in the "George" to Virginia Aug. 21, 1735 (Hotten, p. 124). If this is correct, his birth date would be 1617. However, he was excused from paying levies in Surry County May 6, 1673, and was agin excused July 7, 1674, as "an old impotent man" (Order Bk. 1, pp. 23, 59), which would indicate that he was born at an earlier date. John Rogers represented James City Co. (then including Surry) in the House of Burgesses in the session of 1644-45 (Journals, I, p. xviii), and was apparently living in James City County in 1658, as Carberry Kegan of Isle of Wight County, in his will dated January 12, 1657, and probated Feb. 9, 1657/8, leaves a bequest to "my countryman John Rogers of the Middle Plantation". John Rogers first appears in the records of Surry on October 1, 1659, when John Dixon left him some property (Book 1, p. 143). On May 14, 1666, he was granted 200 acres in Surry (Nugent, p. 562). His latter years were rather turbulent ones. He is probably identical with a John Rogers, called a Welshman, who on Feb. 26, 1671/2 is stated to have gone into debt and run away (Book 1, p. 404). If that is the case, however, he did not stay away from Surry long, as he appears constantly in the tithables from 1668 on. He was certainly involved rather seriously in Bacon's Rebellion, having gone with the rebels on Sept. 18, 1678, under their commander William Rookings and broken into John Solway's house

(D. &W. 1671-84, p.154). He was also accused of appropriating property during the rebellion that belonged to Robert Caufield and Arthur Allen (Order Bk.1, pp. 165, 167), and he was fined 400 lbs. of tobacco in 1677 by the House of Burgesses for signing a petition entitled "The Grievances of Surry Co." which was "highly scandalous and notoriously injurious to the Justices of Surry Co." (Journals, II, p.114). John Rogers married, probably rather late in life, Mary Booth, sister of Richard Booth of the Lower Parish of Isle of Wight Co., who with his wife Elizabeth made a deed of gift of land to John and Mary Rogers "my sister: Nov. 9, 1681 (Boddie, p.590). He last appears in the records in the latter part of 1682 and early 1683, when as "John Rogers, Sr." with his wife "Mary Rogers ye elder", he deeded to Edward Grantham of Isle of Wight County the land granted him in 1666 (Surry Bk.2, pp.318, 319, 328, 341; Boddie, p.593). John Rogers left no will, but probably died soon after 1683. The names of his three sons are found in the tithables of Surry, 1674 shows "John Rodgers and his sonn"; 1677, "John Rogers and William and John his two sons"; 1678, "John Rogers and John Rogers his son and Danll his son", while the son William is shown as an independent tithable in that year. William Rogers was probably the eldest son, and as indicated by the list of tithables, born about 1657/8; John Rogers, the second son was born 1660-61'and married Hester ---------, who appears with him briefly in 1684 (Order Bk.1, p.467). Daniel Rogers, the third son, was born 1661-2, and probably died in 1678, as he does not appear in the tithables of 1679.

William Rogers, son of John and Mary Rogers, was born in Surry Co. about 1657-8 and died there in 1727. He married first about 1678, when the tithables show him as head of a household, and had one son, William Rogers, mentioned in his will as "son of my former wife." This son was born in 1679 or 1680, as he appears first as a tithable in his father's household in 1696. The name of William Rogers' first wife is unknown. It may have been Mary, as his mother is referred to as "Mary Rogers ye elder" in 1682. However, there is a deed in Isle of Wight Co. from William Rogers and Dorothy his wife during the 1680's which may identify this couple, though they are called "of Isle of Wight" rather than Surry (Isle of Wight D.&W. 1661-1719, p.365). In any case, his first wife died after a few years, and he married second in 1686 Elizabeth daughter of Robert Cartwright of Surry Co. Robert Cartwright first appears May 3, 1664, when he gave bond for the estate of Elizabeth Chivers, daughter of Thomas Chivers, decd. (Book 1, p.234). A grant of land to Arthur Allen August 24, 1665, mentions the importation into the colony of Robert and Richard Cartwright (Nugent, p.485). Robert Cartwright's wife was probably a relative of Hezekiah Bunnill and wife Joan of Surry (see Williams Family). Robert Cartwright's will, dated Feb.19, 1676, and probated in Surry Co. April 10, 1676, mentions his friend Benjamin Harrison; brother Richard Cartwright; Hezekiah Bunnill; his eldest daughter Elizabeth, to whom gifts by John Orchard, Richard Cartwright and Joan Bunnill are mentioned; his son Robert Cartwright to whom he leaves all his lands; William Carpender, who is to have the keeping of his son Hezekiah and his daughter Elizabeth; and his daughter

Mary, whom he entrusts to his brother Richard Cartwright (Book 2, p. 106). On Jan. 6, 1679 Hezekiah Bunnill gave bond for the estate of Elizabeth Cartwright, and on Sept. 7, 1686 William Rogers, having married Elizabeth Cartwright, orphan, receipted Mr. Bunnill for his wife's estate (O.B. 1, p. 530). Elizabeth's brother, Robert Cartwright, died in Surry Co. in 1699. His will, dated Oct. 1699 and probated Nov. 7, 1699, mentions his sister Elizabeth Rogers; his sister Mary; his goddaughter Sarah Rogers; and William Rogers. William Rogers' will, dated Jan. 28, 1725 and probated in Surry May 17, 1727, mentions son William, "son of my former wife" and children Benjamin, Robert, Elizabeth Ellis, Mary Bennett, Sarah Bennett, Priscilla Proctor, Joseph, Jane, and "my youngest son William which I had by my wife Elizabeth". Mary Bennett was the wife of James Bennett who died in Brunswick in 1752. (Vol. 1, p. 59)

Beside Joseph Rogers, who will be treated later, the Albemarle Parish Register shows the death of Benjamin Rogers May 28, 1744. This was apparently Benjamin, son of William and Elizabeth. The records of Sussex Co. and the Albemarle Parish Register also show the following, apparently the descendants of the two sons named William Rogers, though as there is some discrepancy between the wills and parish records, the separate records will simply be listed here:

(1) The will of William Rogers, probated in Sussex Co. in 1770, mentions sons William and Benjamin; Joseph Rogers son of Reuben Rogers; wife Prudence; daughter Priscilla wife of George Barrack.

(2) The will of another William Rogers, probated in Sussex Co. in 1778, mentions wife Mary, daughter Elizabeth, sons Nathan, Reuben and Jesse.

The Albemarle Parish Register shows the following, corrensponding more or less with the above wills:

(1) Children of William Rogers, Sr. and Frances his wife:
   a. Martha, born May 26, 1741.
   b. Joseph, born November 4, 1743 (Joseph Rogers godfather).
   c. John, b. Jan. 12, 1749/50.
(2) Children of William Rogers, Jr. and Catherine his wife:
   a. Frederick b. Aug. 26, 1741.
   b. William b. Nov. 20, 1743.
   c. Levi b. Jan. 11, 1745/6.
   d. Agnes b. May 16, 1748.
   e. Sterling b. Oct. 15, 1753.
   f. Archibald b. Dec. 26, 1754.
(3) Children of Nathan and Elizabeth Rogers:
   a. Randolph b. June 13, 1759.
   b. Anne b. Aug. 12, 1762.
   c. Allen b. March 13, 1770.
(4) Children of Reuben and Elizabeth Rogers:
   a. Lucy b. Oct. 17, 1758.
   b. Thomas b. Aug. 16, 1762.
   c. Molly, b. June 17, 1775.
(5) Children of David and Jane Rogers:
   a. Anne b. June 17, 1761.
   b. Allen b. 1765, christened Mar. 17, 1765.

(6) Children of Jesse and Faith Rogers:
   a. Richard, born Aug.17,1768.
   b. John b.June 28, 1770.
   c. Langston b.Oct.23,1762.

Joseph Rogers, probably the next youngest son of William and Elizabeth (Cartwright) Rogers, was born in Surry County about 1700. He and his wife Mary were living in Albemarle Parish, Surry Co. in 1740, when their youngest daughter, Faith, was born. While still living in Surry Co. he was deeded land in Bertie Co. N.C. on May 6, 1741 by Thomas Moyle and John Phillips (Bertie D.B.F. p.215). He was still living in Surry in 1743, when he stood godfather to Joseph, son of William and Frances Rogers, in Albemarle Parish; and in the same year, he and Thomas Clifton were engaged in a suit in chancery in Surry, which was finally dismissed on the agreement of the two parties (Surry O.B. 1741-3). Soon after this he moved to North Carolina, and died in Northampton Co., N.C. in 1752. His will, dated Feb.18, 1752, and probated at the February Court, 1752, leaves his son John 5 s.; to son Joseph 300 acres of land; sons Aaron and Isham a horse, saddle and bridle and 20 s. each; sons Reuben and Drury, a mare, saddle and bridle each; son Michael a horse and one great Bible; daughter Sarah Tarver 5 s.; daughter Mary Lowrey two ewes, a ram and a loom "upon Learning Faithey to weave well"; the rest of the land to be sold and the money remaining to be equally divided between Reuben, Drury, Michael and Faith Rogers, Reuben and Drury to go to school two years, Faith one year, and Michael as long as possible; sons John and Joseph Rogers, executors. Issue of Joseph and Mary Rogers:

I.   John Rogers, probably identical with a John Rogers who was a sergeant in the French and Indian War in North Carolina; perhaps identical with a John Rogers who died in Wake Co., N.C. in 1779, his heirs being James, Josiah, Sarah, John, Priscilla, Rebecca, and Penelope Rogers, and daughter Mary Hillman.

II.   Joseph Rogers, continued to live in Northampton Co., N.C.; where he died in 1791. His will, dated Sept. 20, 1788 and probated March 15, 1791, mentions as his heirs Mark, Olive, Michael, John and Mary.

III.   Aaron Rogers had moved by 1754 to Johnston Co., N.C. with his younger brothers, Isham, Reuben, Drury and Michael; in that year Aaron Rogers was Ensign in Capt. James Wooten's Co. of the Johnston Co. Regiment, his brother Isham was Drummer, Drury a Sergeant, and Michael a private, in the same company (N.C. Col. and State Rec., 22, p.332)

IV.   Isham Rogers, nothing further known except the above reference.

V.   Mary Rogers m. -------- Lowry.

VI.   Sarah Rogers m.-------- Tarver.

VII.   Reuben Rogers, born Nov.1, 1735, in Surry Co., Va., d. 1829 in Georgia; m. Dec.15, 1767 in Johnston Co., N.C. Temperance James (b.Aug.24, 1751). Reuben Rogers moved to Georgia, probably just prior to the Revolution, and served as a soldier in the Revolution there (Knight "Ga.Roster of the Rev." p.150). He fought in the Battle of Kettle Creek and

361

other skirmishes, and he and his wife had the following children: (cf. L. L. Cody " Cody-Rogers of Georgia")
1. John Rogers, born April 25, 1769, m. Nancy Swain.
2. Faith Rogers, b. May 19, 1771, m. Mr. Darden.
3. Mary Rogers, b. Oct. 28, 1772.
4. Clary Rogers, b. Aug 11, 1774.
5. Nancy Rogers, b. Mar. 3, 1776, m. Mr. Saxon.
6. Phoebe Rogers, b. Jan. 15, 1778, m. Frederick Brown.
7. Temperance Rogers b. Oct. 21, 1780, m. Thomas Lockett.
8. Reuben Rogers, Jr., b. Sept. 10, 1782, m. 1810 Elizabeth
   Emerson.
9. Joseph Rogers born Feb. 9, 1784, m. Frances Gardener.
10. Rebecca Rogers b. Jan. 2, 1786, m. Jan. 18, 1818 Michael
    Cody.
11. Abner Rogers b. Oct. 19, 1788.
12. Cullen Rogers b. May 7, 1790, m. his cousin Jane Wom-
    mack, daughter of Sherwood Wommack and Nancy Rogers.
13. Asenath Rogers b. Nov. 11, 1792.
14. Sarah Rogers, b. Oct. 15, 1794, m. Josiah Swain.
VIII. Drury Rogers, b. abt. 1737. See later.
IX. Michael Rogers, youngest son, was old enough to be a private
    in Capt. Wooten's Co. of Johnston Co. militia in 1754. Rec-
    ords of Michael Rogers appear both in Wake Co., N. C. and
    in Greene Co., Ga. Olds "Abstracts of N. C. Wills" shows a
    Michael Rogers who died in Wake Co., N. C. in 1797, his
    will mentioning wife Celia, and children Tabitha, Rebecca,
    Allen, Bennett, Alice, Willis, Mary and Sarah. Willie or
    Willis Rogers is given as making his will in 1803 in Wake
    County, N. C., and mentioning his mother Celia, and heirs,
    Allen, Berry, Willis, Mary, Talitha, Rebecca and Sarah.
    On the other hand, the records of Greene Co., Ga. show
    that Michael Rogers was one of the original settlers of the
    county, was a captain of militia in 1787, a Justice of Greene
    Co. in 1790, and a Captain of militia of Hancock Co. in 1796.
    In Hancock Co. Michael Rogers made a deed of gift to his
    children in 1804, naming as legatees sons John, James,
    Willis, Cacle and Berry Rogers, daughters Becky and Sally
    Rogers; and wife Priscilla (Book G, p. 154, Clerks Office).
    There is some confusion in the above records, but the sim-
    ilarity of names seems to indicate that they were all the
    same family.
X. Faith Rogers, born Aug. 20, 1740, christened Dec. 7, 1740
   in Albemarle Parish, Surry County, Va.

Drury Rogers, son of Joseph and Mary Rogers, was born about
1737 in Surry Co., Va., and died in 1791 in Wilkes Co., Ga. Soon
after his father's death in Northampton Co., N. C. in 1752, he
moved with several of his brothers to Johnston Co., N. C., and
was a Sergeant in Capt. James Wooten's militia company there in
1754 (N. C. Col. and State Rec., 22, p. 332). He married about
1758 or 1759 Tabitha ------- of Johnston Co. On Feb. 3, 1773
he sold his land in Johnston Co., N. C. and on Oct. 15th of the
same year he made application for land before the Ceded Lands
Commission of Georgia, stating that his family consisted of his

wife, three sons and five daughters, the children being from 13
to 1 year of age (Davidson, "Records of Ga.", Vol. I, p.12). He
was settled near the Quaker Colony of Wrightsboro in 1774, and
joined a number of others in the vicinity in signing a protest re-
pudiating resolutions passed Aug.10, 1774 by the hot-headed patri-
ots of the coast (Knight "Landmarks of Ga.",I, p.766). When the
Revolution actually broke out, however, he gave up his pacifist
tendencies, and he and his three oldest sons, Drury, Jr., Brittain
and Burwell, all served in the Revolution in the Georgia troops,
for which service he was granted land on the Ogeechee River in
Wilkes and Washington Cos. (Knight "Ga. Roster of the Revolution"
pp.149, 275, 237, 238, 391). His eldest son, Drury, Jr., was
dead by 1785, and his land bounty was granted to his father, in addition to the latter's own bounty. Drury Rogers was living in Wilkes
Co. during the Revolution. In 1779 he gave evidence against Tories
(Saunders "Early History of Alabama", p.420) and was in that
year appointed a Justice of the Peace in Wilkes Co. (Joseph Ha-
bersham Chapter D.A.R. Hist.Collections, III, p.152). Drury
Rogers died in Wilkes Co., Ga. in 1791, his wife Tabitha being
appointed his administratrix Feb.5, 1791. Tabitha Rogers died in
Wilkes Co. in 1794, her will, dated Oct.28, 1793 and probated Feb.
11, 1794, mentioning 10 children, Burwell, Faith, Polly, Michael,
John (under 21), Tillatha Stokes, Tabby Kendrick, Sally Wommack,
Cilla Rimes, and Brittain. An account of her estate given by Brittain Rogers, executor, July 6, 1797, shows receipts for their
shares of the property from Samuel Stokes and John Rimes, and
a receipt from Thomas Criddle for the tuition of Michael Rogers
in 1796 (Davidson, op.cit., p.281). Issue of Drury and Tabitha
Rogers:
I.   Drury Rogers, Jr., born about 1759-60,d.s.p. before 1785.
II.   Brittain Rogers, born Oct.11, 1781, in Johnston Co., N.C.,
      died April 22, 1835 in Monroe Co., Ga., married Elizabeth
      Lockett (b.July 19, 1767,d.Feb.25,1845); they were ancestors
      of Mrs. H.H. Trottie of Decatur, Ga.
III. Burwell Rogers, born about 1762-3.
IV.   Talitha Rogers, born about 1764-5, m. Samuel Stokes.
V.   Tabitha Rogers, born about 1766-7, m. James Kendricks.
      (See later)
VI.   Sarah Rogers, born about 1768-9, m.Mr.Wommack.
VII. Cilla (Priscilla?) Rogers, born abt.1770-71, m.John Rimes.
VIII. Faith Rogers, b.1772, m.Mr.Stevens.
IX.   Mary Rogers, born about 1774.
X.   Michael Rogers, born about 1776.
XI.   John Rogers, born about 1778.

    Tabitha Rogers, daughter of Drury and Tabitha Rogers, mar-
ried prior to 1793 in Wilkes Co., Ga. James Kendrick, born probably in Chatham Co., N.C. 1765-1770, died in Putnam Co., Ga.
1817-1820. Tabitha Rogers Kendrick died in Putnam Co. in late
Oct. or early Nov., 1833. James Kendrick appears in the tax-lists
of Putnam Co. in 1817, but was dead by the time of the U.S. Census
of 1820. James Kendrick was living in Wilkes Co., Ga., in 1793,
but had moved to Baldwin (later Putnam) Co., by 1805. He was
probably the son of Burwell and Catherine Kendrick of Chatham Co.,

363

N.C. and Wilkes and Washington Counties, Ga.

Issue of James and Tabitha (Rogers) Kendrick:

I.   Isham Kendrick, born about 1795, m. Ann Stubbs in Putnam County Sept. 1827.

II.   Drury Kendrick m. Amy Holland in Putnam Co. 1808-1816; moved to Troup Co., Ga., where he was a Captain of Cavalry under Gen. Scott in the Creek Indian War of 1836.

III. James Kendrick.

IV.   Susan Kendrick, m. Mr. Stubbs.

V.   Tabitha Kendrick, m. Samuel Holland 1808-1816 in Putnam Co.

VI.   Elizabeth Kendrick, m. Rev. John H. CLARK. (See Clark Family)

VII. Celia Kendrick m. Pleasant J. Mullens and lived in Jasper Co., Ga. Issue:

1. Catherine Mullens m. Dr. King.
2. Mary T. Mullens, m. Henry Lawrence.
3. Blandina Mullens, m. Mr. Roberts.

VIII. Julia Caroline Kendrick, born 1813, m. Benjamin W. CLARK. (See Clark Family)

IX.   Catherine Kendrick m. Mr. Baisden, and had a son Thomas Baisden.

SORRELL, EARLE, WARREN
of
Westmoreland

Robert Sorrell, who patented 800 acres in James City County,
April 10, 1651, "being an island within Warrancy Creek, towards
Joyner's neck, bounded by the lands of Edward Cole and Bennett
Freeman, was the ancestor of this family. (C.P. 212).
    A Robert Sorrell was a headright of Benjamin Harrison who
patented land on the Surry side of James City in 1637. Also a
Robert and John Sorrell were headrights of Thomas Wright of
Lower Norfolk who patented land there in 1647. Francis Fleetwood
used three of Thomas Wright's headrights for patenting land in
Lower Norfolk in 1652, including Robert and John Sorrell (C.P.
166, 274). These headrights may have been Robert of James City
and John his son who were returning from England.
    Robert Sorrell, who patented land in 1651, is said to be a son
of Robert Sorrell of Essex Co., England, who married a Miss
Everard (37V 159). This Sorrell family appears in the Visitations
of Essex in 1634. Robert had a brother John who married Mary
Aylett. This supposition is not authenticated by any wills or parish
register records but is said to have been taken from a manuscript
in the Archives of the State of Alabama at Montgomery. The family
was seated at Waltham Magna and Stebbing, Essex (Id.160).
    The James City records are lost but Robert Sorrell appears in
the General Court Minutes in several suits previous to 1675. It is
probable that he married a daughter of William Hockaday or of
William Hockaday Jr. of New Kent for on Jan.20, 1670, the General Court ordered that "in the difference between Mr. John Waters, executor of William Hockaday, Jr., decd., and Robert Sorrell
on behalf of himself and children about certain legacies given unto
them by the will of the said Hockaday that the order of the New Kent
Court for payment of the legacies be confirmed and the said Waters
ordered to pay cost (M.C.G.C. 223). William Hockaday Sr. received large grants of land in New Kent (See C.P. index).
    Robert[1] Sorrell patented 700 acres of land in James City, Nov.
20, 1653 "on the Southernmost Branch of Warrancy Creek next to
Henry Soanes" (C.P. 240). He was one of Berkeley's adherents
and fell "in his Majesty's service before James City". This was
in Berkeley's siege of Jamestown. The General Court ordered
Feb.20, 1682, that "Rebecca Sorrell, the widow of Captain Robert
Sorrell, who was lately killed in his Majesty's service, and his
estate since plundered and taken away by the Rebells, be allowed
out of the public levy 4000 lbs. tbco and what of her goods can be
found returned to her" (B.J. 1682).
    The only known child of Robert Sorrell was his son JOHN SOR-
RELL mentioned in the will of John Erwin of Westmoreland in 1716.
and in the will of THOMAS[3] SORREL. son of John[2] in 1726. Thomas[2]

Sorrell also mentioned his brother JOHN[3] SORRELL in the same will (See later).

Thomas[3] Sorrell moved to Westmoreland where he was Deputy Clerk of the Court. He married Elizabeth, daughter of Daniel Ocanny of Westmoreland who in his will dated and probated in 1716 mentions his "son in law Thomas Sorrell", and also his Crabbe grandchildren (Fotherfill p. 61). Osman Crabbe, son in law of John Ocanny, died in 1713 and in his will appointed his "brother in law Thomas Sorrell" trustee (Id. 69).

Thomas[3] Sorrell made his will in Westmoreland Jan. 12, 1725; probated Feb. 22, 1726, as follows: "to son JAMES the land I live on; to son JOHN all my lands at the head of the Nominy where I formerly lived and the land devised to me by my father in law Daniel Ocanny; to son JAMES the land in James City Co. which my honored FATHER JOHN SORRELL devised to me and also one third of my mill; two thirds of mill to son JOHN. To my nephew THOMAS SORRELL, land where John Holloway now lives on condition that my nephew quit claim title to land adjoining my dwelling seat as promised.

"I have purchased land in James City devised by my father to my BROTHER JOHN SORRELL, deceased. To wife all personal property during children's minority to be divided equally between all my children. To my aforesaid nephew and his sisters, ELIZABETH and FRANCES a mourning ring apiece. to daughters ANN and WINIFRED (35V33).

His children were:
I. Elizabeth, mentioned in will of John Erwin 1716, but not in father's will evidently died young; 2. John
II. John
III. James
IV. Winifred
V. Ann, given a legacy in will of John Wright 1713, married SAMUEL EARLE. Burgess from Fauquier 1742 (37V 159).

John[2] Sorrell, son of Robert and brother of Thomas[2], evidently died in James City Co. His wife was named "Anne" for John Erwin mentions his goddaughter, FRANCES, daughter of John and Anne Sorrell, in his will (Fothergill-57). The date of John[2] Sorrell's death is not known. He may have been the John sorrell mentioned as a headright with his father, Robert Sorrell.

His children were:
I. Elizabeth Sorrell.
II. Thomas Sorrell who whith his wife, Martha, deeded John Tuberville, Dec. 24, 1772, 186 acres (except family burying ground) on the north side of Nominy mill pond and south side of John A. Washington's mill pond, adjoining land purchased of Mr. JOHN BUSHROD from John Sorrell, the said land being inherited by the said Thomas from his father, JOHN SORREL (id.)
III. Frances Sorrell.

Ann Sorrell, daughter of Elizabeth (O'Canny) and Thomas Sorrell, married Samuel[3] Earle, son of Phillis and Samuel[2] Earle of Westmoreland County. Samuel Earle was born in Westmoreland in 1692; was educated at the College of William and

Mary and was a Member of the House of Burgesses, 1743-44. (B.
J. VI-p. 83). He was also High Sheriff of Frederick County; Church
Warden of the Parish in 1751; Major of Col. George William Fair-
fax's Colonial Regiment and Justice of the County Court. Anna
Sorrell Earle died in 1748 and is buried in what is now Warren
County near "Greenway Court". Mr. Earle is said to have married
secondly Elizabeth Hilbrock.
   Children of first wife:
I.   Samuel Earle, born 1727.
II.   Judge Baylis Earle, born 1734, married Mary Prince.
III. Col. John Earle, born June 5, 1737; m. (1) Thomasine
      Prince, (see later); (2) Rebecca Wood.
IV.   Rachel Earle, m. Wilcox in Virginia.
Vm   Hannah Earle, m. Wilcox in Virginia.

   Colonel John Earle, son of Ann (Sorrell) and Samuel Earle,
was born in Westmoreland County, Va., June 5, 1737, and died
in Rutherford County, N.C. between Jan.12, 1799 and Nov.5, 1804.
He married, first, Thomasine Prince, born ca.1746, died in Rutherford County between 1777 and 1785. He married secondly Rebecca
(Berry) Wood, widow of John, about 1786. Col. John Earle served
on the Committee of Safety for Tryon Co., N.C., in October 1775,
and was a Justice of the Peace in Rutherford from July 4, 1781
to 1794 (Griffin: Hist. of Tryon, pp.28, 129).
   Children of first wife:
I.   General John Baylis Earle, born Oct.23, 1766, m.(1) Sarah
      Taylor; (2) Nancy Ann Douglas.
II.   Anna Berry Earle, born Aug.3, 1768, m. Major John Lewis.
III. Elizabeth Sorrell Earle, born Aug.3, 1771, m.(1) Gray
      Briggs; (2) William Hannon. (See later)
IV.   Caroline Matilda Earle, born Feb.23, 1774, m. Edwin Hannon.
V.   George Washington Earle, born Feb.22, 1777, m. Elizabeth
      Earle.
   Children of second wife:
VI.   Dr. Joseph Berry Earle, born Feb.29, 1788, m. Rebecca
      Sloan.
VII. Lydia Maverick Earle, born Jan.4, 1790, m. William B.
      Prince.
VIII. Eleanor Kay Earle, born Jan.7,1791, m. Silas Whitten.
IX.   Letitia Sorrell Earle, born Jan.16, 1793, m. Laban Poole.
X.   Amaryllis Earle, born Feb.16, 1795, m. Elisha Bomar.
XI.   Harriet Harrison Earle, born Aug.27, 1797, m. Ephraim
      Roddy.

   Elizabeth Sorrell Earle, daughter of Colonel John Earl and his
first wife, Thomasine Prince, was born August 3, 1771, married
ca.1788-1789, Gray Briggs of Rutherford County, N.C. Gray
Briggs was a surety on the marriage bond of Jesse Briggs and
Esther Miller, Dec.7, 1781. This indicates some relationship between Jesse and Gray Briggs.
   Jesse came from Brunswick County, Va., for Jan.1, 1794, he
deeded land in Brunswick while a resident of Stokes County (D.B.
15, p.532). Howell Briggs of Brunswick on July 13, 1774, made
his will in Brunswick Co., same probated Aug.22, 1774. His le-

gatees were wife (not named), dau. Betsy, nephew JESSE, son of Thomas Briggs, father-in-law, John Quarles was executor. (W. B. 4, 401).

Another Howell Briggs who married Lucy Gray made his will Dec. 16, 1722, probated Sept. 21, 1775, in Sussex. He named wife Lucy; son GRAY BRIGGS; dau. Elizabeth, wife of George Kerr; granddaus. Elizabeth and Mary Pride, daughter of Mary Briggs and her husband Hallcott Pride; grandson John Howell Briggs (W. B. C-1772-85). The above Gray Briggs is said to have died in Nottoway County, Va.

Gray Briggs of Rutherford patented (subject of this sketch) 200 acres in Rutherford in 1796 but sold that in the same year. He evidently died in 1796 for his widow Elizabeth married William Hannon March 2, 1797 (Marriage bonds).

Children of Elizabeth (Sorrell) Earle and Gray Briggs:

I.   Robert H. Briggs.
II. Thomasine E. Briggs, m. William Holcombe. (See later)
III. Elizabeth Briggs, m. James Hunter.
     (Above children's names taken from Minute Docket 1807-1830, page 9, Superior Court of Rutherford)

Thomasine Earle Briggs, daughter of Gray Briggs and Elizabeth Sorrell Earle, was born Nov. 22, 1791, Rutherford Co, , N. C. died June 4, 1842, Anderson Dist. , S. C.; married August 13, 1816, Rutherford County, N. C. William Holcombe, born April 7, 1792, Greenville Dist., S. C.; died May 14, 1842, Anderson Dist. , S. C. He served for several terms as Judge of Probate for Pickens District, S. C.

Children:

I.   Addison Warren Holcombe, born May 23, 1817, m. Mary Catherine Benson.
II.   Washington Earle Holcombe, born April 20, 1819; m. Elizabeth Caroline Robinson. (See later)
III. Elias James Holcombe, born Feb. 19, 1821, m. (1) Narcissus Whitten; (2) Fannie Cleveland.
IV.   Robert Elliott Holcombe, born Aug. 4, 1823, m. (1) Eliza Caroline Arnold; (2) Martha Elvira Bowen.
V.   Elizabeth Maria Holcombe, born Aug. 24, 1825, m. Bluford D. Smith.
VI.   Minor Brown Holcombe, born Oct. 17, 1827.
VII. Eliza Jane Holcombe, born July 2, 1830, m. (1) Fletcher Smith, (2) John D. Lowry.
VIII. Essie Cleveland Holcombe, m. Rufus Alexander Childs.

Washington Earle Holcombe, born April 20, 1819, Greenville Dist. , S. C.; died May 5, 1888, near Atlanta, Ga.; married Nov. 17, 1839, S. C. , Elizabeth Caroline Robinson, daughter of Dr. John and Eliza (Blassingame) Robinson, born 1819 Old Pendleton Dist. , S. C.: died 1885 near Atlanta, Ga.

Children:

I. William Henry Holcombe, born Feb. 22, 1841; m. Laura West.
II. Eliza Earle Holcombe, born Feb. 2, 1843, m. Dr. Thomas Alexander Evins (See later).

III.   Robert Elliott Holcombe, born 1843.
IV.   J.H. Holcombe, born 1846.
V.   John V. Robinson Holcombe, born Jan.23. 1849; m.Lucy
        Williams.
VI.   Samuel Maxwell Holcombe, born Oct.2, 1850.
VII.   Elias Earle Holcombe, born Feb.12, 1853.
VIII.   Ella Janie Holcombe, born Sept. 11, 1856.
IX.   Essie Cleveland Holcombe, born Nov.3, 1859.

    Eliza Earle Holcombe, daughter of Washington Earle and Eliza-
beth Caroline (Robinson) Holcombe, was born Feb.2, 1843, Pickens
Dist., S.C.; died Sept.3, 1915, New York City, N.Y. m.1866, S.C.
Dr. Thomas Alexander Evins, son of Samuel Nesbitt Evins and Eliza-
beth Cunningham Moore, born Nov.30, 1825, Spartanburg Dist,,
D.C.; died Nov.15, 1872, Anderson Co., S.C. Dr. Evins was a
physician and was commissioned a surgeon in the Confederate Army
July 20, 1860, and served throughout the War and was surrendered
by Gen. Robert E. Lee at Appomattox Court House.
        Children:
I.   Thomas Earle Evins, born April, 1867, m. Mary Margaret
        Woodward. (See later).
II.   Elizabeth Evins, born Oct.26, 1869, d.Nov.1, 1873.
III.   Samuel Holcombe Evins, born Dec.16, 1871; m.Ann Charity
        Johnson.

    Thomas Earle Evins, son of Dr. Thomas Alexander Evins
and Eliza Earle Holcombe, was born April 1867, Anderson Co.,
S.C., died July 18, 1900, aboard U.S. transport Sherman en route
from Phillipines to U.S.; m.Oct.25, 1893, Birmingham, Jefferson
Co., Ala., Mary Margaret Woodward, daughter of Joseph Hersey
Woodward and Martha Burt Metcalf, born July 4, 1872, Wheeling
Co., W.Va.; died March 17, 1930, Orlando, Orange Co., Fla. Dr.
Thomas Earle Evins was a physician. He served as Major and Chief
Surgeon of the U.S. Volunteers in Cuba and during the Philippine
Insurrection.
        Children:
I.   Margaret Woodward Evins, born Nov.24, 1895, m. William
        Micajah Spencer, Jr. (See later)
II.   Josephine Woodward Evins, born Oct.3, 1897, m.James
        Alexander Simpson, died May 3, 1921.

    Margaret Woodward Evins, daughter of Dr. Thomas Earle
Evins and Mary Margaret Woodward, was born Nov.24, 1895,
Birmingham, Ala.; m.June 23, 1915, Birmingham, Ala., William
Micajah Spencer, Jr.,, son of William Micajah Spencer and Bertha
Gracey Steele, born June 29, 1890, Gallion, Hale County, Ala.
Mrs. Spencer is a member of the D.A.R. by right of descent from
Colonel John Earle. (For an account of Mr. and Mrs. Spencer and
family see Vol. I, p.234).
        Children:
I.   Margaret Woodward Spencer, born June 15, 1916, m.Edgar
        G. Givhan, Jr.
II.   William Micajah Spencer, III, born Dec.10, 1920, m.Evalina
        Sommerville Brown.
III.   Bertha Underwood Spencer, born Oct.17, 1923, m.Adrian

A. Ringland, Jr.

Frances Sorrell, born Dec. 17, 1739, in North Carolina, d. 1827 in Robertson County, Tenn.; m. approx. 1761 in North Carolina, William Moss, born Nov. 12, 1729, in North Carolina; died Jan. 1, 1817 in Greenbrier, Robertson Co., Tenn. William Moss received a grant of 5000 acres of land in 1784 and 1794 in Western North Carolina, now Tennessee. Both dates appear on the grant.
Children:
I.   Katherine Moss, born 1763; m. Richard Swift. (See later)
II.   Thomas Ballard Sorrell Moss.
III.   Hannah Bushrod Moss, born Nov. 16, 1768; m. Reuben White.
IV.   Peggy Blanton, born Dec. 9, 1797.
V.   Spencer Swift, born Jan. 23, 1773.
VI.   William Swift, married Susie?

Katherine Moss, daughter of William and Frances (Sorrell) Moss, born 1763 in North Carolina, died Nov. 20, 1816, Greenbriar, Robertson Co., Tenn.; m. approx. 1788, Caswell (?) Co., North Carolina, Richard Swift, born 1766, North Carolina; died 1831, Greenbriar, Robertson Co., Tenn.
Children:
I.   Frances Bushrod Swift, born June 2, 1791; m. Sebirt Warren (See later)
II.   Sidney Swift, m. Susan ?
III.   Anthony Augustus (Gustavus?) Swift, born Aug. 8, 1804, m. Elizabeth England.
IV.   Park Bailey Swift, m.   Bryant.
V.   William Swift, m. Lucy Vaughn.
VI.   Richard Swift Jr., b. 1807, m. Mary Gargent Fulcher.
VII.   George A. Swift, b. 1812, m. Margaret McMurtry.
VIII.   Harriett Swift m. Daniel Murry.
IX.   Elizabeth Swift, m.   Warren.
X.   Peggy Swift, m. Thomas Dulin.
XI.   Mack Swift.

Frances Bushrod Swift, daughter of Richard and Katherine (Moss) Swift, was born June 2, 1791, Caswell (?) Co., N.C.; died Sept. 13, 1865, Walnut Hill, Marion County, Illinois; married March 1810 Robertson County, Tenn., Sebirt Asher Warren, born July 2, 1790, in Virginia; died Sept. 12, 1853, Bolivar, Polk Co., Missouri. Sebirt Warren served in the War of 1812-14. He was a Private under Capt. Gabriel Mastin, 2nd. Regiment, Gen. Andrew Jackson's W. Tennessee Militia. Enlisted Sept. 20, 1814, at Fayetteville, Tenn., and was discharged April 25, 1815, at Wilson Springs, Madison County, Mississippi Territory. On March 29, 1832, he was commissioned Captain in 62nd Regiment, Tennessee Militia by Wm. Carroll, Governor. Descendants still living in Tennessee say he was called "Colonel". He was a Whig and Abolitionist and gave up his slaves when he moved to Illinois. He was a plantation owner and a Methodist, a member of the Old Gideon Church at Greenbrier. He came to Robertson Co., Tenn., before 1810 and lived there until the summer of 1851 when he went to Illinois and Missouri in 1851.

Children:
I.   Hessa Warren, born Dec.17, 1811, m.Samuel Smiley.
II.   Anderson Warren, b.Oct.11, 1813, m.Susan Holman.
III. Jackson Warren, born May 21, 1816, m.Winnifred Shaw.
IV.   Lemual Warren, b.Oct.13, 1818, m.(1) Charity Wynn, (2)?
V.   John Wesley Warren, born Dec.12, 1820, m.(1) Jane Holman, (2) Melissa Collier.
VI.   Franklin Warren, b.July 19, 1823, m.(1)?; (2) Polly?
VII. William Warren, born Dec.16, 1825, m. Mrs. Margaret Agnes Poague Cross. (See later)
VIII. Lewis Warren, born Feb.9, 1829; m. (1) Polly Henry; (2)?
IX.   Stith Meade Warren, born Dec.17, 1832; d.Jan.22, 1864.
X.   Mary Ann Warren, b.Jan.10, 1835; m.Thomas Jefferson Sawyer.
XI.   Richard Swift Warren, b.Apr.22,1831 or 1837; seems to have died in infancy.

William Warren, son of Sebirt Asher and Frances Bushrod (Swift) Warren, was born Dec.16, 1825, Greenbrier, Robertson Co., Tenn.; died June 4, 1890, Pineville, McDonald Co., Missouri; married March 14, 1861, Princeton, Mercer Co., Missouri, Mrs. Agnes Poague Cross, daughter of James Moore Poague and Sarah Boyd Moore, born Dec.1, 1830, at Buchanan, Botetourt Co., Va., died Jan.19, 1890, at Pineville, McDonald Co., Missouri. William Warren was a farmer and a Methodist. He emigrated from Robertson Co., Tenn. to Illinois and Missouri in 1851.
Children:
I.   James Rutherford Warren, born Dec.26, 1861; d.Aug.23,1883.
II.   Lewis Warren, b.Mar.20,1863; m.Clara E. Fullerton. (See later).
III. Columbus Warren, b.Dec.22,1864; d.Nov.23, 1865.
IV.   Rosetta Warren, born July 5, 1867; m.Rice Shelton Eubank.
V.   Charles Wesley Warren, born April 12, 1869, died Jan.12, 1890.
VI.   Hessa Ann Warren, born March 1, 1871; m.Thomas Benton Hannon.

Lewis Warren, son of William and Margaret Agnes (Poague) Cross Warren, was born March 20, 1863, in Princeton, Mercer County, Missouri; died June 19, 1955, Seattle, Mt Co., Wash.; married March 30, 1897, Mt. Vernon, Lawrence Co., Missouri, Clara Elberta Fullerton, daughter of John William Fullerton and Martha Elizabeth Cagle, born July 2, 1869, Carthage, Jasper Co., Missouri; died June 27, 1949, Copalis Beach, Grays Harbor, Co., Washington (Residence at Colville, Wash.). Lewis Warren received his education at Pea Ridge Academy, Pea Ridge, Arkansas. He was a Presbyterian and a farmer. He resided in Mercer Co., Mo., Marion Co., Ill., and McDonald Co., Mo., came to Stevens Co., Wash., in 1902. He died at the age of 92 years and is buried in Acacia Memorial Park.
Children:
I.   Merle Eleanor Warren, born Aug.17, 1900; m.Paul Rees Ratliffe. (See later).
II.   Fleetwood Warren, b.Feb.19, 1902; m.Gladys Evelyn Goss.

III.   Sybil Warren, b. Oct. 5, 1903, m. Chester LeRoy Seeley.
IV.   Hubert Kenneth Warren, b. April 23, 1907, m. Reta Younker.

Merle Eleanor Warren, daughter of Lewis and Clara Elberta (Fullerton) Warren, was born August 17, 1900, in McDonald Co., Missouri; married Dec. 25, 1923 at Colville, Stevens Co., Wash., Paul Rees Ratliffe, son of Francis Asbury Ratliffe and Irena Rees, born Nov. 1, 1900 at LeRoy, McLean Co., Illinois.

Mrs. Ratliffe came to Washington with her parents and baby brother Fleetwood in 1902. She attended Western Washington College of Education, the University of Washington and was graduated from the Wastern Washington College of Education in 1922. She is a member of the O.E.S., D.A.R. and Delphian Society. Mr. Ratliffe was raised on a large wheat farm in the "Palouse" Country, attended Washington State College and is a Realtor in Seattle. They reside at 4742 - 11th Avenue, Seattle, Washington, and are members of the University Presbyterian Church.

Children:
I.   Paul Robert Ratliffe, born Aug. 6, 1925; m. Elizabeth Louise Risbell.
II.   Mark Warren Ratliffe, born Feb. 12, 1931; m. Jenny Evelyn Forrest.
III.   Francis Merle Ratliffe, born May 24, 1932; died Aug. 16, 1939.

372

ELIZABETH STOVER
Born 1786 or 1787
Married to William McKain, March 13, 1806
Lost on Orlean St. John on March 5, 1850

STOVER-McKAIN of SOUTH CAROLINA
(Continued from Page 162, Virginia Historical Genealogies)

Elizabeth Stover, daughter of Mary (Bradford) and John Stover of Lancaster County, S.C., born c.1786, died September 26, 1806, married William McKain, born May 26, 1778, died Dec.23, 1852, in Camden, S.C. His father Robert McKain died Sept.26, 1826; his mother, Abagail McKain died Sept.26, 1806.

The McKain family Bible shows that Mrs. Elizabeth Stover McKain was lost on the "Orlean St.John" on the Alabama River, March 5, 1850. This was listed in the World Almanac as the greatest steamboat disaster of its time. She was probably on her way to visit her brother William Bradford Stover of Wilcox County, Alabama, who was ill and died that same year. Her portrait is the frontspiece of this chapter.

Children:
I.   James R. McKain (1812-1850), druggist, intendant of Camden, m. Sarah Donalson, and had the following children:
    1. John J. McKain (1837-1862) killed in Peninsula Campaign.
    2. William McKain (1839-1866) m. Miss Patterson of Liberty Hill, S.C.
    3. Elizabeth McKain (1841-1876) m. Major E. E. Sill.
    4. Henrietta McKain (1844-1905) well known teacher of Memphis, Tenn.
    James is said to have perished in the "Orlean St.John" disaster.
II.   John McKain, moved West in early life.
III.   Dr. Wiley J. McKain, born Jan.12, 1818, died Feb.22, 1866; m. Anna A. Kennedy. (See later)
IV.   Martha McKain, m.Alphonse Catonnet.
V.   Mary McKain (1824-1910) m. George Shaw.
VI.   Sarah McKain (1826-1915), m.Capt. James I. Villepigue of Camden, N.C.

Dr. Wiley Jackson McKain, son of Elizabeth (Stover) and Robert McKain, was born Jan.12, 1818, and died Feb.22, 1866 in Camden, S.C.; on Jan.5, 1853 in Charleston, S.C. he married Anna Adela, daughter of Holly (Young) and Francis L. Kennedy, born Oct.6, 1831, died July 8, 1898 in Lee Co., S.C.

Dr. McKain graduated at the South Carolina Medical College at Charleston; he practiced in Liberty Hill and later in Camden, S.C.

Children:
I.   Frances Holly McKain, born June 21, 1855; m.Edward J. Dunne.
II.   Wiley James McKain, born July 17, 1863; m.(1) Jennie Carroll; (2) Rosa Melton. (See later)

Wiley James McKain, son of Anna Adela (Kennedy) and Dr. Wiley Jackson McKain, was born on a plantation in Lee County, S.C. July 17, 1863, and died in Georgetown, S.C. in December, 1952. On Nov. 24, 1887, in Columbia, S.C., he married Jennie Carroll, who was born in Columbia, and died on the plantation in Lee County, March 16, 1902. Wiley James McKain married the second time, Rosa Melton, of Spartanburgh, S.C.

Children of 1st. wife, Jennie (Carroll) McKain:

I.   Lorette McKain, born April 8, 1891; m. Benjamin Mood Badger.
II.   Emily Dennison McKain, born Dec. 24, 1893; m. Edward
q   Dunne.
III.   Maida McKain, June 14, 1900; m. L. E. Adams. (See later)

Children of 2nd. wife, Rosa (Melton) McKain:

IV.   Katherine McKain, born 1910.
V.   Ruth McKain, b. 1912, m. Alex Conrad.
VI.   Wylie McKain, b. 1914.
VII.   Adelaida McKain, b. 1916; m. John Fischer.
VIII. Martha McKain, b. 1918, m. John Williams.

Maida McKain, daughter of Jennie (Carroll) and Wiley James McKain was born on the plantation in Lee County, 16 miles from Sumter, S.C. on June 14, 1900; on Feb. 28, 1925 in Columbia, S.C. she married Lacy E. Adams, son of Martha (McLean) and Dr. Charles E. Adams, who was born Feb. 14, 1899, in Gastonia, N.C., now divorced.

Mrs. Adams is an A.B. graduate of Winthrop College, Rock Hill, S.C. is Director of Public Relations for the Citizens National Bank in Gastonia, North Carolina, where she now resides.

Children:

I.   Edith Carroll Adams, born 1927; m. R. S. Brisendine.

TYAS of ENGLAND
and
SURRY COUNTY, VIRGINIA

The family De Tyas was early established in Yorkshire, "At a short distance from the battlefield of Towton stands the antique and diminutive chapel of Leed or Lede, which seems to have been domestic to the adjoining manor house. This was one of the seats of the ancient family of Tyas, styling themselves, in Latin, "Teutonius", five of whose tombs still remain in the chapel which is little more than eighteen feet in length within. The inscriptions are partly visible and four of the five bear the arms of Tyus-'a fesse with three mullets in chief.' " (Vol.III,p.177, Battle Abby Roll by the Duchess of Cleveland.)

Sir Francis Tyus owned the manor house at Lede and is buried in the little chapel. A flag stone has an inscription in very rude characters: "Priez pur Lalme Franconis Ties hi ici gist chevalier" (Heraldry and Genealogy, by Nichols.)

In the oldest part of London is a street called "Tyas Road" that leads out to a district in Essex, and the village of Leighton. Not far away is the Cathedral of Chelmsford. Richard Tyes and Ann Clarke were married there, Aug. 9, 1551. Several hundred years ago Leighton was called, "Low Laydon" and the oldest parish church was "St. Mary of the Virgin".

From an old book of birth records the following children were copied. It is probable that these were the children of Robert Tyus of St. Andrew Wardrobe, London, and Millicent Browne, spinster of St. Dustan in the West, who were married on December 8, 1573.

I.   William Tyus, son of Robert Tyus, Baptized 1589.
II.   Margaret Tyus, dau. of Robert Tyus, Baptized Feb. 1593.
III. John Tyus, son of Robert Tyus, Baptized Feb.17, 1600.
IV.   George Tyus, son of Robert Tyus, Baptized Mar.3, 1604.

Margaret Tyus married Thomas Sandys, fifth son of Rev. Edwin Sandys, formerly Bishop of London, and one of the first Bishops to conform to the Protestant religion and assisted in the new translation of the Bible in 1565. Another son was Sir Edwin Sandys, popular at the court of Queen Elizabeth, and president of "The Virginia Company". The youngest son, George Sandys, a famous Latin scholar, came to the Virginia Colony and was made Treasurer. (Col.Surry, p.36)

At the Herald's Visitation of London in 1633-34 Thomas Sandys recorded his pedigree. He was married to Margaret, daughter of Robert Tyus of the Wardrobe, Clerk Comptroller there. His eldest son, Robert Sandys, married Alice, daughter of Mr. Lawrence Washington of Sulgrave, and aunt of Col. John Washington, who was the emigrant ancestor of General George Washington.

The above records were obtained by Mrs. Annie Laurie Smith of Tucson, Ariz., while on a visit to the Library of the British Museum in London.

An account of the life of George Sandys, Treasurer of Virginia, is given if "Colonial Surry, pages 36 to 39. His niece, Margaret Sandys, married Sir Francis Wyatt, Governor of Virginia. George Sandys received the first recorded land grant in Surry County. (Id.)

John Tyus, born at Lowe Laydon, Feb.17, 1600, evidently came to America with George Sandys, for he was living at Sandy's plantation in James City when the Muster Roll of Settlers was taken, January 23, 1624, in Virginia after the Great Massacre of November 1622. (Hotten 259) The name of the ship on which he came was not given in the Muster, but he apparently came on Mr. Ewen's ship the "George" with George Sandys in 1621.

In a law suit before the Court at James City, February 7, 1627, John Tyus stated that he was aged "26 yeares and borne at Lowe Layton, in Essex". Jane, wife of John Tyus testified that she was "aged about 22 years, borne at Wombarne in Staffordshire". (M. C.G.C.-163)

John Tyus in May, 1634, patented 50 acres in James City on a creek parting it from land of Bridges Freeman, extending northerly upon the Chickahominy River. (C.P. -19) This was on the north side of the James River.

Richard Tyus of Surry, south of the James River, owned land in Surry and an investigation was made of the land grants in the vicinity to determine how he obtained same. Francis Sowerby patented 211 acres in Surry May 21, 1666, "upon heads of the two northermost branches of Greyes Creek, NE and SE upon land of THOMAS WOODHOUSE; JAMES MASON; and JOHN WATKINS; granted to Mr. John Jennings April 11, 1649, assigned to William Rose who assigned to Mathew Battle and RICHARD TYUS." Tyus assigned his one half (105½) to Daniel Massengill and by divers transactions Francis Sowerby finally acquired both halves of 105½ acres each hence his patent of 211 acres. (C.P. 563)

John Twy, probably John Tyus, previously patented 200 acres in James City, (later Surry), July 6, 1648.....adjacent to lands of Thomas Hart, orphan, and William Foster. (C.P.176)

The above mentioned JOHN WATKINS patented 850 acres of land on July 3, 1648, three days previously "lying at the head of FREYS CREEK". (Id.176). Thomas Hart, son unto Henry Hart, decd., also patented 100 acres of land at SMITHS FORT CREEK on July 3, 1648 "about 2 miles distant from James River, adjacent HENRY HART". (C.P. 176). Mr. THOMAS WARREN also patented 400 acres at Smith's Fort Creek on the same July 3, 1648. (C.P.176) THOMAS WOODHOUSE also patented 400 acres at Smiths Fort Creek on the same day. (C.P.176) JAMES MASON also patented 60 acres and 250 acres at Smith's Fort ant Greys Creek, July 8, 1648. (C.P. 177)

These persons were settlers in that vicinity at about the same time.

In a law suit of 1677, Richard Tyus, evidently son of John Twy, or Tyus (Tyas) who patented the above 200 acres on July 6, 1648, made the following depositions: "Richard Tyus, aged about forty-nine years, Sworne, saith: 'That Mr. Thomas Warren, his heirs and assigns have peaceably and quietly possessed an enjoyed in their own rights that plantation called 'Smith's Fort' about 34 years, without any suits, troubles or molestations concerning same, and further about twenty-five or twenty-six years since ye said Mr. Warren did begin to build ye fifty foot brick house which now stands upon ye said land and finished same without being forewarned or disturbed by any person, and Mr. Rolfe was then living and lived several yeares afterwards and was commonly at ye said Warren's house on ye said plantation with Mr. Warren, Mr. Thomas Rolfe, aforesaid and Mr. Mason and several others some certain time before the said Warren built ye said brick house where he saw ye said Mr. Rolfe write a bill of sale with his owne hands wherein he did make over and sell him and his heires and his assigns forever ye said plantation called 'Smith's Forte' and further ye said Warren payed ye said Rolfe parte of ye consideration which he gave for said lands in Corne......"

Richard Tyus, according to his deposition, was born in 1628. He did not patent land nor was he a "headright"; therefore evidently was born in Virginia. In another law suit concerning the same property, in a Court held Dec.17, 1712, a jury found that "One Thomas Hart, son of Henry Hart, patented the land July 3, 1648, citing the above patent next to that of John Twy.

A fairly complete account of the early generations of the Tyus family is given in Vol.I, page 385 of "Southside Virginia Families" which it does not seem necessary to repeat.

In 1663, Richard[2] Tyus bound out his son, Thomas[3], to a John Braddy and wife until Thomas[3] was aged 14. (BK.1-244) He had another son Richard[3], Jr. who was a titheable in 1677. The date of Richard, Sr.'s death is not known.

Thomas[3] Tyus married the widow of William Scarborough in 1679. She appears to be Annie, the daughter of Walter Houldsworth, Sr. Thomas[3] Tyus died in 1726 and John[4] Tyus receipted for his share of his father's estate. (D.B.8, Vol.II, part 1, p.199)

The name of John[4] Tyus' first wife is unknown. He married secondly before March 2, 1718, Mrs. Mary (Jordan) Sowerby, relict of Francis Sowerby and daughter of Thomas Jordan. John Tyus will was probated March 16, 1726. His children by first marriage were: Elizabeth; Priscilla; Joanna; Thomas; Grace Moss; and John. By his second marriage: Richard Tyus. Mary Jordan Sowersby is mentioned in the will of her grandfather Major Wm. Browne, as "Mary Sowersby" in 1704. Her mother was Jane Browne who married Thomas Jordan. (See Browne and Jordan in Vol. I) They had two daughters, Mary and Jane.

John[5] Tyus, son of John[4] Tyus married Ann Branch, daughter of Francis Branch and his wife Lydia Norwood, daughter of William (Norwood). (See Branch and Norwood) John[5] Tyus' will was probated March 17, 1763. His children are given in full in Vol.1, p. 387.

Thomas[6] Tyus, son of John[5] who died in 1763, predeceased his father. Absalom[6] Tyus, brother of Thomas[6] died in 1765. In his will he leaves two slaves to John and Thomas Tyus, sons of his brother Thomas.

Thomas[7] Tyus, son of Thomas[6] and nephew of Absalom[6], was born Jan.14, 1763 (A.P.R.) Thomas was born after the death of his father, and Captain Richard Hill was his God-father. It appears that his mother was Elizabeth, daughter of Captain Hill. (See Hill) Thomas[7] Tyus married Dec.10, 1788, Nancy, daughter of James Hall of Sussex.

Thomas[8] G. Tyus, son of Nancy (Hall) and Thomas[7] Tyus was born Sept.6, 1800, in Sussex Co., Va; and died 1862 at Athens, Limestone County, Alabama. About 1829 he married Annie Mozelle Lark, who was born in Virginia, and died after 1862 in Athens.

Thomas G. Tyus was Register and Master in Chancery 1846; and Judge of the Probate Court for over twenty-five years.

Children:
I.   Capt. Robert Booth Tyus, born 1831, died 1877; m. Mary Meredith of Tuscumbia, Ala.
II. Mary Frances Tyus, born 1833, died 1853; m. on her death bed Thos. J. Cox.
III. Elizabeth Hill Tyus, born 1834, died 1871; m. Thomas J. Cox. (See later)
IV. Major William Tyus, born 1837, d.s.p. in Los Angeles, Calif., about 1877.
V.   Thomas G. Tyus, born 1839, d.s.p.
VI. Egbert Jones Tyus, born 1842, d.s.p.
VII. Martha A. Tyus, born 1844; m. Robert Brandon of Athens, Alabama.
VIII. James H. Tyus, born 1847, died in infancy.
IX. Ellen Miranda Tyus, born 1850; died early.

Elizabeth[9] Hill Tyus, daughter of Anne Mozelle (Lark) and Thomas[8] G. Tyus, was born in 1834 at Athens, Limestone County, Alabama, and died there in 1871. She was graduated at Athens, Female College 1851, and married July 15, 1852, Thomas Jefferson Cox, who had married her sister, Mary, on her death bed. He was born at Brown's Ferry Plantation in Limestone County, Ala., April 19, 1832; graduated at Jefferson Medical College in Penn; and died in Athens, Ala., May 17, 1833. His second wife died in 1871 and he married, thirdly, Mrs. Harriet Andrews Dawson.

Children of Elizabeth (Tyus) and Thomas J. Cox:
I.   Mary Frances Cox, born June, 1853, d.s.p. 1884.
II. James Ford Cox, born 1854, died in infancy.
III. Emma May Cox, born 1857; died 1890; m.Silas Wright.(See later)
IV. Annie Laurie Cox, born 1859; died 1883; m.Thomas Russel.
V.   Elizabeth Maclin Cox, born 1862, d.s.p. 1885.
VI. Sarah Martha Cox, born 1865; died 1884; m. Owen Black.
VII. Thomas Tyus Cox, died in early manhood.
VIII. Byrd Julia Cox, devoted her life to deaf children at Central Institute, St. Louis, retired and lived in the school, dying at 84 years.
Children of Mrs. Harriet (Andrews) Dawson and Thomas J. Cox:
IX. Eugene Andrews Cox, graduated Vanderbilt A.B.; LLB; See "Who's Who in America", 1930-31.

Emma May[10] Cox, the daughter of Elizabeth[9] (Tyus) and Dr. Thomas Jefferson Cox, was born May 1, 1857, in Athens, Alabama;

and died in Little Rock, Ark., Jan. 10, 1890; on Nov. 7, 1877 in Athens, Ala., she married Silas Henry Wright, who was born on "Woodlawn" Plantation, Nash County, North Carolina, May 8, 1849 and died in Little Rock, Ark., Dec. 4, 1938.

Mrs. Wright attended Athens Female Institute, one of the oldest girls schools in the United States. Mr. Wright was educated by tutors on the plantation, attended college at Louisburg, N.C. and was a fine Latin and Greek scholar. He was president of the Wright Bros. Tobacco Co, at St. Charles, Mo.; later went in the lumber business in Arkansas and Missouri.

Children:

I. Byrd Arrington Wright, m. (1) Augustine Feeny; (2) J. C. Anderson.

II. Arch Tyus Wright, m. Aileen Brooks.

III. Annie Laurie Wright, m. William E. Smith. (See later)

IV. Emma May Wright, m. Ernest A. Green.

Annie Laurie Wright, the daughter of Emma May (Cox) and Silas Henry Wright was born in Athens, Ala., and on June 26, at 10 Washington Terrace, St. Louis, Mo., she married William Edward Smith of Madison, Wisconsin, who was born July 22, 1881 in Woodstock County, Illinois, and died May 25, 1939 at Sudbury, Ontario, Canada.

Mr. Smith graduated at the University of Wisconsin B.A. in 1902; LL.B in 1904.

Mrs. Smith now resides at 2532 East Third Street, Tucson, Arizona.

Children:

I. Adelaide Smith, m. Dr. Willis Joret Nelson of New Orleans, La.

II. Lawrence Smith, m. Elsa Lilystrand of Santa Fe, New Mexico.

WESTBROOK of ISLE OF WIGHT

John Westbrook was living in Isle of Wight about 1720. He may have moved there from some other county. He made his will Feb. 13, 1719, same was probated July 23, 1733, and mentioned the following children and wife: ANN; JOHN, will 1761, m. (1) Foster, (2) Honour Ramsey; THOMAS, will 1767, m. Helvia ; SARAH, m. Wm. Vaughan; WILLIAM; JAMES, will 1749, m. Elizabeth (Vaughan); sister ELIZABETH, and "beloved wife" without naming her. (W.B.3, p.357).

John Westbrook, son of John Westbrook, born by 1716 and married by 1737, probably in Isle of Wight County, Foster, dau. of Christopher Foster and wife, Alice Fort, dau. of Elias Fort✓ (See FORT and BAKER families) His second wife was Honour Ramsey. He made his will in Southampton Co., April 7, 1761, probated Aug.13, 1761, and named the following children: (W.B.1-391) WILLIAM; JOHN; MOSES; JAMES, b. ca. 1750, Southampton, d. 1815/20, m. Mary (Lee). (See later) The children by his second wife were: BURWELL; GRAY.

James Westbrook, son of John Westbrook and his wife, a dau. of Christopher Foster, b.ca.1750, m.ca.1774. He died in Sampson Co., N.C. between 1815 and 1820. His wife's name was Mary, last name probably "Lee". She died about 1830. Children: MOSES, b. ca.1775, in N.C., d. 1835, m.ca.1798 Edna Ganey. (See later); CHARLES, WILLIAM; JOSEPH; URIAH; PERCIS.

Moses Westbrook, b.ca.1775, N.C., d.ca.1835, Fayette Co., Ga., m. ca.1798 Sampson Co., N.C., Edna Ganey, dau. of Bartholomew Ganey,b.ca.1774,N.C., d.1835, Fayette Co., Ga.

Children:

I. Sarah Westbrook, b.ca.1799, m.Eldridge Thornton.
II. Ganey Westbrook, b.ca.1801, m.Abigail Marshall.
III. Ananias Westbrook, b.ca.1803.
IV. Abraham Westbrook, b.ca.1805, m. Mary Ann West.
V. Mary Jane Westbrook, b.ca.1807, m.Isiah Warren.
VI. Joseph Westbrook, b.ca.1808, m.Eliza Hill.
VII. Bartholomew Westbrook,b.ca.1809, m.Elizabeth Hill.
VIII. James Westbrook, b.ca.1811.
IX. Moses Westbrook, b.ca.1813, d.1835, unmarried.
X. Barney Westbrook, b.ca.1815, m.Eliza Frances Christian.
XI. Edna Westbrook.
XII. Rufus Westbrook.
XIII. John Charles Westbrook. (See later)

John Charles Westbrook, born August 25, 1819, Sampson Co., N.C., died August 18, 1888, Birmingham, Ala., m. Nov.25, 1840, Tallapoosa, Ala., Elizabeth Ann Lamberth, born Dec.5, 1819, Fayette County, Ga., died Feb.7, 1905, Birmingham, Ala.

Children:
I.   Jane Edna Westbrook, born Nov.7, 1841, m.Samuel Torrey.
II.   Sarah Catherine Westbrook, born July 31, 1843, m. Wm.
      Henry Naff. (See later)
III. William Joseph Westbrook, b.1845, d.unmarried, C.S.A.
IV. Amie Abigail Westbrook, b.Dec.7, 1847, m.Wm.T.Burney.
V.   Frances E. Westbrook, b.Jan.17, 1850, d.July 14, 1859.
VI. Maria J. Westbrook, b.Feb.18, 1852, d.July 12, 1859.
VII. Elvira L. Westbrook, b.June 25, 1855, d.July 21, 1859.
VIII. Estelle A.L. Westbrook, b.Dec.15, 1857, d.Aug.5, 1859.
IX. Rosa Favor Westbrook, b.1860, m.Stephen J. Darby.

Sarah Catherine Westbrook, b.July 31, 1843, Kowaliga, Ala., died Jan.23, 1923, Birmingham, Ala., m.July 12, 1860, Tallapoosa, Ala., William Henry Naff, b.May 26, 1838, d.April 17, 1917, Birmingham, son of Jonathan Neff (1771-1853), b. Md. or Tenn., and Eliza Caroline Massengill, b. Tenn. William Henry Naff was a teacher and Private, Co. A, 1st Ala.Reg. C.S.A.
Children:
I.   John Mortimer Naff, b.June 30, 1861, m.Nina May.
II.   Annie Eliza Naff, b.June 23, 1864, m.Hardy Jones.(See later)
III. Jodie Virginia Naff, b.April 15, 1866, m.W.E.Hansberger.
IV. William Talbott Naff, b.Jan.11, 1869, m.Lucile Timmons.
V.   Jane Augusta Naff, born Jan.14,1871, m.W.M.Marriner.
VI. Henry Julian Naff, b.July 17, 1872, m.Mary E. Sentell.
VII. Katherine Rosalie Naff, b.May 24, 1874, m.Hardie Mills.
VIII. Samuel Torrey Naff, b.April 27, 1876, m.Edna Jennie Frank.
IX. Stephen Burney Naff, b.June 22,1884, m.Helen Clare Davis.

Annie Eliza Naff, born June 23, 1864, Kowaliga, Elmore Co., Ala., d.Mar.19, 1936, Cropwell, Ala., m.Jan.11, 1888, Birmingham, Ala., Hardy Jones, b.March 12, 1864, Loudon, Tenn., d. Jan.4, 1920, Cropwell, Ala. He was a merchant and farmer.
Children:
I.   William Blair Jones, b.March 14, 1889, m.Dixie B. Mays.
      (See later)
II.   Sarah Katherine Jones, b.June 14, 1891, m.W.T. Naff, Jr.
III. Annie Laurie Jones, b.March 3, 1893, m.G.D. Hawkins.'
IV. Rose Amie Jones, b.Oct.12, 1894, m.R. F. Favre.
V.   Lucile, b.Dec.17, 1896, m.C. W. Winn.

William Blair Jones of Pell City, Ala., b.March 14, 1889, Birmingham, Ala., m.Oct.9, 1912, Cropwell, Ala., Dixie Buchanan Mays, b.Aug.17, 1893, Anniston, Ala., dau. of James Campbell Mays, and Flora Dickson Buchanan. Mr. Jones is a member of the firm of Mays and Jones in Pell City.
Children:
I.   James Hardy Jones, b.April 15, 1915, d.Sept.18, 1915.
II.   Dixie Ann Jones, b.Oct.3, 1918, m.Jas.H.Newman.

WORSHAM-MARSHALL of CHESTERFIELD

William and George Worsham patented 400 acres in Henrico Feb. 15, 1652, "200 acres lying at Olde Towne at Appomattox.... and 200 acres being part of a patent granted to Wm. Clarke, decd., May 6, 1638 and by Clarke sold to Seth Ward who sold to William Worsham Nov. 2, 1640. " (C. P. -239, 556) John Wilson patented 100 acres in Henrico June 6, 1666, bought of Seth Ward. This land lay next to the above patent, and Wilson's patent recites that the said 100 acres began at the river side......running along an old known fence" being the line parting said Wilson and the OR-PHANTS OF GEORGE and WILLIAM WORSHAM. (C. P. 556) It seems that George Worsham, died before June 6, 1666, and had a son, George Worsham, Jr., for a jury was called in Henrico on May 15, 1678, to determine the dividing line between John Wilson and the land of "Mr. George Worsham", evidently one of the orphans of 1666. (BK. 2, p. 48) George[1] Worsham was Justice for Henrico in 1656 and his son, Captain George[2] Worsham of Henrico, born in 1648 (deposition) married Mary, daughter of John Pigott of that county, who may have come from Norfolk County, Va. Captain George was a Justice in 1707. (See 33 V 185 for descendants.)

William Worsham was deceased several years before May 15, 1678, for his widow married Colonel Francis Epes, who died in 1678, and had three children by him.

It is said that Mrs. Elizabeth Worsham Epes was a widow before she married Mr. Worsham. She made two wills, one dated July 28, 1678, and the other one dated Sept. 23, 1678. The Worsham children were, ELIZABETH KENNON to whom she gave a stone ring, her black gown, green silk petticoat, green satin bodice and $\frac{1}{4}$ of her money in the hands of Samuel Claphamson in London; to grandaughter Mary Kennon a stone ring "given me by my sister KING; to daughter MARY WORSHAM, $\frac{1}{4}$ of her money; to daughter Mary Epes" a new suite which came this year"; to sons JOHN and CHARLES WORSHAM each $\frac{1}{4}$ of her money. In her second will she describes herself as the widow of Colonel Francis Epes. What estate was given her by his verbal will she wishes divided between her Epes children, viz., William, Littlebury and Mary when they come of age. Executors, Francis Epes, (step-son) and Richard Kennon, son-in-law. (33V-185)

Children of William and Elizabeth Worsham:
I.   John Worsham, m. Mary Wynne. (See later)
II. Charles Worsham, d. 1719.
III. Mary Worsham, m. before Apr. 1, 1680, Richard Ligon, b. 1657; d. 1724; (Ligon Book-329)
IV. Elizabeth Worsham, m. Richard Kennon of "Conjuror's Neck".

John² Worsham was a Justice in Henrico in 1685 and later; also Sheriff for Henrico 1696-97. He held 1104 acres in the Quit Rents of 1704 for Henrico. He married Mary Wynne, daughter of Major Joshua Wynne, and his wife Mary Jones, daughter of Major Peter Jones, and Margaret Wood, daughter of Major Gen. Abraham Wood. Margaret Wood Jones married secondly Capt. Thomas Cocke. (See S.V.F. Vol I, p.221) (V.H.G. p.180, "daughter," Margaret Jones, should read "granddaughter")

Captain John Worsham died in 1729. A copy of his will was not furnished, but according to pages 185-86, 33 Virginia Magazine, his children were as follows:

Children:

I.	John of Henrico; m. Agnes Osborne, widow; d.1745.	
II.	William of Henrico; married; d. 1748.	
III.	Daniel of Henrico, married and died before 1729.	
IV.	Elizabeth; m.(1) Thomas Ligon; (2) Alexander Marshall. (See later)	
V.	Mary, m.	Robertson.
VI.	Martha, m.	Ward.
VII.	Anne; m.	Osborne.
VIII.	; m.	Poythress.
IX.	Elizabeth; m. William Epes. (See Francis Epes Lineage, by Clarke, p.224)	

Elizabeth Worsham, daughter of Captain John Worsham, married Alexander Marshall of Henrico as her second husband. She is mentioned as "my daughter, Elizabeth Marshall..." in Captain Worsham's will.

Alexander Marshall was born in 1676 and died May 3, 1743 at the age of 67. His wife Elizabeth was also born either 1676 or 1677, as she died in February 1743/44, aged 67 years. On August 10, 1706, in a proceeding in the Orphans Court of Henrico, "Alexander Marshall, who lately married Mrs. Elizabeth Ligon", was given the care and custody of Lodowick Tanner. (Vol.1694-1739, p.48) The inventory of the estate of Thomas Ligon was filed May 7, 1705, by John Worsham.

Alexander Marshall received large grants of land in Henrico. On Jan.7, 1725, he patented 2000 acres of land on the north side of Appomattox River, and the south side of Butterwood Creek. This land fell in Goochland and on Sept.28, 1730, he patented 3000 acres of land in Goochland, including the 1000 acres of his former patent and in the same locality. Goochland was cut off Henrico in 1728. Alexander, however, re-patented, on June 3, 1731, 2528 acres on Swift Creek in Henrico, adjacent to Wm. Pride, James Atkins, Francis Flournoys and John Woodbridges; 628 acres heretofore granted June 2, 1721. (PB11-71; 12-334; 14-152) On July 31, 1725, Henry Walthall and Phoebe, his wife, of Henrico, deeded land called "Powell's Tract" which land they had from their father, Thomas Ligon, to Alexander Marshall. (BK 1-192). James Anderson and Elizabeth, his wife of Prince George County, deeded Alexander Marshall lands called "Powells" which their deceased father Thomas Ligon held. (BK 1-192) These two deeds to Alexander Marshall were from the surviving children of his wife Elizabeth, formerly the wife of Thomas Ligon. Two other children were unmarried.

Alexander Marshall was a vestryman in Bristol Parish, 1723-24. Mr. Marshall and his wife are buried on the left bank of the Appomattox River near its mouth, upon a highland which belonged to Mr. Richard Eppes. A double head stone still stands there (1955) with the following inscriptions:

"Here lyeth th Body of Mr. Alexander Marshall who departed this life May 3rd. 1743, Aged 67 years.	Here lyeth the body of Mrs. Elizabeth Marshall who departed this life Feb. 1743/44 Aged 67 years.

Children:

I. Alexander Marshall; m. Sarah   (she married secondly John Robards, July 9, 1772). He made his will in Chesterfield County, Aug. 27, 1771, proven Dec. 1771, as follows: to son ALEXANDER MARSHALL, the land I live on after the death of his mother; son WILLIAM MARSHALL two lots and a house in Bermuda Hundred and lots in Gatesville at Osborne's Warehouse; to sons THOMAS and JOHN land which I bought of William Worsham on Buckskin Creek in Amelia County; sons DANIEL and ARCHIBALD, daughters (not named) to have their part of personal estate given them by their mother. Wife SARAH MARSHALL. Wits: Richard, Thomas, and Henry Batte; Richard Baugh. (W.B. 2-322) In 1787, Alexander Marshall of Chesterfield, William Marshall of Powhattan, Daniel Marshall of Amelia, Archibald Marshall of Chesterfield, sold John Marshall of Amelia, evidently their brother, 160 acres on Great Buckskin Creek in Raleigh Parish, Amelia, ... part of a tract he now lives on".

II. William Marshall; m. (1) Phoebe Farmer; (2) Mrs. Lucy Green Clay. (See later)

III. Elizabeth Marshall; m. John Todd.

IV. John Marshall; d. 1770 in Amelia (?).

V. Francis Marshall (Sr.) of Powhatan County, on Feb. 4, 1779, sold Joseph Gayle of Essex County, Va., 149 acres in Chesterfield on Marshall's line, (BK 8-324) Robert Marshall sold him for Ł. 880, 440 acres in Cumberland on the Appomattox River adjacent William Marshall, Arthur Moseley and George Williamson. (BK 5-266).

Francis Marshall's land fell in Powhatan where he made his will dated May 7, 1779, proven Nov. 15, 1781. His legatees were: wife MARY; son ROBERT, land on the Roanoke River in Mecklenburg County; sons FRANCIS and ALEXANDER; to sons JOSIAH and BENJAMIN "land I now live on" daughters: ELIZABETH; MARY; SALLY; REBECCA; and NANCY. The last named seven children are referred to as "my youngest children" also mentions "My children who are married and off". Sons Robert, Francis and Alexander, executors. (BK 1-54)

Alexander Marshall of Prince Edward County, on Jan. 9, 1782, as eldest son and heir at law of Francis Marshall, deeded to his brothers, Josiah and Benjamin Marshall a certain tract of land for the reason that whereon Francis Marshall father of the above parties, in his will bequeathed them a plantation on the mouth of Butterwood Creek and Appomattox River of 450 acres, lent to his wife for her lifetime and then to her above mentioned sons," but for proper words of inheritance they can only hold a life interest" so Alexander Marshall releases his right and title. (BH 1-166)

William Marshall, son of Elizabeth (Worsham) and Alexander Marshall, lived in Cumberland County. It is stated that he was possibly married three times. He married Phoebe Farmer, daughter of John Farmer of Lunenburg County, who, on Feb.13, 1759, "for love and good will I do bear to my daughter, Phoebe Marshall the wife of William Marshall of Cumberland County, do give her a negro boy named Allen." (BK 2-459). William's last wife was Lucy Green, widow of Henry Clay. (No children.)

William Marshall made his will in Parish of Southam, Cumberland Co., Oct. 2, 1768, proven March 27, 1769, as follows: to wife LUCY all my right to plantation and house I had by her on Fighting Creek; son JOHN 350 acres on Barebone Creek, Amelia; son WILLIAM 300 acres I now live on also 149 acres in Chesterfield. Remainder of estate to be equally divided between my ten children, viz.: JOHN; WILLIAM; ELIZABETH; ANN; PHEBE; MARY; TABITHA; SARAH; MARTHA; SUSANNAH; when my son WILLIAM comes to age of 18 years. Francis Marshall and Edward Bass to be guardians; Thomas Worsham, William Archer, Henry Moody to be executors. Wits.: Dancy Mac Craw, Abner Lockett, Joseph Taylor. (W.B. 1-444)

It will be noted that William2 Marshall devised 300 acres to his son William. John, the first son mentioned in the above will was evidently his eldest son. It appears that William, Sr., had no right to devise this land to William, Jr., as it had been entailed by the will of Alexander1 Marshall to William2 and then to William's eldest son, John Marshall, probably not born at that time. John brought a suit of ejectment against William, then a minor. This was finally compromised by John agreeing to break the entail, sell the land and divide the proceeds with William. William quit claimed the land so John could take possession as heir entail. The agreement was signed by William Marshall, and the following persons: Dancy McCraw, Abner Lockett, Drury Williams and John Robards. The first three persons appear to be sons-in-law of William Marshall, Sr. John Robards was the second husband of Sarah Marshall, widow of William, Sr.

John Marshall and his wife Rebecca of Parish of St. James, Mecklenburgh County, sold this 300 acres to Edward Parish of Cumberland, Aug.14, 1776. (D.B. 5-p.430, 482)

The marriages of six of William's above mentioned children are recorded.
I.   Ann Marshall, m. Abner Lockett, b.1743 who d. in Mecklenburgh, will proven 1793.
II.   Sarah Marshall, m. John Robards, 1772.
III. Elizabeth Marshall, m. Henry Moody. Lucy, the surviving wife of Wm. Marshall, sold her dower rights to Henry Moody.
IV.   Phoebe Marshall, m. Dancy McCraw of Lunenburg. (See Mr. Bell's book)

386
V.   Tabitha Marshall, m.Nov.8, 1770, Drury Williams. (Doug.
        Reg.p.137) (See later) ((M.B. in Cumberland Co., Va.)
VI.   William Marshall, m. Lucy Goode. (deeds)

Tabitha Marshall, daughter of Phoebe (Farmer) and William
Marshall, was married Nov.8, 1770, by the Reverand Douglas in
Goochland County, (Reg.137) to Drury Williams, the son of William
Williams and wife Mary of Goochland. William Williams' will was
probated in Goochland in 1783, and therein he mentions his son
Drury.

Drury Williams moved to Franklin County, Ga., where he obtained a headright grant of 1000 acres in 1786. He settled in Wilkes
County, where he bought 250 acres on Heard's Mill on Fishing
Creek, Aug.10, 1788. (Davidson's Wilkes Co. 1-284) He died pre-
vious to March 4, 1806, for his will was dated Sept. 6, 1805, and
probated March 4, 1806. Tabitha Williams, Jonathan Webster and
John Dyson were appointed administrators of his estate. A division
of the estate was made in 1809 and agreed to by six sons and sons-
in law of Drury in the following order:
I.   Polly Williams, m. Jonathan Webster.
II.   Zachariah Williams, (son of Drury) m. Miss Walton, sister
        of A. G. Walton.
III.   Nancy Williams, b. April, 1774, m. (1) John R. Anderson,
        one of the above signers; m. (2) Nelson Powell; (3) Mr. Ken-
        drick.
IV.   John Williams. (Son of Drury)
V.   Jesse Williams. (Son of Drury) (See later)
VI.   Sally Williams, m. A. G. Walton.
VII.   William Marshall Williams, b.Nov.8, 1771, d.1800, previous
        to his father, leaving children: William Marshall, Nancy, and
        Zachariah.
VIII.   Mary, born July 1776.
IX.   Willis, probably d.s.p.

Jesse Williams, son of Tabitha (Marshall) and Drury Williams,
married possibly Elizabeth Heard. John Dyson, one of the administrators of Drury Williams, married Annie Heard, daughter of
John Heard who died about 1792.

Jesse bought the 1000 acres belonging to the estate of his father,
Drury, in Franklin County, as he was the highest bidder, for $102.00.
However, Tabitha, second wife and widow of Drury, married secondly
James Gresham, who claimed 1/3 of the land for the life of his wife.
James Gresham died in 1807 and willed to wife Tabitha, "Slaves,
land, cattle, furniture which I received from the estate of Drury
Williams." Tabitha evidently lived until 1821 for Jesse took posses-
sion in that year. Women could not hold property in Georgia until
1866.

        Children of Jesse Williams, not in order of birth:
I.   Ann Williams, d.1901; m.Ben Blakey.
II.   Jesse Clark Williams, b.1882; d.1884; m.(1) Caroline Shumate;
        m.(2) Mary Truitt.
III.   Martha Marshall Williams, m. Booker Shelton Terrill; moved
        to Grenada, Miss.
IV.   Mary Williams, b.1810, d.1895; m. Pope Muse.

V. George Williams, b.1807; d.1896; m.Minnie Thurmond.
VI. Joseph Marshall Williams, b.1820; d.1901; m.Lucy Kendall.
    (See later)
VII. William Marshall Williams, b.1825; d.1898; m.Annie Sutton
    and had Ida, m. James Harnes Allen, Temple, Ga., and had
    Harry A. Allen, editor and owner of the "Charlotte Observer,"
    Charlotte, N.C.
VIII. Sarah.

Joseph Marshall Williams, the son of Elizabeth Heard and Jesse
Williams, was born April 13, 1820, in Danbury, Wilkes County, Ga.,
and died March 25, 1901, at Grenada, Miss. In 1850 at Chochuma,
Miss., he married Lucy, the daughter of Mary Adkins (Tomlinson)
and James Kendall. She was born Jan.10, 1826 in Stanley County,
N.C., and died Sept.24, 1921, at Grenada, Miss.
    Dr. Williams was a graduate of South Carolina College of Medi-
cine, and the owner of Belleview Plantation; also property in Grenada.
Dr. Williams home is now owned by his grandaughter, Mrs. Fred
Giles.
    Children:
I. Mary Ida Williams, b.1853, m. Robert Nason.
II. Georgia Williams, b.1855; m.Lafayette Holcomb.
III. Mattie Lee Williams, b.1860; m.Rev. Henry Morehead.
IV. Lucy (Ludie) Eggleston Williams, born 1868; m.Archibald
    W. Stokes. (See later)

Archibald Wade Stokes, owner of Oakachickana and Riverdale
Plantations, as well as a merchant in Grenada, one of "Stokes
Bros.", was born on Riverdale Plantation near Grenada, Miss.,
in 1861; and died in Grenada in 1928. In 1895, at Grenada, he married Ludie Eggleston Williams, the daughter of Lucy Kendall and
Dr. Joseph M. Williams. She was born at the Belleview Plantation
near Chochuma, Miss., and died in 1950 at Grenada.
    Mrs. Stokes was educated at Grenada College and the University
of Mississippi, at Oxford; she returned to teach at Grenada College.
She also taught Men's Bible Class at the Grenada Methodist Church
and was an outstanding leader in the church and the community.
    Children:
I. Helen Louise Stokes, m. Frederic P. Giles. (See later)
II. Ruth Crotin Stokes, m. George Garner. (See later)
III. Rebecca Martin Stokes, d.1942; m. Pete Embry, d.1954.
    No issue.

Helen Louise Stokes, the daughter of Ludie E. Williams and
Archibald Wade Stokes, was married at Grenada, Miss. in 1932
to Frederic Parker Giles, who was born at Anna, Texas, the son
of Mary Frances (Smith) and Jeremiah Hamilton Giles. He received his A.B. degree at the Southern Methodist University, Dallas, Texas, and his M.A. and Ph.D. at Peabody College in Nashville, Tenn., and is now head of Art. Dept. at Eastern Ky. State
College.
    Mrs. Giles received her A.B. degree at Wesleyan College,
Macon, Ga., and her M.A. at the University of Colorado, at
Boulder, and did graduate study at Northwestern University, at
Evanston, Ill. She taught English at Weatherford College in

Texas, 1927-33.

Dr. and Mrs. Giles reside at 323 S. Second Street, Richmond, Ky., and to Mrs. Giles is due credit for furnishing this data concerning the Marshall family.

Children:

I. Frederic Stokes Giles.

II. Henry Wade Giles.

Ruth Cratin Stokes, daughter of Ludie E. (Williams) and Archibald Wade Stokes, was born at Hardy, Grenada County, Miss., Aug. 17, 1903, and married Aug. 20, 1924, at Grenada, Miss., George Merrill Garner, who was born September 18, 1896 at Grenada, Miss., the son of Dodie (Sherman) and Walter Williams Garner.

Mr. and Mrs. George Merrill Garner now reside in Grenada, Miss.

Children:

I. George Merrill Garner, Jr., born March 26, 1930, m. Mary Alice McRee.

II. Wade Stokes Garner, born January 28, 1932.

SUPPLEMENT TO HARVIN FAMILY

(Continued from Page 158)

tember 8th 1801. Shadrach E. Dickey was born April 22nd, 1804.
Henry D. Dickey was born February 9th, 1806 and departed this
life August 30th 1820. Sophronia D. Dickey was born October 10th,
1808. Anne Dickey Departed this life September 17th 1809. Harriet James Dickey was born in the year of our Lord August 11th
day 1810. Mary Ann Neilson Dickey was born November 27th 1813
and departed this Life 27th August 1837.

STATE OF GEORGIA, COUNTY OF GRADY. Before me, a
Notary Public in and for said State and County, personally appeared
Mrs. Blanche M. Dickey, to me personally known, who, after being
by me first duly sworn, on oath deposes and says: That she is cus-
todian of the "Jame E. Harvin Bible" which Bible contains entries
in long hand as follows:

FAMILY RECORD

MARRIAGES

Richard & Francefs Harvin Snr. was married August A.D.1775.
James E. Harvin & Naomi his wife m.18th March A.D.1800.
Michael I. Blackwell, son of Michael and Caroline E.F. Harvin
now Blackwell was married the 10th of December 1818
Shadrach E. Dickey & Susannah his wife was married 8th March
A.D.1827
Thomas E. Harvin and Sarah his wife were married 25th April
1833
Shadrach E. Dickey and Harreet Davis now Dickey were married
April 25th 1841
William James Dickey & Anna Maria Reynolds were married June
28th. A.D.1849
Thomas B. Dickey and Emily McLauchlin were married the 30th
of January A.D.1851.

BIRTHS of

The children of Rich'd F. Harvin Snr.
1st. James E. Harvin was born the 17th day of May Anno domini
1776
2nd. Richard Harvin was born 10th January A.D.1778
3rd. Charles Harvin was born the 12th of October A.D.1779
4th. Nancey Harvin was born the 1st of November A.D.1781
5th. John Harvin was born the 15th of October A.D.1783
6th. William R. Harvin was born the 29th March A.D.1786
7th. Tabitha L.E. Harvin was born the 19th May A.D.1789
8th. Thomas E. Harvin was born the 27th of August A.D.1790
9th. Samuel Harvin was born the 1st. of November A.D.1793.
10th. Sarah J. Harvin was born 28th January A.D.1796.

BIRTHS of

The children of James E. Harvin and Naomi Harvin his wife
1st. Caroline E.F. Harvin was born the 7th February A.D. 1801
2nd. Richard W. Harvin was born the 3rd of June A.D.1802

3rd. James A.Harvin was born the 14th of March A.D.1804
4th. William N.Harvin was born the 18th of December A.D.1805
5th. Hampton F.Harvin was born the 28th December A.D.1807
6th. Thomas E.Harvin was born the 15th September A.D.1809
7th. Susannah E.Harvin was born the 11th July A.D.1811
 Births of M.J. & Caroline E.Blackwell's children
1st. Elizabeth N.Blackwell was born September 25th 1819 15 min.
after 12 o'clock P.M.
 Transferred
 BIRTHS of

John & wife Naomi Harvins Children
John & Naomi married 12th Feby 1807
1. Eliza Ann Harvin born 15th Feby 1808
2. Lucy A.Harvin born 10th April 1809
3. Matilda Hampton Harvin born 6th April 1811
4. Rich S. Harvin born 10th June 1813
5. Charles Harvin born 19th July 1815
6. James Amos Harvin born 1st Dec.1816
 2 & 3 James H. & Emily H.Blackwell were born Nov. 11th 1821
 fifteen minutes before 3 o'clock A.M.
 4th Sarah Savinia Blackwell was born Dec.12th 1823 at 2 o'clock
 P.M. on Friday
1st. William James Dickey was born January 31st Anno domini 1828
 Sarah C. Harvin was born 27th December 1828
2nd. Thomas E.Dickey was born December 3, 1829 Anno Domini
3rd. Patrick Henry Dickey was born January 27th 1832 Anno Domini
4th. Mary Ann Naomi Dickey was born March 10th 1834
 Susan E.Harvin was born 8th Day of February 45 minutes after
 four o'clock Anno Domini 1834
 Shadrach A.Dickey was born April 26th 1837
 John Edwin Dickey was born May 6th Anno domini 1840
 Susannah E.Dickey was born February 5th 1843
 Mary Ann Tabitha Dickey was born the 26th of April A.D.1850
 William Shadrach Dickey was born the 29th of January 1852
 Edwin James Dickey was born the 5th of November 1854
 Susan Ellen Dickey was born the 6th of October 1857
 James E.Harvin departed this life Nov.20th 1821 aged 45 years
 6 mo & 3 days
 Naomi Harvin Departed this life Sept.27th 1826 at 20 minutes
 after 6 o'clock A.M. aged 51 years & 6 mo.
 Susannah E.Dickey Departed this life September 5th 1840 age
 29 years one month & twenty five days
 William N.W.Dickey departed this life October 12th 1813
 Mary Simons departed this life August 11th 1821
 Shadrach E.Dickey departed this life the 30th of November 1847
 Arthur White departed this life Dec.1804
 Ellen White departed this life July 11th 1809
 Frederick J.W.Atkinson departed this life April 3rd.1836
 Henry D.Atkinson died the 17th of April 1842
 Sarah O.Copeland died November 23 1847
 Mary N.McGriffe died the 5th of April 1851
 William Shadrich Dickey died the 28th of December 1855

That said Bible is in fair condition and shows that it was published by M. Carey in the year 1815.

That affiant is the widow of A. C. Dickey Sr., son of James W. Dickey, son of Shadrach E. Dickey.

That said Bible has been recovered with home tanned doe skin.

Dated at Cairo, Georgia, this 13 day of August A.D. 1955

(Signed) Mrs. Blanche M. Dickey

Sworn to and subscribed before me at Cairo, Ga. County of Grady, this 13th day of August, A.D. 1955.

(Signed) Lottie B. Levie

N. P. Grady Co. Ga.

My Commission expires March 25, 1958

(SEAL)

Frances Ragan was daughter of William Ragan, etux, Lucy See Wm. Ragan's Will (St. Mark's Parish, Craven Co., S.C. dated 1/5/1785, W.B. Al. p. 384). Wit: Josiah Furman, Thomas Cassity, Sarah Furman, Executors: John James, Samuel Little, William Saunders. Mentioned: wife, Lucy; daughters, Lucy married to Ragan; Elizabeth, wife of Edward Broughton; Jemimey, wife of William Griffen; Sarah, wife of William Saunders; Frances, wife of Richard Harvin; Tabitha, wife of Richard Rodgers; _____, wife of _____ Gibson; Sons, William, evidently young; John, already married, with issue: grandchildren, Mary Ragan (daughter of Lucy); John Broughton; issue of daughter, Jemimey Griffen; William Saunders (Jr.), William Ragan "exhibited a Memorial", (Vol. 9, p. 217, 4/4/1767) for 100 acres in Craven County near St. Mark's Church, adj. Ephrain Clark, Vacant land, Memorialist's other land, 6/11/1760-2/17/1767 - 4/4/1767.

On pp. 286, 287 "Historic Camden, Colonial and Revolutionary" - Kirkland and Kennedy, lists John Ragan (identity unknown to this writer) as one of many signers (many were Revolutionary War Veterans) of a Petition to the S.C. Legislature to forgive "the Tory, John Adamson."

There are several descendants of Richard Harvin who are members of D.A.R., S.A.R. and Sons of the Revolution, based on Richard Harvin's services. From pp. 174, 175, S.C.N. & G. Mag., Vol. 1, "First Council of Safety of the Revolutionary Party, subscribers in a volunteer Company of Horse commanded by Capt. Matthew Singleton, were Isham Moore, John Singleton, in the Parish of St. Marks, 8/26/1775, and Richard Harvin and Robert Fleming."

Of the issue of Richard Harvin[1] and Frances Ragan
1. James Edwin[2] (5/17/1776-11/20/1821) m. 3/18/1800, Naomi (said to be Dickey or White. No proof.) More later.
2. Richard, Jr.[2] (1/10/1778- *) Nothing further
3. Charles[2] (10/12/1779- *) Nothing further
4. Nancy[2] (11/1/1781-6/20/1813) Apparently d. s. p.
5. John (Tarleton?)[2] (10/15/1783- *) m. 2/12/1807, Naomi Nowell
6. William R.[2] (3/29/1786-5/11/1857). Nothing further
7. Tabitha Lucy Elizabeth[2] (5/19/1789-10/8/1789)
8. Thomas N.[2] (8/27/1790-6/11/1809)

392

9. Samuel^2 (11/1/1793-11/1/1860) m. 1815, Sarah Spears
10. Sarah J.^{2} (1/28/1796-5/17/1830) m. Post 12/12/1807
Davis.
*Living 12/12/1807, date of Richard Harvin's will.

James Edwin^2 Harvin (5/17/1776-11/20/1821), will 10/18/1821-
12/3/1821, Sumter Co., S.C., W.B. AA. 1774-1849, pp. 174 to
178, Incl.) State of South Carolina, Sumter Distric. I, James E.
Harvin, of the State and District aforesaid, Planter, being sick and
weak in body,......Item, I give and bequeath unto my loving wife,
Naomi Harvin, during the term of her natural life, and no longer,
the use of the plantation whereon I now live, and all the adjoining
lands:......Item. I give and bequeath unto my loving daughter,
Caroline E. Blackwell, Three Hundred Acres of land lying on Black
River & Bear Creek, joining Robt. R. White's land, ...and the
money that Michael I. Blackwell is owing me which is ninety two
dollars fifty six & a half cents, clear of interest or hire, untill my
son, James A. Harvin, is of age or marrys. Item. I give & bequeath unto my loving son, Richard W. Harvin, Six Hundred &
Seventy Acres of land, lying on Spring Branch and Farecoat in
Black River Fork whereon William Eveleigh now lives, provided
said Eveleigh should fail in complying with his contract with me.
Should he pay for said land, then Richard W. Harvin is to be paid
out of my estate the principle amount of the land, which is two
thousand nine hundred & three dollars - to him & his lawful issue
forever, but he, the said, is to pay to Susanna E. Harvin the sum
of eight hundred and forty dollars. Item. I give & bequeath unto my
loving son, James A. Harvin, the lower part of the land where I
now live, which is supposed, will be one thousand acres--adjoining
Sam. Harvin's land,......He, the said James A. Harvin, is to pay
to Susanne E. Harvin the sum of four hundred & fifty dollars. Item:
I give & bequeath unto my loving son, William N. Harvin, all the
balance and remaining part of the land whereon I now live, not already bequeathed - to him & his lawfull issue forever. He, the
said William N. Harvin, is to pay to Susanna E. Harvin the sum
of four hundred and fifty dollars. I give & bequeath unto my loving
son, Thomas E. Harvin, all my land, supposed to be one thousand
acres, lying on Big Branch, South side of Black River; also all the
remaining part of my Swamp Surveys, not already bequeathed -
to him & his lawfull issue forever. Item. I give and bequeath unto
my loving daughter, Susanne E. Harvin, one hundred & fourteen
acres of land, lying on Maning Branch that I bought from Elijah
Windom:......I hereby make, ordain, constitute and appoint Mr.
Sam. E. Plowden, my brother, Richard Harvin, my son-in-law,
Michael I. Blackwell, and my loving son, William N. Harvin, -
Executors to this my Last Will and Testament,......this eighteenth
day of October, in the year of our Lord, one thousand, eight hun-
dred and twenty-one, and in the forty-sixth year of Independence of
the United States of America.   James E. Harvin (Seal)
Witnesses: William R. Harvin, Daniel Delany, Thomas Davis, John
Harvin, Sam. H. Gibson

James Edwin^2 Harvin m. 3/18/1800, Naomi (White or Dickey?)
(3/27/1775-9/27/1826) and apparently spent his live in the vicinity

of Sumter, S.C. Issue (Family Bible):
A. Caroline E.F.[3] (2/7/1801-*) m. 12/10/1818, Michael I.Blackwell.
B. Richard W.[3] (6/3/1802*) Nothing further.
C. James A.[3] (3/14/1804-*) Nothing further.
D. Col. Wm. N.[3] (12/18/1805-7/6/1867 in Thomas Co. , Ga.) m. Harriett James Dickey (8/11/1810-). Nothing further.
E. Hampton F.[3] (12/28/1807-) apparently predeceased his father.
F. Thomas E.[3] (9/15/1809-*) m. 4/25/1833, Sarah Nothing further.
G. Susannah Ellen[3] (7/11/1811-9/5/1840) m. 3/8/1827, Shadrach Edward Dickey, brother of Harriett James Dickey, above.
*Living, 11/16/1821, date of Codicil James E. Harvin's Will.

Susannah Ellen[3] Harvin (7-11/1811-9/5/1840) m. 3/8/1827, as his first wife, and mother of all but one of his children, Shadrich Edward Dickey, who had previously moved from Sumter, S.C. to Thomas Co. , Ga. He was a Juror, 1826, (4/22/1804-11/30/1847). See Harvin Bible records. Issue:
a William James[4] Dickey (1/31/1828-12/12/1906) m. (1) 6/28/1849, Anna Maria Reynolds, by whom, apparently, all of his children were born (1/24/1831-10/31/1871): (2) 4/20/1876 Elizabeth J. Everett. See later.
b. Thomas Edward[4] Dickey (12/3/1829-). He is reported to have married 4 times and to have had 18 children by some or all wives. All issue is not known to this writer. m. (1) 1/31/1851, Emily McLauchlin, (2) Feb.1854, Mary Ann Tabitha Hayes, (3) Missouri Norton, (4) Mattie Tyus.
c. Patrick Henry[4] Dickey (1/27/1832-) m. Jan.1856, Sarah Frances McGrift, by whom he had 7 children.
d. Mary Ann Naomi[4] Dickey (3/10/1834-8/27/1872) m.July 1851, William Heir, born 11/28/1828, in Leon Co. , Fla. No record.
e. Shadrach Arthur[4] Dickey (4/26/1837-8/3/1881) m. July 7, 1863, Maria Louise Mitchell, who bore him 5 children.
f. John Edwin[4] Dickey (5/6/1840-9/29/1913) m. June 1, 1865, Mary Ann Tabitha Hayes, whose first cousin, of like name, was 2nd wife of Thomas Edward Dickey. These Misses Hayes were descendants of Southside Virginia families of Hayes (Amelia, Prince George, Henrico), Hamilton (Brunswick, Sussex, Prince George, Surry, Charles City), Sturdivant (Henrico, Surry, Prince George, Charles City), Thweatt (Brunswick, Prince George, Charles City, Henrico, Isle of Wight, Peterson (Prince George, Brunswick, Isle of Wight, Charles City), Soane (New Kent, James City).
Shadrach Edward Dickey's second wife, m. 4/25/1841, Harriett Davis. Issue: Susanna Ellen Dickey (2/5/1843-1/5/1875), m. 5/1/1861, Thomas Jefferson Brown (6/29/1838-11/25/1877).

John Edwin[4] Dickey (5/6/1840-9/29/1913), m.6/1/1865, Mary Ann Tabitha Hayes (10/20/1842-11/16/1910), daughter of Marmaduke Hamilton Hayes of Thomas Co. , Ga. , and his first wife, Sarah Ann Munson (See previous reference to this family et al.) John Edwin Dickey served in the Army of the Confederacy, Co.E, 29th Ga. Reg. , Capt. W.J. Young, Col. Spaulding. Issue:

AA. Mary Hayes[5] (3/28/1866-8/6/1936) m. as his 3rd wife April 15, 1891, Henry Cumming Quarterman (9/27/1854-2/15/1945), son of Robert Young Quarterman and Sarah Howe Handley, of Liberty Co., Ga. She was a granddaughter of Col. George Handley, Governor of Georgia about 1788, aged 36.

BB. William Heir[5] (4/8/1868-1893) dsp

CC. Ida Belle[5] (12/26/1871-8/29/1874).

DD. Walter Lee[5] (12/12/1873-12/31/1873).

EE. John Edwin[5] (10/4/1874-3/26/1912) m May 1904, Virginia Warren.

FF. Leroy Hamilton[5] (10/1/1877) living, 1955, Thomasville, Ga. m. 12/14/1905, Mamie Butler.

GG. Mitchel Harvin[5] (1/26/1883-) m. Elizabeth Pratt.

Mary Hayes[5] Dickey (3/28/1866-8/6/1936), great-great-granddaughter of Richard Harvin, m., as his 3rd wife, 4/15/1891, Henry Cumming Quarterman. Issue:

aa. Mary Belle[6] Quarterman (5/8/1892-9/21/1948), m. as his 1st wife, April 22, 1922, Benjamin Jefferson Kincaid (4/18/1894-living, 1955, Miami, Fla.) The latter m. (2) 4/15/1954, as her 3rd husband, Mrs. William Dewey (Olive Marguerite, "Gretchen", Hand) Hilsabeck (12/10/1896-).

bb. Ellen Leona[6] Quarterman (8/23/1893- living, 1955, at Black Mountain, N.C.) m. April 11, 1923, George Bradford Field. No issue.

cc. Hattie Hayes[6] Quarterman (11/26/1896-9/26/1898).

dd. Theodosia[6] Quarterman (12/23/1899- living, 1955, at Black Mountain, N.C.), m. October 18, 1924, Wade Morrow.

May Belle[6] Quarterman (5/8/1892-9/21/1948), m. April 22, 1922, Benjamin Jefferson Kincaid (A.E.F., W.W. I, 1917-1918), son of James Gordon Kincaid, M.D., and Elbana Cumi Barrett. Issue:

I. Mary Hayes[7] Kincaid (8/6/1923-) m. (1) December 19, 1943, Wayman Horace Lytle, by whom no issue. (2) September 13, 1949, Charles Bernard Karl Schultz of Atlantic City, N.J. (12/12/1923-). She earned A.B., Chemistry, at W.C., U. of N.C., Greensboro, N.C., 1944.

II. Benjamin Jefferson[7] Kincaid, Jr. (2/15/1926 - living, 1955, at Miami, Fla.) He earned B.S., Physics, U. of Miami, Fla. 1949 (W.W. II, E.T.O., Combat Eng.).

Mary Hayes[7] Kincaid, m. Charles Bernard Karl Schultz. Issue:
Issue: Michael Karl[8] Schultz (8/6/1950)
            Roderick Kincaid[8] Schultz (1/2/1955)

Theodosia[6] Quarterman (12/23/1899) married 10/18/1924, Wade Morrow. Issue:

I. Barbara[7] Morrow (12/14/1927 - Living, 1955, Charlotte, N.C.), m. May 8, 1953, James N.E. Helgreen. No issue in 1955.

II. Richard[7] Morrow (3/21/1930 - In U.S. Navy, 1955), m. Aug. 11, 1951, Mary Catherine Hall of Rose Hill, N.C. Issue:
            Richard[8] Morrow Jr. (8-24-1952 - Living 1955)

(Above family records received too late to index)

Thos. 123; 125.
Driggers, Cora, 114; Teresa, 114, Walter, 114.
Drury, John, 2.
DuBose, Alfred, 265; George, 265, Col. J.J. 265; Jesse, 265; Julius, 265; Mary, 265; Sarah, 265; Tasker, 265.
Duck, Wm. 312.
Duckworth, Mr. 327; Mary, 327.
Dudley, Col. 169.
Durden, Darden, Maj. Jacob, 182; Mary, 182.
Duke, Earnest, 77; Eliz. 123; 124; 125; Henry, 122; 123; 124; Jane, 123; John, 123; 279; Lila, 77; Margaret, 179; Ruth, 77; Sam. C. 77; Sarah, 77-179.
Dulan, Peggy, 369; Thos. 369.
Duncan, Geo. 94; Mary E. 94; Wm. 54.
Dunn, Agnes, 37; Allen, 289; Berney, 289; Blanche, 373; David, 120; Rdw. 373; Frances, 373; Margaret, 107; Mary, 289; Thos. 289.
Dunne, Edw. 374; Emily, 374.
Dunstar, John, 275; Master, 30.
Duren, Dorcas, 345; Thos. 345.
Durham, Walter, 127.
Dyke, Jane, 29.
Dyson, Annie, 386; John, 386.

- E -

Earle, Amaryllis, 365-366; Anna, 366; Bayliss, 366; Eleanor, 366; Eliz. 366; Frances, 203; Hannah, 366; Harriet, 366; Jas. 203; John, 366; Joseph, 366; Letitia, 366; Lydia, 366; Mary, 366; Nancy, 366; Phillis, 365; Rachel, 366; Reb. 366; Rochelle, 203; Sam. 365-366; Sarah, 366; Tamesine, 366.
Eaton, Laura, 207; Signora, 327; Susan, 14; Wm. 207-327.
Edgar, Eliz. 245; Jas. 245; John, 245; Joseph, 245.
Edgerton, John, 99.
Edlee, Matthew, 326.
Edmunds, Edmonds, Ann, 119; Chris. 119; David, 119; Elias, 120; Eliz. 119-120; Faith, 119; Gray, 119; Howell, 34; 119; John, 119-120; Mary, 119; Nich. 120; Phillis, 119; Sam. 119-120; Sterling, 120; Thos. 119-120; Wm. 119.
Eduards, Eliz. 277; Henry, 334; Holland, 90; Jesse, 90; John, 90-350; Mary, 350; Thos. 26-28-277; Wm. 90-102-164.
Edwards, Alma, 253; deWilda, 253; Emilie, 253; Henry, 188; Hilliard, 253; John, 177-253; Marguerite, 253; Mary, 253.
Eelback, Jane, 294; Lane, 294.
Egbert, Carol, 147; David, 147; Fran. 147; Kendal, 147; La-Larne 147; Lou. 147; Merl, 147; Myrna, 147; Xenia, 147.
Egerton, Anna, 246; Annie, 202; Benj. 202; Chas. 202; Eliz. 202; Flo. 202; Hugh, 202; Junius, 202-218; Laura, 202; Lucy, 202-218-219; Martha, 202; Robt. 202; Walter, 202.
Elcan, Eliz. 271; Geo. 271; Herbert, 272; Martha, 272.
Eldridge, Eliz. 120; Sarah, 120; Thos. 120.

Eley, Benj. 98; John, 98.
Elgin, Cassandra, 62.
Ellen, C.F. 228; Lucy, 229; Temperance, 229; Tempie,228.
Ellinor, J. P. 320; Lilla, 320.
Elliott, Fannie, 42; Maria, 125.
Ellis, Caleb, 35; Eliz. 359; Faithy, 34; Joseph, 292; Mary, 34; Reb. 70; Sarah, 34-135-136; Wm. 136.
Ellison, Burrell M. 77; Eliz. J. 77; Laura C. 77.
Elliston, Wm. 126.
Ellsbury, Abner F. 5-6; Benj. R. 6-7; Ed. 6; Eliza, 5-6; Laura, 6; Lida, 6; Louise, 6; Mary L. 6; Michael, 5-6; Palmer R. 6; Sam. 6.
Emerson, Annie, 145; Bessie, 27-144-145; Chas. 145.
Emrey, Ben. 34; Faith, 34.
England, Ann, 43-45; Francis, 43-44; Joyce, 44; Sarah, 43.
English, Joseph, 98.
Epes, Eliz. 382-383; Francis, 382; Richard, 382; Littlebury, 382; Mary, 382; Wm. 382-383.
Epps, Caroline, 249; Geo. 249; Wayne, 249.
Erickson, Laura, 62.
Erskin, Charlotte, 139-140; John, 140; Levi, 140; Martha, 139.
Erwin, Elvira, 213; Helen, 213; John, 365; Joseph, 213; Josephine, 157-158; Susan, 213; Walter, 213.
Evans, Arabella, 353; Abraham, 308; Anthony, 85; Benj. 309; Eliz. 353; Frederick, 35; John, 353; Mary, 309; Susan, 13; Wm. 166.
Everard, Ann, 295.
Evers, Robt. 275.
Evins, Ann, 368; Eliza, 367-368; Eliz. 368; Mary, 368; Sam. 368; Thos. 367-368.
Eubank, Rice, 370; Rosetta, 370.
Exum, Jeremiah, 49-295; John, 2-352; Mary, 295; Micajah, 351; Sarah, 351-352; Thos. 352.

- F -

Fairchild, Benj. 99.
Fairies, Ella, 225; Thos. 225.
Falcon, Lucy, 191-199; Nich. 191-199;
Falkner, Andrew, 15.
Farmer, John, 385; Matt. 100; Phoebe, 384-385.
Faris, Eliza, 17.
Farnum, Ava. 64; Clevern, 64; Mary, 64; Wm. 64.
Faulkner, Earl, 151.
Feeny, Angus, 12; Jack, 12; Jos. 12; Martha, 12.
Fenster, Norvin Wilford, 200; Robert Lee, 200; Susan Whitmel, 200.
Fenton, Ellen, 146; John, 146.
Fellows, Margaret,339; Wm. 339.
Ferguson, Carrie, 274; Guila; 274; Gilbert, 274; Robt.41-274.
Field, Eliz. 262; Jane, 35; John 36; Moses, 340; Rich. 262; Sarah, 340.
Fields, Annie, 63; Betty, 17; Minerva, 95.
Figures, Eliz. 32; Mary, 37.
Finley, Eliza, 304; Jas. 304; John, 304; Mary, 304; 4 children.
Fillmore, Joan, 234; Martina, 234; Wm. 234.

401

Fisher, Alma, 145; Earnest, 145; Ed. 28; Garth, 146; Ger. 146, Gordon, 146; Horace, 146; Irene 145; Jane, 145; Jos. 146; Judith, 146; Karla, 146; Kelly, 145; Newell, 145; Priscilla, 145; Sam. 145; Sarah, 28; Wm. 22-144-145.
Fitsgerald, John, 336; Julia, 336.
Fitts, Annie, 18.
Flake, Joice, 43; Mary, 26; Robt. 26-43.
Flanagan, J.W. 57.
Fletcher, Carter, 283; Eliz. 50; Lavinia, 281; Joseph, 281; Ralph, 50; Temperance, 283.
Flewellen, Ann, 55.
Flicker, Mary, 274; Nich. 274.
Flint, David, 300; Ida, 142; Mary, 300.
Flood, Eliz. 120; 291; Jane. 291; John, 135-291; Walter, 120-291.
Flowers, Anna, 273; Dorothy. 273; Jas. 273; John, 78; Kate, 273; Katrina, 273; Lizette, 273.
Flournoy, Francis, 383; Jane,132.
Floyd, Harry, 80; Inez, 329; Jane Ann, 329; Margaret Long, 329; Mr. 86; Wm. 329.
Foley, Geo. 150; Rich. 150.
Ford, Benj. 74; Jack, 64; Jos. 88; Mary, 58; Mickey, 64; Rebecca, 301; Sarah, 301; Sin. 74; Steela, 64; Wm. 74.
Fort, Alice, 33-380; Diana, 181; Cynthia, 181; Elias, 181-350; Eliz. 54-181; Grace, 23-143; Jacob, 181; James, 181; Jane, 181; Jeremiah, 181; John, 33-181; Josiah, 33-181; Mary, 33-181; Sarah, 181; Temperance, 181; Wm. 181.
Forster, Robt. 177.
Foster, Ada, 195; Alice, 33-380; Amy, 33; Anne, 153; Arthur, 33; Chris. 32-33-380; Elias, 33; Eliz. 32-153-154; Faith, 32; Fortune, 32; Grace, 32; Geo. 153-164; Jas. 33; John, 32-33; Mary, 33-153-154; Miss. 380; Moses, 33; Newitt, 33; Robt. 32; Solon, 194; Thos. 154; Wm. 165-166.
Fought, Claude, 254; Dortch, 254.
Fowler, Ethel A.
Foy, Belle, 212; Clara, 212.
Fox, Alice, 151; Magdalene, 131.
Foxworth, Sarah, 116.
Fraile, Maria.
Franklin, Ann, 247; Ernest, 247; Tempie, 247.
Frazier, Adrian, 217; Helen,217.
Freeman, Amanda, 300; Bennett, 364; Cynthia, Eliz., John, 235; Josiah, 300; Margaret, 235; Mary, 298-300; Sarah, 300; Wm. 300.
Fry, Fielding, 241; Howell, 241; Martha, 241; Mary, 241.
Fulton, George Henry, 197; Mamie Clyde Snow, 197; Nancy Kathryn, 197; Nancy, 5.
Fullwood, Josephine, 76.
Fullerton, Clara, 370; John, 370; Martha, 370.
Fuquay, Aldrich, 342; Cora, 342; Dora, 342, Eloise, 342; Emma, 342; Ethlyn, 342; Janice, 342; Judith, 342; Margaret, 342; Martha, 342;

- G -

Gage, Ellenor, 345; John, 345.
Gale, Ed. 48; Thos. 96.

Jno. Waters 364